Praise for *The Boys in the Boat*

"This riveting tale of beating the odds (and the Germans) at the 1936 Olympics is a rousing story of American can-do-ism. It's also a portrait of the nine boys who first rowed together for the University of Washington, and of the one in particular who made the sport his family and his home." —*Parade*

"For those who like adventure stories straight up, *The Boys in the Boat* . . . is this year's closest approximation of *Unbroken*." —*The New York Times*

"The astonishing story of the University of Washington's 1936 eight-oar varsity crew and its rise from obscurity to fame . . . The individual stories of these young men are almost as compelling as the rise of the team itself. Brown excels at weaving those stories with the larger narrative, all culminating in the 1936 Olympic Games. . . . A story this breathtaking demands an equally compelling author, and Brown does not disappoint. The narrative rises inexorably, with the final fifty pages blurring by with white-knuckled suspense as these all-American underdogs pull off the unimaginable." —*The Seattle Times*

"This riveting and inspiring saga evokes that of Seabiscuit. . . . Readers need neither background nor interest in competitive rowing to be captivated by this remarkable and beautifully crafted history. Written with the drama of a compelling novel, it's a quintessentially American story that burnishes the esteem in which we embrace what has come to be known as the Greatest Generation." —*Associated Press*

"A stirring tale of nine Depression-era athletes beating the odds and their inner demons to compete at the 1936 Berlin Olympics. You can Google the result and spoil the sport, but that won't dull the many pleasures in Daniel James Brown's colorful, highly readable celebration of a grueling collegiate challenge." —*Bloomberg*

"If you imagined a great regatta of books about rowing, then Brown's *The Boys in the Boat* certainly makes the final heat." —*The Boston Globe*

"Brown's book juxtaposes the coming together of the Washington crew team against the Nazis' preparations for the games, weaving together a history that feels both intimately personal and weighty in its larger historical implications. This book has already been bought for cinematic development, and it's easy to see why: When Brown describes a race, you feel the splash as the oars slice the water, the burning in the young men's muscles, and the incredible drive that propelled these rowers to glory." —*Smithsonian*

"Superb." —*Library Journal* (starred review)

"[Brown] offers a vivid picture of the socioeconomic landscape of 1930s America (brutal), the relentlessly demanding effort required of an Olympic-level rower, the exquisite brainpower and materials that go into making a first-rate boat, and the wiles of a coach who somehow found a way to first beat archrival University of California, then conquer a national field of qualifiers, and finally, defeat the best rowing teams in the world. A book that informs as it inspires."
—*Booklist* (starred review)

"In evocative, cinematic prose . . . [Brown] makes his heroes' struggle as fascinating as the best Olympic sagas." —*Publishers Weekly*

"The story deserves a more visible place in history, and Brown has brought it to light in a way that will appeal to readers regardless of their knowledge of or interest in rowing or wooden boats. It's a story about universal human values: striving for excellence and the triumph of teamwork." —*WoodenBoat*

"A thrilling, heart-thumping tale of a most remarkable band of rowing brothers who upstaged Adolf Hitler at the 1936 Olympics. Well-told history, packed with suspense and a likable bunch of underdogs at the heart of an improbable triumph." —Timothy Egan, author of *The Worst Hard Time*

"For years I've stared and wondered about the old wooden boat resting on the top rack of the University of Washington's boathouse. I knew the names of the men that rowed it but never really knew who they were. After reading this book, I feel like I got to relive their journey and witness what it was truly like earning a seat in that Pocock shell. The passion and determination showed by Joe and the rest of the boys in the boat are what every rower aspires to. I will never look at that wooden boat the same again."
—Mary Whipple, Olympic gold medal–winning coxswain, women's eight-oared crew, 2008 and 2012

"*The Boys in the Boat* is not only a great and inspiring true story; it is a fascinating work of history."
—Nathaniel Philbrick, author of *Mayflower* and *In the Heart of the Sea*

"In 1936 nine working-class American boys burst from their small towns into the international limelight, unexpectedly wiping the smile off Adolph Hitler's face by beating his vaunted German team to capture the Olympic gold medal. Daniel James Brown has written a robust, emotional snapshot of an era, a book you will recommend to your best friends."

—James Bradley, author of *Flags of Our Fathers* and *Flyboys*

"*The Boys in the Boat* is an exciting blend of history and Olympic sport. I was drawn in as much by the personal stories as I was by the Olympic glory. A must-read for anyone looking to be inspired!"

—Luke McGee, coach, USRowing Men's National Team

"A lovingly crafted saga of sweat and idealism that raised goose bumps from the first page. I was enthralled by the story's play of light and shadow, of mortality and immortality, and its multidimensional re-creation of the pursuit of excellence. This meditation on human frailty and possibility sneaks up on you until it rushes past with the speed of an eight-oared boat."

—Laurence Bergreen, author of *Columbus* and *Over the Edge of the World*

"Daniel Brown's book tells the dramatic story of the crew that set the stage for Seattle emerging as a world-class city. Their lives define the tradition that is still University of Washington rowing today."

—Bob Ernst, director of rowing, University of Washington

"I really can't rave enough about this book. Daniel James Brown has not only captured the hearts and souls of the University of Washington rowers who raced in the 1936 Olympics, he has conjured up an era of history. Brown's evocation of Seattle in the Depression years is dazzling, his limning of character, especially the hardscrabble hero Joe Rantz, is novelistic, his narration of the boat races and the sinister-exalted atmosphere of Berlin in 1936 is cinematic. I read the last fifty pages with white knuckles, and the last twenty-five with tears in my eyes. History, sports, human interest, weather, suspense, design, physics, oppression, and inspiration—*The Boys in the Boat* has it all and Brown does full justice to his terrific material. This is *Chariots of Fire* with oars."

—David Laskin, author of *The Family, The Children's Blizzard,* and *The Long Way Home*

ABOUT THE AUTHOR

Daniel James Brown is the author of *Facing the Mountain*, *The Indifferent Stars Above*, and *Under a Flaming Sky*, in addition to the number one *New York Times* bestseller *The Boys in the Boat*. He lives outside Seattle and in Carmel, California.

Penguin Readers Guide available
online at penguinrandomhouse.com

THE BOYS IN THE BOAT

Nine Americans and Their Epic
Quest for Gold at the 1936 Berlin Olympics

Daniel James Brown

PENGUIN BOOKS

PENGUIN BOOKS
An imprint of Penguin Random House LLC
penguinrandomhouse.com

First published in the United States of America by Viking, an imprint of Penguin Random House LLC, 2013
Published in Penguin Books 2014
This edition published 2023

Photo credits: p. xii: Photo by Josef Scaylea. Used by permission. Josef Scaylea Collection, Museum of History & Industry, Seattle, All Rights Reserved; pp. 6 and 16: *Seattle Post-Intelligencer* Collection, Museum of History & Industry, Seattle, All Rights Reserved; pp. 8 and 206: PEMCO Webster & Stevens Collection, Museum of History & Industry, Seattle, All Rights Reserved; pp. 24, 33, 64, 69, 82, 104, 148, 236, 292, 312, 320, 329, 356, 362, 365, and 369: Judith Willman Materials; p. 38: University of Washington Libraries, Special Collections, UW 33403; p. 52: University of Washington Libraries, Special Collections, A. Curtis 45236; p. 70: University of Washington Libraries, Special Collections, UW 20148z; p. 102: Bundesarchiv, Bild 183-S34639 / Rolf Lantin; p. 124: University of Washington Libraries, Special Collections, UW 3559; p. 164: © Bettmann/CORBIS; p. 172: Photo by Josef Scaylea. Used by permission; p. 192: University of Washington Libraries, Special Collections, UW 33402; p. 228: By permission of *Seattle Post-Intelligencer*; p. 250: Courtesy of Heather White; p. 274: Courtesy of the family of Bob Moch; pp. 299, 301, 327, 336, 342, 344, 345, and 352: Limpert Verlag GmbH; p. 306: United States Holocaust Memorial Museum, Courtesy of Gerhard Vogel; p. 351: University of Washington Libraries, Special Collections, UW 1705; p. 360: Bundesarchiv, Bild 183-R80425 / o.Ang; p. 372: Joshua Huffman.

ISBN 9780593512302 (paperback movie tie-in)

THE LIBRARY OF CONGRESS HAS CATALOGED THE HARDCOVER EDITION AS FOLLOWS:
Brown, Daniel, 1951–
The boys in the boat : nine Americans and their epic quest for gold at the 1936 Olympics / Daniel James Brown.
pages cm
Includes bibliographical references and index.
ISBN 9780670025817 (hardcover)
1. Rowing—United States—History. 2. Rowers—United States—Biography. 3. University of Washington—Rowing—History. 4. Olympic Games (11th : 1936 : Berlin, Germany). I. Title.
GV791.B844 2013
797.12'30973—dc23
2013001560

Printed in the United States of America
2nd Printing

Book design by Carla Bolte

For

Gordon Adam

Chuck Day

Don Hume

George "Shorty" Hunt

Jim "Stub" McMillin

Bob Moch

Roger Morris

Joe Rantz

John White Jr.

and all those other bright, shining boys of the 1930s—
our fathers, our grandfathers, our uncles, our old friends

CONTENTS

Prologue

— 1 —

PART FOUR

1936

Touching the Divine

— 227 —

Epilogue

— 357 —

It's a great art, is rowing. It's the finest art there is. It's a symphony of motion. And when you're rowing well, why it's nearing perfection. And when you near perfection, you're touching the Divine. It touches the you of yous. Which is your soul.

—George Yeoman Pocock

οἴκαδέ τ' ἐλθέμεναι καὶ νόστιμον ἦμαρ ἰδέσθαι . . .
ἤδη γὰρ μάλα πολλὰ πάθον καὶ πολλὰ μόγησα
κύμασι . . .

(But I desire and I long every day to go home and to look upon the day of my return . . . for already I have suffered and labored at so many things on the waves.)

—Homer

Dawn row on Lake Washington

PROLOGUE

In a sport like this—hard work, not much glory, but still popular in every century—well, there must be some beauty which ordinary men can't see, but extraordinary men do.

—George Yeoman Pocock

This book was born on a cold, drizzly, late spring day when I clambered over the split-rail cedar fence that surrounds my pasture and made my way through wet woods to the modest frame house where Joe Rantz lay dying.

I knew only two things about Joe when I knocked on his daughter Judy's door that day. I knew that in his midseventies he had single-handedly hauled a number of cedar logs down a mountain, then hand-split the rails and cut the posts and installed all 2,224 linear feet of the pasture fence I had just climbed over—a task so herculean I shake my head in wonderment whenever I think about it. And I knew that he had been one of nine young men from the state of Washington—farm boys, fishermen, and loggers—who shocked both the rowing world and Adolf Hitler by winning the gold medal in eight-oared rowing at the 1936 Olympics.

When Judy opened the door and ushered me into her cozy living room, Joe was stretched out in a recliner with his feet up, all six foot three of him. He was wearing a gray sweat suit and bright red, down-filled booties. He had a thin white beard. His skin was sallow, his eyes puffy—results of the congestive heart failure from which he was dying. An oxygen tank stood nearby. A fire was popping and hissing in the woodstove. The walls were covered with old family photos. A glass display case crammed with dolls and porcelain horses and rose-patterned china stood against the far wall. Rain flecked a window that looked out into the woods. Jazz tunes from the thirties and forties were playing quietly on the stereo.

Judy introduced me, and Joe offered me an extraordinarily long, thin hand. Judy had been reading one of my books aloud to Joe, and he wanted to meet me and talk about it. As a young man, he had, by extraordinary coincidence, been a friend of Angus Hay Jr.—the son of a person central to the story of that book. So we talked about that for a while. Then the conversation began to turn to his own life.

His voice was reedy, fragile, and attenuated almost to the breaking point. From time to time he faded into silence. Slowly, though, with cautious prompting from his daughter, he began to spin out some of the threads of his life story. Recalling his childhood and his young adulthood during the Great Depression, he spoke haltingly but resolutely about a series of hardships he had endured and obstacles he had overcome, a tale that, as I sat taking notes, at first surprised and then astonished me.

But it wasn't until he began to talk about his rowing career at the University of Washington that he started, from time to time, to cry. He talked about learning the art of rowing, about shells and oars, about tactics and technique. He reminisced about long, cold hours on the water under steel-gray skies, about smashing victories and defeats narrowly averted, about traveling to Germany and marching under Hitler's eyes into the Olympic Stadium in Berlin, and about his crewmates. None of these recollections brought him to tears, though. It was when he tried to talk about "the boat" that his words began to falter and tears welled up in his bright eyes.

At first I thought he meant the *Husky Clipper*, the racing shell in which he had rowed his way to glory. Or did he mean his teammates, the improbable assemblage of young men who had pulled off one of rowing's greatest achievements? Finally, watching Joe struggle for composure over and over, I realized that "the boat" was something more than just the shell or its crew. To Joe, it encompassed but transcended both—it was something mysterious and almost beyond definition. It was a shared experience—a singular thing that had unfolded in a golden sliver of time long gone, when nine good-hearted young men strove together, pulled together as one, gave everything they had for one another, bound together forever by pride and respect and love. Joe was crying, at least in part, for the loss of that vanished moment but much more, I think, for the sheer beauty of it.

As I was preparing to leave that afternoon, Judy removed Joe's gold medal from the glass case against the wall and handed it to me. While I was admiring it, she told me that it had vanished years before. The family had searched Joe's house high and low but had finally given it up as lost. Only many years later, when they were remodeling the house, had they finally found it concealed in

A Washington crew working out, circa 1929

some insulating material in the attic. A squirrel had apparently taken a liking to the glimmer of the gold and hidden the medal away in its nest as a personal treasure. As Judy was telling me this, it occurred to me that Joe's story, like the medal, had been squirreled away out of sight for too long.

I shook Joe's hand again and told him I would like to come back and talk to him some more, and that I'd like to write a book about his rowing days. Joe grasped my hand again and said he'd like that, but then his voice broke once more and he admonished me gently, "But not just about me. It has to be about the boat."

PART ONE

1899–1933

What Seasons They Have Been Through

The Washington shell house, 1930s

CHAPTER ONE

Having rowed myself since the tender age of twelve and having been around rowing ever since, I believe I can speak authoritatively on what we may call the unseen values of rowing—the social, moral, and spiritual values of this oldest of chronicled sports in the world. No didactic teaching will place these values in a young man's soul. He has to get them by his own observation and lessons.

—George Yeoman Pocock

Monday, October 9, 1933, began as a gray day in Seattle. A gray day in a gray time.

Along the waterfront, seaplanes from the Gorst Air Transport company rose slowly from the surface of Puget Sound and droned westward, flying low under the cloud cover, beginning their short hops over to the naval shipyard at Bremerton. Ferries crawled away from Colman Dock on water as flat and dull as old pewter. Downtown, the Smith Tower pointed, like an upraised finger, toward somber skies. On the streets below the tower, men in fraying suit coats, worn-out shoes, and battered felt fedoras wheeled wooden carts toward the street corners where they would spend the day selling apples and oranges and packages of gum for a few pennies apiece. Around the corner, on the steep incline of Yesler Way, Seattle's old, original Skid Road, more men stood in long lines, heads bent, regarding the wet sidewalks and talking softly among themselves as they waited for the soup kitchens to open. Trucks from the *Seattle Post-Intelligencer* rattled along cobblestone streets, dropping off bundles of newspapers. Newsboys in woolen caps lugged the bundles to busy intersections, to trolley stops, and to hotel entrances, where they held the papers aloft, hawking them for two cents a copy, shouting out the day's headline: "15,000,000 to Get U.S. Relief."

A few blocks south of Yesler, in a shantytown sprawling along the edge of Elliott Bay, children awoke in damp cardboard boxes that served as beds. Their parents crawled out of tin-and-tar-paper shacks and into the stench of

Seattle's Hooverville

sewage and rotting seaweed from the mudflats to the west. They broke apart wooden crates and stooped over smoky campfires, feeding the flames. They looked up at the uniform gray skies and, seeing in them tokens of much colder weather ahead, wondered how they would make it through another winter.

Northwest of downtown, in the old Scandinavian neighborhood of Ballard, tugboats belching plumes of black smoke nosed long rafts of logs into the locks that would raise them to the level of Lake Washington. But the gritty shipyards and boat works clustered around the locks were largely quiet, nearly abandoned in fact. In Salmon Bay, just to the east, dozens of fishing boats, unused for months, sat bobbing at moorage, the paint peeling from their weathered hulls. On Phinney Ridge, looming above Ballard, wood smoke curled up from the stovepipes and chimneys of hundreds of modest homes and dissolved into the mist overhead.

It was the fourth year of the Great Depression. One in four working Americans—ten million people—had no job and no prospects of finding one, and only a quarter of them were receiving any kind of relief. Industrial production had fallen by half in those four years. At least one million, and perhaps as many as two million, were homeless, living on the streets or in shantytowns like Seattle's Hooverville. In many American towns, it was impossible to find a bank whose doors weren't permanently shuttered; behind those doors the savings of countless American families had disappeared forever. Nobody could say when, or if, the hard times would ever end.

And perhaps that was the worst of it. Whether you were a banker or a baker, a homemaker or homeless, it was with you night and day—a terrible, unrelenting uncertainty about the future, a feeling that the ground could drop out from under you for good at any moment. In March an oddly appropriate movie had come out and quickly become a smash hit: *King Kong*. Long lines formed in front of movie theaters around the country, people of all ages shelling out precious quarters and dimes to see the story of a huge, irrational beast that had invaded the civilized world, taken its inhabitants into its clutches, and left them dangling over the abyss.

There were glimmers of better times to come, but they were just glimmers. The stock market had rebounded earlier in the year, the Dow Jones Industrial Average climbing an all-time record of 15.34 percent in one day on March 15 to close at 62.10. But Americans had seen so much capital destroyed between 1929 and the end of 1932 that almost everyone believed, correctly as it would turn out, that it might take the better part of a generation—twenty-five years—before the Dow once again saw its previous high of 381 points. And, at any rate, the price of a share of General Electric didn't mean a thing to the vast majority of Americans, who owned no stock at all. What mattered to them was that the strongboxes and mason jars under their beds, in which they now kept what remained of their life savings, were often perilously close to empty.

A new president was in the White House, Franklin Delano Roosevelt, a distant cousin of that most upbeat and energetic of presidents, Teddy Roosevelt. FDR had come into office brimming with optimism and trumpeting a raft of slogans and programs. But Herbert Hoover had come in spouting equal optimism, buoyantly predicting that a day would soon come when poverty would be washed out of American life forever. "Ours is a land rich in resources; stimulating in its glorious beauty; filled with millions of happy homes; blessed with comfort and opportunity," Hoover had said at his inaugural, before adding words that would soon prove particularly ironic: "In no nation are the fruits of accomplishment more secure."

At any rate, it was hard to know what to make of the new President Roosevelt. As he began putting programs into place over the summer, a rising chorus of hostile voices had begun to call him a radical, a socialist, even a Bolshevik. It was unnerving to hear: as bad as things were, few Americans wanted to go down the Russian path.

There was a new man in Germany too, brought into power in January by the National Socialist German Workers' Party, a group with a reputation for thuggish behavior. It was even harder to know what that meant. But Adolf Hitler was hell-bent on rearming his country despite the Treaty of Versailles. And while most Americans were distinctly uninterested in European affairs, the British were increasingly worked up about it all, and one had to wonder whether the horrors of the Great War were about to be replayed. It seemed unlikely, but the possibility hung there, a persistent and troubling cloud.

The day before, October 8, 1933, the *American Weekly*, a Sunday supplement in the *Seattle Post-Intelligencer* and dozens of other American newspapers, had run a single-frame, half-page cartoon, one in a series titled *City Shadows*. Dark, drawn in charcoal, chiaroscuro in style, it depicted a man in a derby sitting dejectedly on a sidewalk by his candy stand with his wife, behind him, dressed in rags and his son, beside him, holding some newspapers. The caption read, "Ah don't give up, Pop. Maybe ya didn't make a sale all week, but it ain't as if I didn't have my paper route." But it was the expression on the man's face that was most arresting. Haunted, haggard, somewhere beyond hopeless, it suggested starkly that he no longer believed in himself. For many of the millions of Americans who read the *American Weekly* every Sunday, it was an all too familiar expression—one they saw every morning when they glanced in the mirror.

But the overcast didn't last, nor did the gloom, in Seattle that day. By late morning, seams began to open in the cloud cover. The still waters of Lake Washington, stretched out at the city's back, slowly shifted from gray to green to blue. On the campus of the University of Washington, perched on a bluff overlooking the lake, slanting rays of sunlight began to warm the shoulders of students lounging on a wide quadrangle of grass in front of the university's massive new stone library, eating their lunches, poring over books, chatting idly. Sleek black crows strutted among the students, hoping for a morsel of bologna or cheese left unguarded. High above the library's stained-glass windows and soaring neo-Gothic spires, screeching seagulls whirled in white loops against the slowly bluing sky.

For the most part, the young men and women sat in separate groups. The men wore pressed slacks and freshly shined oxfords and cardigan sweaters. As they ate, they talked earnestly about classes, about the big upcoming football game with the University of Oregon, and about the improbable ending of the World Series two days before, when little Mel Ott had come to the plate for the New York Giants with two out in the tenth inning. Ott had run the count out to two and two, and then smashed a long line drive into the center field seats to score the series-winning run over the Washington Senators. It was the kind of thing that showed you that a little guy could still make all the difference, and it reminded you how suddenly events could turn around in this world, for better or for worse. Some of the young men sucked lazily on briar pipes, and the sweet smell of Prince Albert tobacco smoke drifted among them. Others dangled cigarettes from their lips, and as they paged through the day's *Seattle Post-Intelligencer* they could take satisfaction in a half-page ad that trumpeted the latest proof of the health benefits of smoking: "21 of 23 Giants World Champions Smoke Camels. It Takes Healthy Nerves to Win the World Series."

The young women, sitting in their own clusters on the lawn, wore short-heeled pumps and rayon hose, calf-length skirts, and loose-fitting blouses with ruffles and flounces on the sleeves and at the necklines. Their hair was sculpted into a wide variety of shapes and styles. Like the young men, the women talked about classes and sometimes about baseball too. Those who had had dates over the weekend talked about the new movies in town—Gary Cooper in *One Sunday Afternoon*, at the Paramount, and a Frank Capra film, *Lady for a Day*, at the Roxy. Like the boys, some of them smoked cigarettes.

By midafternoon the sun had broken through, unfurling a warm, translucent day of golden light. Two young men, taller than most, loped across the grassy quad in front of the library, in a hurry. One of them, a six-foot-three freshman named Roger Morris, had a loose, gangly build; a tousle of dark hair with a forelock that perpetually threatened to fall over his long face; and heavy black eyebrows that lent him, at first glance, a bit of a glowering look. The other young man, Joe Rantz, also a freshman, was nearly as tall, at six foot two and a half, but more tautly built, with broad shoulders and solid, powerful legs. He wore his blond hair in a crew cut. He had a strong jawline, fine, regular features, gray eyes verging into blue, and he drew covert glances from many of the young women sitting on the grass.

The two young men were taking the same engineering class and had a common and audacious objective that radiant afternoon. They rounded a corner of the library, skirted the concrete circle of Frosh Pond, descended a long grassy slope, and then crossed Montlake Boulevard, dodging a steady stream of black coupes, sedans, and roadsters. The pair made their way eastward between the basketball pavilion and the horseshoe-shaped excavation that served as the campus football stadium. Then they turned south again, following a dirt road through open woods and into a marshy area fringing Lake Washington. As they walked they began to overtake other boys heading in the same direction.

They finally came to a point of land located just where the canal known as the Montlake Cut—simply the Cut, in local parlance—entered Union Bay on the west side of Lake Washington. Perched on the point was an odd-looking building. Its sides—clad in weather-beaten shingles and inset with a series of large windows—slanted obliquely inward, rising toward a gambrel roof. When the boys moved around to the front of the building, they found an enormous pair of sliding doors, the upper halves of which consisted almost entirely of windowpanes. A wide wooden ramp ran from the sliding doors down to a long dock floating parallel to the shore of the Cut.

It was an old airplane hangar built by the U.S. Navy in 1918 to house seaplanes for the Naval Aviation Training Corps during the Great War. The war had ended before the building could actually be used, so it had been turned over to the University of Washington in the fall of 1919. Ever since, it had served as the shell house for the school's rowing team. Now both the wide wooden ramp leading down to the water and a narrow ledge of land to the east of the building were crowded with boys milling about nervously, 175 of them, mostly tall and lean, though a dozen or so of them were notably short and slight. A handful of older boys were there too, leaning against the building in white jerseys emblazoned with large purple Ws, their arms crossed, sizing up the newcomers.

Joe Rantz and Roger Morris stepped into the building. Along each side of the cavernous room, long, sleek racing shells were stacked four high on wooden racks. With their burnished wooden hulls turned upward, they gleamed in white shafts of light that fell from the windows overhead, giving the place the feel of a cathedral. The air was dry and still. It smelled sweetly of varnish and freshly sawn cedar. Collegiate banners, faded but still colorful, hung from the high rafters: California, Yale, Princeton, Navy, Cornell, Columbia, Harvard, Syracuse, MIT. In the corners of the room, dozens of yellow-spruce oars stood on end, each ten to twelve feet long and tipped with a white blade. At the back of the room, up in a loft, came the sound of someone at work with a wood rasp.

Joe and Roger signed the freshman crew registration book, then returned to the bright light outside and sat on a bench, waiting for instructions. Joe glanced at Roger, who seemed relaxed and confident.

"Aren't you nervous?" Joe whispered.

Roger glanced back at him. "I'm panicked. I just look like this to demoralize the competition." Joe smiled briefly, too close to panic himself to hold the smile for long.

For Joe Rantz, perhaps more than for any of the other young men sitting by the Montlake Cut, something hung in the balance that afternoon, and he was all too aware of it. The girls on the library lawn who had glanced appreciatively his way had had to overlook what was painfully obvious to him: that his clothes were not like those of most of the other students—his trousers not neatly creased, his oxfords neither new nor freshly polished, his sweater neither crisp nor clean but rather an old and rumpled hand-me-down. Joe understood cold reality. He knew he might not belong here at all, and he certainly couldn't stay long in this world of pressed trousers, of briar pipes and cardigan sweaters, of interesting ideas, sophisticated conversation, and intriguing opportunities, if things did not go well in the shell house. He would never be a chemical engineer, and he would not be able to marry his high school sweetheart, who had followed him to Seattle so they could begin to build a life together. To fail at this rowing business would mean, at best, returning to a small, bleak town on the Olympic Peninsula with nothing ahead of him but the prospect of living alone in a cold, empty, half-built house, surviving as best he could on odd jobs, foraging for food, and maybe, if he was very lucky, finding another highway construction job with the Civilian Conservation Corps. At worst it would mean joining a long line of broken men standing outside a soup kitchen like the one down on Yesler Way.

A spot on the freshman crew would not mean a rowing scholarship, for there was no such thing at Washington in 1933, but it would mean the guarantee of a part-time job somewhere on campus, and that—combined with the little Joe had been able to save during the long year of hard manual labor he had endured since graduating from high school—just might get him through college. But he knew that within a few short weeks only a handful of the crowd of boys gathered around him would still be contenders for the freshman crew. In the end, there were only nine seats in the first freshman shell.

The rest of the afternoon was largely consumed by the collection of facts and figures. Joe Rantz and Roger Morris and all the other hopefuls were told to step onto scales, to stand next to measuring sticks, to fill out forms detailing their medical backgrounds. Assistant coaches and older students carrying clipboards stood by eyeing them and recording the information. Thirty of the freshmen, it turned out, were six feet or taller, twenty-five were six one or more, fourteen were six two or more, six were six three or more, one was six four, and two "reached six feet five into the atmosphere," as one of the sports-writers present noted.

Directing the proceedings was a slim young man toting a large mega-phone. Tom Bolles, the freshman coach, was a former Washington oarsman himself. With a bland, pleasant face, a bit lean in the jowls, and given to wearing wire-rimmed glasses, Bolles had been a history major, was working on a master's degree, and had a distinctly scholarly look about him—a look that had spurred some of Seattle's sportswriters to begin referring to him as "the professor." And in many ways, the role that lay ahead of him that fall, as it did every fall, was that of an educator. When his colleagues in the basketball pavilion or on the football field first encountered their freshman prospects each fall, they could assume that the boys had played the sport in high school and knew at least the rudiments of their respective games. But almost none of the young men assembled outside the shell house that afternoon had ever rowed a stroke in his life, certainly not in a vessel as delicate and unforgiving as a racing shell, pulling oars twice as long as the young men were tall.

Most of them were city boys like the boys lounging up on the quad—the sons of lawyers and businessmen—dressed neatly in woolen slacks and car-digan sweaters. A few, like Joe, were farm boys or lumberjacks or fishermen, the products of foggy coastal villages, damp dairy farms, and smoky lumber towns all over the state. Growing up, they had wielded axes and fishing gaffs and pitchforks expertly, and they had built up strong arms and broad shoul-ders doing so. Their strength would be an asset, Bolles knew, but rowing—he understood as well as anyone—was at least as much art as brawn, and a keen intelligence was just as important as brute strength. There were a thousand and one small things that had to be learned, mastered, and brought to bear in precisely the right way to propel a twenty-four-inch-wide cedar shell, carrying three-quarters of a ton of human flesh and bone, through the water with any semblance of speed and grace. Over the next few months, he would need to teach these boys, or those few among them who made the freshman team, every last one of those thousand and one small things. And some big ones as well: Would the farm boys be able to keep up with the intellectual side of the sport? Would the city boys have the toughness simply to survive? Most of them, Bolles knew, would not.

Another tall man stood watching quietly from the broad doorway of the shell house, dressed impeccably, as he always was, in a dark three-piece business suit, a crisp white shirt, a tie, and a fedora, spinning a Phi Beta Kappa key on a lanyard he held in one hand. Al Ulbrickson, head coach of the University of Washington rowing program, was a stickler for detail, and his style of dress sent a simple message: that he was the boss, and that he was all business. He was just thirty—young enough that he needed to draw a line of demarcation between himself and the boys he commanded. The suit and the Phi Beta Kappa key helped in that regard. It also helped that he was strikingly good-looking and built like the oarsman he had been, the former stroke oar of a Washington crew that had won national championships in 1924 and 1926. He was tall, muscular, broad shouldered, and distinctly Nordic in his features, with high cheekbones, a chiseled jawline, and cold slate-gray eyes. They were the kind of eyes that shut you up fast if you were a young man inclined to challenge something he had just said.

He had been born right here in the Montlake district of Seattle, not far from the shell house. And he had grown up just a few miles down Lake Washington on Mercer Island, long before it became an enclave for the wealthy. His family, in fact, had been of very modest means, straining to make ends meet. In order to attend Franklin High School, he had had to row a small boat two miles over to Seattle and back every day for four years. He had excelled at Franklin, but he never really felt challenged by his teachers. It wasn't until he arrived at the University of Washington and turned out for crew that he came into his own. Finally challenged in the classroom and on the water, he excelled in both areas, and when he graduated in 1926, Washington quickly hired him as the freshman crew coach, and then as head coach. Now he lived and breathed Washington rowing. The university, and rowing, had made him

Al Ulbrickson

who he was. Now they were almost a religion to him. His job was to win converts.

Ulbrickson was also the least talkative man on campus, perhaps in the state, legendary for his reticence and the inscrutability of his countenance. He was half Danish and half Welsh by ancestry, and New York sportswriters, both frustrated and somewhat charmed by how hard they had to work to get a decent quote out of him, had taken to calling him the "Dour Dane." His oarsmen also found the name apt, but none of them was likely to call him it to his face. He commanded enormous respect among his boys, but he did so almost entirely without raising his voice, almost, in fact, without speaking to them. His few words were so carefully chosen and so effectively delivered that every one of them fell like a blade or a balm on the boy to whom they were delivered. He strictly forbade his boys from smoking, cursing, or drinking, though he was known occasionally to do all three himself when safely out of sight or earshot of his crews. To the boys, he seemed at times almost devoid of emotion, yet year after year he somehow managed to stir the deepest and most affirmative emotions many of them had ever known.

As Ulbrickson stood watching the new crop of freshmen that afternoon, Royal Brougham, the sports editor at the *Post-Intelligencer,* edged close to him. Brougham was a slight man, whom many years later ABC's Keith Jackson would call "a jolly little elf." But if he was jolly, he was also crafty. He was well acquainted with Ulbrickson's perpetual solemnity, and he had his own names for the coach: sometimes he was the "Deadpan Kid," sometimes the "Man with the Stone Face." Now he peered up at Ulbrickson's granitic face and began to pepper him with questions—probing, pestering questions—determined to find out what the Husky coach thought about the new crop of freshmen, all this "tall timber," as Brougham put it. Ulbrickson remained quiet a long while, gazing at the boys on the ramp and squinting at the sunlight on the Cut. The temperature had climbed into the high seventies, unusually warm for an October afternoon in Seattle, and some of the new boys had taken off their shirts to soak up the sun. A few of them sauntered along the dock, bending over to hoist long, yellow-spruce oars, getting the feel of them, contemplating their considerable heft. In the golden afternoon light, the boys moved gracefully—lithe and fit, ready to take something on.

When Ulbrickson finally turned to Brougham and replied, it was with a single, none-too-helpful word: "Pleasing."

Royal Brougham had come to know Al Ulbrickson pretty well, and he did a quick double take. There was something about the way Ulbrickson delivered the response, a note in his voice or a glint in his eye or a twitch at the corner of his mouth, that arrested Brougham's attention. The following day he offered his readers this translation of Ulbrickson's reply: "which in less guarded terms means ... 'very good indeed.'"

Royal Brougham's interest in what Al Ulbrickson was thinking was far from casual—much more than just a desire to fill out his daily column with yet another terse Ulbrickson quote. Brougham was on a quest—one of many he would launch in his sixty-eight-year career with the *Post-Intelligencer.*

Since he had started at the paper in 1910, Brougham had become something of a local legend, renowned for his uncanny ability to extract information from storied figures like Babe Ruth and Jack Dempsey. His opinion, his connections, and his tenacity were so well regarded that he was quickly becoming something of a ringmaster of civic life in Seattle, sought out by grandees of all stripes—politicians, star athletes, university presidents, fight promoters, coaches, even bookies. But above all, Brougham was a masterful promoter. "Part poet, part P. T. Barnum," Emmett Watson, another legendary Seattle scribe, called him. What he wanted to promote above all else was Seattle. He wanted to transform the world's view of his gray, sleepy, logging-and-fishing town into something far grander and more sophisticated.

When Brougham first arrived at the *Post-Intelligencer,* Washington's crew program had consisted of little more than a handful of rough-and-tumble country boys lurching around Lake Washington in leaky, tublike shells, coached by what appeared to many to be a red-haired lunatic named Hiram Conibear. In the intervening years, the program had advanced a great deal, but it still got little respect beyond the West Coast. Brougham figured the time was right to change all that. After all, for grandness and sophistication nothing could match a world-class rowing team. The sport reeked of classiness. And crew was a good way for a school, or a city, to get noticed.

In the 1920s and 1930s, collegiate crew was wildly popular, often ranking right up there with baseball and collegiate football in the amount of press it received and the crowds it drew. Outstanding oarsmen were lionized in the national press, even in the era of Babe Ruth, Lou Gehrig, and Joe DiMaggio. Top sportswriters like Grantland Rice and the *New York Times*'s Robert Kelley covered all the major regattas. Millions of fans diligently followed their crews' progress throughout the training and racing seasons, particularly in the East, where something as minor as a coxswain's sore throat could make headlines. Eastern private schools, modeling themselves after elite British institutions like Eton, taught rowing as a gentleman's sport and fed their young-gentlemen oarsmen into the nation's most prestigious universities, places like Harvard, Yale, and Princeton. The most devoted fans even collected trading cards of their favorite crews.

By the 1920s western fans had begun to take a similar interest in their own crews—spurred on by a heated rivalry, which dated back to 1903, between two large public universities, the University of California at Berkeley and the University of Washington. After years of struggling for funding and recognition even on their own campuses, the crew programs at both schools had finally begun to have occasional successes competing with their eastern counterparts. Recently crews from California had even won Olympic gold twice. Both schools could now count on tens of thousands of students, alumni, and excited citizens to turn out for their annual dual regattas in April, when they battled for preeminence in West Coast rowing. But western coaches were paid a fraction of what eastern coaches made, and western crews still rowed mostly against one another. Neither school had a penny for recruitment, nor virtually anything in the way of well-heeled patrons. Everyone knew that the center of gravity in American collegiate rowing still lay somewhere between Cambridge, New Haven, Princeton, Ithaca, and Annapolis. Royal Brougham figured if it could somehow be shifted west, it might land squarely in Seattle and bring the city a lot of much-needed respect. He also knew that, given the way things were going, it might very well land in California instead.

As Al Ulbrickson studied his new freshmen at the shell house in Seattle that afternoon, five thousand miles to the east, a thirty-nine-year-old architect named Werner March worked late into the night, hunched over a drafting table in an office somewhere in Berlin.

A few days before, on October 5, he and Adolf Hitler had stepped out of a black, armored Mercedes-Benz in the countryside west of Berlin. They were accompanied by Dr. Theodor Lewald, president of the German Olympic Organizing Committee, and Wilhelm Frick, Reich minister of the interior. The spot where they emerged from the car was slightly elevated, about a hundred feet higher than the heart of the city. To the west lay the ancient Grunewald forest, where sixteenth-century German princes hunted stags and wild boars and where Berliners of all classes nowadays enjoyed hiking, picnicking, and foraging for mushrooms. To the east, the ancient church spires and peaked rooflines of central Berlin rose above a sea of trees turned red and gold in the crisp autumn air.

They had come to inspect the old Deutsches Stadion, built in 1916 for the ill-fated Olympic Games of that year. Werner March's father, Otto, had designed and overseen construction of the structure—the largest stadium in the world at the time—but the games had been canceled because of the Great War, the war that had so humiliated Germany. Now, under the younger March's direction, the stadium was undergoing renovations in preparation for the 1936 Olympics, which Germany was to host.

Hitler had not originally wanted to host the games at all. Almost everything about the idea, in fact, had offended him. The year before, he had damned the games as the invention of "Jews and Freemasons." The very heart of the Olympic ideal—that athletes of all nations and all races should commingle and compete on equal terms—was antithetical to his National Socialist Party's core belief: that the Aryan people were manifestly superior to all others. And he was filled with revulsion by the notion that Jews, Negroes, and other vagabond races from around the world would come traipsing through Germany. But in the eight months since he had come to power in January, Hitler had begun to change his mind.

The man who, more than any other, was responsible for this transformation was Dr. Joseph Goebbels, minister of public enlightenment and propaganda. Goebbels—a particularly vicious anti-Semite who had engineered much of Hitler's political rise—was now systematically dismantling what remained of a free press in Germany. Just over five feet tall, with a deformed and shortened right leg, a club foot, and an oddly shaped head that seemed too large for his small body, Goebbels did not look the part of a power broker, but he in fact was among the most important and influential members of Hitler's inner circle. He was intelligent, articulate, and remarkably cunning. Many who knew him in social settings—among them, the American ambassador to Germany, William Dodd; his wife, Mattie; and his daughter, Martha—found him "delightful," "infectious," "one of the few men in Germany with a sense of humor." He had a surprisingly compelling speaking voice for so small a man, an instrument that he wielded like a rapier when he addressed large crowds in person or spoke on the radio.

That very week he had assembled three hundred Berlin journalists to instruct them on the provisions of the Nazis' new National Press Law. First and foremost, he had announced, to practice journalism in Germany one would henceforth have to do so as a licensed member of his press organization, the Reichsverband der Deutschen Presse, and no one would be licensed who had, or was married to someone who had, so much as one Jewish grandparent. As for editorial content, no one was to publish anything that was not consecrated by the party. Specifically, nothing was to be published that was "calculated to weaken the power of the Reich at home or abroad, the community will of the German people, its military spirit, or its culture and economy." None of this should be any problem, Goebbels had calmly assured his audience of dumbstruck journalists that day: "I don't see why you should have the slightest difficulty in adjusting the trend of what you write to the interests of the State. It is possible that the Government may sometimes be mistaken—as to individual measures—but it is absurd to suggest that anything superior to the Government might take its place. What is the use, therefore, of editorial skepticism? It can only make people uneasy." But just to make sure, the same week, the new Nazi government had enacted a separate measure imposing the death penalty on those who published "treasonable articles."

Goebbels had his sights set on far more than controlling the German press, however. Always attentive to new and better opportunities to shape the larger message emanating from Berlin, he had seen at once that hosting the Olympics would offer the Nazis a singular opportunity to portray Germany to the world as a civilized and modern state, a friendly but powerful nation that the larger world would do well to recognize and respect. And Hitler, as he listened to Goebbels, and knowing full well what he had planned for Germany in the days, months, and years ahead, had slowly begun to recognize the value in presenting a more attractive face to the world than his brown-shirted storm troopers and his black-shirted security forces had displayed thus far. At the very least, an Olympic interlude would help buy him time—time to convince the world of his peaceful intentions, even as he began to rebuild Germany's military and industrial power for the titanic struggle to come.

Hitler had stood hatless at the Olympic site that afternoon, listening quietly as Werner March explained that the horse-racing track adjoining the old stadium prevented a major expansion. Glancing for a moment at the racetrack, Hitler made an announcement that astonished March. The racetrack must "disappear." A vastly larger stadium was to be built, one that would hold at least a hundred thousand people. And more than that, there must be a massive surrounding sports complex to provide venues for a wide variety of competitions, a single, unified *Reichssportfeld*. "It will be the task of the nation," Hitler said. It was to be a testament to German ingenuity, to its cultural superiority, and to its growing power. When the world assembled here, on this elevated ground overlooking Berlin, in 1936, it would behold the future not just of Germany but of Western civilization.

Five days later, Werner March, stooping over his drafting table, had only until morning before he must lay preliminary plans in front of Hitler.

In Seattle, at about the same hour, Tom Bolles and his assistant coaches released the freshmen. The days were already beginning to grow short, and at 5:30 p.m. the sun sank behind Montlake Bridge just to the west of the shell house. The boys began to straggle back up the hill toward the main campus in small groups, shaking their heads, talking softly among themselves about their chances of making the team.

Al Ulbrickson stood on the floating dock, listening to the lake water lap at the shore, watching them go. Behind his implacable gaze, wheels were turning at an even faster rate than usual. To some extent he remained haunted by the more or less disastrous season of 1932. More than one hundred thousand people had turned out to view the annual contest between California and Washington, crowding along the shores of the lake. A strong wind was blowing by the time the main event, the varsity race, was set to start, and the lake was frothy with whitecaps. Almost as soon as the race got under way, the Washington boat had begun to ship water. By the halfway mark, the oarsmen in their sliding seats were sloshing back and forth in several inches of it. When the Washington boat neared the finish line, it was eighteen lengths behind Cal, and the only real question was whether it would sink before crossing. It stayed more or less afloat, but the outcome was the worst defeat in Washington's history.

In June of that year, Ulbrickson's varsity had attempted to redeem itself at the annual Intercollegiate Rowing Association regatta in Poughkeepsie, New York, but Cal had trounced them again, by five lengths this time. Later in the summer, the Washington varsity had ventured to the Olympic trials at Lake Quinsigamond in Massachusetts, to try once more. This time they were eliminated in a preliminary contest. And to top things off, in August, in Los Angeles, Ulbrickson had watched his counterpart at Cal, Ky Ebright, win the sport's most coveted award, an Olympic gold medal.

Ulbrickson's boys had regrouped quickly. In April of 1933, a fresh and re-constituted varsity crew promptly exacted its revenge, sweeping the Olympic champion Cal Bears from their home waters on the Oakland Estuary. A week later, they did it again, defeating Cal and UCLA on a two-thousand-meter course in Long Beach, California. The 1933 Poughkeepsie Regatta had been canceled due to the Depression, but Washington returned to Long Beach that summer to race against the best crews the East had to offer: Yale, Cornell, and Harvard. Washington edged second-place Yale by eight feet to emerge as de facto national champion. That varsity crew, Ulbrickson told *Esquire* magazine, was by far the best he had ever put together. It had what newspapermen called "plenty of swift." Given that recent history, and the promising look of some of the freshmen walking away from the shell house that evening, Ulbrickson had plenty of reasons to be optimistic about the upcoming season.

But there remained one particularly galling fact of life. No Washington coach had ever even come close to going to the Olympics. With the bad blood that had lately arisen between the Washington and California crew programs, Cal's two gold medals had been bitter pills to swallow. Ulbrickson was already looking forward to 1936. He wanted to bring gold home to Seattle more than he could say—certainly more than he would say.

To pull it off, Ulbrickson knew, he was going to have to clear a series of imposing hurdles. Despite his setbacks the previous year, Cal's head coach Ky Ebright remained an extraordinarily wily opponent, widely regarded as the intellectual master of the sport. He possessed an uncanny knack for winning the big races, the ones that really counted. Ulbrickson needed to find a crew that could beat Ebright's best and keep them beat in an Olympic year. Then he was going to have to find a way to again beat the elite eastern schools— particularly Cornell, Syracuse, Pennsylvania, and Columbia—at the Intercollegiate Rowing Association regatta in Poughkeepsie in 1936. Then he might well have to face Yale, Harvard, or Princeton—schools that did not even deign to row at Poughkeepsie—at the Olympic trials. Yale, after all, had won gold in 1924. The eastern private rowing clubs, particularly the Pennsylvania Athletic Club and the New York Athletic Club, would also likely be in the mix at the 1936 trials. Finally, if he made it to Berlin, he would have to beat the best oarsmen in the world—probably British boys from Oxford and Cambridge, though the Germans were said to be building extraordinarily powerful and disciplined crews under the new Nazi system, and the Italians had very nearly taken the gold in 1932.

All that, Ulbrickson knew, had to start here on this dock, with the boys who were now wandering off into the waning light. Somewhere among them—those green and untested boys—lay much of the stock from which he would have to select a crew capable of going all the way. The trick would be to find which few of them had the potential for raw power, the nearly superhuman stamina, the indomitable willpower, and the intellectual capacity necessary to master the details of technique. And which of them, coupled improbably with all those other qualities, had the most important one: the ability to disregard his own ambitions, to throw his ego over the gunwales, to leave it swirling in the wake of his shell, and to pull, not just for himself, not just for glory, but for the other boys in the boat.

Harry, Fred, Nellie, and Joe Rantz, circa 1917

CHAPTER TWO

These giants of the forest are something to behold. Some have been growing for a thousand years, and each tree contains its own story of the centuries' long struggle for survival. Looking at the annular rings of the wood, you can tell what seasons they have been through. In some drought years they almost perished, as growth is barely perceptible. In others, the growth was far greater.

—George Yeoman Pocock

The path Joe Rantz followed across the quad and down to the shell house that afternoon in 1933 was only the last few hundred yards of a much longer, harder, and at times darker path he had traveled for much of his young life.

His beginnings had been auspicious enough. He was the second son of Harry Rantz and Nellie Maxwell. Harry was a big man, well over six feet tall, large in the hands and feet, heavy in the bones. His face was open and ordinary, its features unremarkable but pleasant and regular. Women found him attractive. He looked you straight in the eye with a simple, earnest expression. But the placidity of his face belied an unusually active mind. He was an inveterate tinkerer and inventor, a lover of gadgetry and mechanical devices, a designer of machines and contraptions of all sorts, a dreamer of big dreams. He thrived on solving complex problems, prided himself on coming up with novel solutions, the kinds of things other people would never think of in a million years.

Harry's was an age that spawned bold dreams and audacious dreamers. In 1903 a pair of tinkerers not unlike Harry, Wilbur and Orville Wright, climbed aboard a device of their own invention near Kitty Hawk, North Carolina, and flew ten feet above the sand for twelve full seconds. In the same year, a Californian named George Adams Wyman rode into New York City aboard a motorcycle that had carried him all the way from San Francisco. He was the first person to cross the continent on a motorized vehicle, and he had done it in only fifty days. Twenty days later, Horatio Nelson Jackson and his bulldog, Bud, arrived from San Francisco in their battered and muddy Winton, becoming the first to accomplish the feat in an automobile. In Milwaukee twenty-one-year-old Bill Harley and twenty-year-old Arthur Davidson attached an engine of their own design to a modified bicycle, hung a sign on the front of their workshop, and went into business selling production motorcycles. And on July 23 of that same year, Henry Ford sold Dr. Ernst Pfenning a shiny red Model A, the first of 1,750 that he would sell in the next year and a half.

In an age of such technological triumphs, it seemed clear to Harry that a man with enough ingenuity and gumption could accomplish almost anything, and he did not intend to be left out of the new gold rush. Before the end of the year, he had designed and built from scratch his own version of an automobile and, to the astonishment of his neighbors, proudly maneuvered it down the street, using a tiller rather than a wheel for steering.

He had gotten married over the telephone in 1899, just for the novelty and wonderment of exchanging vows in two different cities by means of such an exciting new invention. Nellie Maxwell was a piano teacher, the daughter of a no-nonsense Disciples of Christ minister. The couple's first son, Fred, was born later in 1899. In 1906, looking for a place where Harry could make his mark on the world, the young family had left Williamsport, Pennsylvania, headed west, and settled down in Spokane, Washington.

In many ways Spokane was not then far removed from the rough-and-tumble lumber town it had been in the nineteenth century. Located where the cold, clear Spokane River tumbled in a white froth over a series of low falls, the town was surrounded by ponderosa pine forest and open range country. The summers were crackling hot, the air dry and perfumed with the vanilla scent of ponderosa bark. In the autumn towering brown dust storms sometimes blew in from the rolling wheat country to the west. The winters were bitter cold, the springs stingy and slow in coming. And on Saturday nights all year round, cowboys and lumberjacks crowded the downtown bars and honky-tonks, swilled whiskey, and tumbled, brawling, out into the city's streets.

But since the Northern Pacific Railway had arrived, late in the nineteenth century, bringing tens of thousands of Americans to the Northwest for the first time, Spokane's population had quickly soared past a hundred thousand, and a newer, more genteel community had begun to sprout alongside the old lumber town. A thriving commercial center had taken root on the south side of the river, replete with stately brick hotels, sturdy limestone banks, and a wide variety of fine emporiums and reputable mercantile establishments. On the north side of the river, tidy neighborhoods of small frame houses now perched on neat squares of lawn. Harry and Nellie and Fred Rantz moved into one of those houses, at 1023 East Nora Avenue, and Joe was born there in March of 1914.

Harry immediately opened an automobile manufacturing and repair shop. He could fix pretty much any sort of car that sputtered or was dragged by a mule up to his garage door. He specialized, though, in making new ones, sometimes assembling the popular one-cylinder McIntyre Imp cycle-cars, sometimes fabricating new vehicles entirely of his own contrivance. Soon he and his partner, Charles Halstead, also secured the local sales agency for much more substantial cars—brand-new Franklins—and with the town booming they quickly had as much business as they could handle, both in the repair shop and in the sales office.

Harry arose at four thirty each morning to go to the shop, and often he didn't return home until well after seven in the evening. Nellie taught piano to neighborhood children and tended to Joe on weekdays. She doted on her sons, watched over them carefully, and made it her business to keep them away from sin and foolishness. Fred went to school and helped out at the shop on Saturdays. On Sunday mornings the whole family attended Central Christian Church, where Nellie was the principal pianist and Harry sang in the choir. On Sunday afternoons they took their ease, sometimes walking downtown for ice cream, or driving out to Medical Lake, west of town, for a picnic, or strolling through the cool and shady refuge of Natatorium Park, among cottonwood trees down by the river. There they could take in entertainment as lazy and familiar as a semiprofessional baseball game, as carefree as a ride on the dazzling new Looff Carousel, or as stirring as a John Philip Sousa concert at the bandstand. All in all it was a most satisfactory life—a slice, at least, of the dream Harry had come west to live.

But that wasn't at all the way Joe remembered his early childhood. Instead he had a kaleidoscope of broken images, starting in the spring of 1918, when he was just about to turn four, with a memory of his mother standing by his side, in an overgrown field, coughing violently into a handkerchief, and the handkerchief turning bright red with blood. He remembered a doctor with a black leather bag, and the lingering smell of camphor in the house. He remembered sitting on a hard church pew swinging his legs while his mother lay in a box at the front of the church and would not get up. He remembered lying on a bed with his big brother, Fred, perched on the edge, in the upstairs room on Nora Avenue, as the spring winds rattled the windows and Fred spoke softly, talking about dying and about angels and about college and why he couldn't go east to Pennsylvania with Joe. He remembered sitting quietly alone on a train for long days and nights, with blue mountains and green muddy fields and rusty rail yards and dark cities full of smokestacks all flashing past the window by his seat. He remembered a rotund black man, with a bald head and a crisp blue uniform, watching over him on the train, bringing him sandwiches, and tucking him into his berth at night. He remembered meeting the woman who said she was his aunt Alma. And then, almost immediately, a rash on his face and chest, a sore throat, a high fever, and another doctor with another black leather bag. Then, for days stretching into weeks, nothing but lying in a bed in an unfamiliar attic room with the shades always pulled down—no light, no movement, no sound except occasionally the lonely moaning of a train in the distance. No Ma, no Pa, no Fred. Only the sound of a train now and then, and a strange room spinning round him. Plus the beginnings of something else—a new heaviness, a dull sense of apprehension, a burden of doubt and fear pressing down on his small shoulders and his perpetually congested chest.

As he lay ill with scarlet fever in the attic of a woman he did not really know, the last remnants of his former world were dissolving in Spokane. His mother lay in an untended grave, a victim of throat cancer. Fred had gone off to finish college. His father, Harry, his dreams shattered, had fled for the wilds of Canada, unable to cope with what he had seen in his wife's last moments. He could only say that there had been more blood than he had imagined a body could hold and more than he would ever be able to wash from his memory.

A little more than a year later, in the summer of 1919, five-year-old Joe found himself on a train for the second time in his life. He was heading back west this time, summoned by Fred. Since Joe had been sent to Pennsylvania, Fred had graduated from college and, though only twenty-one, secured a job as superintendent of schools in Nezperce, Idaho. Fred had also acquired a wife, Thelma LaFollette, one of a pair of twin sisters from a prosperous eastern

Washington wheat-farming family. Now he hoped to provide his little brother with something like the safe and secure home they had both known before their mother had died and their grief-stricken father had fled north. When a porter helped Joe off the train in Nezperce and set him down on the platform, though, he could barely remember Fred, and he knew not what to make of Thelma. He thought, in fact, that she was his mother and ran to her and threw his arms around her legs.

That fall Harry Rantz abruptly returned from Canada, bought a lot in Spokane, and began to construct a new house, trying to piece his life back together. Like his older son, he needed a wife to make the new house a home, and like his son he found just what he was looking for in the other LaFollette twin. Thelma's sister, Thula, at twenty-two, was a lovely, slender, elfin-faced girl with a whimsical pile of black curls and a fetching smile. Harry was seventeen years her senior, but that was not about to stop him, or her. The basis of Harry's attraction was obvious. The basis of Thula's was less so, and somewhat mysterious to her family.

The elder Rantz must have seemed a romantic figure to her. She had lived thus far in an isolated farmhouse surrounded by vast fields of wheat, with little to entertain her beyond the sound of the wind rustling the bone-dry stalks each autumn. Harry was tall and good-looking, he had a glint in his eye, he was relatively worldly, he was full of restless energy, he was abundantly creative in a mechanical sense, and most of all he seemed to be a kind of visionary. Just by talking about them he could make you see things off in the future, things nobody else had even thought of.

Matters proceeded apace. Harry completed the house in Spokane. He and Thula slipped across the state line and married on the shores of Lake Coeur d'Alene, Idaho, in April 1921, to the great displeasure of Thula's parents. In a stroke Thula became her twin sister's mother-in-law.

For Joe, all this marrying meant another new home and another adjustment. He left Nezperce and moved in with a father he hardly knew, and a young stepmother he knew not at all.

For a time, it seemed as if something like normalcy was returning to his life. The house his father had built was spacious and well lit and smelled sweetly of fresh-sawn wood. Out back there was a swing with a seat wide enough for him and his father and Thula to ride three at a time on warm summer nights. He could walk to school, cutting through a field where he would sometimes filch a ripe melon for an after-school snack. On some vacant land nearby, he could while away long summer days by digging elaborate underground tunnels—cool, dark, subterranean retreats from Spokane's sometimes searing dry heat. And as the old house had been when his mother was alive, the new house was always filled with music. Harry had kept Nellie's most precious possession, her parlor grand piano, and he delighted in sitting at it with Joe, belting out popular tunes, as Joe gleefully sang along: "Ain't We Got Fun" or "Yaaka Hula Hickey Dula" or "Mighty Lak' a Rose" or Harry's favorite, "Yes! We Have No Bananas."

Thula considered the music that Harry and Joe enjoyed coarse, she was not particularly happy to have Nellie's piano in her house, and she disdained to join in. She was an accomplished violinist, far out of the ordinary in fact, her talent so highly valued in her home that growing up she had never had to do the dishes for fear that her fingers would be damaged by soap and water. She and her parents all harbored the conviction that someday she would play in a major orchestra, in New York or Los Angeles perhaps, or even in Berlin or Vienna. Now in the afternoons, when Joe was at school and Harry was at work, she practiced for hours on end—lovely classical pieces that rose and fell and floated out through the screened windows and drifted across the dusty, dry city of Spokane.

In January 1922, Harry and Thula had their first child together, Harry Junior, and in April 1923, they had a second son, Mike. By the time Mike was born, though, family life had begun to fray in the Rantz household. The age of the big dreamer was passing into history before Harry's eyes. Henry Ford had figured out how to manufacture his automobiles on a moving assembly line, and soon others were following suit. Mass production, cheap labor, and big capital were the watchwords of the day now. Harry found himself on the cheap-labor side of the equation. For the past year, he had been living and working weekdays at a gold mine in Idaho, then traveling 140 miles on twisting mountain roads home to Spokane each Friday in his long, black four-door Franklin touring convertible, returning to Idaho again each Sunday afternoon. Harry was glad to have the work. It meant a steady income, and it made use of his mechanical skills. For Thula, though, the change meant long, dismal weeks alone in the house, with nobody to help out, nobody to talk to at night, nobody to sit down to dinner with except for three clamoring boys—an infant, a toddler, and a strangely guarded and watchful young stepson.

Then, not long after Mike was born, during one of Harry's weekend visits, in the middle of a dark, moonless night, Joe suddenly awoke to the smell of smoke and the sound of flames crackling somewhere in the house. He snatched up the baby and grabbed Harry Junior by the arm, yanking him out of bed and stumbling out of the house with his little half brothers. A few moments later, his father and Thula also emerged from the house in singed nightshirts, bewildered, calling out for their children. When Harry saw that his family was intact, he dashed back into the smoke and flames. Several long minutes passed before he reappeared, silhouetted against the fire at the garage entrance to the house. He was pushing Nellie's piano—the only thing of hers he had left from their marriage. His sweat-slick face was a mask of anguish, his every muscle straining as he leaned into the big piano, moving it by brute strength inch by inch through the wide doorway. When the piano was finally out of harm's way, Harry Rantz and his family gathered around it and watched, awestruck, as their house burned to the ground.

Standing in the glare of the flickering light, as the last remnants of the roof tumbled into the fire, Thula Rantz must have wondered why in God's name Harry had chosen an old piano as the one thing he would risk his life to save. Joe, now nine, standing by her side, felt again what he had first felt in his aunt's attic in Pennsylvania five years before—the same coldness, fear, and insecurity. Home, it was beginning to seem, was something you couldn't necessarily count on.

With no place else to go, Harry Rantz packed his family into his Franklin touring car and headed northeast, to the mining camp where he had been working as a master mechanic for the past year. Founded in 1910 by a character named John M. Schnatterly, the mine was located in the far northern panhandle of Idaho, squarely on the Idaho-Montana border, where the Kootenai River flowed south out of British Columbia. Originally the business had been named the Idaho Gold and Radium Mining Company, after Schnatterly claimed to have found a vein of radium worth millions. When none materialized, the government ordered Schnatterly to stop calling it a radium mine, so he blithely renamed the concern the Idaho Gold and Ruby Mining Company, the rubies apparently being small garnets that were occasionally found among the mine's tailings. By the early twenties, the mine still had not produced much, if anything, in the way of gold, or rubies, or even garnets for that matter. That, however, did not keep Schnatterly from importing a steady stream of well-heeled eastern investors, feting them on his luxury yacht as he transported them up the Kootenai to his mining camp and ultimately bilking them out of millions of investment dollars. Along the way he alienated more than a few people, managed to get into three gunfights, and collected three gunshot wounds for his efforts before finally dying a fiery death when an explosion rocked his yacht. Nobody could say for sure whether it was an accident or revenge, but it had the smell of the latter.

Virtually all of the company's three dozen employees and their families lived in Schnatterly's mining camp, Boulder City. Its various ramshackle buildings—thirty-five small, identical, rough-hewn cabins with attached outhouses, a blacksmith shop, a machine shop, a bunkhouse for single men, a church, a water-powered sawmill, and a modest homemade hydroelectric plant—clung to the mountainside along Boulder Creek, linked together by a network of wooden sidewalks. A one-room schoolhouse sided with cedar shingles stood among pines on a flat piece of land above the camp, but there were few children, and the school was sparsely and irregularly attended. A rutted dirt wagon road plunged from the schoolhouse down the mountainside through a long series of tortuous switchbacks before straightening out and crossing a bridge over the Kootenai to the Montana side of the river, where stood the company store and a cook shack.

It was a dismal settlement, but to Harry it was a tinkerer's paradise and the perfect place to try to forget Spokane. With his prodigious mechanical aptitude, he happily set about repairing and maintaining the water-driven sawmill, an electrically driven rock-crushing plant, a forty-five-ton Marion steam shovel, and the mine's many assorted vehicles and odd pieces of machinery.

For nine-year-old Joe, Boulder City offered an astounding cornucopia of delights. When his father operated the huge steam shovel, Joe perched happily on the rear end of the machine and took merry-go-round rides as Harry spun the steam-belching behemoth around and around. When Joe tired of this, Harry spent a long evening in the company shop constructing a go-cart. The next afternoon Joe laboriously dragged it all the way up the wagon road, to the top of the mountain, pointed the contraption downhill, climbed in, and released the brake. He raced down the road at breakneck speed, careening around the hairpin turns, whooping at the top of his lungs all the way to the river and across the bridge. Then he climbed out and began the long trek back to the top of the mountain and did it again and again until it was finally too dark to see the road. Being in motion, outdoors, with wind in his face made him feel alive—it brushed away the anxiety that since his mother's death had seemed to be nibbling continuously at the corners of his mind.

Joe with Harry, Thula, Mike, and Harry Jr. at the Gold and Ruby mine

When winter closed in and the mountainside was deep in powdery snow, his father got out the welding equipment and built Joe a sled on which he could sluice down the wagon road at even more terrifying speeds. And eventually Joe discovered that when no one was watching he could take Harry Junior up the mountain, help him into an ore car at the top of a rickety trestle that ran alongside Boulder Creek, give the car a shove, hop in himself, and again rattle down the mountain at terrifying speeds with his little half brother in front of him, shrieking in delight.

When he wasn't hurtling down the mountain, helping out at the mill, or attending the one-room school above the camp, Joe could explore the woods or climb among the 6,400-foot-tall mountains in the Kaniksu National Forest just to the west. He could hunt for deer antlers and other treasures in the woods, swim in the Kootenai, or tend the vegetable garden he nurtured on a small plot of ground inside the picket fence surrounding his family's cabin.

For Thula, however, Boulder City was about as forlorn a place as could be found on earth. It was unbearably hot and dusty in the summer, wet and muddy in spring and fall, and filthy pretty much all year round. Winter brought the worst of it. Come December, bitterly cold air flowed down the

Kootenai Valley from British Columbia, made its way through every crack and crevice in the walls of her flimsy cabin, and sliced through whatever layers of clothing or bedding she tried to take refuge in. She was still saddled with a screaming infant, a bored and complaining toddler, and a stepson whom, as he grew older and more difficult to control, she was starting to think of as an unwanted reminder of her husband's previous and all too precious marriage. It did not help that to pass the time Joe plucked incessantly at a ukulele, singing and whistling the campy tunes that he and his father enjoyed so much. Nor did it help that when Harry came home from work he often tracked grease and sawdust into the cabin. That came abruptly to an end one chilly mountain evening when Harry came trudging up the hill in his greasy overalls at the end of the day. When he entered the cabin, Thula took one look at him, shrieked, and pushed him back out through the front door. "Take those filthy things off, go down to the creek, and wash yourself off," she commanded. Sheepishly, Harry sat down on a log, took off his boots, stripped down to a pair of white cotton long johns, and hobbled barefoot down a rocky trail toward Boulder Creek. From then on, regardless of temperature or time of year, Harry dutifully bathed in the creek and came into the house carrying his boots, with his overalls draped over his arm.

Growing up, Thula had always been treasured by her family, not only for her beauty—which exceeded that of her twin, Thelma, by a wide margin—and for her extraordinary talent with the violin, but also for the refinement of her taste and the sensitivity of her nature. She was so exquisitely sensitive, in fact, that everyone in her family believed her to possess "second sight," an idea that was dramatically reinforced when they read the newspaper on the morning of April 15, 1912. The night before, Thula had awakened suddenly, screaming about icebergs and a huge ship sinking and people calling out for help.

Thula was educated and artistic and determined to seek finer things than a wheat farm had to offer. Now that she was marooned in Boulder City, her few social companions consisted of the ill-educated and hardscrabble wives of sawyers and miners. Increasingly, she was painfully aware that she was about as far as she could imagine from any means of fulfilling her dream of sitting proudly front and center, as first violin in a major symphony orchestra. She could hardly even practice. In the winter her fingers were too cold to dance up and down the fingerboard; in the summer they were so cracked and sore from the dry Idaho air that she could hardly hold the bow. Her violin mostly sat on a shelf these days, calling out to her, almost mocking her as she washed end-less piles of dishes and dirty diapers. This was the kind of thing her sister, Thelma, had been raised to do, not her. Yet Thelma now lived comfortably in a nice house in Seattle. The more she thought about the unfairness of it, the more tensions mounted in the cabin.

Finally one warm summer afternoon, those tensions boiled over. Thula was pregnant with her third child. She had spent much of the afternoon on her hands and knees, scrubbing the cabin's pinewood floor, and her back was throbbing with pain. As dinnertime approached she began the nightly rou-tine of laboring over the hot woodstove, feeding kindling into the firebox, trying to get enough flame to draw a draft up the chimney. Smoke billowed out from under the cooktop and clawed at her eyes. When she finally got a fire going, she set about trying to cobble together an evening meal for Harry and the boys. Between her limited budget and the scant selection of foods avail-able at the company store, it was hard to put a decent meal on the table every night. It was even harder to keep it on the table long enough for her children to eat a square meal. Joe was growing like a weed, and he inhaled food as fast as Thula could make it. She worried constantly that her own boys wouldn't get enough.

She began shoving pans around on the stovetop angrily, trying to make room, not sure what she was going to cook. Then suddenly she heard a shout from outside the cabin, followed by a long, painful wailing sound—little Mike's voice. Thula dropped a pot on the stove and bolted for the front door.

Joe was outside, down on his hands and knees, tending his vegetable garden that afternoon. The garden was a kind of sanctuary for him, a place where he, not Thula, was in charge, and it was a source of enormous pride. When he brought a basket of fresh tomatoes or an armful of sweet corn into the cabin, and then saw them on the dinner table that night, it made him feel that he was making a contribution to the family, helping Thula, maybe making up for whatever he might have done most recently to annoy her. Working his way down a row in the garden that afternoon, pulling weeds, he had turned around to find eighteen-month-old Mike following him, imitating him, happily plucking half-grown carrots out of the ground. Joe turned and bellowed at him in rage, and Mike unleashed a heart-rending scream. A mo-ment later Joe looked up at the porch and saw Thula, red faced and seething. She ran down the steps, snatched Mike up from the ground, whisked him into the cabin, and slammed the door behind her.

When Harry came home from work later that evening, Thula was waiting for him in the doorway. She demanded that Harry take Joe out back, out of her sight, and give him a good hiding. Instead Harry merely took Joe upstairs, sat him down, and gave him a good talking-to. Thula exploded in the face of what she saw as lax discipline. Feeling trapped, growing desperate, she finally declared that she would not live under the same roof with Joe, that it was him or her, that Joe had to move out if she were to stay in such a godforsaken place. Harry could not calm her down, and he could not abide the thought of losing a second wife, certainly not one as lovely as Thula. He went back upstairs and told his son he would have to move out of the house. Joe was ten.

Early the next morning, his father led him up the wagon road to the shingle-sided schoolhouse at the top of the hill. He left Joe sitting outside on the steps and went in to talk to the male schoolteacher. Joe sat and waited in the morning sunlight, drawing circles in the dust with a stick and staring morosely at a Steller's jay that had perched on a nearby branch and begun screeching at him as if scolding him. After a long while, his father and the teacher emerged from the schoolhouse and shook hands. They had struck a deal. In return for a place to sleep in the building, Joe was to chop enough kindling and split enough wood to keep the school's huge stone fireplace stoked day and night.

So began Joe's life in exile. Thula would no longer cook for him, so every morning before school and again every evening he trudged down the wagon road to the cookhouse at the bottom of the mountain to work for the company cook, Mother Cleveland, in exchange for breakfast and dinner. His job was to carry heavy trays of food—plates heaped high with hotcakes and bacon in the morning and with slabs of meat and steaming potatoes in the evenings—from the cookhouse to the adjoining dining hall, where miners and sawyers in dirty coveralls sat at long tables covered with white butcher paper, talking loudly and eating ravenously. As the men finished their meals, Joe hauled their dirty dishes back to the cookhouse. In the evenings he trudged back up the mountain to the schoolhouse to chop more wood, do his schoolwork, and sleep as best he could.

He fed himself and made his way, but his world had grown dark, narrow, and lonely. There were no boys his age whom he could befriend in the camp. His closest companions—his only companions since moving to Boulder City—had always been his father and Harry Junior. Now, living in the schoolhouse, he pined for the times when the three of them had formed a kind of confederation of resistance to Thula's increasing sourness, sneaking out behind the cabin to toss a ball around among the pine trees or to roughhouse in the dust, or sitting at the piano, pounding out their favorite songs whenever she was safely out of earshot. Even more he missed the times he'd spent alone with his father, sitting and playing gin rummy at the kitchen table while Thula practiced on her violin, or poking around under the hood of the Franklin, tightening and adjusting all the parts of the engine as his father explained the purpose and function of each of them. Most of all he missed the times he and his father would sit out at night on the cabin's porch and stare up into the astonishing swirls of stars shimmering in the black vault of the Idaho night sky, saying nothing, just being together, breathing in the cold air, waiting for a falling star to wish upon. "Keep on watching," his father would say. "Keep your eyes peeled. You never know when one is going to fall. The only time you don't see them is when you stop watching for them." Joe missed that, something terrible. Sitting alone on the schoolhouse steps at night and watching the sky alone just didn't seem the same.

Joe grew rapidly that summer, mostly vertically, though the treks up and down the mountain quickly built up muscle mass in his legs and thighs, and the constant swinging of an axe at the schoolhouse and the hoisting of trays in the cookhouse began to sculpt his upper body. He ate ravenously at Mother Cleveland's table. Yet he still always seemed to be hungry for more, and food was seldom far from his thoughts.

One autumn day the schoolteacher took Joe and the rest of his students on a natural-history field trip into the woods. He led them to an old, rotten stump on which a large white fungus was growing—a rounded, convoluted mass of creamy folds and wrinkles. The teacher plucked the fungus off the stump, held it aloft, and proclaimed it a cauliflower mushroom, *Sparassis radicata*. Not only was it edible, the teacher exclaimed, but it was delicious when stewed slowly. The revelation that one could find free food just sitting on a stump in the woods landed on Joe like a thunderbolt. That night he lay in his bunk in the schoolhouse, staring into the dark rafters above, thinking. There seemed to be more than a schoolroom science lesson in the discovery of the fungus. If you simply kept your eyes open, it seemed, you just might find something valuable in the most unlikely of places. The trick was to recognize a good thing when you saw it, no matter how odd or worthless it might at first appear, no matter who else might just walk away and leave it behind.

George Pocock, Rusty Callow, Ky Ebright, and Al Ulbrickson

CHAPTER THREE

Every good rowing coach, in his own way, imparts to his men the kind of self-discipline required to achieve the ultimate from mind, heart, and body. Which is why most ex-oarsmen will tell you they learned more fundamentally important lessons in the racing shell than in the classroom.

—George Yeoman Pocock

Competitive rowing is an undertaking of extraordinary beauty preceded by brutal punishment. Unlike most sports, which draw primarily on particular muscle groups, rowing makes heavy and repeated use of virtually every muscle in the body, despite the fact that a rower, as Al Ulbrickson liked to put it, "scrimmages on his posterior annex." And rowing makes these muscular demands not at odd intervals but in rapid sequence, over a protracted period of time, repeatedly and without respite. On one occasion, after watching the Washington freshmen practice, the *Seattle Post-Intelligencer*'s Royal Brougham marveled at the relentlessness of the sport: "Nobody ever took time out in a boat race," he noted. "There's no place to stop and get a satisfying drink of water or a lungful of cool, invigorating air. You just keep your eyes glued on the red, perspiring neck of the fellow ahead of you and row until they tell you it's all over . . . Neighbor, it's no game for a softy."

When you row, the major muscles in your arms, legs, and back—particularly the quadriceps, triceps, biceps, deltoids, latissimus dorsi, abdominals, hamstrings, and gluteal muscles—do most of the grunt work, propelling the boat forward against the unrelenting resistance of water and wind. At the same time, scores of smaller muscles in the neck, wrists, hands, and even feet continually fine-tune your efforts, holding the body in constant equipoise in order to maintain the exquisite balance necessary to keep a twenty-four-inch-wide vessel—roughly the width of a man's waist—on an even keel. The result of all this muscular effort, on both the larger scale and the smaller, is that your body burns calories and consumes oxygen at a rate that is unmatched in almost any other human endeavor. Physiologists, in fact, have calculated that rowing a two-thousand-meter race—the Olympic standard—takes the same physiological toll as playing two basketball games back-to-back. And it exacts that toll in about six minutes.

A well-conditioned oarsman or oarswoman competing at the highest levels must be able to take in and consume as much as eight liters of oxygen per minute; an average male is capable of taking in roughly four to five liters at most. Pound for pound, Olympic oarsmen may take in and process as much oxygen as a thoroughbred racehorse. This extraordinary rate of oxygen intake is of only so much value, it should be noted. While 75–80 percent of the energy a rower produces in a two-thousand-meter race is aerobic energy fueled by oxygen, races always begin, and usually end, with hard sprints. These sprints require levels of energy production that far exceed the body's capacity to produce aerobic energy, regardless of oxygen intake. Instead the body must immediately produce anaerobic energy. This, in turn, produces large quantities of lactic acid, and that acid rapidly builds up in the tissue of the muscles. The consequence is that the muscles often begin to scream in agony almost from the outset of a race and continue screaming until the very end.

And it's not only the muscles that scream. The skeletal system to which all those muscles are attached also undergoes tremendous strains and stresses. Without proper training and conditioning—and sometimes even with them—competitive rowers are apt to experience a wide variety of ills in the knees, hips, shoulders, elbows, ribs, neck, and above all the spine. These injuries and complaints range from blisters to severe tendonitis, bursitis, slipped vertebrae, rotator cuff dysfunction, and stress fractures, particularly fractures of the ribs.

The common denominator in all these conditions—whether in the lungs, the muscles, or the bones—is overwhelming pain. And that is perhaps the first and most fundamental thing that all novice oarsmen must learn about competitive rowing in the upper echelons of the sport: that pain is part and parcel of the deal. It's not a question of whether you will hurt, or of how much you will hurt; it's a question of what you will do, and how well you will do it, while pain has her wanton way with you.

All this soon became potently evident to Joe Rantz and the other boys trying out for the University of Washington's freshman crew in the fall of 1933.

Every afternoon, after classes, Joe made the long trek down to the shell house. He donned his jersey and shorts. He weighed in, a daily ritual. The weigh-ins were designed, on the one hand, to remind the boys that every extra ounce that went into the boat needed to be justified in terms of power produced and, on the other hand, to make sure the boys weren't overtraining and dropping below their optimal weight. Joe checked a chalkboard to see which crew he was assigned to for the day and then joined the crowd of boys gathered on the wooden ramp in front of the shell house, to hear what Coach Bolles had to say before practice began.

In those first weeks, Bolles's topic varied each day, depending on factors as unpredictable as the Seattle weather or what particular infelicities of technique he had noticed in the previous practice. Joe soon noted that two larger and intertwined themes inevitably came up in these talks. The boys heard time and again that the course they had chosen to embark on was difficult almost beyond imagining, that both their bodies and their moral characters would be tested in the months ahead, that only a very few of them who possessed near superhuman physical endurance and mental toughness would prove good enough to wear a W on their chests, and that by Christmas break most of them would have given up, perhaps to play something less physically and intellectually demanding, like football. But Bolles sometimes spoke of life-transforming experiences. He held out the prospect of becoming part of something larger than themselves, of finding in themselves something they did not yet know they possessed, of growing from boyhood to manhood. At times he dropped his voice a bit and shifted his tone and cadence and talked of near mystical moments on the water— moments of pride, elation, and deep affection for one's fellow oarsmen, moments they would remember, cherish, and recount to their grandchildren when they were old men. Moments, even, that would bring them nearer to God.

Occasionally, as Bolles spoke with them, the boys noticed a figure standing in the background, watching quietly and listening intently. A man in his early forties, tall like nearly everyone on the boat ramp, he wore horn-rimmed spectacles behind which lurked sharp, penetrating eyes. His forehead was high and he sported an odd haircut—his dark, wavy hair was long on top but cropped high over his ears and around behind his head so his ears looked overlarge and he seemed to be wearing a bowl atop his head. Almost invariably he wore a carpenter's apron covered with red sawdust and curls of cedar shavings. He spoke with a crisp British accent, an upper-crust accent, the kind of voice you might hear at Oxford or Cambridge. Many of the boys knew that his name was George Pocock and that he built racing shells in the loft of their shell house, not just for Washington, but for rowing programs across the country. None of them, though, yet knew that much of what they had just heard Bolles say—the very heart and soul of it—had its origins in the quiet philosophy and deep musings of the Briton.

George Yeoman Pocock was all but born with an oar in his hands. He came into the world at Kingston upon Thames on March 23, 1891, within sight of some of the finest rowing water in the world. He was descended from a long line of boatbuilders. His paternal grandfather had made his living hand-crafting rowboats for the professional watermen who plied the Thames in London, providing water-taxi and ferry services as their predecessors had done for centuries.

Since early in the eighteenth century, the London watermen had also made a sport of racing their dories in impromptu competitions. They were rough-and-tumble events. The friends of competitors sometimes maneuvered large boats or barges into their opponents' paths or positioned themselves on bridges over the racecourse in order to drop heavy stones into their opponents' boats as they passed underneath. Since 1715, the most skilled of the watermen had also held a much more genteel event, an annual race from London Bridge to Chelsea, in which the prize was the right to wear a spectacularly colorful and utterly British bit of regalia: a bright-crimson coat with a silver badge nearly the size of a dinner plate sewn on the left arm, matching crimson knee britches, and white knee-high hosiery. To this day, the race, Doggett's Coat and Badge, is still rowed on the Thames each July amid much ceremony and grandeur.

Pocock's maternal grandfather also worked in the boatbuilding trade, designing and constructing a wide variety of small craft, among them the *Lady Alice*, the custom-built sectional boat that Sir Henry Stanley used to search for Dr. David Livingstone in Central Africa in 1874. His uncle Bill had built the first keel-less shell, in his boatbuilding shop under London Bridge. His father, Aaron, had taken up the trade as well, building racing shells for Eton College, where gentlemen's sons had been rowing competitively since the 1790s. And it was in Eton's ancient boathouse, just across the river from the looming eminence of Windsor Castle, that George had grown up. At the age of fifteen, he signed papers formally apprenticing himself to his father, and for the next six years he worked side by side with him, laboring with hand tools to maintain and add to Eton's prodigious fleet of racing shells.

But George didn't just build boats; he also learned to row them, and to row them very well. He carefully studied the rowing style of the Thames watermen—a style characterized by short but powerful strokes with a quick catch and a quick release—and adapted it to the purpose of racing in a shell. The style he developed soon proved to be in many ways superior to the traditional longer stroke taught at Eton. Messing about on the Thames after formal practice, the aristocratic Eton boys discovered that George and his brother, Dick, although their social inferiors, could be counted on to leave them in their wakes time and again. It wasn't long before the Pocock boys found themselves giving informal rowing lessons to the likes of the young Anthony Eden, to Prince Prajadipok of Siam, and to Lord Grosvenor, son of the Duke of Westminster.

George Pocock, in turn, learned something from the highborn Eton lads. He was inclined by nature to do whatever he attempted on the highest possible level—to master each and every tool he laid hands on in his father's shop, to learn how to row the most efficient stroke, to build the most elegant and best-performing racing shells possible. Now, feeling the sting of British class distinctions, pondering the difference between how he and his father spoke and how they were spoken to, he decided to put in the effort to learn to speak, not with his natural cockney accent, but with the crisp "educated" accent of the boys they served. And, to almost everyone's amazement, he did it. His crisp voice soon stood out in the boathouse, not as an affectation but as a point of pride and a demonstration of his deep commitment to grace, precision, and what would turn out to be a lifelong pursuit of the ideal.

Impressed by George's perseverance, and by his ability on the water, Aaron Pocock entered him in a professional race, the Sportsman Handicap, at Putney on the Thames, when he was seventeen. He told his son he could build his own boat for the contest from scrap lumber in the Eton boathouse and gave him some advice that George never forgot: "No one will ask you *how long* it took to build; they will only ask *who* built it." So George took his time, carefully and meticulously handcrafting a single sculling shell from Norwegian pine and mahogany. At Putney he slipped his boat into the water, leaned deep into his oars, and over the course of three heats defeated a field of fifty-eight oarsmen. He came home with a small fortune: fifty pounds in prize money. Shortly thereafter, George's brother, Dick, one-upped him, winning the biggest of rowing prizes, the nearly two-hundred-year-old Doggett's Coat and Badge itself.

George was just going into training for his own shot at the Doggett's Coat and Badge when, late in 1910, his father abruptly lost his job at Eton, discharged because he had developed a reputation for being too easy on the men who worked for him. Suddenly without means, his father began casting around for boatbuilding work on the London waterfront. George and Dick, not wanting to be a burden on their father, abruptly decided to emigrate to western Canada, where they had heard it was possible to make as much as ten pounds a week working in the woods. They packed their clothes and a few boatbuilding tools, used their winnings from their races to book passage in steerage to Halifax, aboard the steamship *Tunisian*, and set sail from Liverpool.

Two weeks later, on March 11, 1911, after crossing Canada by rail, the Pococks arrived in Vancouver, with forty Canadian dollars between them. Filthy, dazed, and hungry, they wandered on foot from the train station to Vancouver's brick downtown in a cold, dismal rain. It was George's twentieth birthday. Dick was a year older. Set suddenly and unexpectedly adrift in the world, uncertain of what they would do next, both were ill at ease in what seemed to them a primitive frontier town utterly unlike the staid but comfortable environs of Eton. Though still in the King's dominions, they felt as if they had landed on another planet. They finally found a dingy room in a building downtown, rented it for eighteen dollars a week, and immediately went out looking for work. With only two weeks' rent money in their pockets, they tried their hands at whatever they could find. Dick worked as a carpenter at the local "bughouse," a mental hospital in nearby Coquitlam. George went to work in a logging camp on the Adams River outside Vancouver, where he soon found himself scrambling madly up and down a mountain, trying to satisfy a steam donkey's mechanically relentless appetite for firewood and water. After a month of frantically sawing wood and lugging tin pails of water up from the river two at a time, he quit and returned to Vancouver, where he got a relatively cushy job working in the shipyards—one in which he did not have to work quite at the pace of a steam engine. But it was grim, dangerous work that soon cost him two of his fingers.

In 1912 things started looking up for the Pocock boys. The Vancouver Rowing Club, hearing of their reputation in England, commissioned them to build two single sculls for one hundred dollars apiece. The Pococks set up shop in an old, derelict shed floating on timbers fifty yards offshore in Coal

Harbour and then finally resumed what would be their life's work—crafting fine racing shells. They set to work tirelessly in their shop downstairs, stopping only at night, to sleep in an unheated room above the shop.

Conditions were not ideal. Daylight showed through the roof, and wind and rain shuddered through wide gaps between the wallboards. To bathe, they had to dive out their bedroom window and into the cold salt chuck of the harbor. For drinking water, they had to row over to a public fountain in Stanley Park. From time to time, the shed slipped its anchor and drifted aimlessly among inbound and outbound ocean liners while the Pococks slept. At low tide the shed sat on a sloping mud bank, listing twenty-five degrees from bow to stern. When the tide surged back in, the waterlogged timbers on which the structure was built weighed it down and held it fast to the mud. George later described the daily routine: "The water would rise in the shop while we took refuge in the room above and tried to estimate when the next act of the drama would occur. Eventually, with a swish and a roar, the logs would break the mud's hold, and up would come the building, like a surfacing submarine, with the water rushing out the doors at each end. Then we could start working again, until the next change of tide." The brothers completed the work nonetheless, and as word of their craftsmanship spread across Canada they began to get new commissions. By mid-1912 the two of them— just twenty and twenty-one—were beginning to feel that they had their feet under them.

One blustery gray day, George Pocock looked out the window of the floating workshop and saw a gangly and awkward man with a shock of reddish but graying hair flying in the wind, rowing as if he were all elbows and knees. He flailed at his oars, George noted, "like a bewildered crab." The fellow was apparently trying to reach them, though he seemed to be making little progress in that direction. The rowing was so awkward and ineffective, in fact, that the Pococks concluded the man must be drunk. Eventually they found a boathook, snagged the man's boat, and dragged it alongside the workshop. When they warily helped him aboard, he grinned, stuck out a large hand, and boomed out, "My name is Hiram Conibear. I am the rowing coach at the University of Washington."

Conibear—who would come to be called the father of Washington rowing—had become Washington's coach because nobody else was available to take the job, not because he knew the first thing about rowing. He had been a professional bicycle rider at a time when as many as eight men might mount a single multiseated bicycle and careen around rough dirt racetracks in wild melees that often ended in spectacular and bloody collisions. He had moved on to become an athletic trainer for collegiate football and track-and-field teams and, most recently, the athletic trainer for the world champion Chicago White Sox in 1906. When he arrived at Washington in 1907, as coach of the track team and athletic trainer for the football team, his only rowing experience was four weeks in the summer of 1905 when he had trained on a four-oared barge on Lake Chautauqua in New York. Nevertheless, in 1908 he stepped into the position of crew coach more or less by default, replacing a pair of part-time volunteers.

Conibear was, according to those who knew him well, "simple, direct, and fearless." He attacked his new job with characteristic gusto—what George Pocock later called "inflammable enthusiasm." Lacking a coach's launch, he ran up and down the shores of Lake Washington, yelling at his boys through his megaphone, freely mixing baseball slang with rowing terminology and a wide variety of exuberant profanity. He cussed so loudly, so frequently, and so colorfully that offended lakeside residents soon began complaining to the university. Convinced that rowing instruction needed to be more scientific, he pored over anatomy books and physics texts. Then he appropriated a human skeleton from the biology lab, strapped it in a rowing seat, wired its hands to a broom handle, and carefully observed its movements as his student-assistants manipulated it to simulate various rowing strokes. Once he was convinced that he was on the right track with the mechanics of the sport, he turned his focus to the boats themselves. Washington had relied on home-built shells, many of which were notably tubby and slow, some of which had a tendency to fall apart when rowed hard, and one of which was so round bottomed and prone to tip over that Homer Kirby, stroke oar of the 1908 crew, said if you wanted to keep her on an even keel, you had to part your hair in the middle and divide your chewing tobacco evenly between your cheeks.

What Conibear wanted now was the kind of shells they made in England: long, sleek, elegant shells. Fast shells. When he learned that a pair of English boatbuilders had taken up residence just to the north, in Vancouver, he set out in search of them.

When he found their floating shop in Coal Harbour, he told the Pococks that he planned to establish a veritable rowing navy. He needed to purchase a fleet, perhaps as many as fifty, but certainly no fewer than twelve, eight-oared shells. He wanted the Pococks to move down to Seattle forthwith, where he would provide them with a shop on campus—a dry shop on terra firma—in which to build the fleet.

Stunned, but delighted at the size of the potential order, the Pococks visited Seattle, and then wired their father in England, telling him to make haste to Washington, as they had found work enough for the three of them. Only after Aaron was on his way across the Atlantic did George and Dick receive a sobering letter from Conibear. He had spoken a bit prematurely, it seemed. He had only enough funds, it turned out, to buy one shell, not twelve. When told of the setback, Aaron responded to his sons dryly, "You must remember that Mr. Conibear is an American."

Despite the radically lowered expectations, the Pococks were soon ensconced on the Washington campus, and Hiram Conibear began to realize that he had hired much more than a skilled boatbuilder in George Pocock. When George began to watch the Washington oarsmen on the water, he quickly spotted inefficiencies and deficiencies in the mechanics of their stroke that no amount of fiddling with a skeleton could fix. At first he held his peace, not inclined by nature to offer unsolicited advice. But when Conibear began to ask the Pococks for their opinion about his boys' rowing, George gradually spoke up. He began to teach Conibear elements of the stroke that he had learned from Thames watermen in his boyhood and taught to the boys at Eton. Conibear listened eagerly, learned quickly, and what came to be called the "Conibear stroke" soon evolved from those discussions. It featured a shorter layback, a quicker catch, and a shorter but more powerful pull in the water. It left the oarsmen sitting more upright at the end of the stroke, ready to slide forward and begin the next stroke more quickly and with less fuss and bother. It differed conspicuously from the rowing stroke long used by the eastern schools (and Eton), with its exaggerated layback and long recovery, and it began almost immediately to result in Washington's first significant victories. Before long, even the eastern schools were taking note of the Conibear stroke, trying to figure out how something so unorthodox could be so successful.

Conibear died just a few years later, in 1917, when he climbed too far out on a limb, while reaching for a plum in a tree in his backyard, and plunged head-first to the ground. By then, however, Washington had become a serious contender in crew on the West Coast, a worthy opponent for Stanford and California and British Columbia, if not yet quite what Conibear had dreamed of making the program: "the Cornell of the Pacific."

After the Great War, Dick Pocock moved east to build shells for Yale University, while George remained in Seattle and orders for his exquisitely crafted shells began to pour in from around the country. Over the next several decades, a succession of Washington coaches and crews came to learn that the Englishman quietly at work up in the loft of their shell house had much to teach them about rowing. They came to see him as something new under the sun, what in modern parlance might be termed a rowing "geek." His understanding of the details of the sport—the physics of water, wood, and wind; the biomechanics of muscle and bone—was unmatched.

But Pocock's influence didn't end with his command of the technical side of the sport. It really only began there. Over the years, as he saw successive classes of oarsmen come and go, as he watched immensely powerful and proud boys strive to master the vexing subtleties of their sport, as he studied them and worked with them and counseled them and heard them declare their dreams and confess their shortcomings, George Pocock learned much about the hearts and souls of young men. He learned to see hope where a boy thought there was no hope, to see skill where skill was obscured by ego or by anxiety. He observed the fragility of confidence and the redemptive power of trust. He detected the strength of the gossamer threads of affection that sometimes grew between a pair of young men or among a boatload of them striving honestly to do their best. And he came to understand how those almost mystical bonds of trust and affection, if nurtured correctly, might lift a crew above the ordinary sphere, transport it to a place where nine boys somehow became one thing—a thing that could not quite be defined, a thing that was so in tune with the water and the earth and the sky above that, as they rowed, effort was replaced by ecstasy. It was a rare thing, a sacred thing, a thing devoutly to be hoped for. And in the years since coming to Washington, George Pocock had quietly become its high priest.

Years later a Washington coxswain would sum up the sentiment of hundreds of boys who felt his influence: "In his presence Washington crewmen always stood, for he symbolized that for which God's children always stand."

Each day, after Tom Bolles finished talking and George Pocock made his way back up into his shop, the boys wrestled the long, white-bladed oars from their racks, carried them down to the water, and prepared to row. They were not remotely ready to step into the delicate confines of a racing shell, so they waited turns to board the school's venerable training barge, *Old Nero*. The vessel—a wide, flat-bottomed scow with a long walkway running down the middle and seats for sixteen novice oarsmen—had served as an initial proving ground for freshmen since 1907, virtually the whole of the thirty years that Washington had maintained a crew program.

As the freshmen of 1933 flailed at their oars in the first few days, Tom Bolles and Al Ulbrickson strode up and down *Old Nero*'s walkway in gray flannel suits and fedoras. Ulbrickson mostly just watched the boys quietly, still sizing them up. Bolles, however, barked at them continuously—to grip the oar this way and not that, to square their blades to the water, to straighten their backs, to bend their knees, to straighten their knees, to pull harder one moment, to ease up another. It was bewildering and backbreaking. *Old Nero* was designed, in part, to drive boys who, by temperament, weren't cut out for crew—"mollycoddles," Ulbrickson called them—to an early realization of that fact, before they could break expensive oars and racing shells. The boys strained and heaved and gasped for breath, but for all their efforts they moved *Old Nero* only slowly and erratically out of the Cut and onto the ruffled expanse of Lake Washington. As they tried to absorb their lessons and experience, and to synchronize their efforts, they lived in constant fear of making any of the many egregious errors Bolles kept pointing out to them.

One error in particular required no scolding. They soon learned that if the blades of their oars entered the water too deeply, at the wrong angle, or out of time with the others, or if they remained in the water a fraction of a second too long at the end of a stroke, they were apt to "catch a crab": the oar would suddenly and irretrievably become stuck in the water, immobilized as surely as if some sort of gargantuan crustacean had reached up from the depths and seized the blade, holding it fast. *Old Nero* would keep going but the oar would not. The boy holding the oar would either be smacked hard in the chest and knocked out of his seat or, if he held on to the oar too long, be catapulted unceremoniously into the water. Every stroke he took thus offered each boy the possibility of a wet, cold, and spectacularly public form of humiliation.

Of the whole freshman lot, the only one who had ever rowed a lick in his life was Roger Morris. Before the Depression, the Morris family had maintained a small, rustic cabin on the western side of Bainbridge Island in the Puget Sound. As a boy Roger had idled away his summers rowing lazily about in Manzanita Bay, a lovely blue cove lying in the lee of the Olympic Mountains. But he was tall and strong and, when he wished to, Roger could go pretty much as far as he wanted to in that rowboat, a fact he had demonstrated one day when he was twelve. Suffering from a toothache and wanting to return to the comforts of his family home in Seattle's Fremont neighborhood, he rowed some fifteen miles—north through Agate Passage, six miles southeast across the relatively open water of Puget Sound, among freighters and ferries, then east through the Ballard Locks, where he wedged his small rowboat in among salmon trawlers and tugboats and rafts of logs, and finally through Salmon Bay—before walking into the house to the utter astonishment of his mother. But aboard *Old Nero*, Roger quickly found that his freewheeling rowing style was more hindrance than help when it came to mastering the racing stroke that Tom Bolles and Al Ulbrickson taught in the 1930s.

None of the freshmen, in fact, found it easy to master it. To achieve even a reasonably smooth and powerful stroke, they had to learn to execute a series of precisely timed and carefully coordinated moves. Facing the stern of the boat, each boy began with his chest bent over his knees, his arms stretched out in front of him, and both hands gripping the handle of his one long oar. At the beginning of the stroke, the "catch," he dropped the blade of his oar into the water and leaned his torso back hard, toward the bow, keeping his back ramrod straight. As his shoulders came vertical over the center of his body, he began the "leg drive" by propelling his legs forward, his seat sliding toward the bow on greased runners beneath him. Simultaneously, he pulled the oar toward his chest against the resistance of the water, throwing all the strength of his combined arm, back, and leg muscles into the stroke. As the oar came to his chest, and with his back inclined about fifteen degrees toward the bow, he reached the full extent of his "layback." Then he began the "release." He dropped his hands toward his waist and pulled the blade quickly and decisively from the water while at the same time rolling the wrist of the hand nearest the water in order to "feather" the blade parallel to the surface of the water. Next, to begin the "recovery," he rotated his shoulders forward and pushed his arms sternward against the oar while pulling his knees up toward his chest, thus propelling his body forward on the sliders back into the crouched position in which he had begun. Finally, as the boat moved forward beneath him, he again rotated the oar to bring the blade perpendicular to the surface for the next catch, dropped it cleanly back into the water at precisely the same moment as the other boys, and immediately repeated the entire procedure over and over again at whatever rate the coxswain was calling for through the small megaphone strapped on his head. Done correctly, this process levered the boat forward in the water smoothly and powerfully. But it had to be done in one continuous and unbroken cycle of uncoiling and coiling the body. It had to be done rapidly, and it had to be done in precisely the same manner—at the same rate and with the same amount of applied power—as everyone else in the boat was doing it. It was maddeningly diffi-cult, as if eight men standing on a floating log that threatened to roll over whenever they moved had to hit eight golf balls at exactly the same moment, with exactly the same amount of force, directing the ball to exactly the same point on a green, and doing so over and over, every two or three seconds.

The workouts went on for three hours every afternoon, and as the days grew shorter they stretched into the dark and increasingly chilly October eve-nings. By the time the boys came in off the water each night, their hands were blistered and bleeding, their arms and legs throbbed, their backs ached, and they were soaked through and through with a clammy mixture of sweat and lake water. They racked their oars, hung their rowing clothes up to dry in a steam-heated locker in the shell house, dressed, and began the long trudge back up the hill to campus.

Each evening, Joe Rantz noted with mounting satisfaction, there were fewer boys making the climb. And he noted something else. The first to drop out had been the boys with impeccably creased trousers and freshly polished oxfords. At a time when images of successful oarsmen appeared on the covers of *Life* and the *Saturday Evening Post,* varsity crew had seemed to many of them to be a way to build up their social status, to become big men on campus. But they had not reckoned on the sport's extreme physical and psychological de-mands. As Joe made his way down to the shell house every afternoon, he saw more and more familiar boys—boys who had abandoned their boats—lounging on the grass in front of Suzzallo Library, casting him quick glances as he passed. The hurting was taking its toll, and that was just fine with Joe. Hurting was nothing new to him.

Downtown Sequim

CHAPTER FOUR

It is hard to make that boat go as fast as you want to. The enemy, of course, is resistance of the water, as you have to displace the amount of water equal to the weight of men and equipment, but that very water is what supports you and that very enemy is your friend. So is life: the very problems you must overcome also support you and make you stronger in overcoming them.

—George Yeoman Pocock

On a stormy night in November 1924, Thula Rantz went into labor in her cabin at the Gold and Ruby mine. As she lay moaning in her bed, Harry set off for Bonners Ferry, Idaho, eighteen miles away on twisting mountain roads, to fetch a doctor. He promptly came to a washed-out bridge on the only road out of town. With help from some of the miners, he rebuilt the bridge, made it to Bonners Ferry, and returned just in time for the doctor to deliver his first daughter, Rose. But it had taken all night.

That was the last straw for Thula. She was done with the cabin, done with the mine, done with Idaho. A few weeks later, they packed up the Franklin, picked up Joe from the schoolhouse, drove to Seattle, and moved into the basement of Thula's parents' home on Alki Point. For the first time in a year, they all lived under one roof.

It didn't go well. Thula, with yet another infant to tend to, was no happier in their cramped quarters in the basement than she had been in the cabin. Once again Joe in particular seemed to be always underfoot. So when Harry got a job as a mechanic with the Hama Hama Logging Company out on the Hood Canal—a half day's journey west of Seattle by car and ferry—Joe had to leave too. Harry took his son, still ten, to live with a family, named Schwartz, near the logging camp.

By 1925 Harry had saved up a bit of money from the Hama Hama job and used it to put a down payment on an auto repair and tire shop in Sequim, on the north side of the Olympic Peninsula. The shop was located right down-town on Washington Street, the main thoroughfare through town, squarely on the route of anyone traveling from Seattle to Port Angeles or farther out onto the peninsula. It seemed a good location, and it got Harry back to doing what he loved most, tinkering with cars. The whole family moved into a small apartment over the shop. Joe enrolled at the Sequim school. He spent his weekends helping his father work on cars, tinkering with carburetors and learning to vulcanize rubber, partly out of eagerness to exercise his own ex-panding mechanical aptitude and partly out of eagerness to stay out of Thu-la's way upstairs. When the mayor of Sequim smashed up Harry's Franklin while ogling a passing girl—breaking its wooden frame—he bought Harry a newer model, and Harry gave Joe the older Franklin so he could learn by re-pairing it. A second daughter, Polly, was born that year, and as his business took root Harry bought a stump farm—160 acres of recently logged land southwest of town. There he began to build, with his own hands, a large farm-house.

Sequim sat on a wide expanse of prairie between the snowcapped Olympic Mountains to the south and the broad, blue Strait of Juan de Fuca to the north. Vancouver Island was just visible on the horizon. Nestled in the lee of the mountains, sheltered from the storms that rotated in off the Pacific from the southwest, the area was far less rainy than most of western Washington, and the skies were blue more often than gray. The weather was so dry, in fact, that early settlers had found cacti growing in places. It was the kind of town where people got together on weekends to build a new church, to hold Sunday-afternoon ice cream socials, or to kick up their heels at Saturday-night square dances. In Sequim your butcher might also be the volunteer firefighter who saved your house or barn, as well as the neighbor who helped you rebuild it. It was a place where native women from the nearby Jamestown S'Klallam tribe might share recipes with a Protestant minister's wife over a cup of coffee at Dryke's Café, where old men sat in front of the post office on Saturday after-noon spitting brown arcs of tobacco juice into strategically arranged spit-toons, where boys could sell melons purloined from local vegetable patches to Honolulu Pete at his fruit truck parked on Seal Street, where children could wander into Lehman's Meat Market and be given a free hot dog in a bun just because they looked hungry, or where they might stop by Brayton Drug Store and be handed a piece of candy just because they said "please."

The farmhouse that Harry set about building amid the tree stumps outside of town became a work perpetually in progress. With Joe's help, he dug a ditch to divert water, illegally, from an irrigation canal flowing out of the nearby Dungeness River. He rigged up a sawmill powered by the water he had diverted. He felled the few crooked trees left behind by the lumber company that had recently logged off the property, and then milled enough rough-cut lumber to frame the two-story house and apply cedar siding to part of it. He and Joe collected smooth river rocks from the Dungeness and laboriously erected an enormous stone fireplace. The house was still only half completed when he decided to sell the car repair shop and move his family out to the stump farm.

Over the next few years, Harry and Joe kept pounding nails when they had the time. They built a wide front porch and a woodshed, a ramshackle henhouse that soon became home to more than four hundred chickens, and a rickety milking barn for half a dozen dairy cows that grazed among the stumps. Harry rigged a flywheel and generator to the waterwheel that powered his sawmill, ran electrical wire into the house, and dangled lightbulbs from the rafters. As the supply of water from the irrigation ditch waxed and waned, the lights flickered on and off and glowed with varying degrees of intensity. But he never quite got around to finishing the house.

To Joe the condition of the house made little difference. Once again he had the semblance of a home and a new world to explore. Behind the house there was a meadow of nearly an acre, carpeted in summer with sweet wild strawberries. During the spring, water flowed over his father's waterwheel with such force that it excavated a pool nearly ten feet deep and twenty-five feet long. Soon salmon and steelhead and trout from the Dungeness made their way up the irrigation ditch and gathered in schools in the pond. Joe rigged up a net on a long pole, and whenever he wanted fish for dinner he simply took the net out behind the house, picked out a fish, and hauled it in. The woods just beyond the property were full of bears and cougars. That troubled Thula and made her understandably nervous about her flock of small children, but Joe thrilled at night when he heard the bears splashing as they fished in the pond or the cougars screeching as they met their mates in the dark.

Joe was a good and popular student. His classmates found him outgoing, freewheeling, handy with a joke, and fun to be around. A few who got to know him better found that he could suddenly and unexpectedly turn somber—never nasty or hostile, but guarded, as if there was a part of him he didn't want you to touch.

He was a particular favorite of Miss Flatebo, the music teacher. Through barter and the generosity of a few friends, he soon owned a ragged collection of old stringed instruments—a mandolin, several guitars, an old ukulele, and two banjos. Sitting on the front porch every day after school, working at it again at night when his schoolwork was finished, he patiently and painstakingly taught himself to play each instrument proficiently. He took to carrying one of the guitars onto the school bus every day. He sat in the back, playing and singing the songs he loved—boisterous tunes from vaudeville acts he had heard on the radio, long comical ballads, and sad, lilting cowboy songs—entertaining the other students, drawing groups of them toward the rear of the bus to listen and sing along with him. It wasn't long before he found that he had one particular devotee, a pretty slip of a girl named Joyce Simdars—with blond curls, a button nose, and a fetching smile—who more and more often sat next to him, singing along in perfect two-part harmony.

To Joe, Sequim was shaping up to be near paradise. For Thula, though, it was yet another disappointment, not much of an improvement over Boulder City, her parents' basement, or the apartment over the tire shop. Stuck in a half-finished house surrounded by rotting stumps and wild animals of all sorts, she felt as far removed as ever from the sophisticated life that she envisioned for herself. Everything about farm life appalled her—the daily milking of cows, the ever-present stench of manure, the relentless collecting of eggs, the daily cleaning of the cream separator, the always flickering light fixtures hung from the rafters. She despised the endless chopping of kindling to feed the woodstove, the early mornings and the late nights. And she was perpetually irritated by Joe and his teenaged friends and their makeshift bands, out on the wide front porch, making a racket day and night.

All these miseries seemed compounded into a single horrific moment one misty winter morning when she turned from the woodstove with an iron skillet full of hot bacon grease, potatoes, and onions and tripped over Harry Junior, who was lying on his back on the floor. She dropped the skillet and its contents directly onto the boy's neck and chest. She and her son screamed simultaneously. Harry ran out the door, tore off his shirt, and threw himself into a snowbank, but the damage was done—his chest was hideously burned and blistered. He survived, but only after contracting pneumonia, spending weeks in a nearby hospital, and missing a full year of school.

After that, things began to sour once more for the whole family. In the fall of 1929, a hole opened up in Joe's life. Joyce Simdars's family home burned to the ground on the night of September 29, while the family was away. Joyce was sent off to live with an aunt in Great Falls, Montana, until the house could be rebuilt. All at once, the bus ride to school was not what it had been.

A month later came a much more serious calamity. The rural economy of the United States had already been in desperate straits for some time by that fall. Huge surpluses of wheat, corn, milk, pork, and beef produced in the Midwest had caused the price of farm commodities to crash. Wheat brought in only a tenth of what it had nine or ten years before. In Iowa a bushel of corn fetched less than the price of a packet of gum. And the price collapse began to spread to the Far West. Things in Sequim were not yet as hard as on the Great Plains, but they were hard enough. The Rantz farm, like countless others across the country, had so far barely managed to remain profitable. But when they picked up the *Sequim Press* on October 30 and read what had happened in New York over the last several days, Harry and Thula Rantz knew with cold certainty that the world had utterly changed, that they would not long be sheltered from the storm on Wall Street, not even in Sequim, out in the far northwestern corner of the whole country.

Over the next few weeks, things continued to unravel at the Rantz house on Silberhorn Road. A week after the financial crash, wild dogs began to appear daily on the farm. Dozens of families had simply walked away from their homes and farms in Sequim that fall, many leaving dogs behind to fend for themselves. Now packs of them began chasing the cows all over the Rantz property, relentlessly nipping at their legs. The bellowing, distressed cows lumbered among the stumps until they were exhausted and stopped giving the milk that was the farm's principal cash product. Two weeks later, minks stole into the henhouse and slaughtered dozens of chickens, leaving their bloody corpses piled up in the corners. A few nights later, they did it again, almost as if for sport, and now the egg money dwindled away. Harry Junior would later say of events that fall, "Everything just stopped dead in the water. It was almost as if someone said to God, 'Go after them!'"

Then late one rainy afternoon in November, the school bus dropped off Joe just as darkness was enveloping the house. Walking up the driveway to the house, stepping over potholes full of rainwater, Joe noticed his father's Franklin, its engine running, plumes of white exhaust billowing from the tailpipe. Something was tied to the roof of the car, with a tarpaulin over it. As he drew nearer, he saw that the younger kids were sitting in the backseat, among suitcases, and peering out at him through steamy windows. Thula was sitting in the front seat, staring straight ahead, looking at the house, where Harry stood on the porch, watching Joe approach. Joe mounted the porch steps. His father's face was drawn and white.

"What's up, Pop? Where are we going?" Joe murmured.

Harry looked down at the boards planking the porch, then raised his eyes and gazed off into the dark, wet woods over Joe's shoulder.

"We can't make it here, Joe. There's nothing else for it. Thula won't stay, at any rate. She's insisting."

"Where are we going to go?"

Harry turned to meet Joe's eyes.

"I'm not sure. Seattle, for now, then California maybe. But, Son, the thing is, Thula wants you to stay here. I would stay with you, but I can't. The little kids are going to need a father more than you are. You're pretty much all grown up now anyway."

Joe froze. His gray-blue eyes locked onto his father's face, suddenly blank and expressionless, like stone. Stunned, trying to take in what he had just heard, unable to speak, Joe reached out a hand and laid it on the rough-hewn cedar railing, steadying himself. Rainwater dripping from the roof splattered in the mud below. Joe's stomach lurched. Finally he sputtered, "But can't I just come along?"

"No. That won't work. Look, Son, if there's one thing I've figured out about life, it's that if you want to be happy, you have to learn how to be happy on your own."

With that, Harry strode back to the car, climbed in, closed the door, and started down the driveway. In the backseat, Mike and Harry Junior peered through the oval rearview window. Joe watched the red taillights recede and disappear into a dark shroud of rain. He turned and walked into the house and closed the door behind him. The whole thing had taken less than five minutes. The rain was thundering on the roof now. The house was cold and damp. The lightbulbs hanging from the rafters flickered on for a moment. Then they flickered off and stayed off.

Rain was still pounding the roof of the half-finished house in Sequim when Joe woke up the next morning. A wind had come up during the night, and it moaned in the tops of the fir trees behind the house. Joe lay in bed for a long time, listening, remembering the days he had spent lying in bed in his aunt's attic in Pennsylvania listening to the mournful sound of trains in the distance, with fear and aloneness weighing on him, pressing down on his chest, pushing him into the mattress. The feeling was back. He did not want to get up, did not really care if he ever got up.

Finally, though, he did get up. He made a fire in the woodstove, put water on to boil, fried some bacon, and made some coffee. Very slowly, as he ate the bacon and the coffee cleared his mind, the spinning in his head began to diminish and he found himself creeping up on a new realization. He opened his eyes and seized it, took it in, comprehended it all at once, and found that it came accompanied by a fierce determination, a sense of rising resolution. He was sick and tired of finding himself in this position—scared and hurt and abandoned and endlessly asking himself why. Whatever else came his way, he wasn't going to let anything like this happen again. From now on, he would make his own way, find his own route to happiness, as his father had said. He'd prove to his father and to himself that he could do it. He wouldn't become a hermit. He liked other people too much for that, and friends could help push away the loneliness. He would never again let himself depend on them, though, nor on his family, nor on anyone else, for his sense of who he was. He would survive, and he would do it on his own.

The smell and taste of the bacon had stimulated his appetite mightily, and he was still hungry. He got up and rummaged through the kitchen to take inventory. There wasn't much to be found—a few boxes of oatmeal, a jar of pickles, some eggs from the chickens that had survived the mink attacks, a half a head of cabbage and some bologna in the icebox. Not much for a fifteen-year-old boy already approaching six feet.

He made some oatmeal and sat back down to think further. His father had always taught him that there was a solution to every problem. But he had always stressed that sometimes the solution wasn't where people would ordinarily expect it to be, that you might have to look in unexpected places and think in new and creative ways to find the answers you were looking for. He remembered the mushrooms on the rotten logs in Boulder City. He could survive on his own, he figured, if he just kept his wits about him, if he kept his eyes open for opportunities, and if he didn't allow his life to be dictated by other people's notions of what he should do.

Over the next few weeks and months, Joe began to learn to fend entirely for himself. He drove iron stakes into the ground to fortify the chicken coop against future mink attacks and treasured the few eggs he gathered every morning. He foraged in the dripping woods for mushrooms, and with all the recent rain he found basketfuls of them—beautiful, fluted, orange chanterelles and fat, meaty king boletes that he fried in some bacon grease Thula had saved in a tin can. He gathered the last of the autumn's blackberries, netted the last of the fish from the pool behind the waterwheel, picked watercress and added the berries and made salads of them.

Berries and watercress would only go so far, though. It was clear that he was going to need some money in his pocket. He drove downtown in the old Franklin his father had left behind and parked on Washington Street, where he sat on the hood and played his banjo and sang, hoping for spare change. He soon found that there was no such thing as spare change in 1929.

The crash had started on Wall Street, but it quickly brought down communities from coast to coast. Downtown Sequim was desolate. The State Bank of Sequim was still afloat but would fail within months. More and more storefronts were boarded up every day. As Joe sang, dogs sat on their haunches on the wooden sidewalks watching him idly, scratching their fleas in the rain. Black cars bounced down the unpaved street, splashing through muddy potholes, sending up jets of brown water, but the drivers paid Joe little heed. About the only audience he could count on was a bearded character everyone called the Mad Russian, who had been wandering Sequim's streets barefoot and muttering to himself for as long as anyone could remember.

Joe dug deeper into his imagination. Months before, he and his friend Harry Secor had discovered a spot on the Dungeness River where huge chinook salmon—some as much as four feet long—lay in a deep, green, swirling pool, waiting to spawn. Joe found a gaff hook in the barn and began to carry it secreted in his pocket.

Early one misty Saturday morning, he and Harry worked their way through a dripping tangle of cottonwoods and alders lining the Dungeness, evading the game warden who regularly patrolled the river during salmon-spawning season. They cut a stout pole from a young alder, lashed the gaff hook to it, and then stealthily approached the swift, cold river. Joe took off his shoes, rolled up his pants, and waded quietly into the shallow riffles upstream from the pool. When Joe was in position, Harry started throwing large river rocks into the pool and beating the surface with a stick. In a panic, the fish dashed upstream toward Joe in the shallows. As they flashed by, Joe aimed the gaff at one of the largest of them, thrust the pole into the water, and deftly snagged the fish under the gills, where the hook would leave no telltale marks. Then, amid much shouting and splashing, he stumbled out of the water and dragged the thrashing salmon up onto the gravel bank.

Joe feasted on salmon that night, alone in the house. Then he set about turning the poaching of salmon into a business. Each Saturday afternoon Joe hiked the three miles into town with one or more of the enormous salmon slung over his shoulder on a willow switch, their tails dragging in the dust behind him. He delivered his catch to the back door of Lehman's Meat Market and to the back doors of various households around Sequim, where he sold them for cash or bartered them for butter or meat or gas for the Franklin or whatever else he needed that week, solemnly and good-naturedly assuring his customers that, yes, indeed, he had caught the fish on a hook and line, fair and square.

Later that winter he found another entrepreneurial opportunity. With Prohibition in full swing and Canada just fifteen miles across the Strait of Juan de Fuca, Sequim was a lively port of entry for hard spirits of all sorts. Much of it made its way to the speakeasies of Seattle, but one bootlegger specialized in local customers. Byron Noble roared into the outskirts of town every Friday night in a long, sleek black Chrysler, depositing hip flasks full of gin, rum, or whiskey behind particular fence posts where his customers knew to look for them. Soon Joe and Harry Secor also knew where to look for them.

Dressed in dark, heavy clothes on frosty nights, they followed Noble around on his nocturnal route, pouring the contents of selected flasks into fruit jars and replacing the liquor with dandelion wine that they brewed themselves in Joe's barn. That way, they figured, rather than seeming as if someone had stolen the goods, it would seem to Noble's customers that they had simply gotten a bad batch of hooch. But they were careful not to purloin too often from the same location, fearful that Noble or his customers might be lying in the weeds, waiting for them with a shotgun. After a night's work, Joe silently delivered the fruit jars full of the good stuff to the fence posts of his own discreetly cultivated clients.

When he wasn't poaching fish or stealing booze, Joe worked at any kind of legitimate work he could find. He dug tunnels under stumps in his neighbors' pastures and pried them out of the earth with long iron bars. When prying didn't work, he stuffed sticks of dynamite under them, lit a fuse, and ran like hell as the dynamite sent the stumps and a black plume of dirt and rocks high into the air. He stooped and scraped with a shovel, digging irrigation ditches by hand. With a long-handled, double-edged axe, he split fence rails from massive cedar logs that washed down the Dungeness in the spring. He dug wells. He built barns, crawling around in the rafters and pounding nails. He hand-cranked cream separators and lugged 120-pound cans of milk and sweet cream around dairy farms, loading them onto trucks for delivery to the Dungeness-Sequim Cooperative Creamery. As summer came on, he labored under pale blue skies in the dry fields surrounding Sequim, cutting hay with a scythe, forking it onto wagons, and hoisting it by the ton into the lofts of his neighbors' barns.

In all of this Joe grew continually stronger and ever more self-reliant. Through it all he stayed in school and earned good grades. At the end of the day, though, he remained stoically alone, returning each night to the empty, half-finished house. He ate solitary meals, sitting at one end of the large dining table where his family had previously gathered for boisterous dinners. Each night he washed the one plate he used and wiped it dry and set it back in its place on top of the stack of dishes Thula had left behind in a kitchen cabinet. He sat down at his mother's old piano in the front room and plinked at the keys and floated simple melodies through the dark, empty spaces of the house. He sat on the front steps and played his banjo and sang quietly to himself.

In the months that followed, Joe hunted for new opportunities in Sequim. Just down Silberhorn Road, he found part-time work helping his older neighbor, Charlie McDonald. McDonald made his living logging—harvesting enormous cottonwood trees that grew in the gravelly bottomlands along the Dungeness River. The work was backbreaking. The cottonwoods were so immense—their diameters so great—that it sometimes took an hour or more for Joe and Charlie to fell just one, pulling an eighty-four-inch two-man saw back and forth through the soft white heartwood. In the spring, when the sap was running, it jetted up out of the stumps three or four feet into the air after the trees finally toppled over. Then Joe and Charlie lopped off all the branches with axes, pried the bark from the logs with long iron bars, and harnessed them to Charlie's draft horses, Fritz and Dick, so they could be dragged out of the woods and sent off to a pulp mill in Port Angeles.

Charlie had been gassed in the Great War, his vocal cords all but destroyed. At best he could manage croaks and whispers. As they worked together, Joe marveled at how Charlie could command the ponderous draft horses to do his bidding with a barely audible "gee" or "haw" or, as often as not, simply a whistle and nod of his head. Charlie would give a signal, and in unison Fritz and Dick would squat down on their haunches while he chained them up. He'd give another signal, and the two would rise and pull as if they were one horse, their movements crisply synchronized. And they pulled with all their hearts. When horses pulled like that, Charlie told Joe, they could pull far more than twice what each could pull alone. They'd pull, he said, till the log moved, the harness broke, or their hearts gave out.

In time Joe began to take some of his evening meals with the McDonald family, in exchange for his labor. He quickly became enormously popular with their preteen daughters—Margaret and Pearlie—staying after dinner and late into the evenings most nights, strumming his banjo and singing for the girls, or lying on the braided carpet in the front parlor, playing dominos, mah-jongg, or pickup sticks with them.

He soon found another way to make a few dollars, while entertaining himself as well. He and two of his school friends, Eddie Blake and Angus Hay Jr., formed a three-man band, with Joe on banjo, Eddie on drums, and Angus on saxophone. The trio played jazz tunes during intermissions at the Olympic movie theater in Sequim in exchange for an opportunity to watch the films. They played for square dances at the Grange Hall in Carlsborg. On Saturday nights they played at a dance hall in nearby Blyn, where a farmer had turned, with the addition of some strings of electric lights, his chicken coop into Sequim's most popular dance venue. Girls were admitted to the Chicken Coop free of charge, boys for twenty-five cents, but Joe and his bandmates paid no admission when they performed. That meant a lot to Joe; several weeks earlier, Joyce Simdars had returned from Montana, and free admission meant that he could afford to bring her along on dates. He soon found, to his chagrin, though, that she was allowed to go only rarely—only when her mother was available to accompany her, riding primly and vigilantly in the wide, plush backseat of the Franklin, taking control of the dangerous territory.

If there was one thing in the world Joyce Simdars wanted, it was for her mother to be less vigilant.

The Simdars household was austere, Joyce's upbringing severe. Descended from German and Scottish immigrants who had settled in Sequim as pioneers, her parents both believed that work was an end in itself, that it straightened a wayward soul, and that no amount of it was too much. Joyce's father, in

Joyce Simdars at sixteen

fact, was well on his way to working himself to death. Suffering from an enlarged heart and inflammatory rheumatism, he nevertheless continued to plow his fields the old-fashioned way—behind a team of mules. By the end of his life, the mules would be more or less dragging him across the field from shortly after dawn till evening, sometimes six days a week during planting season.

But it was Joyce's mother, and in particular her mother's religious views, that most oppressed Joyce. Enid Simdars embraced the strictures of Christian Science, a faith that taught that the material world and all the evil that attended it were illusory, that the only reality was spiritual. This meant, among other things, that prayer and only prayer could heal afflictions like the rheumatism that afflicted Joyce's father, and that doctors were a waste of time. It also meant something that affected Joyce even more personally as she was growing up. Enid believed there was only a "good Joyce," that a "bad Joyce" was a theological impossibility, that any such person who might appear was by definition an imposter in the guise of her daughter. When Joyce misbehaved, she simply ceased to exist for her mother. The bad Joyce was made to sit on a chair and was not acknowledged in any way, or allowed to leave the chair until the good Joyce spontaneously reappeared. As a result, Joyce had spent much of her childhood wrestling with the notion that any wicked thought or misbehavior on her part meant that she was not worthy of love and, in fact, was in imminent danger of ceasing to exist. Years later she remembered sitting in the chair, sobbing and checking on herself over and over again, thinking, "But I'm still here. I'm still here."

If she had a refuge, it was in working out-of-doors rather than in the house. She detested housework, in part because it had no end in the Simdars household and in part because it held her under the bell jar of her mother's watchful eye. And it did not help that since her midteens Joyce had begun to suffer from arthritis, apparently a genetic gift from her father. The endless washing of dishes and scrubbing of floors and wiping of windows was the kind of repetitious work that aggravated the pain in her hands and wrists. Whenever she had a chance, she slipped outdoors to work in the vegetable garden or to tend to the animals with her father. He was hardly effusive with his affection, more apt to cuddle the family dog than one of his children, but at least he always seemed vaguely glad to have her around, and Joyce found the farmwork he did more interesting than housework. It often involved solving practical problems or making something new, and that appealed to her considerable and burgeoning intellectual curiosity—a curiosity that had already made her an unusually proficient student at school, scholarly even. She was always eager to delve deeply into whatever piqued her interest, everything from photography to Latin. She loved logic, loved to take things apart and put them back together, whether it was a speech by Cicero or a windmill. At the end of the day, though, dishes and more housework and her mother's vigilant eye always waited for Joyce in the dark and close confines of the house.

And so when Joyce had first laid eyes on Joe Rantz, sitting in the back of the school bus strumming a guitar, singing some funny old song and flashing his big white toothy grin, when she had first heard his boisterous laugh and seen mirth in his eyes as he glanced up the aisle at her, she had been drawn to him, seen in him at once a window to a wider and sunnier world. He seemed the very embodiment of freedom.

She knew what his circumstances were, knew how marginal his existence was, how poor his prospects. She knew that many girls would turn away from a boy like this, and that perhaps she should as well. And yet the more she observed how he handled those circumstances, how strong he was, how resourceful he could be, how he, like she, enjoyed the challenge of solving practical problems, the more she came to admire him. In time she also came to understand that he, like she, lived with self-doubt gnawing continually at his heart. Most of all, she marveled at and exulted in the simple and undeniable fact that he seemed to care for her just as she was, good or bad. Slowly she resolved that someday she would find a way to compensate for the way the world had so far treated Joe Rantz.

In the summer of 1931, Joe received a letter from his brother Fred, now a chemistry teacher at Roosevelt High School in Seattle. Fred wanted Joe to come to Seattle, to live with him and Thelma and take his senior year at Roosevelt. If Joe graduated from a school as highly regarded as Roosevelt, Fred said, he just might be able to get into the University of Washington. From there, anything might be possible.

Joe was wary. Since Fred had first taken him in, back in Nezperce when he was five, Joe had always felt that Fred was a bit overbearing, bent perhaps as much on directing Joe's life as helping him out. Fred had long seemed to think that his little brother was just a bit inept, and that he needed to set him straight on any number of things. Now, just as Joe was finally beginning to get his feet under himself, to make it on his own, he wasn't at all sure he wanted Fred, or anyone else for that matter, telling him how to live his life. He wasn't sure he wanted to live with Thula's twin sister either. And he had not really contemplated going to the university before. Still, as he pondered Fred's letter, the notion began to work on him. He'd always done well in his classes, he was insatiably curious about any number of subjects, and he liked the idea of testing his intellectual abilities. More than that, though, he knew that Sequim was never likely to offer him a path to the future he was starting to imagine, a future that centered on Joyce Simdars and a family of his own. To get there, he knew, he would have to leave Joyce behind, at least for now.

In the end he boarded up the house in Sequim, told Joyce he'd be back at the end of the school year, took the ferry to Seattle, moved in with Fred and Thelma, and started attending Roosevelt. It was a strange turn: for the first time in as long as he could remember, he found himself with three square meals a day and little to do except attend school and explore his interests. He threw himself into both. Again he excelled in the classroom and quickly worked his way onto the dean's honor roll. He joined the glee club and relished the opportunity it gave him to sing and perform in plays and make music. He signed up for the men's gymnastics team, where his prodigious upper-body strength made him a standout on the rings, the high bar, and the parallel bars. At the end of the day, he sometimes went out on the town with Fred and Thelma, eating in real restaurants, taking in Hollywood movies, even going to musicals at the 5th Avenue Theatre. It seemed, to Joe, a life of extraordinary ease and privilege, and it confirmed what he had been thinking—he did want something more out of life than what Sequim could offer.

One spring day in 1932, as Joe was practicing "giants" on the high bar in the gym, he noticed a tall man in a dark gray suit and a fedora, standing in the doorway and watching him intently. The man disappeared, but a few minutes later Fred walked into the gym and called Joe over to the door.

"A fellow just came into my classroom and asked who you were," Fred said. "Said he was from the university. He gave me this. Said you should look him up when you get to the U. That he might be able to use a fellow like you."

Fred handed Joe a card, and Joe glanced down at it:

ALVIN M. ULBRICKSON
HEAD COACH, CREW
UNIVERSITY OF WASHINGTON ATHLETIC DEPARTMENT

Joe pondered the card for a moment, then walked to his locker and put it in his wallet. It couldn't hurt to give it a try. Rowing couldn't be any harder than cutting cottonwoods.

By the summer of 1932, Joe had graduated from Roosevelt with honors and was back in Sequim. If he was really going to attend the university, he was going to need to scrape together enough money for rent and books and tuition. It would take him a year just to earn enough for his freshman year. He'd worry about the second year, and the third, and the fourth, later.

Joe was glad to be home. As he had feared, in Seattle Fred had directed his every move. It had been with the best of intentions, Joe was sure, but he had felt suffocated by the ceaseless rejoinders and advice—on everything from what classes to take to how to tie his necktie. Fred had even suggested that he date particular girls at Roosevelt, suggesting that the Simdars girl out in Sequim might be a bit of a country bumpkin, and that perhaps he should set his sights a little higher, on a city girl. And there had been something else. As the year went by, Joe had gradually begun to suspect and then to believe that Fred and Thelma knew exactly where his father, stepmother, and half siblings were, and that they were not far away. There had been bits of conversation overheard, topics abruptly dropped, glances hastily averted, phone calls carried out with muffled voices. Joe had thought about confronting them, but he'd always reconsidered, pushed the subject out of his mind. The last thing he wanted to know was that his father was nearby and making no effort to reach out to him.

In Sequim, Joe worked continuously. He counted himself lucky when he landed a summer job with the Civilian Conservation Corps, laying asphalt for the new Olympic Highway for fifty cents an hour. The money was decent, the work brutal. For eight hours a day, he shoveled steaming asphalt out of trucks and raked it out flat in advance of the steamrollers, the unrelenting heat rising from the black asphalt melding with the heat from the sun overhead, as if the two sources were competing to see which would kill him first. On weekends he cut hay again with Harry Secor and dug irrigation ditches for local farmers. By winter he was back in the woods with Charlie McDonald, cutting cottonwoods, chaining them to the draft horses, and skidding them out of the woods in snow and sleet.

But there was a saving grace. Almost every afternoon now, Joyce got off the school bus on Silberhorn, down by the river, rather than at her home in Happy Valley. She rushed through the woods looking for Joe. When she found him, he always hugged her tight, smelling, as she would remember seventy years later on her deathbed, of wet wood and sweat and the sweet wildness of the outdoors.

One radiant day in late April, she hurried to Joe as usual. When she found him, he took her hand and led her to a small meadow among the cottonwoods on the south bank of the Dungeness. Joe sat her down in the grass and asked her to wait a moment. He wandered a few feet off and sat down and began to inspect the ground carefully, pawing through the grass. Joyce knew what he was doing. He had always had an uncanny knack for finding four-leaf clovers, and he loved to present them to her as small tokens of his affection. How he found them so easily mystified her, but he always told her that it wasn't a matter of luck at all, that it was just a matter of keeping your eyes open. "The only time you *don't* find a four-leaf clover," he liked to say, "is when you stop looking for one." She loved that. It summed up in a few words what she most loved about him.

She lay back in the grass and closed her eyes, enjoying the warmth of the sun on her face and legs. After a short while, shorter than usual, she heard Joe approaching. She sat up and smiled at him.

"Found one," he said, beaming.

He held out a closed fist, and she reached out to receive the clover. But as he slowly unfolded his hand, she saw that it held not a clover but a golden ring with a small but perfect diamond sparkling in the rare spring sunshine.

Joe and Joyce at the beach

Freshmen on *Old Nero*

CHAPTER FIVE

Rowing is perhaps the toughest of sports. Once the race starts, there are no time-outs, no substitutions. It calls upon the limits of human endurance. The coach must therefore impart the secrets of the special kind of endurance that comes from mind, heart, and body.

—George Yeoman Pocock

As the autumn of 1933 began to wane, daytime temperatures in Seattle sagged into the low forties, evening temperatures into the twenties. The perpetually somber skies began to drizzle relentlessly. Biting winds blew in from the southwest, kicking up legions of whitecaps on Lake Washington. On October 22 gale winds ripped display signs from buildings downtown, tossed houseboats around on Lake Union, and necessitated the rescue of thirty-three people from various storm-tossed pleasure craft on Puget Sound.

For the boys still competing for a spot on the freshman crew, the deteriorating weather meant new forms of misery as they labored at their oars aboard *Old Nero*. Rain pelted their bare heads and shoulders. Their oars slapped against wind-tossed waves, sending up plumes of icy spray that blew back into their faces and stung their eyes. Their hands grew so numb that they could never be sure they had a proper hold on their oars. They could not feel their ears or noses. The icy water of the lake beneath them seemed to suck warmth and energy out of them more quickly than they could produce it. Their aching muscles cramped up the moment they stopped moving them. And they dropped like flies.

By October 30 the original 175 had been whittled down to 80 boys competing for a seat in the first two freshman boats. There would be a third boat and a fourth boat too, but nobody sitting in them would be likely to find himself racing in the spring or having a shot at eventually making the varsity crew. Tom Bolles decided it was time to move the best of them out of *Old Nero* and into shell barges. Both Joe Rantz and Roger Morris were among those he chose.

The shell barges were much like the racing shells the boys aspired to sit in, but they were a few inches broader in the beam, with flatter bottoms and keels. Considerably more stable than racing shells, they were nevertheless eccentric craft, easy to capsize and difficult to maneuver. What had been true before was true all over again: they would have to master an entirely new set of skills simply to remain upright in them. For now, though, it was enough simply to be out of *Old Nero* and in something resembling a shell, and Joe for one was bursting with pride as he first sat down in one and laced his feet into the foot stretchers.

For both Joe and Roger, making it into the shell barges was sweet recompense for days that had been, ever since school began, brutally long and demanding. Every weekday Roger slogged on foot the two and a half miles from his parents' house in Fremont to school, labored at his engineering classes until crew practice, and when practice was over, walked back home again to help out with family chores and do his homework. On Friday and Saturday nights, to pay his tuition and help with the home finances, he played saxophone and clarinet in a swing band, the Blue Lyres, he had started in high school. On weekends he worked for his family's moving business, the Franklin Transfer Company, hoisting sofas and bed sets and pianos in and out of homes all over town. With almost half the mortgages in America delinquent that fall, and a thousand foreclosures occurring every day, it was often sad work as he moved families out of homes they had worked a lifetime to acquire. Too often men stood hollow-eyed and women wept in doorways as Roger loaded onto a truck the last of their possessions, destined not for another home but for an auction house. Each time it happened, Roger whispered a little prayer of gratitude that so far his own family had managed to hang on to their house. Like so many, they had slipped, in a few short years, from a comfortable, secure middle-class existence to one in which every dime seemed harder to come by than the one before. But at least they still had their home.

Roger was a funny sort of fellow—kind of gruff, apt to speak bluntly, almost rudely. He wasn't easy to buddy up to, but sometimes Joe sat with him in the cafeteria. They talked sporadically, mostly chatting awkwardly about their engineering classes. As often as not, they ate in silence. There seemed to be a tenuous, if unspoken, strand of affection and respect growing between them, but otherwise Joe didn't feel much kinship with most of the boys in the shell house. Even with the most nattily dressed boys now gone, he still felt that he stuck out among the survivors. He showed up every day in the same rumpled sweater, the only one he owned, and almost every day there were snide remarks about it in the locker room. "Hobo Joe," the boys snickered. "How's life down in Hooverville?" "You trying to catch moths with that thing, Rantz?" Joe took to arriving early to change into his rowing clothes before the others showed up.

Every afternoon he hurried from his engineering classes to crew practice. Directly afterward he rushed again, this time to his job in the student athletic store, where he worked until midnight selling everything from candy bars to what an ad for the store euphemistically termed "those guardians of the vital zone." After work he trudged up University Avenue in the rain and the dark to the YMCA, where he worked as a janitor in exchange for a small, cell-like room just big enough for a desk and a bed. It was just one in a warren of such rooms that had been partitioned off in a converted coal storage basement. The dank, dingy rooms housed an eclectic collection of students, both male and female. Among them was a precocious and stunning young drama student named Frances Farmer, who less than two years later the rest of them would be watching on the silver screen. But there was little in the way of socializing among the denizens of the basement, and for Joe his room represented little more than a place to do his homework and stretch out his aching frame for a few hours before heading off to classes again in the morning. It was not like anything one could call a home.

As grueling as the fall of 1933 was for Joe, it wasn't quite all work and loneliness. Joyce was nearby, and that was a consolation.

She had come to Seattle to be with Joe, but also to pursue her own dreams. Her academic success set her on a course that was different from those of most of the farm girls with whom she had gone to high school in Sequim. She didn't seek a career outside her home; she wanted to raise a family and to do it very well. But she had no intention of living a life like her mother's, in which housework defined and limited the horizon of her worldview. She wanted to live a life of the mind, and the university was her ticket to that life.

Ironically, though, the only route to her goal lay through still more housework. She walked off a ferry and arrived in downtown Seattle that September desperately needing a place to live and a way to pay for her tuition, her food, and her books. She enrolled at the university and moved in briefly with her aunt Laura, but it was soon clear that, what with the hard times, another mouth to feed was an unwelcome burden on her aunt's already crimped budget. For the next two weeks, Joyce arose every morning at dawn and hurriedly scanned the all too meager offerings of the help-wanted ads in the *Seattle Post-Intelligencer*. Many days fewer than half a dozen ads appeared, alongside long columns of work-wanted ads.

Aside from a bright mind, all Joyce could reasonably offer the world of employers was her skill at doing what she least liked to do, cleaning and cooking. So she focused on ads for domestic service. Unwilling to pay for bus fare, dressed in her Sunday best, she walked miles each time she found an ad for a maid, trekking far out into the fashionable Laurelhurst neighborhood east of the campus or climbing the steep incline up to the crest of Capitol Hill, where stately Victorian houses stood on quiet, shady side streets. Time and again, she was met at the door by the haughty wives of the city's elite, who ushered her into stuffy front rooms, perched her on ornate sofas, and then demanded references and evidence of her employment experience, neither of which Joyce could offer.

Finally, one hot afternoon, after another disheartening interview in Laurelhurst, Joyce decided simply to start knocking on doors. The houses here were massive and elegant. Perhaps someone needed help and hadn't gotten around to placing an ad. She walked up and down the street, her swollen and arthritic feet aching, sweat building up under her arms, her hair growing damp and disheveled as she traipsed up long walkways to formidable front doors and rapped gently.

Late that day a gaunt-looking elderly gentleman, a prominent local judge, came to his door, heard her out, cocked his head, studied her carefully, but asked no difficult questions about references or experience. There was a long, awkward silence as the judge contemplated her. Finally he croaked, "Come back in the morning, and we'll see if you fit in the last maid's uniform."

The uniform fit, and with that Joyce had landed a job.

Now on weekend evenings, when she could get some time off, she and Joe could board a streetcar for a few cents and go downtown to catch a Charlie Chan or Mae West movie for forty cents more. Friday nights were college nights at Club Victor, which meant no cover charge and a chance to dance to the offerings of a local bandmaster, Vic Meyers. Saturdays often brought a football game, and every football game called for a dance afterward in the women's gym. Joe and Joyce went to nearly all of them, Joe springing for the twenty-five-cent admission. But dancing on a basketball court to the blaring of the school band wasn't particularly romantic, wasn't really much better than dancing in the close, sweaty confines of the Chicken Coop back in Sequim. Joe couldn't do what he most wanted to do, to take Joyce out to the swank places downtown that many of her friends frequented. They were the kinds of places where Joyce might have worn a chiffon gown, and Joe a suit, if either had had such a thing—places like the Trianon Ballroom at Third and Wall, with its vast polished-maple dance floor capable of holding five thousand at a time, its glittering chandeliers, its pink walls painted with tropical scenes, and its silver clamshell hood suspended over the bandstand. At places like that, you could dance all night to the likes of the Dorsey Brothers and Guy Lombardo. Joyce professed not to care, but it pained Joe that he could not take her there.

In mid-November the campus crackled with excitement and anticipation as the annual homecoming game with the University of Oregon approached. As a prelude Joe and his freshman crewmates took on the varsity crew in a football game of their own and were unceremoniously crushed by the older boys. It was a loss the freshmen wouldn't forget, and they swore they would have their revenge on the water. In the meantime, though, tradition demanded that the losers prepare a banquet for the victors, and the student paper, the University of Washington Daily, seized on the opportunity to gibe the freshman crew: "their menu should be easy to select for they caught plenty of crabs on Sunday."

On November 17 a pall fell over the campus when, just at the height of the festivities, tragedy struck. A freshman, Willis Thompson, attempting to start a bonfire for a rally, splashed gasoline on his clothes and set himself afire. After lingering in great pain for several days, Thompson died the following week.

A pall of another, quite literal, sort continued to hang over the larger world as well that month. On November 11 farmers in the Dakotas awoke after a windy night to find something they had never seen before—daytime skies turned black by topsoil scoured from their fields and carried aloft by the wind. The next day the skies over Chicago grew dark as the dust cloud traveled eastward, and a few days later people in upstate New York looked up, astonished, into skies the color of rust. Nobody knew it yet, but the dust that month, that first "black blizzard," was merely a harbinger of what would come to be called the Dust Bowl, the second great act in the long tragedy of the 1930s and early 1940s. The winds of November 1933 would soon be followed by others, even stronger, that would blow away much of the topsoil of the American plains and send hundreds of thousands of refugees streaming westward across the continent in search of jobs that did not exist—adrift, rootless, homeless, dispossessed in their own land, their confidence as well as their livelihoods carried away on the wind.

And increasingly there were distant but dark rumblings from Germany, intimations of the third and most tragic act. On October 14, Hitler had abruptly quit the League of Nations and discontinued Germany's ongoing disarmament talks with France and her allies. It was a deeply disturbing turn of events, essentially abrogating the Treaty of Versailles and undermining the foundations on which European peace had been built since 1919. Krupp, Germany's legendary armament and munitions manufacturer, had begun secretly working on an initial order of 135 Panzer I tanks. Observers in Panama had recently noted an enormous surge in the number of shipments of nitrates—used in the manufacturing of munitions—passing through the canal under blind sailing orders, en route from Chile to the Azores, heading in the direction of Europe, ultimate destination unknown.

On the streets of German cities that fall, Americans and other foreign nationals were assaulted by storm troopers when they refused to give Nazi salutes, prompting the United States, Britain, and Holland to issue warnings to Berlin of "most serious consequences" should the attacks continue. By late fall reports were reaching as far as Seattle. Richard Tyler, dean of engineering at the University of Washington, just back from Germany himself, reported his observations in an article in the *Daily*: "The people of Germany today are afraid to express opinions even on trivial matters," he said, before going on to observe that anyone saying anything that could be interpreted as unflattering to the Nazis was liable to be arrested and incarcerated without trial. And though neither Tyler nor any of his readers yet knew it, the Nazis had in fact already imprisoned thousands of political dissidents in a camp they had opened in March near the charming little medieval village of Dachau.

Tyler's account and scores of others even more sinister, particularly those by Jewish emigrants from Germany, fell almost entirely on deaf ears in America that fall. When the student body at Washington was polled on the question of whether the United States should ally itself with France and

Britain to oppose Germany, the results were the same as they had been in similar polls nearly everywhere else in the country: 99 percent said no. On November 15, Will Rogers neatly and characteristically summed up the American attitude toward the prospect of a second French-German conflict with a simple, homespun image. The United States, he said, ought to "just let those two old tomcats whose tails are tied together over the fence alone and try to cure the scratches we got the last time we tried to untie 'em."

On the afternoon of November 28, the last practice day of the fall term, the freshmen took one final, frigid workout. When the last of them had returned to the shell house, Coach Bolles told the boys to stick around, that it was time to announce who had made the first and second boats. Then he ducked into Al Ulbrickson's office.

The boys glanced at one another. Through the steamy panes of the glassed-in cubbyhole that served as the coaches' office, they could see Ulbrickson and Bolles hunched over a desk in their flannel suits, studying a piece of paper. The shell house reeked sourly of sweat and damp socks and mildew, as it did every afternoon now that the rainy season had begun. The afternoon's last feeble light filtered down from the windows above. Occasional gusts of wind buffeted the massive sliding door. As the two coaches lingered in the office, the boys' usual post-practice banter and joshing faded away and was replaced by an uncomfortable silence. The only sound was a soft tapping. Up in the loft at the back of the room, Pocock was nailing together the frame for a new shell. Roger Morris drifted over and stood quietly next to Joe, toweling his hair dry.

Bolles emerged from the office and climbed up onto a bench, clutching the piece of paper. The boys shuffled into a semicircle around him.

He began by saying that this was just a preliminary selection, that all of them could continue to compete for the seats he was about to announce, that he encouraged them to do so, that nobody should get all swell headed just because he heard his name called out now. Nobody should think he was a sure thing. There wasn't any such animal. Then he began to read off the names on the list, moving first through the assignments for the second boat, announcing the names of boys who would make up the primary challengers to the presumptive favorites in the first freshman boat.

When Bolles finished announcing the second boat, Joe glanced at Roger, who was staring morosely down at the floor. Neither of them had been called. But neither had long to wait. Bolles began calling out the first-boat assignments: "Bow seat, Roger Morris. Number two seat, Shorty Hunt. Number three seat, Joe Rantz . . ." As Bolles continued, Joe clenched his fist at his side and gave it a subtle little pump, unwilling to celebrate any more demonstrably than that in front of the boys who had not been selected. Next to him, Roger began to exhale softly.

As the rest of the boys headed toward the showers, those selected for the first boat took a shell barge off its rack, hoisted it over their heads, and marched it down to the darkening lake for a celebratory row. A light but cutting wind ruffled the water. As the sun set, they laced their feet into the stretchers and began to row westward through the Cut and Portage Bay and out onto Lake Union, seeking calmer water than could be found on the open expanse of Lake Washington.

The temperatures had fallen into the upper thirties, and it felt even colder out on the water. Joe hardly noticed. As the boat slipped onto the surface of Lake Union, the noise of city traffic fell away, and he entered into a world completely silent except for the rhythmic barking of the coxswain in the stern. Joe's seat slid methodically and silently back and forth on the greased runners beneath him. His arms and legs pulled and pushed smoothly, almost easily. When the white blade of his oar entered the black water, it merely murmured.

At the north end of the lake, the coxswain called out, "Way . . . 'nuff!" The boys stopped rowing and the shell glided to a stop, the long oars trailing in the water alongside them. Dark clouds fringed with silver moonlight scudded by overhead, carried briskly along by the winds aloft. The boys sat without talking, breathing heavily, exhaling plumes of white breath. Even now that they had stopped rowing, their breathing was synchronized, and for a brief, fragile moment it seemed to Joe as if all of them were part of a single thing, something alive with breath and spirit of its own. To the west, silver headlights crawled slowly across the spidery steel arch of the new Aurora Bridge. To the south, the amber lights of downtown Seattle danced on the waves. Atop Queen Anne Hill, ruby-red lights on radio towers winked on and off. Joe gulped huge drafts of the frigid air and sat staring at the scene, watching it turn into a soft blur of colors as, for the first time since his family had left him, tears filled his eyes.

He turned his face to the water, fiddling with his oarlock so the others would not see. He didn't know where the tears had come from, what they were all about. But something inside him had shifted, if only for a few moments.

The boys had caught their breaths, and they were talking softly, not joking for a change, not horsing around, just talking quietly about the lights and what lay before them. Then the coxswain called out, "Ready all!" Joe turned and faced the rear of the boat, slid his seat forward, sank the white blade of his oar into the oil-black water, tensed his muscles, and waited for the command that would propel him forward into the glimmering darkness.

On the second day of December 1933, it began to rain in Seattle as it had never rained before and has never rained since. Over the next thirty days, there was only one day when the skies were not leaden with clouds, only four when it did not rain. By the end of the month, fourteen and a quarter inches of rain had fallen at the University of Washington. Fifteen and a third inches had fallen downtown, still the all-time record for any month of the year. Some days it drizzled; some days it poured. Either way, it just kept coming.

Rivers all across western Washington—the Chehalis, the Snoqualmie, the Duwamish, the Skykomish, the Stillaguamish, the Skokomish, the Snohomish—overflowed their banks, sweeping away farmhouses, washing millions of tons of topsoil into Puget Sound, flooding the commercial districts of riverside communities from the Canadian border all the way south to the Columbia. North of Seattle the swollen Skagit River sliced though earthen dikes near its mouth and sent tidal salt water spilling across twenty thousand acres of the richest farmland in the state.

In many of Seattle's nicest hillside neighborhoods—places like Alki and Madrona and Magnolia—homes slid from eroding bluffs and tumbled into Lake Washington or Puget Sound. Roadways cracked and followed the homes downhill. Downtown, storm water overwhelmed the sewers, bubbled up through manholes, and flooded the streets and businesses of the low-lying International District. In the miserable shantytown spread out along the shore of Elliott Bay, unrelenting rain dissolved newspaper that had been wadded into chinks in flimsy walls, worked its way through the weather-beaten fabric of old tents, and dripped through rusty corrugated steel roofs, soaking old mattresses lying on muddy floors and chilling to the bone those who tried to sleep on them.

In the midst of this onslaught, as soon as final exams were over for the fall quarter, Joyce took some time off from her job, and she and Joe went home to Sequim for Christmas break. Joe visited with the McDonalds and checked on the house on Silberhorn, but he stayed at Joyce's parents' house, sleeping in a bed in the attic. When he had settled in, Joyce's mother pulled out a clipping from the local newspaper and showed him the headline: "Joe Rantz Makes First Crew." He was, she told him, becoming quite the talk of the town.

PART TWO

1934

Resiliency

Tom Bolles

CHAPTER SIX

My ambition has always been to be the greatest shell builder in the world; and without false modesty, I believe I have attained that goal. If I were to sell the [Boeing] stock, I fear I would lose my incentive and become a wealthy man, but a second-rate artisan. I prefer to remain a first-class artisan.

—George Yeoman Pocock

In January, Joe and Joyce returned to Seattle, where rain continued to fall almost every day. When crew practice started up again on January 8, Joe and the seventeen other boys in the first and second freshman boats learned that they were now entitled to abandon the shell barges and step for the first time into proper racing shells, the sleek and lovely cedar craft built by George Pocock in his loft workshop at the back of the Washington shell house.

They also learned that what had seemed a brutal workout schedule in the fall was merely a whisper of what Al Ulbrickson and Tom Bolles had in mind for them now. In the next few months, they were told, they would mostly race against one another and their junior varsity and varsity counterparts. After that they might race against the University of British Columbia or a handful of other Northwest crews. But the real racing season was short and the stakes high: In mid-April just one boatload of freshmen—whichever emerged as the first freshman boat—would face their primary rival, the University of California at Berkeley, right here on Lake Washington, in the annual Pacific Coast Regatta. If they prevailed in that race—and only if they did so—they could claim supremacy in the West. That would likely earn them a chance to race against Navy and the elite eastern schools for the national freshman championship in Poughkeepsie in June. And that was it. The whole season—nine months of preparation—came down to just two major races.

In his six years as freshman coach, Bolles had never coached a crew that had lost a race to California, or anyone else, on Lake Washington. Bolles didn't intend for this bunch to be the first, no matter how good the Cal freshmen were reputed to be, and he happened to know that they were reputed to be very good indeed. Bolles knew, in fact, that Ky Ebright's boys had been rowing since late August, and that he had been racing them against one another in real shells since late October, when the Washington freshmen had begun tentatively trying out the shell barges. Ebright, Bolles noticed, had been making more than the usual amount of noise in the Bay Area press lately about how thoroughly his freshmen were going to shellac Washington. From now until race day, Bolles told his boys, they would row six days a week, rain or shine.

It rained, and they rowed. They rowed through cutting wind, bitter sleet, and occasional snow, well into the dark of night every evening. They rowed with cold rainwater running down their backs, pooling in the bottom of the boat, and sloshing back and forth under their sliding seats. A local sportswriter who watched them work out that month observed that "it rained and rained and rained. Then it rained and rained and rained." Another commented that they "could have turned their shells upside down and rowed without making much difference in their progress. It was nearly as wet above the surface of the lake as it was below." Through it all, Bolles followed them doggedly back and forth across Lake Washington and down the Montlake Cut into Lake Union, where they rowed past the wet, black hulls and dripping bowsprits of old lumber schooners. Riding through the slop and the chop in the open cockpit of his brass-trimmed, mahogany-planked motor launch, the *Alumnus*, wearing a bright yellow rain slicker, he bellowed commands at them through his megaphone until his voice grew hoarse and his throat sore.

Once again boys who had endured the bitter cold workouts in October and November now placed their oars in racks at the end of the day, climbed wearily back up the hill, and refused to come back for more. Four boatloads soon became three, and by the end of the month Bolles sometimes had a hard time filling the third boat. All the boys in Joe's boat stuck it out, but the easy camaraderie they had briefly felt the first time they went out together on Lake Union in November quickly evaporated. Anxiety, self-doubt, and bickering replaced that night's buoyant optimism as Bolles scrutinized each of them anew, trying to figure out who to keep in the boat and who to demote.

Al Ulbrickson was working his upperclassmen just as hard, trying to settle on a first junior varsity and a first varsity boat to race against Cal in April and the eastern schools in June. But as soggy January wore on and gave way to a blustery February, he was decidedly unhappy with what he was seeing out on the water, particularly with his varsity. After every workout it was Ulbrickson's habit to sit down in his office and make notations in a logbook. These private comments were more often far more expressive than those his reticent public persona allowed. Amid many entries grumbling about the weather, he grumbled even more about the lack of spirit in the older boys as he raced boatloads of them against one another. Increasingly, he littered the log with stinging commentary: "too many TOLO dates," "too many gripers," "not enough pepper," "They could have been closer by wishing hard."

On February 16, Ulbrickson finally found something he liked, but not where he'd been looking. Returning to the shell house that evening, the first varsity boat fell in alongside Tom Bolles's first freshman boat, which was also returning. Still two miles out, the two crews began, on an impulse, to race for home. At first the freshmen stayed even with the varsity, rowing at the same stroke count. Ulbrickson wasn't terribly surprised. He knew Bolles was working his freshmen hard. But both crews had been rowing for hours, and as he trailed them in his launch Ulbrickson waited for the younger, less experienced boys to fade. Instead of fading, though, a half mile from the shell house the freshmen suddenly began to pull ahead, grabbing a quarter-length lead. That got Ulbrickson's attention. It also got the attention of Harvey Love, the coxswain in the varsity boat, who frantically called for a higher stroke rate. The varsity poured it on for the last thirty seconds, just managing to pull even with the freshmen as they reached the floating dock at the shell house. Ulbrickson's acrid entry in his logbook that night read "First real work the varsity has done."

Six hundred and seventy miles to the south, on the Oakland Estuary—the University of California's home water—Ky Ebright was facing remarkably similar problems. Only one of his 1932 Olympic gold medal crew still rowed for California, and his varsity lineup was turning in indifferent times at best. Ebright couldn't quite figure out what was wrong. "They are just the right size and they have lots of power, but I just can't see them winning," he complained to the San Francisco Chronicle. To top things off, in recent weeks his freshmen had begun to beat his varsity in time trials and head-to-head races.

In a number of ways, Ky Ebright was the opposite of Al Ulbrickson. Ulbrickson, a former stroke oar—one of the best Washington had ever known—was tall, well built, and notably handsome. Ebright, a former coxswain, was short, skinny, bespectacled, and sharp of feature, with a

prominent nose and a receding chin. Ulbrickson dressed conservatively, usually in his fedora and a three-piece flannel suit; Ebright wore flannel suits as
well, but he was apt to pair them improbably with an old oilskin sou'wester or a
wide-brimmed hat, the front of which he pushed up, making him look something like Gene Autry's comedic sidekick, Smiley Burnette, or a younger version of Hopalong Cassidy's equally comic sidekick, Gabby Hayes. Ulbrickson
was reticent, often to the point of rudeness; Ebright was expressive, often also
to the point of rudeness. One of his oarsmen, Buzz Schulte, recalled, "He yelled,
goaded, teased, whatever it took to motivate his boys." Prone to pounding his
megaphone on the gunwales of his coaching launch in exasperation, he once
hurled it at an oarsman who had caught a crab. The megaphone, not being particularly aerodynamic, missed its mark by a wide margin and landed in the lap
of the coxswain, Don Blessing, who, irritated by the assault on his crewmate,
nudged the megaphone over the side of the boat with his knee. As it sank into
the depths, an enraged Ebright exploded, "Blessing! God damn you! That was
an expensive megaphone. Why did you destroy it like that?"

As difficult as he could sometimes be, though, Ky Ebright, like Al
Ulbrickson, was a remarkable coach—destined, like Ulbrickson, for rowing's
hall of fame—and he cared deeply for the young men in his charge. The night
California won Olympic gold in Amsterdam in 1928, an emotional Ebright
came to Blessing, put his arm around the younger man, and said with a
cracking voice, "You know, Don, I cussed you a lot of times and made you
mad a lot of times, but you've been the greatest coxswain, the greatest
student, I've ever had, and I want you to know how much I appreciate that." "It
made me cry," Blessing later said. "I mean, he was God to me." It was a feeling
shared by most of the boys Ebright coached, among them Robert McNamara,
later the U.S. secretary of defense, and the movie star Gregory Peck, who in 1997
donated twenty-five thousand dollars to the Cal crew in Ebright's memory.

Like Ulbrickson, Ebright grew up in Seattle, attended the University of
Washington, and began his rowing life there in 1915, as coxswain. He once
coxed a Washington crew to a humiliating fifteen-length shellacking of California. After graduating, he continued to hang around the Washington shell
house, informally advising students and coaches and generally helping out. In
1923, when Washington's head coach, Ed Leader, left to coach at Yale, Ebright
was among the candidates eager to replace him, but Washington passed him
over in favor of Russell "Rusty" Callow.

Shortly after that, Washington learned that California's coach, Ben Wallis, was leaving Berkeley and that the school was on the verge of abandoning its crew program after years of less than stellar results. The board of stewards for rowing at Washington quickly took note. California had had a rowing team since 1868, making it one of the oldest crew programs in the country. Stanford had abandoned the sport in 1920. If Cal gave it up too, the stewards feared that Washington would have little justification for perpetuating its own program without a serious West Coast rival. But a solution seemed to be at hand: California wanted an effective coach, Ebright wanted a coaching job, Washington wanted a rival, and the upshot was that Ky Ebright became the head coach at California in February 1924, with the mission of rebuilding the school's program. And that he did with a vengeance.

By 1927 the Cal program had improved to the point that Berkeley could reasonably contend with Washington for West Coast supremacy. Friction began to grow between the two programs. From the outset, some in the Washington shell house felt that by agreeing to go to Cal, Ebright had betrayed the institution that had nurtured him. Others felt, rightly or wrongly, that Ebright was bitter about not getting the job at Washington and was bent on evening a personal score. As California continued to improve, other issues surfaced, new resentments arose, and the relationship between the two programs deteriorated further. Before long, the rivalry between them had become, as Ebright later put it bluntly, "vicious and bloody."

Some of the bad blood centered, improbably, on the most gentlemanly of individuals in either shell house. Ky Ebright knew from his own days at Washington what the presence of George Pocock meant to the Washington crew program. And as he built his own program, he began to brood on it.

Part of his resentment involved suspicions about equipment. Like nearly every other crew coach in the country, Ebright was by the late 1920s buying almost all his equipment from Pocock, who ran an independent business from his shop in the Washington shell house. Pocock's cedar shells and spruce oars were by now understood across America to be unsurpassed for craftsmanship, durability, and, most important, speed on the water. They were state-of-the-art, so elegant and streamlined that people liked to say they seemed to be in motion while still on the racks. By the mid-1930s, a Pocock eight-man shell would have the same market price as a brand-new LaSalle built by General Motors' Cadillac division. But Ebright, reacting to rumors his father had heard, had come to suspect that Pocock was sending him second-rate or defective equipment in order to hobble Washington's principal rival. He wrote angrily to Pocock about it: "He heard that you said the shell you hoped Washington would use was a great deal better than the one you made California this year." Over the next few months, a series of increasingly unpleasant and accusatory letters from Berkeley arrived in Pocock's mailbox. Each time, the Englishman responded politely and diplomatically, declaring that the equipment he sent to Cal was identical to that which he provided to Washington or anyone else on his list of customers: "You can take it from me that Washington would gladly swap boats with you," he wrote. "Stamp out any thought among your men that they are getting shells from the enemy. Far from it. My work is absolutely first, then comes the broadening of the rowing game." But Ebright remained suspicious, and he continued to lash out at Pocock: "It is the most natural thing in the world for our men to feel as I say they do—that they are getting their equipment from the enemy. It injures their morale and makes it hard for us to compete on even terms."

In trying to deal with Ebright, Pocock found himself in a quandary. By 1931 the effects of the Depression had caused crew programs across the country to go out of existence or to cut back drastically on the purchase of equipment. As coveted as his shells were, Pocock had begun to find himself struggling to stay in business, reduced to writing plaintive letters to coaches around the country, pleading for orders. Ebright seemed eager to seize the opportunity to exact revenge for the wrongs he had imputed to Pocock. In his correspondence with the boatbuilder, he threatened to buy his equipment from an English supplier, demanded price concessions, and insisted on design modifications if he were to buy. Time and again Pocock explained that he was desperate for business but could not reduce prices: "No one who has ordered a boat this year has asked for it. They know they are worth it." But Ebright only hardened his position: "You will not be able to get your old prices much longer, it will just be impossible to pay them ... the goose that laid the golden egg is gone."

What most seemed to get Ebright's goat, though, when he thought about the Washington program, wasn't the quality or price of the equipment he was receiving from Pocock; it was the quality of advice the Washington boys were receiving and his boys were not. Ebright knew that Pocock possessed deep insights into every aspect of the sport, into specific elements of technique as well as into the psychology of winning and losing at it, and he didn't think Washington should have a monopoly on Pocock's wisdom. When the two schools got together, it griped him to see the Englishman squatting on the dock and talking with the Washington boys or riding along in Ulbrickson's launch, leaning over to him, whispering things in his ears. Somewhat bizarrely, given the geographical situation, he lashed out at Pocock, "I repeat that you have never gone out with our crew in a workout . . . you should ride with us and give us suggestions about rowing the same as you do for Washington."

Pocock's integrity, his craftsmanship, and above all his honor were his life-blood. The letters stung. There was no logical reason why he owed California anything more than the quality equipment he continued to send them. And there was something else. When California had first approached Washington about a new head coach in the fall of 1923, it was George Pocock to whom they had first offered the job. Pocock thought he would be more valuable to the sport if he continued to build shells. It was he who had first recommended Ky Ebright.

Nonetheless, Pocock tried to smooth things out. Whenever the two schools met, he took to going out of his way to talk with the Cal boys. He helped them rig their shells before races. He made a point of chatting with the Cal coaching staff, offering tips. But Ebright's lashing out at Pocock had not gone unnoticed in the Washington shell house, and by 1934 relations between the two programs could not have been any more strained.

By midspring Tom Bolles found himself struggling daily with the freshmen, and the trend seemed to be going the wrong way. "They seem to be getting slower every day," a dour and subdued Bolles complained.

One of the fundamental challenges in rowing is that when any one member of a crew goes into a slump the entire crew goes with him. A baseball team or a basketball team may very well triumph even if its star player is off his game. But the demands of rowing are such that every man or woman in a racing shell depends on his or her crewmates to perform almost flawlessly with each and every pull of the oar. The movements of each rower are so intimately intertwined, so precisely synchronized with the movements of all the others, that any one rower's mistake or subpar performance can throw off the tempo of the stroke, the balance of the boat, and ultimately the success of the whole crew. More often than not, it comes down to a lack of concentration on one person's part.

For just this reason, as they struggled to regain their form the Washington freshmen came up with a mantra that their coxswain, George Morry, chanted as they rowed. Morry shouted, "M-I-B, M-I-B, M-I-B!" over and over to the rhythm of their stroke. The initialism stood for "mind in boat." It was meant as a reminder that from the time an oarsman steps into a racing shell until the moment that the boat crosses the finish line, he must keep his mind focused on what is happening inside the boat. His whole world must shrink down to the small space within the gunwales. He must maintain a singular focus on the rower just ahead of him and the voice of the coxswain calling out commands. Nothing outside the boat—not the boat in the next lane over, not the cheering of a crowd of spectators, not last night's date—can enter the successful oarsman's mind. But no amount of chanting "M-I-B" seemed to be working for the freshmen. Bolles decided he needed to tinker with the fundamentals of the boat, the mechanics of what made it go—or not go.

By and large, every rower in an eight-oared shell does the same thing—pull an oar through the water as smoothly as possible, as hard and as frequently as requested by the coxswain. But there are subtle differences in what is expected of individual rowers depending on which seat they occupy. Because the rest of the boat necessarily goes where the bow goes, any deflection or irregularity in the stroke of the oarsman in the bow seat has the greatest potential to disrupt the course, speed, and stability of the boat. So while the bow oarsman must be strong, like all the others, it's most important that he or she be technically proficient: capable of pulling a perfect oar, stroke after stroke, without fail. The same is true to a lesser extent of the rowers in the number two and three seats. The four, five, and six seats are often called "the engine room" of the crew, and the rowers who occupy these seats are typically the biggest and strongest in the boat. While technique is still important in those seats, the speed of the boat ultimately depends on the raw power of these rowers and how efficiently they transmit it through their oars and into the water. The rower in the number seven seat is something of a hybrid. He or she must be nearly as strong as the rowers in the engine room but must also be particularly alert, constantly aware of and in tune with what is happening in the rest of the boat. He or she must precisely match both the timing and the degree of power set by the rower in the number eight seat, the "stroke oar," and must transmit that information efficiently back into the boat's engine room. The stroke sits directly in front of and face-to-face with the coxswain, who faces the bow and steers the shell. Theoretically the stroke oar always rows at the rate and with the degree of power called for by the coxswain, but in the end it is the stroke who ultimately controls these things. Everyone else in the boat rows at the rate and power at which the stroke rows. When working well, the entire boat operates like a well-lubricated machine, with every rower serving as a vital link in a chain that powers that machine forward, somewhat like a bicycle chain.

To break the freshmen's slump, Bolles had to search vigilantly for and repair weak links in the chain. One potential weak link that spring seemed to be Joe Rantz. Bolles had tried moving Joe back and forth between the number three seat and number seven, but with no effect. The problem looked to be technical. From the beginning of freshman tryouts the previous fall, Bolles had not been able to get Joe to "square up" consistently—to rotate his oar so that the blade was perpendicular to the surface just before inserting it into the water on the catch, the beginning of each stroke. If the blade entered the water at any angle other than ninety degrees, the amount of power generated by the subsequent stroke would be compromised and the efficiency of the whole boat reduced. Squaring up required strong wrists and a fine degree of motor control, and Joe just couldn't seem to get the hang of it. Beyond that, his stroke was generally eccentric. He rowed powerfully but decidedly in his own way, and by any conventional measure his own way looked to be largely ineffective.

In exasperation, Bolles yanked Joe out of the first boat one afternoon before the outbound trip down Lake Washington. The boat slowed down perceptibly. Perplexed, Bolles put Joe back into the boat for the return run. Racing for home, Joe and the reconstituted first boat beat the second boat by a decisive margin. Bolles was flummoxed. Maybe the problem wasn't in Rantz's wrist. Maybe it was in his head.

For Joe, the incident, brief as it was, provided a sudden and cold reminder of how precarious his position on the crew, and therefore his attendance at the university, really was. A few days later, on March 20, when a *Post-Intelligencer* article proclaimed, "Rantz is getting the call at number 3," Joe cut out the article, pasted it in a scrapbook he had just begun keeping, and penned in next to it, "Am I a sure bet? Look what the *PI* says. Can't be too sure, though." Everything he had worked for could be over on any given afternoon.

It didn't help that he continued to feel like everyone's poor cousin. With the weather remaining cool, he still had to wear his ragged sweater to practice almost every day, and the boys still teased him continuously for it.

They found new and fertile grounds for mirth at his expense one evening when a group of them noticed Joe eating a meal in the cafeteria. Joe had piled his plate high with meat loaf and potatoes and creamed corn. He attacked the food with his knife and fork, working at it vigorously, shoveling it into his mouth. The moment he had cleared his plate he turned to the boy next to him, asked him for his leftover meat loaf, and devoured it just as rapidly.

Over the noise of the cafeteria, he didn't notice that someone had come up behind him. Nor did he hear the snickering. When he finally paused and looked up, he saw a smirk on the face of the boy across the table from him. Following his gaze, he turned around to find half a dozen fellows from the shell house standing in a semicircle, holding their dirty plates out to him, grins smeared across their faces. Joe paused, startled and humiliated, but then, with his ears growing red, he turned around, put his head down, and resumed eating—forking the food into his mouth like hay into a barn, his jaw working methodically, his eyes set and cold and defiant. He was hungry nearly all the time, and he wasn't about to walk away from perfectly good food because of a bunch of jackasses in jerseys. He'd dug too many ditches, cut down too many cottonwoods, foraged in the cold, wet woods for too many berries and mushrooms.

By the end of March, the slump appeared to be over. The freshman time trials were improving again as Bolles finally seemed to be zeroing in on the right mix of boys and seating assignments. On April 2, with Joe still sitting in the number three seat, Bolles put the clock to them. That night Joe went home and wrote in his scrapbook, "Two miles: 10:36. Gotta take eight seconds off to be the fastest frosh crew ever!!!"

For much of the rest of that week, it was too windy to row, but on April 6 the winds died down, and Ulbrickson decided to pit the varsity, junior varsity, and freshman crews against one another on Lake Washington. It was the perfect opportunity to get all three crews out on the water and see whether the wind delay had affected their performance.

As a handicap, Ulbrickson positioned the junior varsity, which had not thus far shown much promise, three boat lengths out in front of the other two boats at the start. He told the freshman crew to pull up and end its race at the two-mile mark, the standard distance for freshman races. That would allow the coaches to get a final and accurate readout on their time under racing conditions before the confrontation with Cal. The varsity and junior varsity were to continue racing to the three-mile mark.

Ulbrickson lined the boats up and barked, "Ready all . . . row!" through his megaphone. Harvey Love, the varsity coxswain, was talking and missed the signal. The freshmen immediately leapt out a half boat length ahead of the older boys. All three boats fell into a moderately high stroke rate, and for a mile they all held their rates and their relative positions—the junior varsity still three lengths out in front in their handicap position, the freshmen second, and the bow of the varsity boat locked in place, half a length back, alongside the freshman boat's number five seat. Then, slowly, the varsity's bow fell back to the six seat, the seven seat, the stroke seat, and finally the coxswain's seat. By the mile-and-a-half mark, the freshmen had opened a sliver of water between the rear of their boat and the varsity's bow, and they were beginning to close on the junior varsity out front. They had not raised their stroke rate a bit. With a quarter mile to go, sensing he had both boats where he wanted them, knowing his crew had plenty left in the tank, coxswain George Morry told the freshmen to kick the stroke rate up a couple of notches, and they surged past the junior varsity and into the overall lead. At the two-mile mark, Morry barked out, "Way 'nuff," and now two full lengths ahead of both other boats, the freshmen pulled up, let their oars ride the water, and coasted to a stop. As the other two boats finally passed them, the freshman boys raised a lusty cheer and pumped their fists in the air.

Bolles looked down at his stopwatch, saw the freshmen's two-mile time, and looked again. He had known they were getting sharp, but now he knew in no uncertain terms that he had the makings of something exceptional in his boat. What he didn't know was whether California had something even more exceptional, as Ky Ebright seemed to be hinting in the press. That would be revealed a week hence, on April 13. In the meantime, he resolved to keep the time on his stopwatch to himself.

There are certain laws of physics by which all crew coaches live and die. The speed of a racing shell is determined primarily by two factors: the power produced by the combined strokes of the oars, and the stroke rate, the number of strokes the crew takes each minute. So if two boats carrying the same weight have the exact same stroke rate, the one producing more power per stroke will pull ahead. If those two boats have the exact same power per stroke but one has a higher stroke rate, the one with the higher rate will pull ahead. A boat with both a very high stroke rate and very powerful strokes will beat a boat that can't match it on both counts. But, of course, oarsmen are human and no crew can maintain both powerful strokes and a very high rate indefinitely. And, critically, the higher the stroke rate, the harder it is to keep all the many individual movements of the crew synchronized. So every race is a balancing act, a series of delicate and deliberate adjustments of power on one hand and stroke rate on the other. It may be that nobody ever achieves absolutely optimal performance, but what Bolles had seen that day—his crew rowing so comfortably at a high but sustainable rate and with such great power—gave him every reason to think that someday these freshmen just might pull it off.

And it wasn't just their physical prowess. He liked the character of these particular freshmen. The boys who had made it this far were rugged and optimistic in a way that seemed emblematic of their western roots. They were the genuine article, mostly the products of lumber towns, dairy farms, mining camps, fishing boats, and shipyards. They looked, they walked, and they talked as if they had spent most of their lives out-of-doors. Despite the hard times and their pinched circumstances, they smiled easily and openly. They extended calloused hands eagerly to strangers. They looked you in the eye, not as a challenge, but as an invitation. They joshed you at the drop of a hat. They looked at impediments and saw opportunities. All that, Bolles knew, added up to a lot of potential in a crew, particularly if that crew got a chance to row in the East.

That same evening, at the Southern Pacific Railroad Depot in Oakland, Ky Ebright loaded his crews and his racing shells aboard the *Cascade* and headed north to Seattle.

Ebright knew that it had been windy in the Northwest, and he had been fretting to the Bay Area press about his boys' lack of experience with rough water. He was all too familiar with the whims of Lake Washington, from his coxswain days, and the weather on the Oakland Estuary had been typically but frustratingly calm and pleasant. So when windy conditions resumed shortly after California arrived in Seattle, Ebright wasted no time. On April 10 he hustled all three of his crews out onto the frothy lake to see what they could do among the whitecaps. As it turned out, they could do plenty, particularly the freshmen. The Cal frosh fairly skimmed over the water, their oars coming well clear of the waves between strokes and digging cleanly into them on the catch at the beginning of each stroke. They turned in a series of fine time trials, though Ebright declined to make those times available to the press. The outing confirmed what Ebright and his freshman coach, Russ Nagler, another former Washington coxswain, had been hinting for some time now: that their freshmen might be the best they had ever coached, better even than the boys who had gone on to produce an Olympic gold medal in 1932.

When a reporter for the *San Francisco Chronicle* asked him, on April 6, what he thought of his freshmen's prospects, the Cal coach answered with surprising candor: "Ebright took on a radiant look and boomed out, 'Our frosh boat will beat the stuffing out of the Husky yearlings.'"

Tom Bolles and Al Ulbrickson had read that account, and now they watched California's workout from shore with apparent concern. They had taken their own boys out the same day, with the press and Ebright looking on, only to have the freshmen turn back after a mile, their rowing conspicuously lethargic and their shell half full of water from the heavy chop. Bolles had returned gloomily to the dock and gone atypically out of his way to approach the sportswriters assembled at the shell house, giving them a terse but bleak forecast for the freshmen: "It looks as if we'll be rowing from behind."

Misdirection was part of the game. It was easy enough to rig a shell so the oars sat a little too close to the water and easy enough to pull a leisurely oar but make it look hard. When Bolles's quote appeared in the newspaper the next day, Joe cut it out, pasted it in his scrapbook, and wrote next to it, "Coach said Cal had their necks out a foot. He is giving out pessimistic reports so that they will stick them out farther. Makes them easier to cut off."

Race day, Friday, April 13, was one of those rare spring days in Seattle when cotton-puff clouds drift across robin's-egg-blue skies and afternoon temperatures climb into the midseventies.

At 11:00 a.m. a student-chartered ferry left Colman Dock in downtown Seattle and headed through the locks in Ballard en route to Lake Washington. Early in the afternoon, it arrived at the university's Oceanographic Dock, where Joyce Simdars joined fourteen hundred other boisterous students dressed in purple and gold as they piled aboard, accompanied by the blaring brass and rattling drums of the university's varsity band playing fight songs. As the ferry pulled away from the dock, the band switched over to jazz tunes and some of the students poured out onto an upper deck and began to dance.

Joyce settled down on a bench on the foredeck, sipping coffee in the sun, looking forward to watching Joe race and seeing him afterward, however it turned out. She couldn't help but be nervous, though. She knew how much Joe wanted to succeed at crew, how much depended on it for the two of them. In order to root him on, she had taken a rare afternoon off from her live-in job at the judge's house in Laurelhurst. She detested the job as much as she had expected. It was the kind of housework she had always loathed. She was required to wear a ridiculous uniform and creep around the house as quietly as a mouse, lest she disturb the judge in his seemingly endless and sacrosanct deliberations. Between that, studying for her classes, and the unusually long, wet winter, she had grown wan and pale and sometimes depressed, so she luxuriated in the fresh air and bright sunlight on the ferry.

As the boat rounded the Laurelhurst light and headed north, it hugged the west shore of the lake. People on private docks, backyard decks, and grassy slopes all along the western lakeshore spread out blankets, popped open bottles of cold beer or Coca-Cola, pulled lunches out of picnic hampers, snapped open peanuts and popped them in their mouths, and tested out their binoculars. Here and there, on slender patches of beach, shirtless young men tossed footballs back and forth. Young women in modest one-piece bathing suits with frilled skirts splashed in the water or stretched out on warm sand, waiting.

At the northern end of the lake, hundreds of pleasure craft were converging on the same spot. Sleek white sailboats, burnished mahogany-hulled launches, stately yachts trimmed in teak and brass, and humble skiffs and rowboats were already crowding together and dropping anchor, forming an enormous semicircle of boats off Sheridan Beach, just past the barge on which the finish line for the races was marked by a large black arrow pointing down at the water. A coast guard vessel patrolled the racing lanes, her crew sounding a siren and barking orders through megaphones, keeping the lanes clear of small craft.

Joyce got up from her bench and maneuvered herself to a position along the railing, crowding in among other students. She was, she resolved, going to stay calm no matter what.

A few miles to the south, another two thousand fans dressed in purple and gold clambered aboard an observation train at the Northern Pacific Railway's University Station. More than seven hundred of them shelled out two dollars apiece to sit in nine special open-sided viewing cars; the rest paid a dollar fifty for regular coach seats. As each race of the day went off, the train would run north along the western shore of Lake Washington, paralleling the racecourse all the way from Sand Point to the finish line at Sheridan Beach, then returning to the starting line before the next race. All told, nearly eighty thousand Seattleites—far more than Washington's football stadium could hold—had taken an early start to a gorgeous weekend and come out to watch the races.

Farther to the south, in the Bay Area, much of the public's attention was focused that afternoon on a massive federal manhunt for the fugitive John Dillinger, whom someone claimed to have seen eating lunch in a San Jose café the day before. But shortly before 3:00 p.m., thousands of fans around the bay spun their radio dials away from the news broadcasts to listen to coverage of the race up in Seattle, on the Columbia Broadcasting System's radio network.

The Washington and California freshman crews paddled briskly out toward the starting line off Sand Point. They would race first, for a distance of two miles, followed at hourly intervals by the junior varsity and the varsity, each racing for three miles. Joe Rantz sat in the number three seat of Washington's boat; Roger Morris sat in the number seven seat. Both were nervous, as were all the boys. Warm as it was onshore, a moderately stiff north breeze had sprung up out in midlake, and they would be rowing directly into it. That would slow their time and perhaps cramp their style. More than that, though, they were hard up against the fact that a few minutes of extreme exertion were about to tell them whether five and a half months of training had been worthwhile. During those few minutes, each of them would take more than three hundred strokes. With eight oarsmen in the boat, oars would have to enter and exit the water cleanly more than twenty-four hundred times. If just one boy muffed just one of those strokes—if just one of them caught one crab—the race would effectively be over, and none of them would have a chance to travel to New York in June to race against the best crews in the East for the national championship. Joe surveyed the crowd assembled along the shoreline. He wondered whether Joyce was half as nervous as he was.

At 3:00 p.m., in a light chop, the freshmen maneuvered their shell parallel to California's, did their best to settle their minds into the boat, and waited for the start signal. Tom Bolles maneuvered his coaching launch up behind his boys' boat. He was wearing an unusually battered fedora—the brim drooping, the crown riddled with moth holes. He'd picked it up secondhand back in 1930, had come to think of it as his lucky hat, and wore it now for every race.

The band on the ferryboat stopped playing. The students stopped dancing and crowded the near rails, the great boat listing slightly toward the racing lanes. The engineer on the observation train laid a hand on the throttle. Thousands along the shoreline raised binoculars to their eyes. The starter called out, "Ready all!" The Washington boys slid their seats forward, sank their white blades into the water, hunched over their oars, and stared straight ahead. George

Morry, Washington's coxswain, raised his right arm momentarily and then dropped it to signal that his boat was ready. Grover Clark, the Cal coxswain, clenching a whistle between his teeth, did the same. The starter barked, "Row!"

California exploded off the line, lashing the water at a furious thirty-eight strokes per minute. The silver prow of their shell immediately surged a quarter length ahead of Washington's. Having seized the lead, Cal dropped its rate down a bit, to a more sustainable thirty-two, and Grover Clark began blowing his whistle in time with the stroke count. Washington settled in at thirty but held its position at a quarter length back. The two boats churned up the lake for almost a quarter of a mile, locked together in that configuration— Washington's white blades glinting in the sunlight, Cal's flashing shards of blue. Sitting in the number three seat, Joe Rantz was parallel with roughly the six or seven seat in the California boat; in the seven seat, Roger Morris was parallel with nothing but open water. All the boys had their minds fully in the boat now. Facing the stern, the only thing any of them could see was the heaving back of the man in front of him. None had any idea how far ahead Cal's initial surge might have carried them. George Morry, facing forward, knew exactly. He could see Grover Clark's backside in front of him, but he continued to hold Washington steady at thirty strokes per minute.

As they passed the quarter-mile mark, the two boats slowly came even. Then Washington began to overtake California, methodically, seat by seat, the boys still rowing at a remarkably low thirty. By the one-mile mark, Washington had open water on Cal. As the California boat fell into the field of view of the Washington boys, their confidence surged. The pain that had been building in their arms and legs and chests did not abate, but it fled to the backs of their minds, chased there by a sense, almost, of invulnerability.

In the Cal boat, Grover Clark pulled the whistle from his mouth and screamed out, "Gimme ten big ones!"—the standard call in rowing for ten mammoth strokes, strokes as hard and powerful as each oarsman can muster. The California oars bent like bows with the strain, and for those ten strokes the boys from Cal held their position. But Washington remained out in front, their lead—almost two lengths now—essentially undiminished. At the mile-and-a-half mark, Clark called for another big ten, but by now Cal's boys had given everything they had to give, and Washington's boys hadn't. As they entered the last half mile and came into the lee of the hills at the north end of the lake, the headwind died down. Cheers began to rise from the semicircle of boats ahead, from the beaches, from the observation train working its way along the shore, and—loudest of all—from the ferryboat chock-full of students. The California boat labored to catch up, Grover Clark's whistle now shrieking like an out-of-control steam locomotive. Approaching the line and already ahead by four lengths, George Morry finally called for a higher stroke rate. The Washington boys stepped it up to thirty-two and then all the way to thirty-six, just because they knew they could. Washington sliced across the finish line four and a half lengths ahead of California, and almost twenty seconds ahead of the freshman course record, despite the headwind.

Shrill horns and cheers resounded all along the shores of Lake Washington. The Washington freshmen paddled over to the California boat and collected the traditional trophy of victorious crews everywhere—the shirts off the backs of their vanquished rivals. They shook hands with the crestfallen and shirtless Cal boys and then, exultant, paddled off the course to stow their shell. Tom Bolles cheerily loaded them onto the *Alumnus*, then transported them to the student ferry.

Joe, clutching a California jersey, bounded up the steps to the upper deck, beaming, looking around for Joyce. At five foot four, she was hard to find in the crowd that surged forward to congratulate the boys. Joyce had seen him, though. She worked her way through the mass of close-pressed bodies, slipping through small openings, pressing an elbow here, gently shoving against a hip there, until she finally emerged before Joe, who promptly leaned over, enveloped her in an exuberant and sweaty hug, and lifted her off her feet.

A crowd of students ushered the crew into the boat's galley and sat them down at a table piled with a mountain of ice cream, as much as they could eat, courtesy of the Associated Students of the University of Washington. Joe stuffed himself, as he always did when presented with free food, or any sort of food for that matter. When he'd finally had his fill, he took Joyce's hand and pulled her back out onto the deck where the band was again playing loud, brassy dance tunes. Joe, sun bronzed and barefoot in his jersey and shorts, took Joyce, slight and slender in a frilly white summer dress, and twirled her once under his long, outstretched arm. And then they danced, the two of them careening around the deck, swinging, smiling, laughing, giddy for now under a blue Seattle sky.

That same day, in a posh Berlin neighborhood near the Ministry of Public Enlightenment and Propaganda, Joseph and Magda Goebbels welcomed a new daughter into the world—a little brown-haired girl they named Hildegard.

They nicknamed her Hilde, but her father soon began to call her his "little mouse." She was the second of what would become six Goebbels children, all of whom Magda Goebbels would order murdered with cyanide eleven years later.

Life was going swimmingly for Reich minister Goebbels that spring. The old Olympic stadium was being torn down, and Werner March had drawn up elaborate plans for the vast complex that would replace it for the 1936 games—plans that fit the scope of Hitler's ambitions and Goebbels's propaganda objectives. The Reichssportfeld would sprawl over more than 325 acres.

In January and February, in anticipation of the games, Goebbels had formed organizing committees at the propaganda ministry. There were committees for the press, radio, film, transportation, public art, and the budget, each charged with separate responsibilities for extracting the maximum propaganda value from the games. No opportunity was to be overlooked, nothing taken for granted. Everything from how the foreign media would be treated to how the city would be decorated would be subject to rigorous planning. At one of those meetings, one of Goebbels's ministers had proposed an entirely new idea—a potent bit of imagery designed to underscore what the Third Reich saw as its ancestral roots in ancient Greece—a torch relay to carry a flame from Olympia in Greece all the way to Berlin.

Meanwhile Goebbels's work of eliminating any Jewish or otherwise "objectionable" influence from the cultural life of Germany continued inexorably. Since the great bonfires of May 10, 1933, when university students in Berlin, urged on by Goebbels himself, had burned some twenty thousand books—books by, among others, Albert Einstein, Erich Maria Remarque, Thomas Mann, Jack London, H. G. Wells, and Helen Keller—he had been unrelenting in his drive to "purify" German art, music, theater, literature, radio, education, athletics, and film. Jewish actors, writers, performers, teachers, civil servants, lawyers, and doctors had all been forced from their occupations and deprived of their livelihoods, either by the enactment of new laws or by the application of terror at the hands of the Nazis' brown-shirted paramilitary storm troopers, the Sturmabteilung, or SA.

The German film industry had become one of Goebbels's particular interests. He was intrigued by the propaganda potential of motion pictures and ruthless in suppressing any ideas, images, or themes in them that did not conform to the emerging Nazi mythos. To ensure compliance, the film department of the propaganda ministry now directly oversaw the planning and production of all new German films. Goebbels himself—a failed novelist and playwright earlier in life—had taken to reviewing the scripts of nearly all films personally, using a green pencil to strike out or rewrite offending lines or scenes.

Beyond the pragmatic propaganda value of film, Goebbels was also personally enthralled by the glamour of the movie business, and particularly by the allure of German stars who lit up the silver screen in Berlin's cinemas. Because German actors, actresses, producers, and directors were now all beholden to him for their careers, they began to flock around Goebbels, fawning over him and soliciting his favor.

The previous June, Hitler had awarded Goebbels a sumptuous personal residence on the recently renamed Hermann-Göring-Strasse, just a block south of the Brandenburg Gate. Goebbels had promptly remodeled and expanded the house—the hundred-year-old former palace of the marshals of the Prussian court—to make it even grander than it had been. He had added a second story, installed a private cinema, built heated greenhouses, and laid out formal gardens. With an essentially unlimited budget, Magda Goebbels had furnished and decorated it extravagantly—covering the walls with Gobelin tapestries and paintings appropriated from German museums, laying down luxurious carpets, even installing a commode previously owned by Frederick the Great. Thus brought up to the Goebbels's standards, the house served as a venue for both intimate soirees and grand dinner parties for the Nazi elite and those who basked in their light.

Among those who flocked to the house at number 20 Hermann-Göring-Strasse, certain young starlets were of particular interest to Goebbels. A number of them soon found that attending to his erotic desires, despite his dwarfish stature and misshapen physique, went a long way toward enhancing their career prospects. Others he cultivated for their genuine capabilities on the screen, and for the sense of aggrandizement that he derived from associating with them.

One particular young woman who sometimes showed up at the Goebbels house that spring, and who belonged to the second category, was an increasingly close friend of Adolf Hitler and a force to be reckoned with in her own right. Before all was said and done, she would, in fact, become the woman in Germany who more than any other would materially shape the destiny of the Nazi movement.

Leni Riefenstahl was beautiful and brilliant. She knew what she wanted and how to get it. And what she wanted above all was to be at the center of things, in the spotlight, basking in applause.

From her earliest years, she displayed an indomitable will to succeed. When she decided to become a dancer at seventeen, she disregarded all conventional wisdom, which preached that dancers must begin their training as young children. By her early twenties, she was dancing professionally before packed houses all over Germany, drawing rave reviews. When an injury ended her dance career, she turned to acting. She quickly talked her way into a lead role and became an instant star with her first film, *The Holy Mountain* (*Der heilige Berg*). It was characteristic of Riefenstahl that even as she starred in a succession of similar films her ambitions continued to mount. Increasingly unwilling to cede creative control to anyone, in 1931 she founded her own production company and set about—very precociously for a woman in the 1930s—writing, producing, directing, editing, and starring in a film of her own.

The Blue Light (*Das blaue Licht*), released in 1932, was unlike anything anyone had ever seen before. A sort of mystical fairy tale, it romanticized and cele-

Joseph Goebbels and Leni Riefenstahl

brated the simple life of German farmers living harmoniously with nature on their German soil. It condemned the corruption of the modern industrial world. By implication it also condemned intellectuals. It quickly won international acclaim and ran for weeks in London and Paris.

In Germany the response was more tepid, but Adolf Hitler was transported by *The Blue Light*, seeing in it a visual and artistic representation of the very "blood and soil" ideology on which his Nazi Party had been founded—the notion that the nation's strength lay in its simple, pure native stock. Hitler had been aware of Riefenstahl for some time, but now he became her friend. In 1933, at his personal request, she directed a one-hour propaganda film, *Victory of Faith* (*Der Sieg des Glaubens*), documenting the Nazi Party rally that year in Nuremberg. She made the film on short notice, had technical difficulties, and was not pleased with the results, but Hitler remained impressed by her work nonetheless. Now he hoped that in the fall she would produce a more ambitious film about the 1934 Nuremberg Rally.

As her star continued to rise in the months ahead, Riefenstahl and Goebbels frequently came into conflict. Goebbels would grow bitterly jealous of her influence with Hitler and the immunity it gave her from his own authority. And yet, by her account, he was also drawn to her and would pursue her romantically and sexually. In time this oddly matched pair would play a large role in defining how the world viewed the 1936 Olympics in Berlin and, by extension, the very nature of the new Nazi state.

But for now hers was simply one of the swirl of glamorous faces who drifted in and out of Joseph and Magda Goebbels's stately home, popping the corks from champagne bottles, being feted by their host and hostess, celebrating one another and their youth and their good looks, dancing late into the night, singing, watching films, and talking of racial purity while little Hilde Goebbels lay asleep in a cradle in a darkened room upstairs.

Joe with his banjo

CHAPTER SEVEN

Rowing a race is an art, not a frantic scramble. It must be rowed with head power as well as hand power. From the first stroke all thoughts of the other crew must be blocked out. Your thoughts must be directed to you and your own boat, always positive, never negative.

—George Yeoman Pocock

Joe Rantz and his crewmates lined up along the ferry's railing and gazed out over the water, using their hands to shield their eyes against the glare of the late afternoon sun. It had been two hours since they had defeated the California freshmen. Now it was the varsity's turn to take on Ky Ebright's boys.

What transpired over the next several minutes turned out to be one of the great varsity races in the history of the Cal-Washington rivalry. Immediately after the race, Frank G. Gorrie, writing for the Associated Press, wired an exuberant account back east for his national audience: "The famous racing eights flashed down the sun-speckled waters as if they were hooked together. First one then another forged into the lead but never by more than a few feet. California had a shade at the start, lost ground at the mile, poked its bow out again at the mile-and-a-half mark, fell behind as Washington hit 'ten big ones' three successive times at the two-mile mark, came back strong a moment later."

Joe watched with fascination as the drama unfolded. Time and again the students on the ferry called out for Washington to "take it up," to raise the stroke and put California away. Cal was pounding the water white at a vigorous rate of thirty-six strokes per minute, but for more than two and a half miles Washington's coxswain, Harvey Love, kept the stroke steady at a relatively relaxed thirty-one, doing only as much as necessary to keep his boat in contention, sending his boys surging forward by calling for big tens when he was in danger of falling too far behind, but then settling in, holding steady, conserving his crew. It was only as they came within sight of the barge marking the finish line, after California had tried again and again to pull away and failed each time, that Love finally barked out, "Now! Turn on the heat!" The stroke rate went up to thirty-eight, then almost immediately to forty. The Washington boat leapt forward, the California boat hesitated for a moment, and Washington crossed the line a little more than a second ahead of California, with a new course record at 16:33.4.

It was a stirring race, but, more than that, it was a primer for Joe and the other freshmen on how the man who would become their primary coach in the fall, Al Ulbrickson, went about winning. In some ways the lesson was one that Tom Bolles had already illustrated when he had concealed the freshmen's best times from Ebright and explained to his boys the value of letting Cal stick its neck out too far. But watching the varsity race drove the lesson home for Joe. To defeat an adversary who was your equal, maybe even your superior, it wasn't necessarily enough just to give your all from start to finish. You had to master your opponent mentally. When the critical moment in a close race was upon you, you had to know something he did not—that down in your core you still had something in reserve, something you had not yet shown, something that once revealed would make him doubt himself, make him falter just when it counted the most. Like so much in life, crew was partly about confidence, partly about knowing your own heart.

In the days following the 1934 California-Washington race, the freshmen promptly fell into another slump. Day after day they turned in discouraging times. Since beating California, they appeared to have lost all focus. The more Tom Bolles bellowed at them through his megaphone, the sloppier they seemed to get.

One lazy day in early May, with a warm sun beating down on their bare backs, some of the boys rowed so lethargically that they failed to cross quickly in front of an oncoming tugboat pulling a barge. The tug bore down on their shell, belching black smoke, its whistle shrieking, its horn blaring. The coxswain, John Merrill, shouted, "Back! Back!" The boy in the number four seat panicked and threw himself awkwardly overboard, nearly capsizing the shell. The tug swerved hard to port, grazed the bow of the shell, and narrowly missed the boy in the water. Bolles, watching from his launch, was fit to be tied. He plucked the red-faced jumper from the water, gunned the motor on the launch, and headed for the shell house.

The boys rowed back to campus in silence. Bolles was waiting for them. He rampaged up and down the dock, shaking his finger at the boys as they sat in their shell. He was going to rebuild the crew from scratch for the Poughkeepsie Regatta in June, he growled. Nobody's seat was safe just because he had rowed in the boat that had defeated California so impressively. Joe's heart sank. What had seemed briefly like a sure bet was suddenly in jeopardy again. That same week he got a note from the administration announcing that he was failing PE, for which his rowing was supposed to substitute. Joe, who had just seen a Paramount movie short featuring a cartoon character new to the silver screen, Popeye the Sailor, wrote in his scrapbook that night, "I yam disgusted."

By mid-May the weather in Seattle, as it sometimes cruelly does in late spring, reverted from sunny to foul, and the freshmen found themselves once more struggling against headwinds, their hands numb with cold, whitecaps breaking over the bow. And yet to their own and their coaches' surprise, the worse the weather got, the better they began to row.

Rowing against a sharp north wind on one of those wet, gray days in late May, with spray flying off the oars at every release and water sloshing in the bottom of the boat, Joe and his crewmates in the first boat finished a time trial in 10:35, just four seconds off the record for that course. George Pocock watched the performance from aboard the *Alumnus*. When he got back ashore, he walked up to a reporter at the shell house, buttonholed him, and rendered a startling verdict: "Tom Bolles has a fine rough-water boat," he said quietly but forcefully. "It is as good as any I have seen." Coming from Pocock, a reserved and modest man who was not prone to exaggeration in regard to anything, and least of all in regard to the rowing ability of a boatload of freshmen, this was something akin to a divine proclamation. Tom Bolles stopped talking about rebuilding the crew from scratch. The nine freshman boys who had beaten California would go to Poughkeepsie to race for the national championship after all.

On the evening of June 1, 1934, the University of Washington's marching band and more than a thousand fans crammed into the ornate marble lobby of the King Street railroad station in Seattle, cheering and singing fight songs as the freshman and varsity crews boarded a Great Northern train, the *Empire Builder*, on their way to Poughkeepsie. The freshman boys, in particular, were in high spirits. Few of them had ever been outside of western Washington;

most had never been on a train. Yet here they were, about to cross the entire continent. For boys who had been brought up milking cows and swinging axes and stacking lumber, who knew the first names of half the people in the towns they came from, whose parents could tell them about the first time they had seen an automobile or a house with electricity, this was heady stuff.

As he sat in his plush seat, looking out through the green-tinted window of the Pullman coach, Joe could not quite believe the hubbub now spilling from the lobby out onto the platform. He had never been celebrated for anything, and yet here he was, a part of something that was the focus of not just admiration but a kind of adulation. It filled him with pride but also with a strained, churning unease. It brought up things he spent a lot of time trying not to think about these days.

That evening, as the *Empire Builder* climbed over the Cascades at Stevens Pass and set out across the arid wheat country of eastern Washington, the boys were on a lark. They caroused late into the night, playing cards, telling off-color jokes, racing up and down the aisles of the Pullman coach, tossing a football back and forth, until they finally exhausted themselves and tumbled into their berths.

The merriment resumed the next day when someone produced a package of balloons. They filled the balloons with water in the lavatory, positioned themselves on the clattering platforms between coaches, and as they rolled across Montana and into North Dakota, began gleefully lobbing the water balloons at any available target—cows grazing in fields, dusty cars waiting at clanging railroad crossings, sleeping dogs sprawled on platforms in small-town stations—each time breaking into a chorus of "Bow Down to Washington" as they rumbled past their astonished victims.

Later Joe, emboldened by the water-balloon adventure, pulled from its case the guitar he had somewhat nervously brought along. Curious, some of the older boys gathered around him as he started twisting pegs and plucking at strings to tune the instrument. Looking at the frets, concentrating on his fingering, he began to strum chords and sing, launching into the kinds of songs that he had played in high school—camp tunes and cowboy songs he'd learned at the Gold and Ruby mine or picked up listening to the radio back in Sequim.

At first the boys just stared at him as he sang; then they began to glance at one another, then to snicker, and finally to hoot and holler. "Lookee there at Cowboy Joe!" one shouted. Another called down the aisle, "Hey, boys, come and hear Rantz, the rowing troubadour!" Joe looked up, startled, and stopped playing abruptly in the middle of "The Yellow Rose of Texas." Red-faced but with his jaw set and his eyes stone cold, he quickly fumbled the guitar back into its case and retreated to another coach.

Few things could have been more hurtful for Joe. His music was what had brightened the bleakest days of his boyhood. It had drawn people to him in high school, made him friends, and even helped him eke out a living in Sequim. It was his special talent, a particular point of pride. Now, suddenly and unexpectedly, it had turned on him, reminding him of how short he fell in matters of sophistication. Just when he had begun to feel that he was becoming part of something larger than himself, he was cast out again.

When they arrived in New York, on June 6, the Washington crews moved their shells into a dilapidated old boathouse on the western, Highland, side of the Hudson River, across from Poughkeepsie. The boathouse was not much more than a shed, really. It was drafty, rickety, perched on thin stilts over the river, with showers that pumped foul-smelling water directly from the Hudson over the boys' heads.

Tom Bolles hustled his freshmen out onto the water that same day, anxious to see how they would handle the unfamiliar racecourse. This would be the first time they rowed on a river rather than a lake, the first time, in fact, that they rowed anywhere other than Lake Washington. The weather was unlike anything the boys had experienced back home—oppressively hot and sticky. By the time they had carried their shell, the *City of Seattle*, down to the water, they were already drenched in sweat. There was a bit of a breeze on the water, but even the wind seemed molten to them as they climbed into the shell. They stripped off their shirts, dragged them through the Hudson's foul water, and put them back on, but that only seemed to make the humidity more unbearable. Bolles told them to row upriver at a warm-up pace for a few minutes. He climbed into a launch and began to follow them. When he judged them ready, he lifted his megaphone and told them to take it up to a sprint. The boys leaned into their oars and took it up, but Bolles didn't even bother to look at his stopwatch. He could see at a glance that they were rowing well off their best pace. Worse, they looked ragged, clearly knackered by the heat, and were wandering from one side of the course to the other. They could handle almost any amount of wind and wave on Lake Washington, but the waves on the Hudson were different—long, low waves that hit the boat from the side, leaving the blades of their oars flailing at air one moment, sunk too deep in the water the next. The effects of tide and current baffled them. The water itself was not supposed to move under their boat, was not supposed to take them places they did not intend to go. Bolles shouted, "Way 'nuff!" through his megaphone and waved the boys back to the shell house. He was going to need to talk to Pocock.

The boys, discouraged, stowed their shell, showered in caustic river water, and made a long trek on foot up the railroad tracks running along the western shoreline before climbing the face of the Highland bluff to Florence Palmer's boardinghouse, where they were to be lodged. Mrs. Palmer's farmhouse was small, her fare light. The meager products of her kitchen could not begin to satisfy the appetites of two dozen tall, strapping boys and a handful of coaches and coxswains. The boys ate everything in sight and then climbed wearily up to attic bedrooms where, crammed six to a room, they tried to sleep in the wet, suffocating heat on cots that seemed more like torture racks than beds.

The Intercollegiate Rowing Association's regatta at Poughkeepsie was a storied institution, with roots deep in the history of American rowing.

The first great rowing spectacle in America was a dual match in New York Harbor in 1824, between a crew of four New York City watermen racing in a twenty-four-foot Whitehall boat, the *American Star*, taking on four sailors from a visiting British warship, manning a similar boat, the *Certain Death*. With the War of 1812 and the burning of the White House still a reasonably fresh memory, feelings were high, particularly on the American side. The Americans won the race, and the hefty thousand-dollar purse, rowing from the Battery to Hoboken and back before a wildly enthusiastic crowd of somewhere between fifty thousand and one hundred thousand spectators, at the time the largest assemblage of Americans ever to have watched a sporting event.

In the 1830s, private rowing clubs began to appear in various American cities, and by the 1840s a few eastern colleges had assembled crews. The first collegiate crew race in America—and in fact the first American intercollegiate athletic event of any kind—took place between Harvard and Yale in 1852, on Lake Winnipesaukee in New Hampshire. With a few interruptions—major wars that have taken the young men at each school off to other, more hazardous occupations—the Harvard-Yale Regatta has been raced every subsequent year since 1859. For much of that time, the regatta was one of the country's premier sporting events. In 1869, Harvard met Britain's most elite institution, Oxford, in a match on the Thames. Rowing before an immense crowd, Oxford defeated Harvard, but the event was so widely publicized in the United States that it produced an explosion of interest in rowing. It also imbued the sport with an aura of elitism that has lingered to this day.

Other eastern colleges soon launched rowing programs, and many of them began to compete against one another in head-to-head regattas. But Harvard and Yale did not row in any kind of intercollegiate championship regatta beyond their own annual match, and there was no semblance of a national championship event until 1895. Then, spurred on by the New York Central Railroad, Cornell, Columbia, and Pennsylvania agreed to form the Intercollegiate Rowing Association and meet annually on a straight four-mile stretch of the Hudson River at Poughkeepsie, where amateur and professional oarsmen had been racing since the 1860s. Almost immediately following that first meeting—won by Cornell on June 21, 1895—other schools began to be invited to Poughkeepsie, and the regatta came to be seen as the most prestigious crew race in the country, eclipsing even the annual Harvard-Yale boat race and coming to represent the equivalent of a national championship.

By the beginning of the twentieth century, rowing clubs flourished in the enclaves of the well-heeled. Luxury hotels and ocean liners—among them the *Titanic*—installed batteries of rowing machines so their clients could stay in shape and emulate their rowing heroes. By the second decade of the new century, tens of thousands of fans—as many as 125,000 in 1929—came to Poughkeepsie to watch the annual regatta in person; millions more listened to the radio coverage; and the regatta came to rival the Kentucky Derby, the Rose Bowl, and the World Series as a major national sporting event.

For most of the first quarter of the century, the eastern colleges thoroughly dominated the regatta. No western school even dared to compete until Stanford appeared in 1912, only to finish a distant sixth. The following year Hiram Conibear brought a Washington varsity crew east for the first time. Though his rural, homespun western boys did not win, they came in third, an outcome that shocked the eastern fans and press. In 1915 they were shocked again when Stanford came in second. One more or less appalled New York writer that year noted that "if Stanford had not been using a clumsily-built Western shell they might have won." In fact, Stanford had used an Eastern-built boat, having left their sleek Pocock-built shell at home in Palo Alto.

During the next ten years, though, the western schools—California, Stanford, and Washington—only occasionally ventured back to Poughkeepsie. It was hard to justify the trip. Transporting a crew and several delicate racing shells to the East was an expensive proposition, and the western boys were met each time with an uncomfortable mixture of gawking curiosity, subtle condescension, and occasional open derision. Eastern fans, alumni, and sportswriters, and the national press as well, were accustomed to seeing the sons of senators, governors, titans of industry, and even presidents—not farmers and fishermen and lumberjacks—sitting in shells on the Hudson.

Then, on a rainy June evening in 1923, Washington's varsity crew returned to Poughkeepsie under their new head coach, Russell "Rusty" Callow. After pulling away from the rest of the field, Washington and an elite Navy crew entered the home stretch rowing bow to bow. With the roar of the crowd drowning out his commands, Washington's coxswain, Don Grant, suddenly raised a red flag (cut hastily from a Cornell banner just before the race) over his head to signal his boys that this was the moment to give it their all. Washington's stroke oar, Dow Walling, one of his legs grotesquely inflamed by three enormous boils, slid forward on his seat, drove both legs sternward, and took the rate up above the furious forty at which the Washington boys were already rowing. The boat shot forward and Washington narrowly eked out the West's first IRA victory. The exuberant Husky crew gingerly hoisted Walling out of the shell and sent him off to the hospital. Astonished fans and journalists gathered around them on the dock, peppering them with questions: Was the University of Washington in the District of Columbia? Where exactly was Seattle, anyway? Were any of them really lumberjacks? The boys, flashing wide grins, said little but began handing out miniature totem poles.

Watching the conclusion of the race from the coaches' launch, George Pocock whooped and hollered uncharacteristically. Later the typically reserved Englishman confessed, "I must have acted like a child." But he had good reason. He had built the Spanish cedar shell in which Washington had won. It was the first time easterners had had a chance to see his handiwork. Within a few days of returning to Seattle, orders for eight new eight-man shells had arrived at his shop. Less than a decade later, most of the shells in the Poughkeepsie Regatta would be Pocock's. By 1943, all of them—thirty shells in total—would be his.

Dr. Loyal Shoudy, a prominent and fanatically loyal Washington alumnus, was so impressed by the boys' achievement that he took them into New York

City that night and treated them to a stage show and a gala dinner. At the dinner, each boy found a ten-dollar bill at his plate, along with a purple tie. For decades afterward, Washington crewmembers were feted at the end of each rowing year with a Loyal Shoudy banquet, where each found a purple tie waiting at his plate.

The next year, 1924, Washington returned, with a young Al Ulbrickson rowing at stroke, and won the varsity race again, decisively this time. In 1926 they did it yet again, this time with Ulbrickson rowing the final quarter of a mile with a torn muscle in one arm. In 1928, Ky Ebright's California Bears won their first Poughkeepsie title en route to winning the Olympics that year and again in 1932. By 1934 the western schools were finally beginning to be taken seriously. Still, for most who sailed their yachts up the Hudson to watch the races each June, whether from Manhattan or from the Hamptons, it remained a natural assumption that this year the East would once again resume its proper and long-established place atop the rowing world.

The rise of the western crews may have shocked eastern fans, but it delighted newspaper editors across the country in the 1930s. The story fit in with a larger sports narrative that had fueled newspaper and newsreel sales since the rivalry between two boxers—a poor, part-Cherokee Coloradoan named Jack Dempsey and an easterner and ex-Marine named Gene Tunney—had riveted the nation's attention in the 1920s. The East versus West rivalry carried over to football with the annual East-West Shrine Game and added interest every January to the Rose Bowl—then the nearest thing to a national collegiate football championship. And it was about to have additional life breathed into it when an oddly put together but spirited, rough-and-tumble racehorse named Seabiscuit would appear on the western horizon to challenge and defeat the racing establishment's darling, the king of the eastern tracks, War Admiral.

A notable element of all these East-West rivalries was that the western representatives nearly always seemed to embody certain attributes that stood in stark contrast to those of their eastern counterparts. They seemed, as a rule, self-made, rough hewn, wild, native, brawny, simple, and perhaps, in the eyes of some, a bit coarse; their eastern counterparts seemed, as a rule, well bred, sophisticated, moneyed, refined, and perhaps, in their own eyes at least, a bit superior. There was frequently some element of truth in these essential lines of differentiation. But the eastern perceptions of the rivalry often took on an element of snobbery, and this rankled western athletes and fans.

It further rankled the westerners that the prejudices of the East overwhelmingly prevailed in the national press, which often seemed to operate on the assumption that anything west of the Rockies was China. Sometimes the same attitudes prevailed even in the western press. Throughout the 1930s, even after Washington's and California's victories at Poughkeepsie, the *Los Angeles Times*, for instance, spilled far more ink covering the turnouts, boat assignments, coaching changes, and trial heats of eastern crews than the outright victories and increasingly impressive record times of western ones.

Joe and the other freshman boys from Washington who showed up for the 1934 Poughkeepsie Regatta could not have been better cast to play their parts in the ongoing regional conflict. The economic hardships of the last few years had only sharpened the distinctions between them and the boys they were about to take on. And it had only made their story more compelling for the nation at large. The 1934 regatta was once again shaping up to be a clash of eastern privilege and prestige on the one hand and western sincerity and brawn on the other. In financial terms, it was pretty starkly going to be a clash of old money versus no money at all.

In the last few days leading up to the regatta, the coaches of most of the eighteen crews involved began to hold their final workouts late at night, both to spare their boys the cruel heat of midday and to use the cover of darkness to conceal their times and racing strategies from one another and from the legions of inquisitive sportswriters who had descended on the Poughkeepsie riverside.

Race day, Saturday, June 16, dawned clear and warm. By noon, as race fans began to arrive by train and by automobile from all over the East, men were already shedding their coats and ties, women donning broad-brimmed sun hats and sunglasses. By midafternoon, the town of Poughkeepsie was pulsating with humanity. Hotel lobbies and restaurants were jam-packed with fans sipping various icy concoctions, many of them well fortified with alcohol now that Prohibition was finally over. On the streets, vendors with pushcarts made their way through the throngs, hawking hot dogs and ice cream cones.

All afternoon trolleys rattled down the bluff on the steep Poughkeepsie side of the Hudson, transporting fans to the waterside. A gray heat haze hung over the river. White electric ferries made their way back and forth, shuttling fans over to the west side, where an observation train awaited them, its thirteen white-skirted flat cars outfitted with bleachers. By 5:00 p.m., more than seventy-five thousand people lined both banks of the river, sitting on beaches, standing on docks, perched on roofs, bluffs, and palisades along the race-course, sipping lemonade and fanning themselves with copies of the program.

The freshman race was set to go off first, over a two-mile course, followed at hourly intervals by the junior varsity three-mile race and finally the varsity four-miler. As Joe and his crewmates paddled the *City of Seattle* from their boathouse out onto the river, they got their first good look at the spectacle of a Poughkeepsie Regatta. Exactly a mile upriver from the soaring, spidery 6,767-foot-long steel span of the old railroad bridge, built in 1889, a line of stake boats—seven identical rowboats at anchor—was stretched out across the river to form a starting line. In each stake boat, an official sat ready to hold the stern of the shell assigned to that lane until the starting pistol was fired. Half a mile below the railroad bridge was a new automobile bridge on which stood dozens of additional officials. Between the two bridges and down to the finish line, the river was jammed with yachts at anchor, their teak decks crowded with race fans, many of them wearing crisp nautical whites and royal-blue caps with gold braid. Canoes and wooden motorboats darted in and out among the yachts. Only the seven racing lanes in the middle of the river remained clear and open water. Just short of the finish line, a gleaming white 250-foot coast guard cutter, the *Champlain*, was tied up in the shadow of an imposing grim, gray U.S. Navy destroyer, the crew of the latter on hand to cheer on the midshipmen from Annapolis. Up and down the river, an assortment of tall ships with black hulls—schooners and sloops dating from the previous century—also lay at anchor. Bright arrays of nautical pennants dangled from their riggings.

As the freshman boats approached the stake boats at the starting line, the coaches' launches fell in behind their respective crews, their inboard engines sputtering and gurgling as they idled, with white exhaust fumes burbling from the water behind them. The smell of diesel fuel hung faintly over the river. Tom Bolles, wearing his good-luck fedora, bellowed last-minute instructions to George Morry, his coxswain. Washington was in lane three, right next to the Syracuse Orange in lane two. Coached by a rowing legend, eighty-two-year-old Jim Ten Eyck—reputed to have first rowed competitively in 1863, the day after the Battle of Gettysburg—the Orange had won three of the last four freshman titles and were the defending champions and presumed favorites.

The heat had abated by just a degree or two. A hint of a north wind lightly ruffled the water, lead colored now in the late afternoon haze. The pennants on the tall ships stirred lazily. As the Washington boys backed their shell into position, the official in the stake boat for lane three reached out a hand and laid hold of their stern. Morry barked at George Lund, up front, to straighten the bow. Morry lowered his raised hand to signal the starter that his boat was ready to row. Joe Rantz took a deep breath, settling his mind. Roger Morris adjusted his grip on his oar.

At the crack of the starting pistol, Syracuse immediately jumped in front, rowing at thirty-four, followed closely by Washington, rowing at thirty-one. Everyone else—Columbia, Rutgers, Pennsylvania, and Cornell—began to fall behind almost immediately. At a quarter of a mile down the river, it looked as if the Orange of Syracuse would, as predicted, settle into the lead. But by the half-mile mark, Washington had crept up and nosed ahead of them without raising its stroke rate. As the leaders swept under the railroad bridge at a mile, officials on the bridge set off a salvo of three bombs, signifying that the boat in lane three, Washington, was ahead with another mile still to go. Slowly the bow of the Syracuse boat came into Joe's field of view, just beginning to fall away behind him. He ignored it, focused instead on the oar in his hands, pulling hard and pulling smoothly, rowing comfortably, almost without pain. At the mile-and-a-half mark, someone in the middle of the Syracuse boat caught a crab. The Orange faltered for a moment, then immediately recovered their rhythm. But it no longer mattered. Washington was two and a half lengths ahead. Cornell, in third, had all but disappeared, eight lengths farther back. George Morry whipped his head around, took a quick look, and was startled at the length of their lead. Nevertheless, as he had against California in April on Lake Washington, he called up the rate in the last few hundred feet, just for the show of it. Another salvo of three bombs exploded as Tom Bolles's boys passed the finish line an astonishing five lengths ahead of Syracuse.

In Seattle and in Sequim, people huddled around radios in their kitchens and parlors stood and cheered when they heard the final salvo. Just like that, the farm boys and fishermen and shipyard workers from Washington State, boys who just nine months before had never rowed a lick, had whipped the best boats in the East and become national freshman champions.

The boys shook one another's hands, paddled over to the Syracuse boat, collected trophy shirts off the backs of the defeated Orangemen and shook their hands, and then rowed leisurely back to their shell house. They clambered out of the *City of Seattle*, onto the floating dock, and reenacted a universal ritual of winning crews: the dunking of the coxswain. Four of the boys tackled Morry before he could escape up the ramp, swung him back and forth three times by his arms and legs, and launched him far out over the Hudson, where he spiraled through the air, with legs and arms flailing, before landing on his back with a satisfying splash. When Morry had swum back to the dock, the boys helped him out of the fetid water and made their way upstairs into the rickety shell house to take their showers and get their own tastes of the Hudson. Tom Bolles rushed to the Western Union office in Poughkeepsie and fired off telegrams back home. So did George Varnell of the *Seattle Times*: "There is not a happier bunch of lads in this entire country. Take that as the straight dope."

But it wasn't just folks back home who stood up and paid attention to what had just happened. There was something about the way the Washington freshmen had won that caught the attention of nearly everyone in Poughkeepsie that day, just as it caught the attention of race fans around the country who listened on radios or read about it in newspapers the following day. Despite its relative lack of drama, the *New York Times*—the very epitome of the eastern establishment—called the race "stunning." It wasn't the margin of victory or the time of 10:50 that people marveled at. It was how the boys had rowed the race. From the starting gun to the final salvo, they had rowed as if they could keep going at the same pace for another two miles or ten. They had rowed with so much composure, so "serenely" as the *Times* put it, so completely within themselves, that at the finish, rather than slumping in their seats and gasping for breath as oarsmen generally do at the end of a race, they had been sitting bolt upright, looking calmly around. Looking as if they were simply out for an afternoon paddle and wondering what all the fuss was about. Looking, for all the world, like wide-eyed westerners.

An hour later the Syracuse junior varsity improved their ancient coach's day when they withstood a furious come-from-behind charge to fend off Navy—even as sirens wailed on the navy destroyer, urging the midshipmen on—to win the second race of the day.

By the time the third and premier event of the day, the varsity race, approached, the sun had begun to set and a murky, swampish darkness was settling over the river. Al Ulbrickson was quietly pacing the shoreline, waiting to board the press car on the observation train with George Pocock and Tom Bolles, when a reporter approached and asked him whether he was nervous.

Ulbrickson scoffed, said he was perfectly calm, and inserted the wrong end of a cigarette into his mouth. The truth was that Ulbrickson wanted to win the varsity race at Poughkeepsie more than almost anything. He'd yet to do so as a coach, and the people back in Washington who paid his salary had begun to take note of that fact. And Ulbrickson wanted to set the larger world straight on another score. Back in April, moments after his varsity boys had beaten California on Lake Washington, the Associated Press had put out a story that was picked up all over the country the next morning. It read: "Although the Bears failed to overtake the veteran Husky varsity . . . in that last heartbreaking drive they proved that they were headed for the Olympic Games of 1936." It was as if the Washington victory had been held up to the nation as some sort of fluke. It was just the kind of thing that drove Al Ulbrickson crazy.

The 1934 Poughkeepsie varsity race did turn out to be a duel between Ulbrickson's boys and Ebright's. The boats got off cleanly at the start and stayed clustered together for the first hundred yards. But by the end of the first mile of the four-mile varsity course, the two western schools had pulled out well in front of all the easterners. California took the lead, then relinquished it to Washington, then reclaimed it again. By a mile and a half, Washington had moved back ahead. The two boats churned toward the railroad bridge with Washington in the lead, but by the time they passed beneath the steel expanse, California had closed the gap to a matter of inches. They entered the final mile dead even and rowed thus, stroke for stroke, for the next three-quarters of a mile. Then in the last quarter of a mile California unleashed the full power of their gigantic, gangly, but enormously strong stroke oar, six-foot-five Dick Burnley. California surged ahead. Washington wilted and finished three-quarters of a length back. Ebright had his second consecutive IRA title, revenge for his loss on Lake Washington, and validation for the conclusion that the Associated Press writer had come to back in April.

For the varsity boys, it was a long, dismal train ride back to Seattle. By all outward appearances, Al Ulbrickson took the defeat stoically. He joked with the boys on the train, trying to cheer them up. But when the boys drifted away, he sat alone and fumed. The last time Ky Ebright had won the IRA he had gone on to win Olympic gold, a fact that the New York Times promptly pointed out even as it joined the AP in predicting that California would go to the Olympics again in 1936. The comparison wasn't quite apt, as Ulbrickson knew full well. The next Olympic Games were still two years away. But Ulbrickson was left staring at a cold, hard fact: Ebright just seemed to have an uncanny knack for winning the ones that mattered most.

Ten days later, Joe Rantz sat again on a train, looking out through the fly-specked window of the coach, watching a fresh new American calamity begin to unfold.

After his victory in Poughkeepsie, he had journeyed alone to Pennsylvania, where he visited his uncle Sam and aunt Alma Castner, who had taken him in all those years before, when his mother died. Then he had traveled down to New Orleans. He had wandered the steaming city, marveling at the sight of huge ships making their way up the Mississippi above street level, eating huge platters full of cheap shrimp and crab, digging into steaming bowls of gumbo and jambalaya, soaking up the rhythms and the howl of the jazz and the blues that coursed through the streets of the French Quarter on warm, silky nights scented with jasmine and bourbon.

Now he was on his way home, traveling across an America that had begun to dry up and blow away.

That summer was exceptionally hot across much of the United States, though the summer of 1936 would cruelly eclipse even this one. In the Dakotas, Minnesota, and Iowa, summertime temperatures began early. By May 9, it was 109 in Sisseton, South Dakota. By May 30 it was 113. That same day it was 109 in Spencer, Iowa, and 108 in Pipestone, Minnesota. And as the heat rose, the rain stopped falling. Sioux Falls, South Dakota, had only a tenth of an inch of rain that month, right in the middle of corn-growing season.

From the upper plains, the heat and aridity radiated across the country. By June more than half the United States was in the grip of severe heat and extreme drought conditions. In Saint Louis temperatures would rise above 100 for eight straight days that summer. At the airport in Chicago, it would top 100 for six straight days and hit an all-time high of 109 on July 23. In Topeka, Kansas, the mercury would pass the 100 mark forty-seven times that summer. July would be the hottest month ever recorded in Ohio.

In the Far West it was even worse. In Orofino, Idaho, it would hit 118 on July 28. The ten states with the highest average temperatures in the country that summer were all in the West. And the worst of the heat wasn't in the

Southwest, where people expected it and crops and lifestyles were adapted to it. Instead the heat scorched enormous swaths of the Intermountain West and even portions of the normally green Northwest.

Nothing could grow under such conditions, and without corn, wheat, and hay livestock could not survive. Alarmed, the secretary of agriculture, Henry Wallace, dispatched an expedition to the Gobi Desert to see if there were any species of grass there that might be able to survive in the deserts that the American West and Midwest were quickly becoming.

But the heat and the drought were in some ways the least of it. On May 9 a colossal dust storm had swung out of eastern Montana, rolled across the Dakotas and Minnesota, dumped 12 million tons of dirt on Chicago, and then moved on to tower over Boston and New York. As they had in November 1933, people stood in Central Park and looked skyward, aghast at the blackened sky. Somewhere in the neighborhood of 350 million tons of American topsoil had become airborne in that single storm. The New York Times proclaimed it "the greatest dust storm in United States history." But in fact the greater storms, and the greater suffering, were still months ahead.

As Joe traveled north and west across Oklahoma and eastern Colorado, a sepia-toned landscape scrolled by. The whole country seemed to have withered and browned under the searing sun. Except for the motion of the train itself, everything appeared to be standing stock-still, as if waiting for the next assault. Powdery dust stood in deep windrows along fence lines. Stunted stalks of corn, just waist-high, their leaves already russet colored and curling in on themselves, stretched forlornly in broken rows across parched, brown fields. Windmills stood motionless, their galvanized steel blades shimmering in the sun. Gaunt cattle, their ribs protruding and their heads hanging low, stood listless at the bottoms of dried-up stock ponds where the mud had dried and cracked into mosaics of tiles as hard as stone. As his train passed one ranch in Colorado, Joe watched men shooting starved cattle and tipping the carcasses into huge trenches.

It was the people he passed who most arrested Joe's attention, though. Sitting on front porches, standing barefoot in dry fields, perched on fences, wearing faded coveralls or tattered gingham dresses, they raised their hands to their brows and stared at the train as it passed, giving it hard, cold looks—looks that seemed to begrudge the train and those who rode on it their ability to get out of this godforsaken land.

And indeed some of them had decided to do just that. A small, sporadic stream of automobiles with faded paint and patched tires bounced along the rutted roads that paralleled the railroad tracks, all heading the same direction—west. The cars had old chairs and sewing machines and washtubs tied to their roofs. The backseats were packed with dusty children and dogs and toothless grandparents and rolls of bedding and boxes of canned goods. In many cases, their occupants had simply driven away from their homes, leaving their front doors standing open so their neighbors could help themselves to what they had left behind—sofas and pianos and bed frames too big to tie to the top of a car. Some of them—mostly single men—had no cars in which to load their possessions. They simply trudged on foot alongside the tracks, wearing slouch hats and dusty black coats—their Sunday coats—carrying old suitcases bound up with twine or clutching bundles they had slung over their shoulders, and glancing up at Joe as he sped past.

The train rolled on across eastern Washington and climbed into the Cascade Mountains, where fire warnings had been posted throughout the tinder-dry national forest and where in recent months desperate, out-of-work lumberjacks had set fires in order to create jobs fighting them. Then, finally, it descended into the relatively cool, green beneficence of the Puget Sound region, perhaps the only region in America that was not sweltering that summer.

But Joe arrived to find that if temperatures were not hot in Seattle, tempers had risen in their place. A long-simmering labor dispute between nearly thirty-five thousand members of the International Longshoremen's Association and steamship companies had flared up in port cities up and down the West Coast. Before it was over, the conflict would take eight lives. In Seattle it reached its climax along the waterfront on July 18. Twelve hundred ILA members formed flying wedges and smashed through cordons of mounted police armed with tear gas and billy clubs, successfully shutting down the unloading of cargo by strike breakers, among them University of Washington fraternity boys and football players recruited by the steamship companies. All hell broke loose. A pitched battle raged for days along the docks and waterfront streets of Smith Cove, injuring scores on both sides. Strikers armed with two-by-fours charged police positions. Mounted police launched cavalry charges into the massed strikers, swinging at them with batons. The mayor, Charles Smith, ordered the chief of police to set up machine-gun emplacements at Pier 91; the chief refused and handed the mayor his badge.

As the nation baked under the unrelenting sun, and violence spread along the docks and waterfronts of the West, the national political dialogue also grew heated that summer. Franklin Roosevelt had been in office for a year and a half, the stock market had stabilized, for the moment, and employment was up slightly. Yet for millions of Americans—for most Americans—the hard times still seemed as hard as ever. The opposition pounded the new president, zeroing in on his methods rather than his results. In a national radio address on July 2, Henry Fletcher, chairman of the Republican Party, blasted the president's New Deal, calling it "an undemocratic departure from all that is distinctively American." He went on, gloomily and ominously predicting dire consequences from what seemed a radical experiment in socialist-style big-government spending: "The average American is thinking, 'I am perhaps better off than last year but I ask myself, will I be better off when the tax bill comes in, and how about my children and my children's children?'" Two days later, Republican senator William Borah of Idaho, though widely considered a progressive Republican, warned that Roosevelt's policies were endangering the very foundations of American liberty and that their "creeping paralysis of bureaucracy threatens freedom of the press, placing the yoke of torture, colossal expense, and demoralization on the nation."

But in one small corner of the country, something large was beginning to stir that terribly hot summer. Something more affirmative. Early on August 4, in the predawn darkness, Seattleites climbed into their automobiles and headed east, toward the crest of the Cascades. People in Spokane found their picnic hampers and filled them with sandwiches and loaded them in the backseats of their own cars and headed west. Chief George Friedlander and a delegation of Colville Indians donned buckskins and moccasins and ceremonial headdresses and headed south. By late morning, the roads of eastern Washington were black with automobiles converging from all directions on one unlikely spot: Ephrata, a forlorn little town of 516 people, out in the desolate scablands, not far from the Columbia River and a fifty-mile-long dry canyon called the Grand Coulee.

By midafternoon, twenty thousand people had gathered behind a rope line in Ephrata. Packed somewhere in among them were George Pocock and his family. When Franklin D. Roosevelt appeared on the platform before them, his cigarette holder angled jauntily upward, the crowd roared its welcome. Then Roosevelt began to speak, leaning forward on his podium, clutching it. In measured tones, but with rising emotion, he began laying out a vision of the benefits that the new Grand Coulee Dam would bring to this arid land in exchange for the 175 million public dollars it would cost: 1.2 million acres of desert land reclaimed for farming, abundant irrigation water for millions more acres of existing farmland, vast amounts of cheap electrical power that could be exported all across the West, and thousands of new jobs building the hydroelectric and irrigation infrastructure that the dam would necessitate. As he spoke, the crowd interrupted him again and again with waves of applause and choruses of hearty cheers. Speaking of the water of the Columbia running unchecked to the sea, its energy unharnessed, he underscored the commonality of the great task at hand: "It is not a problem of the State of Washington; it is not a problem of the State of Idaho; it is a problem that touches all the states in the union." He paused, removed a handkerchief from his pocket, and dabbed it against his glistening brow. "We are going to see, I believe, with our own eyes, electricity and power made so cheap that they will become a standard article of use . . . for every home within the reach of an electrical transmission line." Then he moved toward his conclusion, addressing the men and women standing before him directly: "You have great opportunities and you are doing nobly in grasping them. . . . So I leave here today with the feeling that this work is well undertaken; that we are going ahead with a useful project; and that we *are* going to see it through for the benefit of our country." When he finished, the crowd again roared their approval.

Many of them would never forget the day. For them, it was a dawning, the first real hint of hope. If there was little they could do individually to turn the situation around, perhaps there was something they could do collectively. Perhaps the seeds of redemption lay not just in perseverance, hard work, and rugged individualism. Perhaps they lay in something more fundamental— the simple notion of everyone pitching in and pulling together.

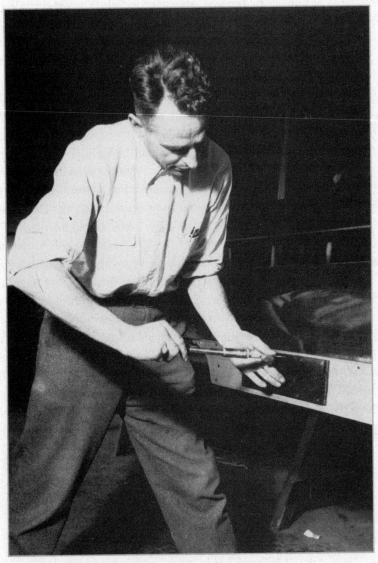

George Pocock at work in his shop

CHAPTER EIGHT

A good shell has to have life and resiliency to get in harmony with the swing of the crew.

—George Yeoman Pocock

The game warden sneaked up on Joe from behind. Joe was standing on a long gravel bar in the Dungeness River, studying a pool, looking for salmon, and the sound of rushing water muffled the warden's footfall. Sizing Joe up and calculating that he might not prevail in a head-to-head contest, the warden picked up a sturdy piece of driftwood, took careful aim, and brought it crashing down on the back of Joe's head. Joe pitched forward onto the gravel bar unconscious. He came to a few moments later, just in time to see an enraged Harry Secor chasing the warden down the river, wielding a gaffing pole like a spear. The warden disappeared into the woods, but Joe and Harry knew he'd be back with reinforcements. The jig was up. They never snagged another salmon.

After his cross-country trip, Joe spent the rest of the summer of 1934 in the still half-finished house on Silberhorn Road in Sequim, desperately trying to conjure up enough money to get himself through another school year. He cut more hay, dug more ditches, dynamited more stumps, and spread more hot, black asphalt on Highway 101. Mostly, though, he worked in the woods with Charlie McDonald. Charlie had decided he needed a new roof on his farmhouse. One afternoon he harnessed his draft horses to a buckboard and took Joe upriver, hunting for cedar. The upper reaches of his property had been logged for the first time just a dozen years before. The loggers had had their pick of the virgin timber still growing along that section of the Dungeness— towering Douglas firs and massive western red cedars. Some of the cedars had been more than two thousand years old, and their stumps—seven or eight feet in diameter and just as tall—rose like ancient monuments from a dense tangle of salal, huckleberry, young cottonwoods, and purple plumes of fireweed. In the face of the extraordinary bounty of the massive cedars, and valuing them primarily for making roofing shakes and shingles, the men who had cut them down had taken only the prime middle section of each, leaving behind long sections from the tops, where the branches were, and the bottoms, where the trunks began to flare out and the grain of the wood no longer ran perfectly straight and true. Much of what they had left could still be used, but only if one knew how to read the wood, to decipher its inner structure.

Charlie led Joe among the stumps and downed trees, teaching him how to understand what lay beneath the bark of the fallen logs. He rolled them over with a peavey and pounded them with the flat face of a splitting maul, testing for the ringing tone that indicated soundness. He ran his hands over them, feeling for hidden knots and irregularities. He crouched down at the cut ends and peered at the annual growth rings, trying to get a nuanced read on how tight and regular the grain within was likely to be. Joe was fascinated, intrigued by the idea that he could learn to see what others could not see in the wood, thrilled as always at the notion that something valuable could be found in what others had passed over and left behind. When Charlie found a log he liked, and explained to Joe why he liked it, the two of them used a crosscut saw to buck the wood into twenty-four-inch bolts—sections the length of a roofing shake—and toted them back to the buckboard.

Later Charlie taught Joe how to decipher the subtle clues of shape, texture, and color that would enable him to cleave the wood into well-formed shakes, to see hidden points of weakness or resilience. He taught the younger man how to split a log neatly into quarters with a maul and iron wedges; how to use a heavy wooden mallet to pound a froe—the shake maker's principal tool: a long, straight blade with an equally long perpendicular handle—into the wood across rather than with the grain; how to work the froe evenly down the length of the wood; how to listen to the wood as it began to "talk" back to him, the fibers crackling and snapping softly as they pulled away from one another, telling him that they were prepared to split along the plane he intended; how to twist the froe in the wood decisively at just the right moment to make the shake pop free, clean and elegant, smooth faced and gently tapered from one end to the other, ready to put on a roof.

Within a few days, Joe had mastered the froe and the mallet and could size up a log and split shakes from it nearly as quickly and decisively as Charlie could. A year of rowing had given him prodigious strength in his arms and shoulders, and he worked his way through the pile of cedar bolts like a machine. A small mountain of shakes soon surrounded him in the McDonalds' barnyard. Proud of his new skill, he found that shaping cedar resonated with him in an elusive but elemental way—it satisfied him down in his core, and gave him peace. Partly it was the old pleasure that he always derived from mastering new tools and solving practical problems—working out the angles and planes at which the cedar would or wouldn't cleave cleanly. And partly it was the deeply sensuous nature of the work. He liked the way that the wood murmured to him before it parted, almost as if it was alive, and when it finally gave way under his hands he liked the way it invariably revealed itself in lovely and unpredictable patterns of color—streaks of orange and burgundy and cream. At the same moment, as the wood opened up, it always perfumed the air. The spicy-sweet aroma that rose from freshly split cedar was the same scent that often filled the shell house in Seattle when Pocock was at work up in his loft. There seemed to Joe to be some kind of connection between what he was doing here among a pile of freshly split shakes, what Pocock was doing in his shop, and what he was trying to do himself in the racing shells Pocock built—something about the deliberate application of strength, the careful coordination of mind and muscle, the sudden unfolding of mystery and beauty.

When Joe arrived at the shell house for fall turnout on October 5, 1934, it was another radiant afternoon, much like the day when he had first shown up as a freshman. The thermometer was hovering just under seventy, and the sun was glinting off the Cut just as it had that day a year before. The scenery was altered in only one regard: the long summer of drought had dramatically lowered the level of the lake, exposing brown earthen banks and leaving the floating dock high, dry, and useless. For a while, at least, the boys were going to have to launch their shells by carrying them down the bank and wading into the water.

But what was most different was the attitude of the bunch of boys Joe had rowed with last year. As they moved in and out of the shell house, in shorts and jerseys, helping Tom Bolles register the new freshmen, there was an unmistakable hint of swagger in their step. After all, they were the national freshman champions. Now, as sophomores, it was their turn to lounge in the broad doorway of the shell house, their arms crossed, grinning as they watched the freshmen lining up nervously for their first weigh-in and bumbling about trying to get oars out of racks without clobbering one another before climbing awkwardly aboard *Old Nero*.

Even beyond the trophy they had brought home from Poughkeepsie, Joe and his fellow sophomores had good reason to be confident and optimistic about the upcoming season. Al Ulbrickson generally made a point of discouraging anyone in the crew house from reading the sports pages during the school year. No good and much ill could come from boys worrying too much about whatever Royal Brougham at the *Post-Intelligencer* or George Varnell at the *Seattle Times* might be speculating about on any given day. But over the summer there was little he could do to police the boys' reading, and there had been much in both papers to catch their eyes. On the morning following the Poughkeepsie Regatta in June, Varnell had come right out and written what many in Seattle were thinking after listening to the race on the radio: "Count this Washington freshman outfit as a potential Olympic lineup in 1936." And there had also been suggestions over the summer that in order to prepare them for such an Olympic bid Al Ulbrickson would be wise to elevate them to varsity status this year, leapfrogging them ahead of the juniors and any returning seniors. It seemed profoundly unlikely, but the idea was out there, in public, and the sophomore boys already had begun to talk quietly about it among themselves.

And, in fact, the notion had indeed been lurking somewhere in the back of Al Ulbrickson's mind for a long while now. There were a number of factors in its favor. First and foremost, there was the stunning ease with which the freshmen had won at Poughkeepsie in June. There was the fact that they were an unusually big and athletic bunch, averaging 190 pounds, beefier and stronger on average than the juniors and seniors. That meant there was a great deal of raw potential for power in the boat. He could see plenty of technical flaws in their mechanics, but those could be dealt with. What was more important was their character. They were a rough-and-tumble bunch, not very worldly, but earnest and used to hard work. And character could still, to some extent, be formed in boys as young as the freshmen. They were still malleable. As important as anything else, he could be sure that none of them would be graduating before the Olympic summer of 1936.

Not that Ulbrickson would let any of them know any of this. The last thing he needed was for a bunch of upstart sophomores to start thinking they were God's gift to rowing. Or that because they had won the two-mile freshman race last June they could win a four-mile varsity race next June. That was a whole nother ball of wax—twice as long and in many ways more than twice as hard. Right now, he needed them to be thinking about building up their bodies, developing mental discipline, learning how to get an oar in and out of the water without splashing half of Lake Washington into their shell. They were good, but they were still green. Eventually, if they were going to become what he hoped they would, he would need to see each of them develop the rare balance of ego and humility that great oarsmen somehow always manage to have. For now, what he saw strutting around the shell house and lounging in the doorway was plenty of ego and not much humility.

Last year these boys had been primarily in Tom Bolles's charge. Now, whether they ultimately rowed as the varsity or the JV, they belonged entirely to Ulbrickson. From what Bolles had told him, he knew already that he would have to look particularly hard at a couple of them. One was the baby of the boat, a seventeen-year-old boy in the number two seat, six-foot-three George "Shorty" Hunt. He was an ox for work and absolutely indispensable. But he was high-strung, nervous, someone you often had to treat with kid gloves to settle him down, like a racehorse.

The other was the blond kid with the crew cut in the number three seat, Rantz—the boy he'd spotted on the rings in the gym at Roosevelt two years before. He was as poor as a church mouse. Anybody could tell that just by looking at him. When he wanted to, though, Bolles had reported, Joe Rantz would row longer and harder than any man in the boat. The problem was that he didn't always seem to want to. All last spring he had been erratic as all get-out—on one day, off the next. He marched to his own drummer. The other boys had taken to calling him Mr. Individuality. He was physically tough, independent, seemingly self-assured, friendly, and yet at the same time strangely sensitive. He seemed to have hidden vulnerabilities, tender spots that you had to watch out for if you wanted him to come through for you, though nobody, not even the other sophomores, could figure out quite what they were, where on earth they had come from, or whether putting up with them was even worth the effort. But Al Ulbrickson wasn't one to waste a lot of time trying to figure out a touchy kid's tender spots.

He picked up a megaphone and barked at the sophomores to assemble down on the ramp. The boys shuffled toward the water. Ulbrickson took a position slightly up the ramp from them, to gain a bit of height advantage over these very tall boys. Things like that mattered to Ulbrickson. To marshal large men who were not all that much younger than him, and in many cases just as strong willed, he needed every advantage he could get. He straightened his tie and took his Phi Beta Kappa key from his vest pocket and began to twirl it on its lanyard, as he often did on such occasions. He gazed out over them for a moment, saying nothing, letting his attitude silence them. And then, without prelude, he began to tell them how it was going to be.

"You will eat no fried meats," he began abruptly. "You will eat no pastries, but you will eat plenty of vegetables. You will eat good, substantial, wholesome food—the kind of food your mother makes. You will go to bed at ten o'clock and arise punctually at seven o'clock. You will not smoke or drink or chew. And you will follow this regimen all year round, for as long as you row for me. A man cannot abuse his body for six months and then expect to row the other six months. He must be a total abstainer all year. You will not use profane language in the shell house, nor anywhere within my hearing. You will keep at your studies and maintain a high grade point average. You will not disappoint your parents, nor your crewmates. Now let's row."

Ulbrickson's effort to knock the sophomores down a peg or two had mixed results. Two weeks later he made a move that inevitably revealed the extent of his high regard for them, though he tried to disguise it. When he first listed the tentative "boatings," or crew rosters, for the new year on the blackboard in the shell house, everyone could see at a glance that four of the five potential varsity boats were crewed, as usual, by a mixture of boys from different classes—some from last year's second freshman boat, some from each of last year's two JV boats, and some from last year's varsity boat. Just one boat was intact from last year, Joe's boat, the freshman first. For now at least, the sophomores were to sit together just as they had in June when bombs signifying their victory had exploded over the automobile bridge at Poughkeepsie: George Lund at bow, Shorty Hunt at two, Joe Rantz at three, Chuck Hartman at four, Delos Schoch at five, Bob Green at six, Roger Morris at seven, Bud Schacht at stroke, and George Morry in the coxswain's seat. The boat assignment seemed tangible and undeniable evidence that what the sophomores had been speculating about was true—something was special about them, and Ulbrickson had unusual confidence in them as a unit. But lest anyone—and particularly the sophomores themselves—read too much into it, Ulbrickson put the boat far down the list that generally signified a crew's status in the program. The sophomore boys were not in the first boat or the second. They were, in fact, in the fifth boat, the lowest rung on the ladder and the last place in which anyone would expect to see serious contenders for next spring's first varsity rowing.

The boys did not know what to make of the mixed message. Although they were not particularly close, they were glad to be rowing together again, if only because they seemed to do it so well. But given their championship, they recognized what seemed an unwarranted demotion and felt more than a little intimidated by their new coach's bearing. The swagger promptly disappeared from their steps. Ulbrickson was a harder man than Bolles, and this season would clearly be harder than the last.

As the fall training season got under way, Joe in particular struggled to keep up his spirits. It wasn't just the status of his boat that worried him. It wasn't just the brutality of the long workouts or the inevitable days of rowing in the rain and bitter cold. It was personal stuff. Despite the long summer of work, he found himself even poorer than he had been the previous year. Even the cost of a movie on a Saturday night now seemed unwisely extravagant to him. His dates with Joyce devolved into bleak meetings in the cafeteria, where they mixed catsup with hot water and called it tomato soup and rounded out the meal with soda crackers. The diamond ring on Joyce's finger comforted both of them, but at times Joe could not help but look at it and wonder whether he would ever be able to live up to its implications.

There were family matters eating at him as well. Joe had finally gone to his brother Fred and asked him point-blank where their father was, and Fred, after some hemming and hawing, had told him. Harry and Thula and Joe's half siblings were living in Seattle. They had been there all along, in fact, since the night in 1929 when they had driven away and left Joe behind in Sequim.

They had moved at first into a dilapidated shed down on the waterfront, on the fringes of Hooverville. It wasn't a tar-paper shanty, but it wasn't much better. There were only two rooms. One, with a toilet and a sink, served as kitchen and bathroom; the other, with a woodstove in a corner, served as living room and bedroom for all six of them. At night trucks rumbled by just a few inches from their front door. Prostitutes and toughs loafed under streetlamps down the way. Rats scurried about in the corners of both rooms. Harry, unable to find the job they had come to Seattle seeking, went on the public dole.

They didn't stay in the waterfront shed for long, but where they went next was only marginally better, an old house on Phinney Ridge, west of Green Lake. The place had been built in 1885 and had not seen a repair or improvement since. It had only one electrical outlet and only a single wood-stove for heat. The stove did them little good anyway because they could not afford firewood to fuel it. Perched on the ridge, the house caught every wintry blast that blew down from the Arctic and into the city. Desperate to heat the house and put a little food on the table, Thula began to frequent local soup kitchens and a neighborhood commissary set up by the Unemployed Citizens League, an organization founded by local socialists. Dedicated to distributing food and firewood to the destitute, members of the league gleaned what they could in the way of partially spoiled crops in the fields of eastern Washington and foraged for firewood in the Cascade Mountains, bringing whatever they could find back to Seattle. The pickings at the commissary were always slim, however. Most of the meals Thula managed to put before her children consisted of thin stews made from parsnips, rutabagas, potatoes, and chipped beef. Lacking wood for the stove most of the time, she took to turning her electric iron upside down, plugging it into the one outlet, and cooking their stew on it.

Thula's father had died in 1926, but her mother lived in a large house just a few blocks down the hill, across Aurora Avenue, near Green Lake. Mary La-Follette had never been happy about Thula's marriage in the first place, and she was decidedly unhappy now with Harry and the way things had unfolded. The single concession she made to recognizing his family's plight was that every Sunday morning Thula was allowed to send her children to the house for bowls of Cream of Wheat. But that was it. One bowl of Cream of Wheat each week and nothing more in the way of support. The ritual seemed designed to send a message. Eighty years later Harry Junior's voice still trembled when he remembered it: "One bowl. Once a week. I never could figure that out." Thula got the message, though. She told Harry to get out of the house, and not to come back until he had a job. Harry headed for Los Angeles. Six months later, he returned with a motorcycle but no job.

Thula gave him another ultimatum, and finally Harry did find a job, as head mechanic with the Golden Rule Dairy and Bakery in Fremont. The Golden Rule was a fiercely nonunion shop—which would, over the next few years, find itself at the center of a citywide boycott and labor battle—and as a result wages were low. But they were wages nonetheless, and Harry couldn't afford to be particular. He moved his family to a small but respectable house at Thirty-Ninth and Bagley, not far from the bakery and not far from the north end of Lake Union where Joe rowed nearly every afternoon. That's where Joe found them in the fall of 1934, at an address that Fred finally provided.

There wasn't much of a reunion. Joe and Joyce climbed into the Franklin and drove over to the house one afternoon. They parked on Bagley, took deep breaths, and climbed a flight of concrete steps to the front porch, holding hands. They could hear someone playing violin inside. Joe knocked on a yellow Dutch door, and the violin fell silent. A shadow moved behind lace curtains on the upper half of the door. There was a moment's hesitation, and then Thula opened the door halfway.

She did not seem particularly surprised to see them. Joe had the sense that she'd been expecting this for a long time. She glanced at Joyce and nodded at her pleasantly enough, but she made no move to invite them in. There was a long moment of silence. Nobody knew quite what to say. Joe thought Thula looked careworn and exhausted, much older than her thirty-six years. Her face was pale and drawn, her eyes a bit sunken. Joe focused for a moment on her fingers, red and chafed.

Finally Joe broke the silence. "Hello, Thula. We just came by to see how you are doing."

Thula peered at him silently for a moment, her expression veiled, then dropped her eyes as she began to speak.

"We're fine, Joe. We're doing fine now. How is school going?"

Joe said it was going well, that he was on the crew now.

Thula responded that she had heard that, and that his father was proud of him. She asked Joyce how her parents were doing, and expressed her regret when Joyce replied that her father was quite ill.

Thula continued to hold the door just half open, her body blocking the entrance. Even as she addressed them, Joe noticed, she continued to look down at the porch, as if studying something at her feet, trying to find the answer to something there.

Finally Joe asked if they could come in to say hello to his father and the kids. Thula said that Harry was at work and the kids were visiting friends.

Joe asked if he and Joyce could come back and visit them another time.

Thula seemed suddenly to find what she had been looking for. She raised her eyes abruptly and leveled them at Joe. "No," she said, her voice colder now.

"Make your own life, Joe. Stay out of ours." And with that she closed the door gently and slid the dead bolt into position with a soft, metallic click.

As they drove away from the house on Bagley that afternoon, Joyce simmered. Over the years she had been slowly learning more about Joe's parents and what exactly had happened back in Sequim and before that, at the Gold and Ruby mine. She'd learned about his mother's death and the long, lonely train ride to Pennsylvania. And stitching it all together, she could not understand how Thula could have been so cold to a motherless child, nor how Joe's father could have been so impassive in the face of it all. She could not understand, either, why Joe seemed to show so little anger about it all, why he continued to try to ingratiate himself with the two of them, as if none of it had ever happened. Finally, as Joe pulled over to the curb to drop her off at the judge's home, Joyce erupted.

She demanded to know why Joe let his parents treat him as they did. Why did he go on pretending that they hadn't done him any harm? What kind of woman would leave a boy alone in the world? What kind of father would let her do that? Why didn't he ever get angry at them? Why didn't he just demand that they let him see his half siblings? She was nearly sobbing by the time she finished.

She glanced across the seat at Joe, and saw at once, through a blur of tears, that his eyes were full of hurt too. But his jaw was set, and he stared ahead over the steering wheel rather than turning to look at her.

"You don't understand," he murmured. "They didn't have any choice. There were just too many mouths to feed."

Joyce pondered that for a moment, then said, "I just don't understand why you don't get angry."

Joe continued to stare ahead through the windshield.

"It takes energy to get angry. It eats you up inside. I can't waste my energy like that and expect to get ahead. When they left, it took everything I had in me just to survive. Now I have to stay focused. I've just gotta take care of it myself."

Joe retreated into the life of the shell house. The boys still might razz him about his low taste in clothes and music, and he really was only comfortable around Roger and Shorty, but at least he felt he had purpose at the shell house. The rituals of rowing, the specialized language of the sport, the details of technique that he was struggling to master, the wisdom of the coaches, even their litany of rules and the various taboos they proscribed—all seemed to Joe to give the world of the shell house a measure of stability and order that for a long time now the outside world had seemed to him to lack. The brutal afternoon workouts left him exhausted and sore but feeling cleansed, as if someone had scrubbed out his soul with a stiff wire brush.

The shell house had become more of a home than the grim confines of his cubicle in the basement of the YMCA or the half-built house out in Sequim. He liked the way the light poured in through the windows of the enormous sliding doors, the stacks of burnished shells on their racks, the hiss of steam in the radiators, the banging of locker doors, the intermingled scents of cedar and varnish and sweat. He often lingered in the building long after practice was over, and more and more he found himself drawn to the back of the room and the stairs that led to Pocock's workshop. Joe would not think of going up the stairs uninvited, for fear of interrupting Pocock. There was a kind of reverence that attached to Mr. Pocock, as the boys invariably called him at all times. Not that Pocock cultivated the attitude. If anything, the opposite was true. He often stood on the floating dock as the boys got ready for a workout, fiddling with the riggers on this boat or that, chatting with the boys, occasionally offering up a nugget of wisdom or two, a suggestion that they try this or that adjustment to their stroke. In point of fact, Pocock, with only a lower-school education, tended to believe that it was he rather than these college men who should be deferential.

But Pocock was learned far beyond his formal education, as was immediately obvious to everyone who met him. He was well read in a wide variety of subjects—religion, literature, history, and philosophy. He could quote Browning or Tennyson or Shakespeare at the drop of a hat, and the quote was always apt and telling, never pretentious or affected. The net effect was that for all his quiet humility the man's wide-ranging knowledge and quiet eloquence commanded absolute respect, and never more than when he was at work in his shop, plying his craft. No one interrupted Pocock at work. Ever.

So Joe remained at the bottom of the stairs, looking up and wondering, but keeping his curiosity to himself. He noticed, though, that Pocock was at work in the shop a great deal these days. Partly because rowing programs everywhere had gone so long, following the crash of 1929, without ordering new equipment, and partly because of the recent successes of Washington crews rowing in Pocock shells at Poughkeepsie, orders had suddenly begun coming into the shop again over the summer. Pocock now had a backlog of eight orders for eight-man shells, including requests from some of the most elite rowing programs in the country: Navy, Syracuse, Princeton, and Pennsylvania. By the beginning of September, he was able to write to Ky Ebright, down in Berkeley, in a tone markedly different from that of just a year before. He was too much the gentleman to be vindictive, but he was now entirely confident: "If you are going to buy anything, old boy, I sure would advise not leaving it too late. We have taken terrific punishment the last two years and the boys back East are waking up to the fact they have got to get some equipment. That means we will be busy." When Ebright responded by questioning his prices, it was Pocock who now pushed back, firmly reiterating the amount: "The price on an eight is $1,150.... One thing is sure, Ky, I refuse to go into competition for the cheapest eight in the country. I cannot build all of them, but I can still have a good shot at building the best."

In fact, George Pocock was already building the best, and doing so by a wide margin. He didn't just build racing shells. He sculpted them.

Looked at one way, a racing shell is a machine with a narrowly defined purpose: to enable a number of large men or women, and one small one, to propel themselves over an expanse of water as quickly and efficiently as possible. Looked at another way, it is a work of art, an expression of the human spirit, with its unbounded hunger for the ideal, for beauty, for purity, for grace. A large part of Pocock's genius as a boatbuilder was that he managed to excel both as a maker of machines and as an artist.

Growing up and learning his trade from his father at Eton, he had used simple hand tools—saws, hammers, chisels, wood planes, and sanding blocks. For the most part, he continued to use those same tools even as more modern, laborsaving power tools came to market in the 1930s. Partly, this was because he tended strongly toward the traditional in all things. Partly, it was because he believed that the hand tools gave him more precise control over the fine details of the work. Partly, it was because he could not abide the noise that power tools made. Craftsmanship required thought, and thought required a quiet environment. Mostly, though, it was because he wanted more intimacy with the wood—he wanted to feel the life in the wood with his hands, and in turn to impart some of himself, his own life, his pride and his caring, into the shell.

Up until 1927, he made his shells precisely as his father had taught him to make them in England. Working on a perfectly straight I beam more than sixty feet long, he constructed a delicate framework of spruce and northern ash. Then he carefully joined and nailed strips of Spanish cedar to the ribs of the frame to form the hull. This required thousands of brass nails and screws, the heads of which had to be patiently and laboriously filed down by hand before he could apply coats of marine varnish to the exterior. The fitting and nailing on of the planks was labor intensive and nerve-racking. At any moment the slip of a chisel or a careless blow from a hammer could ruin days' worth of work.

In 1927 he made an improvement that revolutionized the building of racing shells in America. For a number of years, Ed Leader, who succeeded Hiram Conibear as the Washington crew coach, had suggested that Pocock try making a shell out of the native western red cedar that grew so abundantly, and so large, in Washington and British Columbia. After all, Spanish cedar was expensive, having to be imported from its native South America. (Spanish cedar, *Cedrela odorata*, is in fact neither Spanish nor cedar, being a member of the mahogany family.) It was also notoriously brittle, necessitating the almost continual repair of the school's fleet of shells. Pocock was attracted to the idea of trying the native cedar. He had, for years, taken notice of the lightness and the durability of the old cedar Indian canoes that still occasionally plied the waters of the Puget Sound. But he had been dissuaded from experimenting with it by head coach Rusty Callow. Callow had been a logger in his younger years, and like most lumbermen he believed that cedar was only good for making shakes and shingles. But when Pocock finally followed his own heart and began to experiment with the wood in 1927, he was astonished by the possibilities it opened up.

Western red cedar (*Thuja plicata*) is a kind of wonder wood. Its low density makes it easy to shape, whether with a chisel, a plane, or a handsaw. Its open cell structure makes it light and buoyant, and in rowing lightness means speed. Its tight, even grain makes it strong but flexible, easy to bend yet disinclined to twist, warp, or cup. It is free of pitch or sap, but its fibers contain chemicals called thujaplicins that act as natural preservatives, making it highly resistant to rot while at the same time lending it its lovely scent. It is beautiful to look at, it takes a finish well, and it can be polished to a high degree of luster, essential for providing the smooth, friction-free racing bottom a good shell requires.

Pocock quickly became a convert. Soon he was scouring the Northwest for the highest-quality cedar he could find, making long journeys to smoky saw-mills out on the Olympic Peninsula and far to the north in the still-virgin for-ests of British Columbia. He found just what he wanted in the misty woods surrounding Lake Cowichan on Vancouver Island. From the cedar stock he found there—long, tight-grained, straight sections cut from massive, ancient trees—he could mill elegant planks of wood twenty inches or more wide and sixty feet long. And from these planks he could shave identical pairs of much thinner planks, delicate sheets of cedar just five thirty-seconds of an inch thick, each a mirror image of the other, with the same pattern of grain. By placing these book-matched pairs on either side of the keel, he could ensure perfect symmetry in the boat's appearance and performance.

These flexible sheets of cedar also allowed Pocock to do away with the end-less nailing of planks to the boat's ribs. Instead he could simply strap the sheets of wood over the frame of the boat, forcing them to conform to its shape, then cover the whole assembly with heavy blankets and divert steam from the shell house's heating system under the blankets. The steam caused the cedar to relax and bend to fit itself to the shape of the frame. When he turned off the steam and removed the blankets three days later, the cedar sheets held their new shape perfectly. All he had to do was dry them and glue them to the frame. It was the same technique that the Coast Salish peoples of the Northwest had used for centuries to fashion bentwood boxes out of single planks of cedar. The sleek shells that resulted from the process were not only more beautiful than the Spanish cedar shells but also demonstrably faster. Harvard ordered, as an experiment, one of the first to come out of Pocock's shop and promptly reported back that the boat had taken several full seconds off its crew's best times.

With the cedar skin attached to the shell, Pocock installed the runners and the seats, the riggers, the rudder assembly, and the trim. He took pride in using a variety of Northwest woods in his products—sugar pine for keels, ash for the frames, Sitka spruce for the gunnels and the hand-carved seats, Alaska yellow cedar for the washboards. The last of these he favored mostly because as it aged its color evolved from that of old ivory to a golden honey hue that harmonized with the burnished red of the cedar hulls. He stretched sheer silk fabric over the stern and bow sections and painted the silk with varnish. As the varnish dried and hardened on the fabric, it created a fragile and lovely translucent yellow decking fore and aft. Finally, he worked on the finish, hand-rubbing the cedar hull with powdered pumice and rottenstone for hours, applying thin coats of marine varnish, then rubbing the finish again and again until it gleamed like still water. All told, it took four gallons of varnish to get the finish he was looking for. Only when it fairly shimmered, when it seemed in its sleekness to be alive with the potential for speed, did Pocock pronounce the boat ready for use.

There was one more thing about cedar—a sort of secret that Pocock had discovered accidentally after his first shells made of the wood had been in the water for a while. People had taken to calling them "banana boats," because once they were exposed to water both their bows and sterns tended to curve ever so slightly upward. Pocock pondered this effect and its consequences and gradually came to a startling realization. Although cedar does not expand or swell *across* the grain of the wood when wet, and thus tends not to warp, it does expand slightly *along* the grain. This can amount to as much as an inch of swelling in the length of a sixty-foot shell. Because the cedar was dry when attached to the frame but then became wet after being used regularly, the wood wanted to expand slightly in length. However, the interior frame of the boat, being made of ash that remained perpetually dry and rigid, would not allow it to expand. The cedar skin thus became compressed, forcing the ends of the boat up slightly and lending it what boatbuilders call "camber." The result was that the boat as a whole was under subtle but continual tension caused by the unreleased compression in the skin, something like a drawn bow waiting to be released. This gave it a kind of liveliness, a tendency to spring forward on the catch of the oars in a way that no other design or material could duplicate.

To Pocock, this unflagging resilience—this readiness to bounce back, to keep coming, to persist in the face of resistance—was the magic in cedar, the unseen force that imparted life to the shell. And as far as he was concerned, a shell that did not have life in it was a shell that was unworthy of the young men who gave their hearts to the effort of moving it through the water.

At the end of October, Ebright wrote back to Pocock. If he was going to order a new shell, he wanted it custom designed. He wanted one with less camber. Pocock was horrified. After alleging that Pocock had sent him inferior equipment, Ebright was now demanding a boat that simply would not go as fast as

Pocock's best, a boat that would not reflect well on him as a craftsman. Pocock wrote back with a long, detailed technical explanation of his design and proposed a few minor modifications that he thought might mollify Ebright without compromising the integrity of the shell. Ebright replied testily with technical arguments of his own and then continued, "I think you know as much about boatbuilding as anyone in the world, but perhaps new ideas might be advantageous to all of us. . . . I doubt if you will like the tone of this letter, George." Pocock did not like the tone of the letter at all, but he let it slide. He had orders from virtually every major rowing program in the country. Ebright could order a shell or not, as he chose.

And in time Ebright did finally order one. When it was finished, Pocock paid eight of the boys a dollar each to deliver it to the docks in Seattle, so it could be shipped south.

The boys rowed it through the Cut and to the south end of Lake Union. There they removed it gingerly from the water, inverted it over their heads, and began a mile-and-a-half portage across Seattle. A sixteen-legged cedar turtle, more than sixty feet long, they crossed Mercer Street and headed south on Westlake, plunging into downtown traffic. With their heads under the shell, they could see little except for their own feet and the back of the man ahead of them, so a coxswain ran ahead of them, waving his hands to warn oncoming vehicles to steer clear and simultaneously shouting out instructions in rowing terms: "Way enough, boys! Hard to port. Pick 'er up!" They dodged streetcars and buses, swung wide around each corner, peered out from under the shell from time to time to get their bearings. As they jogged to their right and entered the shopping district on Fourth Avenue, people stopped on the sidewalk or rushed out of storefronts to watch them pass—staring, snickering, and applauding. Finally they turned right on Columbia, followed the steep descent to the waterfront, scurried hastily across railroad tracks, and made it safely to the docks. There they sent the shell on its way to California, where they would soon race against it on the Oakland Estuary.

Tensions began to mount in the Washington shell house that October. The continuing rumors that the sophomores might be pegged for the first varsity boat in the spring had everyone on edge. Al Ulbrickson remained characteristically silent on the topic, but the older boys fretted that that in itself seemed an ominous sign. Why didn't he just put the rumors to rest and say the sophomores would have their crack at the varsity boat the following year, as usual? As boys suited up and hoisted oars in and out of the racks, there was little of the usual banter and joshing. Icy stares began to replace good-natured grins. On the water, occasional catcalls flew from boat to boat when the coaches weren't in earshot.

As the mood in the shell house deteriorated, so too did the weather. At first it was just the usual fall drizzle, but then on the morning of October 21 all hell broke loose as the next in a series of extreme weather events that characterized the mid-1930s unfolded. An enormous cyclonic windstorm—a storm that made the previous fall's windstorm look almost like a spring breeze—slammed into Washington State.

It seemed to come out of nowhere. At nine in the morning, there was nothing more than a light chop on Lake Washington, a typical gray, late fall day with light winds out of the southeast at perhaps five miles per hour. An hour later, sustained winds were blowing out of the southwest at fifty miles per hour. By noon, gusts up to seventy-five miles per hour were screaming over Lake Washington. At Aberdeen, on the coast, winds hit ninety miles per hour. It was the greatest windstorm the Seattle area had ever seen.

At Pier 41 the transpacific ocean liner *President Madison* snapped her hawsers and careened into the steamboat *Harvester*, sinking her. Off Port Townsend, the purse seiner *Agnes* also sank, drowning five Seattle fishermen. Thirty passengers had to be rescued from the *Virginia V*, one of the last of the city's historic Mosquito Fleet, when she smashed into a wharf and her superstructure was crushed. Out in the countryside, barn roofs and entire outhouses flew away. An airplane hangar at Boeing Field—then Seattle's principal airport—collapsed, destroying several aircraft inside. At the Alki Hotel, a brick wall collapsed, killing a Chinese boarder in his bed. In Hooverville tin roofs cartwheeled across the sky and shanties were simply shredded, leaving their denizens standing dazed among the wreckage. At a nearby bakery, hungry men gathered in front of the plate-glass window separating them from racks of freshly baked bread, hoping the window would implode. On the University of Washington campus, the glass skylights at the basketball pavilion caved in, giant Douglas firs toppled over, and five sections of temporary seating in the football stadium blew away. The winds blew for six and a half hours, almost without respite, and when they finally died down millions of board feet of standing timber had fallen, millions of dollars of property damage had been done, eighteen people were dead, and Seattle was largely cut off from communication with the outside world.

Then the rains came again, as they always do. It was not quite the deluge of the previous year, but it rained more days than not for the rest of October and into November. An unusual number of lesser windstorms continued to blow in from the Pacific as well. One of the few advantages West Coast crews were supposed to have over East Coast crews was that the easterners could not train out-of-doors during the winter when their home rivers were frozen. Instead they were usually relegated to indoor rowing tanks, poor substitutes for the real thing. "Like sitting on the edge of a bathtub with a shovel," one western coach scoffed. As a result of all their outdoor exposure, Washington's boys were, year after year, particularly hardy and particularly adept at rowing in rough water. But you could not row at all if your shell sank, and as November of 1934 wore on, the water was so rough that it continually threatened to swamp the boats. Day after day Ulbrickson had to keep them ashore. He drove his boys hard, but he wasn't about to let a boatload of them drown in the middle of Lake Washington. By mid-November he figured he was two weeks behind schedule.

Throughout that month, a world away at the lavish Geyer-Werke film studios on Harzer Strasse in Berlin, Leni Riefenstahl was peering, day and night, with weary but zealous eyes, through the double magnifying lenses of her small Lytax film-editing machine. Dressed in a white smock, she sat at her editing table for up to sixteen hours a day, often until three or four in the morning, seldom eating, surrounded by thousands of filmstrips dangling from hooks in front of backlit glass walls. The immediate task at hand was to carefully review, cut, and splice selections from the four hundred thousand feet of raw film she had shot at the 1934 Nazi Party rally in Nuremberg.

The film that would eventually emerge from her labors, *Triumph of the Will* (*Triumph des Willens*), would come to define the iconography of Nazi Germany. To this day it stands as a monument to the ability of propaganda to foster absolute power and to justify unfettered hatred. And Riefenstahl would be celebrated for it for the rest of her life.

The Nuremberg Rally of 1934 was itself an anthem to power and a carefully designed tool for further concentrating and advancing it. From the moment Adolf Hitler's airplane descended from the clouds into Nuremberg on September 4 of that year, every movement he made, every detail of the imagery that unfolded, every word he and his minions spoke, was carefully calculated to reinforce the notion that the Nazi Party was invincible. And more: that it was the only legitimate object of not just political but religious fervor. And still more: that this new German religion was embodied and made incarnate in the person of its leader.

The rally's principal choreographers were Albert Speer, Hitler's chief architect, who designed the massive movie set Nuremberg became; Joseph Goebbels, who controlled the overall propaganda value of the event, its "messaging" in modern parlance; and Leni Riefenstahl, whose job it was to capture on film not just the rally itself but, more important, its underlying spirit—to amplify its message and convey it to an audience far wider than the three-quarters of a million party members who were actually in Nuremberg that week.

It was a tense, strained alliance, particularly between Riefenstahl and Goebbels. As Riefenstahl's influence continued to grow, Goebbels increasingly struggled to comprehend how a woman could occupy such a situation, much as he struggled to understand why his wife objected so strenuously to his many affairs.

After the war, Riefenstahl said she initially hesitated to make the film, fearing interference from Goebbels and his powerful Ministry of Propaganda. In her enormously self-serving and revisionist autobiography, she asserted that she agreed to make the film only after Hitler promised to keep Goebbels at bay. She also claimed that she had already had to keep Goebbels at bay on a more personal level—that he had become so smitten with her charms, so determined to have her for his mistress, that he had come to her apartment one night and flung himself on his knees at her feet, begging her to have him, only to be unceremoniously shown the door. Goebbels, she said, never forgave her for the humiliation of the rejection.

Despite all this, and regardless of the veracity of Riefenstahl's account of her relationship with Goebbels, the 1934 rally and Riefenstahl's film in particular were enormous successes. *Triumph of the Will* was everything Riefenstahl hoped it would be, and it is still considered by many to be the most successful propaganda film of all time. With a staff of 172, including 18 cameramen dressed as SA men so they would blend into the crowd, Riefenstahl shot the week's events from every conceivable angle, using techniques that had never been tried in a documentary before—cameras on dollies moving along tracks, cameras mounted on elevator platforms for dynamic aerial views, cameras in pits dug at ground level for shots upward at the looming Nazi figures. And the cameras caught it all: a half million uniformed party members marching in thunderous lock step, standing in massed rectangular formations, perfect in their uniformity and conformity; the speeches by Rudolf Hess, Goebbels, and Hitler himself, pounding on the podium, eyes ablaze, spittle flying from his mouth; Speer's monumental architecture, the ponderous stone buildings lending their weight and solidity to the impression of overwhelming might, the vast open spaces suggesting unlimited ambition; the eerie torchlight parade of the SA men on the second night, with flickering torches and magnesium flares and bonfires illuminating their gleaming faces against the black night; the ranks of black-shirted SS men goose-stepping past bespectacled, crab-faced Heinrich Himmler; enormous banners emblazoned with swastikas, fluttering in the background of nearly every shot. If you have in your mind any image of Nazi pageantry and power, it likely comes, directly or indirectly, from *Triumph of the Will*.

But perhaps the most horrifying images from Riefenstahl's film were seemingly the most innocent. They were shot on the third day of the rally, as Hitler addressed tens of thousands of boys from the Hitler-Jugend, the Hitler Youth, and its junior branch, the Deutsches Jungvolk. Service in the Hitler Youth was not yet compulsory, as it would later be; these were boys who were already true believers and they had been indoctrinated with a fierce anti-Semitism. Dressed in short pants and khaki shirts and neckerchiefs, looking for all the world like Boy Scouts with swastikas on their armbands, they ranged in age from eighteen down to ten. Many of them were destined to become members of the SS or SA.

On the podium, Hitler addressed them directly, jabbing at the air with one arm, his fist clenched. "We want our people to be obedient," he ranted, "and you must practice obedience! Before us Germany lies. In us Germany burns. And behind us Germany follows!" On the field, Riefenstahl's cameras moved slowly up and down the ranks of the boys, lenses angled slightly upward toward their faces. A gentle autumn breeze tousled their mostly fair hair. Their eyes shone with zeal, illuminated by trust. Their faces were so full of grace, so free of blemish, so perfect, that even today, even in the old black-and-white film, you can almost see the pink blush of their cheeks. And yet many of these were the faces of young men who would someday pull sobbing children from their mothers' arms and herd them into gas chambers; who would order Polish women to strip naked, line them up at the edge of trenches, and shoot them in the back; who would lock all the women and children of the French town of Oradour-sur-Glane in a church and set it on fire.

Leni Riefenstahl did her work well, and Hitler was pleased. A little less than two years later, in 1936, she had an opportunity to make another propaganda film, one that would again revel in images of youth and beauty and grace, and that would again perpetrate a great and sinister fraud upon the world.

As the fall quarter at the university wound down, Joe headed home to Sequim to spend Christmas with Joyce and her family. All fall he had been looking forward to winter break, and to spending time with Joyce somewhere other than in the dreary student cafeteria.

As he got ready to leave town, though, a headline in the *Daily* caught his attention: "Senior Men Face Life with Debts, Few Jobs." The article made his heart sink. The average debt among graduates was two hundred dollars, it said, and the average four-year tab was more than two thousand. Both were staggering amounts of money for someone like Joe in 1934. But what surprised him most, as he read on, what he remembered years later, was the revelation that "more than half the men interviewed are receiving their university education at no expense to themselves, their expenses being paid by parents or relatives who expect no reimbursement." The whole premise of Joe's struggle to stay in school was the prospect of a more promising future afterward. It had not occurred to him that doors wouldn't just open for a man with a college degree. And once again it was pounded home to him how many of his classmates apparently did not even have to think about money, how many had people watching out for them, shelling out thousands of dollars they never expected to see again. It stirred up the old anxiety and self-doubt that always threatened to bubble to the surface. And it added something new to the mix—a toxic dash of jealousy.

PART THREE

1935

The Parts That Really Matter

Joe and Joyce in Seattle

CHAPTER NINE

One of the first admonitions of a good rowing coach, after the fundamentals are over, is "pull your own weight," and the young oarsman does just that when he finds out that the boat goes better when he does. There is certainly a social implication here.

—George Yeoman Pocock

The boys sat on hard benches, shivering in their mismatched shorts and cotton jerseys. The sun had already set, and the vast interior space of the shell house was drafty and uncomfortable. Outside, it was a bitterly cold night. The panes of glass on the great sliding doors were frosted at the corners. It was the evening of January 14, 1935, the first crew turnout of the new year. The boys and a handful of reporters were waiting for Al Ulbrickson to lay out his plan for the upcoming racing season. After a long, uncomfortable wait, Ulbrickson emerged from his office and began to talk. By the time he finished, nobody in the room was cold any longer.

He had started off simply, announcing a change of basic strategy. Instead of taking it relatively slow for the first few weeks of winter quarter, as they generally did, working on details of form and technique while waiting for the weather to improve, they were going to row all out every day, right from the outset this year, weather be damned. They were going to work themselves into top physical condition first and then worry about refining technique later. More than that, though, all of them—not just the sophomores—were going to start out by racing one another in set crews rather than in constantly changing mixtures of men. And the races would be for the highest of stakes. This was not going to be an ordinary season. "At one time or another," he declared, "Washington crews have won the highest honors in America. They have not, however, participated in the Olympic Games. That's our objective." The push to go to Berlin in 1936, and to win gold there, was to begin that night.

Casting aside his usual reticence, and despite the presence of reporters in

149

the room, Ulbrickson then began to grow animated, almost emotional. There was more potential in this room, he said, than he had ever seen in a shell house in all his years of rowing and coaching, more than he ever expected to see again in his lifetime. Somewhere among them, he told the boys, was the greatest crew that Washington had ever seen. Better than the great 1926 crew that he had himself stroked to victory at Poughkeepsie. Better than the great Cal crews that had won Olympic gold in 1928 and 1932. Maybe the best Washington would ever see. Nine of them, he wound up declaring, as if it was a certainty, were going to be on the medal podium in Berlin in 1936. It was up to each of them whether he would be there or not. When he finished, the boys leapt to their feet and cheered, applauding with their hands held over their heads.

The performance was so uncharacteristic of Al Ulbrickson that everyone in Seattle with any interest in rowing took note. The next morning the *Seattle Post-Intelligencer* exulted, "A New Era in Washington Rowing. Possible Entry in the Olympic Games in Berlin!" The *Washington Daily* reported that "despite the intense cold, the shell house radiated more fire and spirit last night than has been the case for many a year."

All-out war promptly broke out in the shell house. The sullen rivalries that had arisen during the fall season now turned into outright battles. Eyes that had been coolly averted from one another before now locked in icy stares. Accidental bumping of shoulders turned into open pushing matches. Locker doors were slammed. Curses were exchanged. Grudges were nursed. Brothers Sid and George Lund—one in the all-sophomore boat, one in a JV boat—now barely greeted each other with grunts each afternoon.

The nine boys in the all-sophomore boat were sure that Ulbrickson had been talking directly to and about them. They changed their "M-I-B" rowing chant to "L-G-B." When asked what it meant, they smiled and said, "Let's get better." It didn't. It meant, "Let's go to Berlin." It became a kind of secret code embodying their ambitions. But they were still listed on the chalkboard as boat number four out of five, no matter what they chanted out on the water. And Ulbrickson, publicly at least, seemed to have other boys at the front of his mind these days. In particular, over the next few weeks he seemed to make a point of talking to any reporter he could find about the golden prospects of a potential stroke oar for the varsity, a boy named Broussais C. Beck Jr. Beck's father had been the manager of Seattle's iconic Bon Marché department store and a fierce opponent of organized labor, famous for hiring spies who infiltrated the unions and reported back to him. He had also been an outstanding stroke on the Washington crew of his day and later chairman of the Board of Rowing Stewards at Washington. His own father had been one of Seattle's most prominent pioneers, establishing a large homestead in the city's Ravenna Park area, just north of the university. The business community and a good number of alumni very much wanted to see the young Beck stroking the Washington varsity now. He may or may not have had the kind of potential Ulbrickson talked about, but there was no doubt that he was the kind of boy coaches liked to keep around to make the alums happy. Joe, for one, took note of it. Beck was pretty clearly one of the boys who didn't have to worry about money, or about a clean shirt to wear. Joe wondered if he had to worry about much of anything.

Ulbrickson's plan to have the boys row themselves quickly into fighting form ran into trouble starting the day after his fiery speech. The *Daily's* next headline told the tale, or at least the beginning of it: "Sweepsters Turn Out with Icicles on Their Oars." The weather, which had been wet and blustery since late October, now turned arctic. On the night of Ulbrickson's talk, cold north winds blew enormous breakers in off Puget Sound, pushing salt water two blocks inland at Alki Beach and along the waterfront in West Seattle. Over the next several days, temperatures dropped into the teens, snow flurries turned into light snowstorms, which in turn became full-scale blizzards. The siege went on almost continually, well into the third week of January. As he had in the fall, Ulbrickson had to keep his crews in the shell house day after day, or at best turn them out for quick sprints up and down the Cut, rowing in the snow until their hands grew so numb they could no longer hold the oars. He never said so, but he must have begun to wish he had some of those indoor rowing tanks they had back east. The eastern boys at least were at their oars, while his sat cooped up in a shell house, staring out the windows at some of the best rowing water in the world.

As the weather worsened, Tom Bolles watched his freshman squad rapidly shrink from the 210 who had turned out in the fall to 53 on January 14. By the third week of January, the *Daily* noted, "Three more days of blizzard and Tom Bolles won't have a frosh crew." Bolles, though, seemed unperturbed. "Crew is one sport where a cut is not necessary," he observed. And though Bolles wasn't talking much about it yet, he was well aware that among those few boys who were showing up there was some outstanding talent. He was starting to think, in fact, that he might just put together a freshman crew that could beat even last year's bunch.

By the time the snow finally turned to rain, in late January, the campus was mired in 532 acres of slush, and the infirmary was so overrun with students suffering from colds, flu, and pneumonia that all the beds were full and sick students were left lying on cots in the hallways. Ulbrickson hustled all five boatloads of varsity contenders back out onto the water in the wind and the rain.

The war that had been simmering in the shell house became a full-on naval engagement. On January 24 another item in the *Daily* got things started. Under a large photograph of Joe and the sophomores rowing the *City of Seattle*, a bold caption read "They Dream of Poughkeepsie and Olympics." The accompanying headline read "Frosh Crew Champs of Last Year Look Good to Coach Ulbrickson." Last year's varsity boys were outraged. It had seemed for months as if Ulbrickson had been quietly favoring the younger boys, but it had been subtle. Now it was all out in the open, down in black and white, for them and their friends and, worse, their girlfriends to read. By all appearances they were going to be shunted aside, humiliated for the sake of Ulbrickson's all too precious sophomores.

One of the boys in the all-sophomore boat, Bob Green, had the habit of getting excited and shouting encouragement to his crewmates during races. It was something of a breach of protocol, as ordinarily it is only the coxswain who is at all verbal in a shell, and it had the potential to confuse the stroke, especially during a race. But it had seemed to work for the sophomores the year before, and George Morry, the usual sophomore coxswain, had put up with it good-naturedly.

It irritated the hell out of some of the older boys in the other boats, though, particularly Bobby Moch, the savvy little coxswain of what seemed to be shaping up to be the best of the JV boats. As the boats began to compete head-to-head for varsity status in February, Moch, a junior, grew more and more outraged by Green's behavior. But he soon found that he could turn it to his own advantage. Whenever his boat came up alongside Joe and the sophomores, Moch quietly leaned toward his stroke oar and whispered, "Give me twenty really big ones, after five more." Green meanwhile would be hooting and hollering at his own crew, urging them on. Five strokes later, Moch would direct his megaphone over to the sophomore boat and say, "Well, Green just opened his big mouth again. Let's pass them!" By the time he said this, his own boat would already be starting to surge, as if by magic. In the sophomore boat, Green, angry at the name-calling, would start yelling even more loudly. In the coxswain's seat, Morry would chime in, "Give me ten big ones!" but all the while Moch's boat would be silently accelerating away from them. Each time Moch tried it, the sophomores did the same thing—all at once, collectively, and in unison, they lost their cool. They flailed at their oars, digging them too deep in the water or too shallow, out of time with one another, angry and desperate to catch up, losing all semblance of form. Time after time, they got, as Moch called it, "all bloody nosed." And none more so than Joe, to whom the whole thing seemed like another joke at his expense, designed to show him up. But it always worked. Moch wound up each time sitting in the stern of his boat, looking back over his shoulder, chuckling at the suddenly hapless-looking sophomores as they fell out of contention, and giving them a casual farewell wave. Bobby Moch—as everyone concerned would eventually learn—was nobody's fool.

Neither was Al Ulbrickson, though he was starting to have some serious doubts about the sophomores. He had frankly expected that by now they would emerge decisively as the new varsity lineup. But watching them suddenly struggle against even the JV boys, they just didn't look like the crew that had won with such astonishing ease at Poughkeepsie. They seemed to be going all to hell. He studied them for a few days, trying to figure it out, looking for individual faults. Then he called those who seemed to be struggling the most—George Lund, Chuck Hartman, Roger Morris, Shorty Hunt, and Joe Rantz—into his office for a talk. It wasn't quite the whole boat but pretty nearly so.

It was an intimidating thing to be summoned into Al Ulbrickson's office. It didn't happen often, and it left an impression when it did. On this occasion, as on most, he didn't shout or pound on the table, but he sat the boys down, leveled his gray eyes at them, and told them flat out that they were all in danger of falling out of contention for the boat if they didn't shape up. They were messing up his plan to keep their crew intact, and wasn't that what they wanted? If so, then why weren't they rowing as they did at the championship? It looked to him like a case of laziness. They weren't pulling hard enough. They had no pepper. And they were sloppy. They were knifing their oars into the water rather than digging into it. They weren't putting their backs into it. Their spacing was all off. Worst of all, they were letting their emotions climb into the boat with them, losing their cool over little things, and that had to stop. By way of closing, he reminded them that there were at least four boys vying for each seat in the first varsity boat. Then he stopped talking and simply pointed at the door.

The boys came out of the shell house shaken, trying to ignore a cluster of seniors and juniors smirking at them from the doorway. Joe, Roger, and Shorty started up the hill in the rain, talking over what had just happened, beginning to get agitated.

Shorty and Roger had been buddies from day one. Shorty was so naturally garrulous and Roger so naturally reticent and gruff that it seemed an odd combination. But somehow it worked for them. And Joe was grateful that the two of them had never given him a hard time. In fact, more and more Joe could count on the pair of them to come to his side when the older boys teased him. Shorty rowed in the number two seat, right behind Joe, and he'd taken lately to looping an arm over Joe's shoulder whenever he seemed down and saying, "Don't worry, Joe. I've got your back."

Hunt was an extraordinary young man by anybody's reckoning. Just how extraordinary, nobody yet quite knew. But just a few years down the line, Royal Brougham would name him, along with Al Ulbrickson, as one of the two greatest oarsmen ever to sit in a shell for Washington. Like Joe, he had grown up in a small town, Puyallup, between Tacoma and the foothills of Mount Rainier. Unlike Joe's, his family life had been stable, and as a result he'd grown comfortable with himself and highly accomplished. At Puyallup High School, he had been a superstar. He had played football, basketball, and tennis. He was class treasurer, an assistant librarian, a member of the radio club, and he appeared on the honor roll every year that he attended the school. He was active in the honor society and the school's Hi-Y chapter. And he graduated two years early. He was also quite good-looking, with wavy dark hair. People liked to compare him to Cesar Romero. He was six foot three as a freshman, and his fellow students promptly dubbed him Shorty. He'd use the name for the rest of his life. He was something of a fashion plate, always well dressed and forever drawing the eyes of the young women around him, though he did not seem to have a steady girl.

Despite his accomplishments, he was also something of a contradiction. He was garrulous and sociable and loved to be at the center of attention, but at the same time he was extraordinarily guarded about his private life. He liked to keep the many people who swirled around him swirling, but always at a distance. He tended to believe that his opinion was inevitably the right opinion, and he did not have a lot of patience for people who thought otherwise. As with Joe, there was an invisible boundary around him that he would not let others cross. And like Joe, he was sensitive. You could never quite be sure what might set him off, shut him down, or make him lose his focus. Taunts from another boat seemed to be one of the things that did.

Walking up the hill from the shell house together that night, after the meeting with Ulbrickson, Joe and Shorty and Roger talked excitedly but in hushed voices. Al Ulbrickson had a long-established policy that a single training infraction would drop a man two shells; a second infraction would lead to his expulsion from the squad. They weren't sure whether what had just happened represented a training infraction or not, but they feared it might. Either way, they were angry at having been chewed out. Shorty, in particular, was agitated, getting hot under the collar. Roger moped along, looking even more morose than usual. As they rounded Frosh Pond, they muttered to one another: Ulbrickson was unfair, a cold taskmaster, too hard on them, too blind to see how hard they were working. He'd do better to give a fellow an occasional pat on the back than to always demand more. He wasn't likely to change, though. They knew that much. And things were getting dangerous. They agreed that from now on they'd all better be watching one another's backs.

As Joe peeled off from the group and made his way up University Avenue to the YMCA, with his shoulders hunched up and his eyes narrowed against the windblown rain, he passed cheap restaurants packed with giddy students, happy to be out of the cold, eating Chinese or burgers, smoking cigarettes, and drinking beer. Joe cast them sidelong glances but kept walking, leaning against the rain. He had blustered and complained about Ulbrickson right along with Shorty and Roger, but now that he was alone the bluster faded and the old weight of anxiety and self-doubt settled on him again. After all he had been through, it was obvious that he still remained utterly disposable, even at the crew house, the one place he had started to feel more or less at home.

The day after their little chat in his office, Al Ulbrickson happily noted in his logbook that the sophomore boat suddenly snapped back into form, handily beating all four of the other boats on its first outing. Dodging rainsqualls, rowing through whitecaps, stopping between races to bail out their shells—the five potential varsity crews went at it tooth and nail over the next several weeks, and through it all the sophomores seemed to have found themselves again. Ulbrickson decided to put them to the test. He staged a one-mile time trial. The sophomores leapt out to a one-length lead and never looked back, pulling away decisively at the halfway mark and cruising to a seemingly effortless win. But when Ulbrickson looked at his stopwatch, he was disappointed. They were about ten seconds off the pace he was looking for at this point in the season. Nevertheless, they had won, so on the blackboard in the shell house the next day he finally listed the sophomore boat as the first varsity boat for the first time.

The following day they rowed awkwardly and lost badly. Ulbrickson promptly demoted them to third boat. That night, writing in his logbook, a frustrated Ulbrickson tore them apart: "horrible," "every man for himself," "no semblance of teamwork," "have gone to sleep entirely," "too much criticism," "need the old morale." A few days later, he held a three-mile trial. The sophomores trailed the field for the first mile. In the second mile they pulled even with the leading JV boat. Then they simply overpowered the older boys in the last mile to pull away and win by a convincing length and a half. Ulbrickson scratched his head and moved them back to first-boat status on the blackboard. But as soon as he elevated them, they fell apart yet again. "Dead from the bottom up," "timing messed up," "Rantz holding slide and arms too long," he wrote in the logbook. By now Ulbrickson was headed along the road from mild confusion to utter consternation, if not madness. He was, in his quiet way, rapidly becoming obsessed, almost Ahab-like, in his pursuit of the ultimate varsity crew, one that could beat Ky Ebright in California in April and at Poughkeepsie in June and be in a position to go to Berlin the following year.

Ebright was much on his mind. The normally vociferous Cal coach had gone uncharacteristically silent down in Berkeley. One Bay Area sports scribe took to calling him the "sphinx of Berkeley" and wondered if he even so much as said hello to his wife in the evening these days. The last time he had been so reserved was in the run-up to the 1928 and 1932 Olympic seasons. Now all that Ulbrickson could find in the Bay Area papers was the disconcerting tidbit that Dick Burnley—Cal's sensational stroke oar, who had so spectacularly powered Ebright's varsity to victory over Ulbrickson's boys in Poughkeepsie—had grown another half inch in height.

Ebright was far from all that was confusing Ulbrickson, though. Nor was it just the suddenly erratic performance of the sophomores on whom he had staked so much hope. Part of what he was wrestling with was, in fact, good news—an embarrassment of riches. He had begun to see a great deal of unexpected talent in some of his other boats.

For starters, there was Tom Bolles's new crop of freshmen. They were off-limits for now, but Ulbrickson knew he had to factor them into his plans for next year, and next year was what mattered most. Bolles was reporting that the new crop was rowing just seconds off the kinds of record paces Joe and his crew had set the year before, and they seemed to be getting better each time out. There was a curly-haired kid at stroke in the freshman boat, Don Hume, who looked particularly promising. He wasn't polished yet, but he never seemed to tire, never showed pain, just kept going, kept driving forward no matter what, like a well-oiled locomotive. In no position except for coxswain is experience so important as it is at stroke, though, and Hume still had a lot of experience to garner. There were a couple of other kids in the freshman crew that looked real good too—a big, muscular, quiet boy named Gordy Adam in the number five seat, and Johnny White in number two. White's father had once been a standout single sculler, and his boy just lived and breathed rowing.

One of the JV boats—the one Bobby Moch was steering, the one that now and then left the all-sophomore boat in its wake—also contained a couple of promising surprises, also sophomores. There was another curly-headed boy, a six-foot-five, slightly goofy-looking beanpole with a smile that could knock your socks off, named Jim McMillin. His crewmates called him Stub. He had not rowed particularly well in the second freshman boat the previous year. Now suddenly he seemed to be finding his niche in Moch's boat. He was big enough to provide the leverage and power that a great crew needs in the middle of the boat, and he never seemed to believe he was beaten, even if he was. He rowed as hard in a losing cause as in a winning one. He just plain had a lot of pepper, and he'd made it clear that he thought he belonged in the first boat. There was also a bespectacled boy named Chuck Day. Ulbrickson had noticed him as a freshman. He was almost impossible to overlook, in fact, if only because he was a chatterbox and a prankster and he made himself conspicuous. Like Hume, he hadn't yet smoothed out as an oarsman, but his natural inclination was to fight first and ask questions later, and it was starting to pay off for him. There were times when a crew needed that kind of spark plug to get it revved up and firing on all cylinders.

———

As February gave way to March, Ulbrickson decided it was time to change tactics again. He abandoned the notion of set crews and started mixing and matching men in different boats, telling them, "I will change men around until I get a varsity boat that walks off and leaves the other lineups. Then I will know I have the right combination together." He started off by moving Joe out of the all-sophomore boat. But just as it had the year before when Tom Bolles took Joe out, the boat slowed down. The next day Joe was back in the boat. Ulbrickson tried Stub McMillin in the number seven seat in the sophomore boat, but then took him out the next day. He tried taking Joe out again, with the same results. He moved Shorty Hunt into the JV boat Moch was coxing. He swapped boys in and out of each and every boat. As March wore on, he gradually began to settle on two leading contenders for varsity status: one of the previous season's JV boats—the one with Moch, McMillin, and Day in it—and the original sophomore boat, still intact despite his various attempts at dismantling and improving it. Both boats were now logging impressive trial times, but neither seemed able to beat the other decisively. Ulbrickson needed one or the other of them to break through, if only to put him out of his misery, but it just wasn't happening.

Ulbrickson knew what the real problem was. He littered his logbook with the myriad technical faults he was observing: Rantz and Hartman still weren't breaking their arms at the right point in the stroke; Green and Hartman were catching the water too early; Rantz and Lund were catching it too late; and so on. But the real problem wasn't that—wasn't an accumulation of small faults. Back in February he had commented to the *Seattle Times'* George Varnell that "there are more good individual men on this year's squad than on any I have coached." The fundamental problem lay in the fact that he had felt compelled to throw that word "individual" into the sentence. There were too many days when they rowed not as crews but as boatfuls of individuals. The more he scolded them for personal technical issues, even as he preached teamsmanship, the more the boys seemed to sink into their own separate and sometimes defiant little worlds.

The nasty weather that had assaulted Seattle since the previous October finally broke, though not before spitting a late spring snowstorm at the city for good measure on March 21. On April 2 a warm sun blossomed over Lake Washington. On the campus, students emerged from the mustiness of

Suzzallo Library and the dankness of their rented rooms, blinked warily, and looked about for a place to stretch out on a patch of grass. Boys appeared wearing sports shirts and white shoes for the first time since the previous summer. Girls appeared wearing flowery skirts and ankle socks. The many cherry trees on the quad burst into blossom. Robins hopped around on the grass, cocking their heads, listening for worms. The first violet-green swallows of the year swirled among the spires of the library. Sunlight streamed through windows into classrooms where professors gave halting lectures as they gazed out onto the sun-washed campus.

At the shell house, the crew boys stripped off their jerseys and stretched out on the ramp, basking like lithe, white lizards in the sun. The custodian at the canoe house noted a sudden demand for canoes, all of them rented by boy-girl combinations. The *Daily* ran a banner headline: "Campus Blotto with Influx of Love, Birds."

Joe and Joyce were among the first of those to rent a canoe. Joyce was still living and working at the judge's house, and hating the job more with each passing day. Joe figured maybe it would help to get her out on the water. He found her wearing a summer dress, sitting on the lawn in front of the library, chatting with some girlfriends. He took her by the hand and rushed her down to the canoe house. There he stripped off his shirt, helped her into a boat, and paddled briskly across the Cut. He made his way lazily among the green expanse of lily pads and beaver lodges on the south side of Union Bay until he found a spot he liked. Then he let the boat drift.

Joyce reclined in the bow, trailing a hand in the water, soaking up the sun. Joe stretched out as best he could in the stern, gazing up at the translucent blue sky. From time to time, a frog croaked and plopped into the water, alarmed by the slow approach of the drifting boat. Blue dragonflies hovered overhead, their wings rattling dryly. Redwing blackbirds clung to reeds along the shoreline, chortling. Lulled by the subtle rocking of the canoe, Joe began to drift off.

As Joe slept, Joyce sat in the bow, studying the face of the young man to whom she had committed herself. He had grown even more handsome since high school, and at moments like this, when he was fully at ease, his face and his sculpted body were so full of composure and grace that they reminded Joyce of the ancient marble statues of Greek athletes that she had recently studied in her art history class. Looking at him like this, she thought, it was hard to believe that he had ever known a troubled moment.

Sleek, mahogany motorboats roared by, on their way from Lake Washington into the Cut, coeds in bathing suits perched on the rear decks waving at them as they passed. Their wide wakes rippled through the lily pads and rolled the canoe abruptly from side to side, prodding Joe back to alertness. He smiled at Joyce, who was beaming at him from the bow. He sat up, shook his head to clear his mind, took his guitar out of its battered old case, and began to sing. He sang at first the songs he and Joyce had sung together on the school bus back in Sequim—funny, happy-go-lucky songs, songs that made them both laugh—and Joyce joined in joyfully again just as she had back then.

Then Joe slipped into soft, slow, sweet love songs and Joyce grew quiet, listening carefully, happy in a different, deeper way. When Joe stopped playing, they talked about what it would be like when they were married and had a home and maybe kids. They talked earnestly, continuously, without respite and with no sense of time passing until the sun began to sink behind Capitol Hill and Joyce grew cold in her light dress, and Joe paddled them back to the university side of the bay and helped her out of the boat. It was a day that both of them would remember well into old age.

The next day Joe, still feeling awash with goodwill, bought a little gas, drove his old Franklin over to Fremont, and parked in front of the Golden Rule Dairy and Bakery. He rolled the window down and waited, trying to enjoy the rich smell of baking bread but too nervous to really savor it. A little after noon, men dressed in white streamed out of the building and began sitting on the lawn, opening lunch boxes. A bit later a few men in dark coveralls emerged, and Joe spotted his father immediately. At six foot two, he was easily the tallest man in the group. He did not appear to have changed at all. Even his coveralls looked to be the ones he'd always worn back on the farm in Sequim. Joe climbed out of the car and trotted across the street.

Harry looked up, saw him coming, and froze in place, clutching his lunch box. Joe stuck out his hand and said, "Hi, Pop."

Startled, Harry said nothing but took his son's hand. It had been five and a half years since he'd seen Joe. He was no longer the scrawny kid he had left behind in Sequim. He had to wonder. Had Joe come to confront him or forgive him?

"Hi, Joe. It's swell to see you."

The two of them crossed the street and climbed into the front of the Franklin. Harry unwrapped a salami sandwich and silently offered half of it to Joe. They began to eat, and then, after a long, awkward silence, to talk. At first Harry talked mostly about the equipment in the bakery—the huge ovens and dough mixers and the fleet of delivery trucks that he maintained. Joe allowed his father to go on at length, not particularly interested but reveling in the familiar sound of his big, deep voice, the voice that had told him so many stories while sitting at night on the steps of the cabin at the Gold and Ruby mine, the voice that had taught him so much as they tinkered with machinery back in Sequim or hunted for bee trees out in the woods.

When Joe finally started to talk, questions about his half siblings tumbled out: How was Harry Junior doing? Had he ever caught up with his schooling after the accident with the bacon grease? How big was Mike now? How were the girls getting on? Harry assured him they were all well. There was a long pause. Joe asked if he could come by and see them. Harry looked down at his lap and said, "I don't reckon so, Joe." Deep down in Joe's gut, something surged—anger, disappointment, resentment, he wasn't sure what, but it was old and familiar and painful.

But then, after another pause, Harry added, without looking up, "Sometimes Thula and I go off on little excursions, though. Nobody home but the kids then." He looked out the window as if distancing himself from what he'd just said. He seemed relieved—Joe wasn't going to ask him about that awful night in Sequim when they'd left him behind.

There is a thing that sometimes happens in rowing that is hard to achieve and hard to define. Many crews, even winning crews, never really find it. Others find it but can't sustain it. It's called "swing." It only happens when all eight oarsmen are rowing in such perfect unison that no single action by any one is out of synch with those of all the others. It's not just that the oars enter and leave the water at precisely the same instant. Sixteen arms must begin to pull, sixteen knees must begin to fold and unfold, eight bodies must begin to slide forward and backward, eight backs must bend and straighten all at once. Each minute action—each subtle turning of wrists—must be mirrored exactly by each oarsman, from one end of the boat to the other. Only then will the boat continue to run, unchecked, fluidly and gracefully between pulls of the oars. Only then will it feel as if the boat is a part of each of them, moving as if on its own. Only then does pain entirely give way to exultation. Rowing then becomes a kind of perfect language. Poetry, that's what a good swing feels like.

A good swing does not necessarily make crews go faster, except to the extent that if no one's actions check the run of the boat, rowers get more bang for their buck on each stroke. Mainly what it does is allow them to conserve power, to row at a lower stroke rate and still move through the water as efficiently as possible, and often more rapidly than another crew rowing less efficiently at a higher rate. It allows them to possess a reserve of energy for a gut-wrenching, muscle-screaming sprint at the end of a race. It is insanely difficult to keep a good swing as you raise your rate. As the tempo increases, each of the myriad separate actions has to happen at shorter and shorter intervals, so that at some point it becomes virtually impossible to maintain a good swing at a high rate. But the closer a crew can come to that ideal—maintaining a good swing while rowing at a high rate—the closer they are to rowing on another plane, the plane on which champions row.

Joe and his crewmates had found their swing as freshmen the day they'd won in Poughkeepsie, and Al Ulbrickson had not forgotten that. He could not, in fact, get the picture of it out of his mind. There had been something marvelous, almost magical, about how they closed out that race. He had to believe that it was still there.

But as the Pacific Coast Regatta in California approached, in early April, the weather again deteriorated and the sophomore boys could not, for the life of them, seem to regain and hold on to their magic. One day they'd have it; the next day they'd lose it. They would beat the junior varsity on Monday, lose badly on Tuesday, win again on Wednesday, lose on Thursday. When they won, they did so handily; when they lost, they fell apart completely. Fuming, Ulbrickson went public with his dilemma, telling the Seattle Times on April 2, "I have never seen a situation like this. . . . Never before in my experience has a UW training campaign come up to this point without the question of the superiority of a crew being settled long ere this." Still, he had to make a decision.

Finally he did what he had wanted to do all along. He officially proclaimed the entire sophomore boat to be the 1935 first varsity crew. The local papers announced it to the world. And the sophomores promptly lost their next head-to-head race against the JV boat. The JV clamored to be named the varsity boat for the regatta. Ulbrickson, all but throwing his hands in the air, announced that he'd reconsider. They would race one more time in California.

Whoever won the first time trial after they arrived in Oakland would row as the varsity crew in the Pacific Coast Regatta.

Elevating the sophomores to varsity status was an unusual move, but not unheard of. Ky Ebright was, in fact, in the midst of doing essentially the same thing—perhaps in reaction to all he'd been reading about the Washington sophomores. Improbably, as he had moved toward the Pacific Coast Regatta, Ebright had demoted the varsity boys who had won the national title in Poughkeepsie the year before, in favor of a mixed boat of sophomores and juniors. Only one of the previous year's national champions now sat in his varsity boat, and Ebright remained perplexed by the poor performance of the older boys. When Royal Brougham arrived in Oakland to cover the regatta, Ebright pleaded with him, "Will you please tell me why the crew that last June was the best in the U.S. can't row fast enough to beat a pickup boat of sophomores and J.V. oarsmen?" Brougham had no idea why, but he was happy to telegraph the intelligence to Ulbrickson, up in Seattle. And to add a warning. He had put a stopwatch to Ebright's new pickup boat. "Don't get the idea that the new Bear varsity is slow, Mr. Ulbrickson . . . this boat has plenty of get up about it." When Ulbrickson learned the details, particularly the fact that Ebright had replaced even Dick Burnley, the enormous stroke who had powered Cal to victory over his boys in Poughkeepsie, he could only have been stunned. He knew that Ebright was looking beyond this year to '36, looking for younger talent, just as he was. But who on earth could Ebright have found that would knock a machine like Burnley out of a national championship boat?

By eight o'clock on the morning of April 7, all three Washington crews were in California, out on the oil-slicked waters of the Oakland Estuary, rowing in the rain with a thirty-mile-per-hour wind whipping in off San Francisco Bay, pushing salt spray in their faces for the first time. Except for the taste of salt in the water, they felt right at home. They had brought a bit of Seattle south with them. Cal was nowhere to be seen. They rowed the length of the estuary and out along the mudflats on the east shore of the bay. The silver towers of the partially completed Bay Bridge rose dramatically from the water before them, elegant spires stretching with surprising grace across the bay toward Treasure Island and San Francisco. Out in the open bay, though, the chop was even heavier, heavy enough to threaten to swamp the boats. Ulbrickson turned them around.

On the way out, it had seemed to him that the junior varsity boat was moving better than the sophomores. On the way back in, the sophomores seemed to be going better than the junior varsity. Everyone waited for Ulbrickson to stage the decisive time trial that he had promised before leaving Seattle. Nobody in either shell talked much to anybody in the other.

Meanwhile Al Ulbrickson and Ky Ebright performed their practiced dance, the dance of doom. Each tried to outdo the other in gloomy prognostications for the upcoming regatta. Ulbrickson announced that his boys were too heavy, badly out of shape as a result of all the canceled workouts in Seattle. He'd hoped but failed to "boil them down" to fighting trim by now. Rate them "for the dark horses that they are," he said. "My boys are not ready for a race. They started out to row three miles yesterday and they were sitting on their tongues at the end of the first mile. We've never had less work and poorer conditions." Reporters, though, noted that the boys had looked pretty darned fit when they'd stepped off the train. When asked why he'd showed up with a

Ky Ebright

boatload of sophomores, Ulbrickson looked at the reporter balefully and said, "They're the best we've got." Ebright, trying to swing perceptions the other way, said less, but was more direct when he said anything. Talking to the *New York Times*, he claimed flat out, "California has a chance, but I think Washington will win." And added, "Our chances are not so hot. Our varsity is undoubtedly slower than last year's shell, and is inexperienced entirely in racing." He continued to remain oddly silent about his own boys.

On April 10, Ulbrickson finally staged the formal time trial that was to determine who would race as the varsity. Joe and his sophomore crewmates came in almost a length behind the JV. They slumped in their shell in despair and disbelief. The boys in the JV boat were jubilant. Al Ulbrickson went back to the hotel and scrawled in his logbook, "In a hell of a fix now." But he still didn't announce a varsity boating.

On the morning of April 12, the same thing happened, but now Ulbrickson tried one more trick. The sophomores had come south with a new, still-unchristened shell. But they had taken an immediate dislike to it. They had been complaining since they arrived that it just didn't swing for them. So Ulbrickson sent them out one more time, this time in their old shell, the one in which they had won so convincingly at Poughkeepsie, the *City of Seattle*. They rowed beautifully and matched the JV's time. "The old boat made them feel right at home," Ulbrickson noted in his logbook.

After dinner at the Hotel Oakland that night, he dropped the bomb on the JV. He was going to race the sophomores as the varsity despite their repeated defeats. "I'm sorry," he said. "I probably shouldn't do this, but I can't help it." The JV boys walked out of the room enraged, stormed out into the dark, and tried to walk off their anger on the streets of Oakland. Explaining the reversal to the Associated Press, Ulbrickson broke cover, abandoned the dance of doom, and said simply what he believed in his heart about the sophomores. They were, he declared, "potentially the best crew I have ever coached." But in his logbook that night he wrote, miserably, "Hell of a position to be in the day before the race."

Race day, April 13, was again rainy, and a stiff headwind blew out of the south, up the length of the Oakland Estuary. The estuary was not what anyone might call pristine rowing water even on the best of days. A long, narrow slot of water between Oakland and Alameda Island, it was essentially a marine highway through an already aging industrial landscape. Spanned by several steel bridges, the racecourse made a slight curve at Union Point, just before the finish line at the Fruitvale Avenue Bridge. Crumbling brick warehouses, oil storage tanks, rusting cranes, and gritty factories lined both sides of the waterway. Tied up along its shores was every conceivable kind of watercraft—Chinese junks, tugboats, rickety houseboats, old schooners, and barges heaped with jumbles of industrial cargo. The water itself was turgid, gray-green even on sunny days, oil slicked, and reeking of diesel fuel and seaweed. Right next to Cal's shell house a four-inch pipe discharged raw sewage directly into the water.

It was a challenging landscape in which to find a place to watch a crew race, but by midafternoon on April 13 nearly forty thousand spectators had assembled under umbrellas in empty lots, on scattered docks, on warehouse rooftops, and on small craft moored along the racecourse. By far the greatest concentration of fans was at the finish line, on the Fruitvale Avenue Bridge. There thousands of California fans dressed in blue and gold mingled on the span with hundreds of Washington loyalists in purple and gold, everyone jostling to get a good view of the water. Radio announcers sat huddled under a shelter near the bridge, ready to broadcast the results around the nation.

At 3:55 p.m., the regatta got started with the two-mile freshman race. Don Hume, Washington's stroke, was just a few days out of the infirmary and still recovering from severe tonsillitis, but you wouldn't have known it by watching the race. The Washington freshmen jumped out early to a half-length lead. At the halfway mark, they led by a full length, with both crews rowing at thirty-two. As they came around the bend and into the final stretch, the Cal freshmen tried to rally, edging their rate up to thirty-four. Washington upped its rate to match Cal's. With both boats rowing at the same rate, Hume's stroke made all the difference. In the last quarter mile, Hume rowed so smoothly, so powerfully, and so efficiently that, with the boys behind him falling in synch, the Washington boat powered still farther ahead and crossed the line three lengths ahead of California. Officials on the bridge dropped a white flag to signify a win for the white blades of Washington.

The junior varsity race was, for the suddenly demoted older boys from Washington, all about making a point. And about opening up the future. At 4:10 p.m., still seething over Ulbrickson's reversal, they brought their boat up to the starting line at the foot of Webster Street, just south of Jack London Square and three miles from the finish. When the start was called, California jumped out in front and then settled in at thirty-two. With Bobby Moch calling the cadence and big Stub McMillin in the engine room, Washington slowly and methodically pulled even and then began to edge ahead. By the halfway mark, they had open water between themselves and the Cal boat.

Then they started rowing in earnest. Moch barked at them to raise the stroke, and then barked again. They dug hard. With every stroke they began to punish Cal, and Ulbrickson, and the sophomores, and anyone else who might doubt them, unleashing months' worth of frustration, demolishing the course, hurling their backs into the oncoming wind and rain. Bobby Moch had a habit of calling for big tens by attaching someone's name to the call—to give it more emotional impact. Sometimes it was "Give me ten for Al," or "Give me ten for Mr. Pocock." Now he shouted through his megaphone, "Give me ten big ones for Joe Beasley!" Nobody in the boat, including Moch apparently, had ever heard of Joe Beasley, but he was having fun now. They gave him ten big ones. Then he screamed, "And give me ten big ones for those sophomores!" The boat exploded forward. As they came around the bend and within sight of the crowd on the bridge, they were five lengths ahead. As they shot across the line and under the bridge, they were eight lengths ahead and still pulling away.

When it came time for the varsity race, the Cal fans finally got something to cheer about.

As Joe and the sophomore varsity paddled to their starting position, they figured that they pretty much had to win now, after what the JV had just done, not just to justify Ulbrickson's faith in them, but to keep their Olympic aspirations alive. From now on, in fact, they figured they had to win every race or it would be all over for them. Over the next sixteen minutes, they did everything they could to make sure it wasn't all over. After the race, the *San Francisco Chronicle*'s tough-as-nails sports editor, Bill Leiser, said simply, "It was a great battle. The best race I ever saw on the estuary."

Cal had been practicing fast starts all week, but neither boat was quite ready at the start. Once they were away, Washington leapt out to an early lead. Cal responded, quickly and decisively, raising its rate and pulling even, then moving quickly out in front by half a length. Both boats settled in and held their positions for the next mile and a half, with Washington's blades dipping in and out of the water almost stroke for stroke with Cal's at a steady thirty strokes per minute. As they approached Government Island and the halfway mark, California slowly increased its rate and stretched its lead out to a full length. George Morry, in the coxswain's seat, called for more, and the Washington rate went up to thirty-two, but Morry held it there as Cal went up to thirty-four and a half, refusing to yield to the temptation to panic or bolt. Ever so slowly, Washington began to claw its way back, inch by inch, still keeping the rate low but starting to gain on sheer power. By the time they reached the south end of the island, the Cal lead had been whittled down to a quarter of a length. Then they were bow to bow. Approaching the bend in the course, Washington slowly nosed out ahead of the California boat. Washington went up to thirty-four now, Cal to a punishing thirty-eight.

The two boats swung around the bend side by side and surged into view of the fans on the bridge. An armada of launches and pleasure craft was following them. Observers in those boats, studying the boys through binoculars, thought both crews looked tired.

California made a move, starting to sprint, going up to forty strokes per minute and charging forward again, back into the lead. The Cal fans erupted in cheers. Their boys were out in front by a quarter of a length and bearing down on the finish line. But George Morry did what he had been told to do. Ulbrickson had instructed him to keep the stroke rate as low as he could for as long as he possibly could. With his boys still rowing at thirty-four, Morry resisted the temptation to call for a higher rate, even as Cal maintained its frantic forty and the Fruitvale Avenue Bridge began to loom up ahead of them. Stroke rate is one thing and power is another. Morry knew he still had plenty of power at his disposal. He figured that by now Cal almost certainly didn't. He leaned forward and called out, "Gimme ten big ones!" The Washington boys dug hard. The boat leapt forward. At the end of ten strokes, the bows of the boats were dead even again. With the bridge and the finish line closing on them, Morry screamed again, "Gimme ten more!" Joe and Shorty and Roger and everyone with an oar in his hands threw everything he had into the last few pulls. In the coaching launch directly behind his boys, Al Ulbrickson held his breath. The boats shot under the bridge side by side.

A blue flag and a white flag dropped from the bridge simultaneously. The fans fell suddenly silent, confused. Someone in one of the following boats shouted, "Washington by a foot!" The Husky fans roared. Then a voice on the official loudspeaker boomed out, "California by two feet." Now the Cal fans roared. The radio broadcasters huddling under the shelter hesitated, then beamed the news out to the nation: "California Wins." The same message rattled out over the newswires. On the bridge, the Washington fans were adamant, pointing angrily at the water, gesticulating. Their boys had surged ahead at the end—anyone could see that. California fans who had been leaning over the railing as the boats passed below insisted that the nose of the Cal boat had gone under the bridge first, by three feet at least. The pandemonium increased. Long minutes passed. And then, suddenly, the voice on the loudspeaker crackled back to life: "Judges of the finish announce officially that Washington won by six feet." An enormous moan arose from the California fans en masse. In Seattle a news flash from Oakland interrupted regular radio programming, and people who had been sitting dejectedly by the radio stood up and slapped each other on the back and shook hands.

It turned out that neither crew, nor any of the official judges, had ever really had any doubt about the outcome. They just had trouble getting to the loudspeaker through the throng of people on the bridge. What most spectators had not realized was that the bridge ran across the estuary at a slight angle. The finish line, on the other hand, ran straight across the water, just about intersecting the bridge on the California side of the racecourse but intersecting the Washington side several yards short of the bridge. The nose of the California boat had indeed passed under the bridge first, but by then the first six feet of the Washington boat was already well over the line. When Ulbrickson got back to the hotel that night, he jotted a simple commentary in the logbook: "Quite a day."

The train ride home was jubilant. The hard feelings of the long fall and winter were forgotten; everyone had come out a winner. Tom Bolles was sure now he had a freshman crew at least equal to that of the previous year. The junior varsity had made their point, at least for now. The sophomores were the Pacific Coast varsity champions. Together they had swept California from its home water. Anything now seemed possible.

The day following the race it was front-page news in Seattle, a banner headline in the *Seattle Times* trumpeting, "Husky Crews Make Clean Sweep." On April 18 the city held its version of a ticker-tape parade to honor the crews, as well as a girls' swim team that had just returned from Chicago with a handful of medals and six national records and Jack Medica, a superstar swimmer who had himself just returned from victories in the East. Eighty members of the Husky marching band led the procession up Second Avenue and Pike Street as confetti and scraps of paper mixed with a steady, cold rain drifting down from clouds high above. Behind the band, in a flower-bedecked car, Mayor Smith rode with Al Ulbrickson and Tom Bolles, waving at the cheering crowd that lined the street four and five deep. Medica and the girls' swim team rode in a second car. Then came the main attraction—a long logging truck draped in flowers and green foliage carrying the varsity crew and their shell. The boys wore white sweaters with big purple Ws emblazoned on them. Each held a twelve-foot-long oar upright. As it crawled through downtown, the float looked something like an enormous green reptile with a sleek cedar spine and eight wavering spruce quills. From time to time, a relative or friend of one of the boys called out a greeting from the sidewalk or ran out into the street for a quick handshake. Joyce was at work, but Joe scanned the faces in the crowd, looking for his father or his half siblings, but they were nowhere to be seen.

The procession made its way to the Washington Athletic Club on Union Street. There the boys were ushered into a smoky room packed with hundreds of Seattle's leading citizens, each of whom had paid seventy-five cents to attend a special luncheon and get an up-close look at the returning heroes. Royal Brougham was the master of ceremonies, and the proceedings were broadcast live on radio.

The mayor, Tom Bolles, and Al Ulbrickson each gave brief talks. Ulbrickson heaped praise on all three crews and ended by saying, to cheers, "With support like this we'll win at Poughkeepsie and then it will be on to Berlin and the Olympics." The dean of the university spoke, as did the president of the chamber of commerce. Pretty much everyone who was anyone in town wanted in on the act. Then the boys from all three boats were called up onto the stage. They were introduced, one at a time, each to long, sustained applause.

When it was Joe's turn, he stood for a moment looking out over the scene before him. White light poured into the room from tall windows flanked by heavy velvet curtains. Enormous crystal chandeliers hung shimmering from high, ornately plastered ceilings. The beaming faces of large-bellied men in three-piece suits and matronly-looking women bedecked with jewelry gazed up at him. They sat at tables spread with crisp white linen tablecloths and gleaming silverware and crystal stemware and platters heaped with hot food. Waiters in white coats and black bow ties scurried among the tables, carrying trays with still more food.

As Joe raised a hand to acknowledge the wave of applause rising to greet him, he found himself struggling desperately to keep back tears. He had never let himself dream of standing in a place like this, surrounded by people like these. It startled him but at the same time it also filled him with gratitude, and as he stood at the front of the room that day acknowledging the applause, he felt a sudden surge of something unfamiliar—a sense of pride that was deeper and more heartfelt than any he had ever felt before. Now it was on to Poughkeepsie again, and then maybe even Berlin. Everything finally seemed to be starting to turn golden.

Rowing into the Montlake Cut

CHAPTER TEN

A boat is a sensitive thing, an eight-oared shell, and if it isn't let go free, it doesn't work for you.

—George Yeoman Pocock

In an age when Americans enjoy dozens of cable sports channels, when professional athletes often command annual salaries in the tens of millions of dollars, and when the entire nation all but shuts down for a virtual national holiday on Super Bowl Sunday, it's hard to fully appreciate how important the rising prominence of the University of Washington's crew was to the people of Seattle in 1935. Seattle was a city that had long been considered, and was sometimes prone to consider itself, a backwater in many regards, and not least in the world of sports. The university's football team had historically been a winning proposition, with an astonishing accomplishment to its credit—a record sixty-three consecutive games without a defeat between 1907 and 1917. During that streak, under coach Gil Dobie, Washington scored 1,930 points to its opponents' 118. But it must be noted that Dobie's adherence to the rules may have been a wee bit lax. On one occasion he was reputed to have fit a pair of his smaller players with iron shoulder pads, an equipment adjustment that gave the fellows a seemingly uncanny ability to take down much bigger men. At any rate, the Washington Sun Dodgers (rebranded the Huskies at the suggestion of the 1922 crew) played almost entirely on the West Coast and had made it to the national stage of the Rose Bowl only twice, once tying Navy and once losing to Alabama.

Seattle baseball had never really made it onto a national stage at all. There had been a succession of professional ball teams in town since May 24, 1890, when the Seattle Reds took on the Spokane Falls Spokanes. In the years that followed, the city had seen baseball teams variously called the Seattles, the Klondikers, the Rainmakers, the Braves, the Giants, the Rainiers, the Siwashes, the Indians, and, at one unfortunate juncture, the Seattle Clamdiggers. But all these were minor league teams that played only in local and regional contests. And baseball in Seattle had recently experienced a major setback—one of many more to come—when the wooden stands at the Indians' ballpark, Dugdale Park, burned to the ground in July 1932. The team had moved to Civic Field, a high school football stadium. But the field had no grass, was little more than a rectangle of dirt and stones. During and between games, grounds crews scurried about with gunnysacks picking up as many rocks as possible, to keep the players from tripping over them when racing for a fly ball or flaying themselves alive when sliding into a base. It proved to be a hopeless cause and an endless task. One of the high schoolers who played there, Edo Vanni—later the manager of the Rainiers—said of the field, "If a horse got stranded out there, he would have starved to death. It was nothing but rocks." For decades, baseball fans in Seattle had to choose an eastern team to root for if they wanted a stake in the big leagues.

Seattle sports had once risen briefly to international prominence, in 1917, when the city's professional hockey team, the Metropolitans, became the first American team to win the Stanley Cup, defeating the Montreal Canadiens. But the Metropolitans ordinarily played only in the Pacific Coast Hockey Association, and when the owner of their arena did not renew their lease in 1924, the team folded.

Given this meager sports heritage, the Washington crews' victories gave Seattleites something they hadn't had in a long time—something, in fact, that they had never really had. With the sweep in California, recent victories in Poughkeepsie, and now talk even of future victories in the Olympics, any Seattleite could suddenly stick out his chest and crow a bit. He could write to friends and relations back east about it. He could read about it in the Post-Intelligencer in the morning and then enjoy reading about it again in the Seattle Times in the evening. He could talk to the barber about it when getting a haircut and know that the barber cared about it as much as he did. Those boys in their boats were—length by length and victory by victory—suddenly beginning to put Seattle on the map, and they were likely to do more of it in the near future. Everyone in town believed that now, and it pulled them together and made them feel better about themselves in a deeply troubled time.

If they lingered too long over the front page of the Times or the Post-Intelligencer, though, Seattleites could not avoid seeing harbingers of other troubles to come.

On April 14, the day after the Pacific Coast Regatta on the Oakland Estuary, the dust storms of the past several years were suddenly eclipsed by a single catastrophe that is still remembered in the Plains states as Black Sunday. In only a few hours' time, cold, dry winds howling out of the north scoured from dry fields more than two times the amount of soil that had been excavated from the Panama Canal and lifted it eight thousand feet into the sky. Across much of five states, late afternoon sunlight gave way to utter darkness. The dust particles the wind carried generated so much static electricity in the air that barbed-wire fences glowed in the midday darkness. Farmers at work in their fields crumpled to their hands and knees and groped aimlessly about, unable to find their way to their own doorsteps. Cars careened off roads and into ditches, where their occupants clutched cloths to their faces, struggled to breathe, gagged, and coughed up dirt. Sometimes they abandoned their cars and staggered up to the houses of strangers and pounded on their front doors, begging for and receiving shelter.

The next day, Kansas City AP bureau chief Ed Stanley inserted the phrase "the dust bowl" into a wire service account of the devastation, and a new term entered the American lexicon. Over the next few months, as the extent of the devastation settled in, the trickle of ragged refugees that Joe Rantz had witnessed heading west the previous summer became a torrent. Within a few years, two and a half million Americans would pull up stakes and head west into an uncertain future—rootless, dispossessed, bereft of the simple comfort and dignity of having a place to call home.

For months, things had been looking up in America. Job offerings had begun to appear again in the *Seattle Times* and the *Post-Intelligencer* as they had in hundreds of newspapers across the country; men like Harry Rantz had finally begun to find meaningful work. But the winds of April 14 suddenly blew away the slowly accumulating hopes of millions. Within weeks, the *Post-Intelligencer* was warning the locals to expect company, and competition for those jobs, soon. "Great Migration Westward About to Begin: Homeseekers Look Upon Northwest as Promised Land," read a *Post-Intelligencer* headline on May 4. Employment agencies in Seattle received inquiries about the availability of jobs—any kind of job, no matter how low paying—from as far away as Missouri and Arkansas. Most of the migrants were farmers, and real estate offices were flooded with inquiries about the availability of cheap acreage near Seattle. Eager agents answered the inquiries with assurances that there was plenty of inexpensive land available. But they seldom mentioned that around the Puget Sound acreage generally came with stumps—hundreds of stumps per acre—each of which had to be pulled or dug or dynamited out of the earth; nor did they mention that the underlying soil was glacial till, hard-packed clay interlaced with stones; nor that the climate was cool and gray, not suited for growing the kinds of crops that had long sustained the people of the American Midwest.

At the same time, the drumbeat of ominous headlines emanating from Europe had begun to grow steadily louder and more insistent that spring. Four weeks' worth of headlines from the *Seattle Times* alone were reason enough for worry: "Death Penalty for Pacifists Is Decreed as Germany Girds" (April 19); "Nazis Jail Aged Nuns, Monks in New Attack on Christianity" (April 27); "German Move to Build U-Boats Rouses Anxiety in Great Britain" (April 28); "Britain to Match Nazi Planes; Calls on Hitler to Fix Limits" (May 2); "Hitler Warned by Britain Not to Militarize Rhineland Zone" (May 7); "Nazis Have New Weapon: 60-Knot Boat" (May 17); "Hitler Police Jail U.S. Citizen" (May 18). The dark news was difficult to ignore. But not impossible. The vast majority of Americans, in Seattle and elsewhere, did exactly that. The affairs of Europe still seemed a million miles away, and that's exactly where most people wanted to keep them.

On the first day of training for Poughkeepsie, Ulbrickson surprised a gaggle of sportswriters at the shell house by announcing that the sophomores weren't necessarily going to keep their varsity status in Poughkeepsie, despite their win in Oakland. He pointed out that there were older boys in the junior varsity boat with a lot of experience and talent. Some of them deserved a shot at a national varsity championship before they graduated. Insofar as it went, Ulbrickson was probably entirely sincere on that point. He had in fact felt bad about disappointing the older boys in Oakland, especially in light of the fact that they had won the final trials on the estuary after he had broken his word to them. But there was something else. He was well aware that the older boys had utterly dominated their competition in Oakland. The sophomores, on the other hand, had won by the narrowest of margins, and they had caused their coach a good deal of heartburn while he waited for the official results. That hadn't helped their cause at all.

Joe and the other sophomores couldn't believe it. They hadn't just beaten another crew on the estuary; they'd beaten Cal's varsity, the defending national champions. They'd reached beyond themselves to defeat older and much more experienced boys, the same crew that Ebright would presumably take to Poughkeepsie. Yet suddenly their varsity status was back on the line again. Furious, they resolved to put the JV boys in their place as soon as they got out on the water.

Instead they thoroughly sabotaged themselves and their cause. On May 9, Ulbrickson held another head-to-head contest between the two boats. Riding along in Ulbrickson's launch was an important guest: J. Lyman Bingham of the Amateur Athletic Union, a close associate of Avery Brundage, the president of both the AAU and the American Olympic Committee. When Ulbrickson shouted the start command through his megaphone—"Ready all . . . Row!"— the JV boat, with Bobby Moch in the stern, pulled away from the sophomores promptly, easily, and decisively. Ulbrickson gunned the motor on the launch, ran the two boats down, and bellowed, "Way enough!" He lined them up again, and called another start. Again, the JV pulled away decisively. Bingham turned to Ulbrickson and asked, dryly, "Which did you say was the varsity? Maybe I'm watching the wrong crew." Ulbrickson was flummoxed.

Over the next several weeks Ulbrickson raced the two boats against each other again and again. Occasionally the sophomores won, but usually they lost. They rowed well when left on their own, but the moment they got a glimpse of the older boys they fell apart completely. Months of taunting had gotten under their skins.

In April Ulbrickson had all but crowed to both national wire services that this all-sophomore crew was great—"potentially the greatest crew I have coached," he'd said, in front of the whole world. Now they seemed bent on making a fool of him. He marched them into his office, closed the door, and read them the riot act. "If you cannot get to doing business, I will break up the combination," he growled. Ulbrickson hated to even say it. He still had not forgotten the stunning manner in which the sophomores had won the freshman title in Poughkeepsie the year before. Nor had anybody else. Almost every press account that mentioned them still harkened back to that moment in New York when their boat had pulled away from the field as if propelled by young gods rather than by young men. But Ulbrickson knew that, in the end, it wasn't gods but young men who had to win crew races, and, unlike gods, young men were fallible. It was his job to find their failings and remedy them if he could and to replace them if he couldn't.

Rowing is, in a number of ways, a sport of fundamental paradoxes. For one thing, an eight-oared racing shell—powered by unusually large and physically powerful men or women—is commanded, controlled, and directed by the smallest and least powerful person in the boat. The coxswain (nowadays often a female even in an otherwise male crew) must have the force of character to look men or women twice his or her size in the face, bark orders at them, and be confident that the leviathans will respond instantly and unquestioningly to those orders. It is perhaps the most incongruous relationship in sports.

Another paradox lies in the physics of the sport. The object of the endeavor is, of course, to make the boat move through the water as quickly as possible. But the faster the boat goes, the harder it is to row well. The enormously complicated sequence of movements, each of which an oarsman must execute with exquisite precision, becomes exponentially more difficult to perform as the stroke rate increases. Rowing at a beat of thirty-six is vastly more challenging than rowing at a beat of twenty-six. As the tempo accelerates, the penalty of a miscue—an oar touching the water a fraction of a second too early or too late, for instance—becomes ever more severe, the opportunity for disaster ever greater. At the same time, the exertion required to maintain a high rate makes the physical pain all the more devastating and therefore the likelihood of a miscue greater. In this sense, speed is both the rower's ultimate goal and also his greatest foe. Put another way, beautiful and effective rowing often means painful rowing. An unnamed coach is reputed to have said, bluntly, "Rowing is like a beautiful duck. On the surface it is all grace, but underneath the bastard's paddling like mad!"

But the greatest paradox of the sport has to do with the psychological makeup of the people who pull the oars. Great oarsmen and oarswomen are necessarily made of conflicting stuff—of oil and water, fire and earth. On the one hand, they must possess enormous self-confidence, strong egos, and titanic willpower. They must be almost immune to frustration. Nobody who does not believe deeply in himself or herself—in his or her ability to endure hardship and to prevail over adversity—is likely even to attempt something as audacious as competitive rowing at the highest levels. The sport offers so many opportunities for suffering and so few opportunities for glory that only the most tenaciously self-reliant and self-motivated are likely to succeed at it. And yet, at the same time—and this is key—no other sport demands and rewards the complete abandonment of the self the way that rowing does. Great crews may have men or women of exceptional talent or strength; they may have outstanding coxswains or stroke oars or bowmen; but they have no stars. The team effort—the perfectly synchronized flow of muscle, oars, boat, and water; the single, whole, unified, and beautiful symphony that a crew in motion becomes—is all that matters. Not the individual, not the self.

The psychology is complex. Even as rowers must subsume their often fierce sense of independence and self-reliance, at the same time they must hold true to their individuality, their unique capabilities as oarsmen or oarswomen or, for that matter, as human beings. Even if they could, few rowing coaches would simply clone their biggest, strongest, smartest, and most capable rowers. Crew races are not won by clones. They are won by crews, and great crews are carefully balanced blends of both physical abilities and personality types. In physical terms, for instance, one rower's arms might be longer than another's, but the latter might have a stronger back than the former. Neither is necessarily a better or more valuable oarsman than the other; both the long arms and the strong back are assets to the boat. But if they are to row well together, each of these oarsmen must adjust to the needs and capabilities of the other. Each must be prepared to compromise something in the way of optimizing his stroke for the overall benefit of the boat— the shorter-armed man reaching a little farther, the longer-armed man foreshortening his reach just a bit—so that both men's oars remain parallel and both blades enter and exit the water at precisely the same moment. This highly refined coordination and cooperation must be multiplied out across eight individuals of varying statures and physiques to make the most of each individual's strengths. Only in this way can the capabilities that come with diversity—lighter, more technical rowers in the bow and stronger, heavier pullers in the middle of the boat, for instance—be turned to advantage rather than disadvantage.

And capitalizing on diversity is perhaps even more important when it comes to the characters of the oarsmen. A crew composed entirely of eight amped-up, overtly aggressive oarsmen will often degenerate into a dysfunctional brawl in a boat or exhaust itself in the first leg of a long race. Similarly, a boatload of quiet but strong introverts may never find the common core of fiery resolve that causes the boat to explode past its competitors when all seems lost. Good crews are good blends of personalities: someone to lead the charge, someone to hold something in reserve; someone to pick a fight, someone to make peace; someone to think things through, someone to charge ahead without thinking. Somehow all this must mesh. That's the steepest challenge. Even after the right mixture is found, each man or woman in the boat must recognize his or her place in the fabric of the crew, accept it, and accept the others as they are. It is an exquisite thing when it all comes together in just the right way. The intense bonding and the sense of exhilaration that results from it are what many oarsmen row for, far more than for trophies or accolades. But it takes young men or women of extraordinary character as well as extraordinary physical ability to pull it off.

That's what Al Ulbrickson believed he had seen in Washington's sophomore boat in Poughkeepsie the previous June. They had become that perfect thing that all crew coaches seek. He remained almost desperately reluctant now to tear the fabric of what held them together then, but the boys seemed to be leaving him no choice. They seemed to have come unraveled all on their own.

On May 22 he tested both boats again, rowing two miles at a racing beat. The older boys won by a length. The next day he tried them at three miles. The older boys turned in an impressive 15:53, a full 8 seconds faster than the sophomores. Finally, Ulbrickson told the reporters waiting on the ramp what they'd been expecting to hear for weeks now. Barring some kind of miracle, the older boys would race as the varsity crew at Poughkeepsie; the sophomores would almost certainly be demoted to junior varsity status, despite winning in California. But he added that the sophomores would continue to row together. He'd keep an open mind, Ulbrickson said, and see how both boats performed on the Hudson before the regatta. It was clear to everyone, though, including Joe and his dejected crewmates, that his mind was all but made up.

Seattle's sportswriters weren't at all sure that it was the correct decision. The *Post-Intelligencer*'s Royal Brougham had been loudly backing the cause of the sophomores for months, despite their recent sloppiness. George Varnell of the *Seattle Times* had watched the last few trials closely, and he'd noted something that he wondered if Ulbrickson had picked up on. In the two-mile and the three-mile trials, the sophomores had gotten off the line badly, flailing at the water inefficiently, as if overexcited and flustered, and letting the older boys get out ahead of them. But by the end of the first mile, they seemed to row as well as the older boys. What's more, in the three-mile trials the older boys had begun to look decidedly ragged by the time they entered the last mile. Clarence Dirks, a writer for the *Post-Intelligencer*, had already noticed the same thing. The sophomores seemed to get smoother with every pull of the oar, and they had been closing fast at the end of that third mile. The varsity course at Poughkeepsie was four miles long.

The trip to Poughkeepsie was not the boisterous and carefree jaunt of the year before. The weather was hot all the way across the country, the train stuffy and uncomfortable. Al Ulbrickson was on edge. Following the triple victories in California, he had taken to telling Seattle that he would sweep the regatta in Poughkeepsie this year, winning all three events. In response the excited citizenry had shelled out precious nickels and quarters and dollars, raising an astonishing twelve thousand dollars to send the crews east. Ulbrickson figured he needed to repay the debt by making good on his word.

The tension between the sophomores and the older boys was palpable. To the extent that it was possible, they tried to stay out of one another's way, but the train was a confining environment and it was a challenge for both groups all the way east. Day after stifling day, the coaches and crews sat in small, almost sullen groups, playing cards, reading pulp magazines, shooting the bull, choosing whom they went to the dining car with and whom they didn't. Joe and Shorty Hunt and Roger Morris kept largely to themselves in one corner of a coach. There was no singing this time; Joe had left his guitar at home.

Five days later, they arrived in Poughkeepsie. When they stepped off the train, on a Sunday morning, they were all relieved to find themselves in the midst of a cool, refreshing summer rainstorm rather than the sticky, oppressive heat they had been anticipating. As Pocock issued anxious instructions, they gingerly unloaded the shells from the baggage car. A large construction crane lifted the coaching launch from a flatcar and placed it gently in the Hudson. Then the boys began to unload the dozens of milk cans they had brought along. Each contained ten gallons of fresh, clear, sweet Northwest water. They would row on the Hudson's water. They might even shower in it. But they weren't about to drink it again.

Reporters pressed around Ulbrickson as he detrained. He still hadn't officially announced his varsity boat assignments, but he was frank: "The sophomore crew has been a deep disappointment to me." He went on to elaborate: "We can't figure out what happened to them. . . . They began losing their punch a while before the California race . . . unless they come back again they'll row here as the junior varsity." The eastern sportswriters were flabbergasted. They could not believe that Ulbrickson would even consider demoting the boys whom they had seen with their own eyes sweeping to victory so easily a year ago, boys who had gone on to defeat the California varsity just two months ago.

The next day the Husky crews performed a time-honored Poughkeepsie ritual and visited each of their rivals' shell houses to pay grudging respect to their competitors before taking to the river. At each stop Ulbrickson had to explain, all over again, to his coaching counterpart that, yes, indeed, he planned to send the sophomores off in the junior varsity boat. The coaches were as incredulous as the reporters had been. Venerable old Jim Ten Eyck of Syracuse, now eighty-three years old, shook his gray head and said he didn't believe Ulbrickson would really do it, that in his opinion it was a ruse, that on June 18 the sophomores would go off in the varsity boat. After Ulbrickson and his boys left, Ten Eyck shook his head again and said, "Ulbrickson must have two great boats if he can do that."

The sophomore boat was not now, in fact, quite composed entirely of sophomores. Ulbrickson had swapped a senior, Wink Winslow, for George Morry, as coxswain, to capitalize on Winslow's greater experience with river rowing. Other than that, though, it was the crew that had swept to victory here so effortlessly a year before.

By the time they got to rowing, things were tough out on the water. It was still rainy, and a cold, stiff wind was whipping downstream. The river was a heaving mass of rollers, the water dark and oily. These were exactly the kinds of conditions that the Washington boys most dreaded, not because of the rain or the wind, with which they were better acquainted than most, but because of the peculiar sideways motion of the river water when wind-driven waves interacted with a tidal current. Ulbrickson hustled the boys out onto the water twice that day to give them as much exposure as he could to the challenging conditions. The Washington boats were the only ones there. All the other crews—having been visited by the Huskies and having sneaked a peek at them in action—were content to remain in the warmth of their shell houses for the rest of the day.

The warmest and coziest of them were the Bears from California. Ky Ebright and his freshman and varsity crews had arrived several days before and moved into a brand-spanking-new boathouse on the more convenient Poughkeepsie side of the river, complete with city water, hot showers, a dining room, cooking facilities, electric lights, and spacious sleeping quarters. The contrast with their own arrangements did not set well with the Washington boys. As the rain continued to fall and the wind to blow, their rickety old boathouse on the Highland side of the river, with its leaky roof and cold river-water showers, seemed by comparison to have been designed to make them as miserable as possible. And the meager fare at Mother Palmer's boarding-house up on the bluff was proving downright starvation inducing this year. Instead of sleeping six to a room, as they had the year before, they now had to find places to stretch out eight or nine of their long frames in each room. Even absent the stifling heat of the previous year, the accommodations were decidedly uncomfortable.

What likely made Al Ulbrickson most uncomfortable, though, was late-breaking news he had just received from Ebright—that shortly before leaving Berkeley, he had moved four boys from his national championship crew of the previous year back into this year's varsity shell. All told, in fact, six of the boys in the Cal boat were now veterans of last year's championship crew. Ulbrickson had to wonder if Cal's losing crew in Oakland had, to some extent, been a ruse employed by Ebright en route to the greater prize of a national championship in Poughkeepsie. Worse, from Ulbrickson's perspective, was that after a few days of watching the reconstituted Cal varsity boat working out on the Hudson, the throng of bookmakers and sportswriters who had descended on Poughkeepsie had already begun to make comparisons between this Cal crew and the great crew that won Olympic gold for California in 1932. And still worse news, in some ways, was the skinny on Cal's big stroke oar, Eugene Berkenkamp. In the Poughkeepsie cigar shops, where men gathered to exchange the latest news and keep an eye on the odds that bookies were offering, the straight dope was that Berkenkamp was easily the equal of the great Peter Donlon. Donlon had stroked Cal to its other Olympic gold medal, in 1928, and to the fastest time ever on the Poughkeepsie course.

On June 12, six days before the race, Ulbrickson put both boats head-to-head on the river again, and the sophomores fell apart as soon as they saw the older boys. They came in a staggering eight lengths behind them. That finally settled it. Ulbrickson threw in the towel. The sophomores were officially demoted to junior varsity status; the older boys would row as varsity. For Joe and his crewmates, it was a terrible blow, but from Al Ulbrickson's point of view, his new varsity's eight-length margin of victory seemed to betoken good things to come in the climactic race on June 18. And it was the varsity race that he most wanted to win. Washington hadn't managed that since 1926, when he himself stroked the Huskies to victory here. The same afternoon Ulbrickson made the sophomores' demotion final, though, the *New York Times'*

Robert Kelley, watching the newly anointed Washington varsity in a trial, observed the same thing that reporters back in Seattle had noticed earlier—in the fourth and final mile the older boys seemed to be dragging just a bit.

Later that day Ulbrickson received a hand-delivered message from the president of the United States. A few days before, Ulbrickson had invited FDR—an enthusiastic crew fan, whose son Franklin Junior would in a few days be rowing for Harvard against Yale—to ride along in his coaching launch and observe a time trial. The president responded regretfully that he could not make it, as he had to be in Washington, D.C., to sign the extension of the National Recovery Administration into law before going to New London to watch Franklin Junior row. But that evening Ulbrickson got a call from Hyde Park, just up the river. It was John Roosevelt, the president's youngest son. He had also rowed for Harvard, and he wondered if he might ride along in the president's place.

The following day, with John Roosevelt—a tall, good-looking kid with his hair slicked back and a warm, fetching smile—riding along in the launch, Ulbrickson held one final trial, just to see what to expect on race day. He started the older boys, his new varsity, at four miles. At the three-mile mark, Joe and the sophomores joined in. They quickly powered ahead of the varsity. At the two-mile mark, Tom Bolles's exceptional freshmen joined in. For the rest of the way, the sophomores and the freshmen battled for first with a clearly exhausted varsity trailing both. At the end the freshmen came in half a length ahead of Joe and the sophomores, with both boats well ahead of the new varsity. George Pocock, surprised, said, "The sophomores looked like something today for the first time in weeks. It surely looked like a crew that is coming." So far as we know, Al Ulbrickson said nothing—neither publicly nor to those closest to him—but he must have tossed and turned in his bunk that night. By now the die was cast, the programs had been printed, the older boys would still row as the varsity. But he couldn't have liked what he had just seen.

On June 14, Ulbrickson invited Royal Brougham upstairs in the crew quarters to see something. For months, Brougham had been using his daily sports column, "The Morning After," to sing the praises of the sophomores, sometimes at the expense of the older boys who now constituted the varsity. The older boys had taken it as a challenge. Now, in their dressing area, they had put up signs to keep themselves motivated: "Remember the Morning After!" and "Go Get Brougham's Babies!" Furthermore, Ulbrickson told Brougham,

Bobby Moch had a new mantra when he called for extra effort: "Take ten for RB." When Moch resorted to that one, Ulbrickson said, "the boys get so hot they have to wrap asbestos around their oar handles to keep the boat from burning up."

What Ulbrickson likely didn't know was that Bobby Moch had worked out an elaborate set of verbal codes to which only he and his crew knew the real meanings. Some of them were simply abbreviated versions of longer commands he sometimes called out in the boat. "SOS," for instance, meant "slow on slides." "OK" meant "keep the boat on keel." Most, though, were coded because neither Moch nor his boys wanted the other crews or the coaches to know their exact meaning. "WTA" meant "wax their ass." "BS" meant "beat the sophs." And another, along the same lines, "BAB," meant "beat Al's babies."

All was quiet at the Washington shell house on the morning of the regatta. Unlike football coaches, who often try to key their players up for a big game, rowing coaches sometimes take the opposite tack. Well-trained oarsmen, in Ulbrickson's experience, were like high-strung racehorses. Once they were in motion, they'd bust their hearts to win. Their willpower was indomitable. But you didn't want to bring them to the gate in a lather. He always kept things low-key before a race, and the boys spent the morning dozing, playing cards, and shooting the bull.

As many as a hundred thousand people had been expected for the regatta, but by midafternoon only perhaps a third of that number had showed up. It was a miserably wet, blustery day, with rain slanting down out of dark skies in torrents—no kind of day for standing out in the elements and watching a race. A navy destroyer and a coast guard cutter, the 240-foot *Tampa*, were on hand, but fewer than a hundred smaller craft—sailboats, houseboats, and yachts—had made their way to the finish line, where they lay swaying and bobbing at anchor. Nearly everyone aboard them stayed belowdecks for as long as possible while waiting for the races to begin.

Late in the afternoon, they began to emerge onto their decks in peacoats and slickers. In Poughkeepsie a group of fans bought bright pink oilskin tablecloths and fashioned capes and hoods out of them. Another group raided a hardware store, bought a roll of tar paper, and contrived to make raincoats out of it. Gradually, dark masses of people huddled under umbrellas made their way down the steep descent from Main Street to the water, where they took up positions along the shore or waited in line to cross the river on ferries. The observation train began to fill up, though this year the open-sided cars were not as popular as the enclosed coaches, which promptly reached capacity. At the shell houses on both sides of the river, boys finished rigging their shells. Of the sixteen shells on the river that day, George Pocock had built fifteen.

A little before 4:00 p.m., in a driving rain, Tom Bolles's freshmen paddled upriver to the stake boats and took their starting position, with Columbia on one side and California on the other. Tom Bolles and Al Ulbrickson climbed into the train's press car, along with John Roosevelt, who had overnight become an enthusiastic Husky fan. Water was dripping from the brim of Bolles's raggedy old good-luck hat. Since he had started wearing it on race days in 1930, he hadn't lost a race.

It was even more miserable out on the water than onshore. The boats lined up, the starting gun fired, and the regatta—and Washington's quest to sweep the Hudson—was under way almost before anyone realized it. Royal Brougham, hunched over an NBC microphone, began to call the race. Fans along the shoreline peered through the curtain of rain, struggling to distinguish one boat from another.

For thirty strokes, it was a race. Then, with Don Hume at stroke, big Gordy Adam in the middle of the boat, and the tenacious Johnny White up in seat number two all settling into their rhythms, the Washington freshmen began to pull ahead, easing out in front of the others as if effortlessly, stroke by stroke.

By the end of a half mile, it was all but decided. The rest of the way was a cakewalk. In the last mile, the Washington boat lengthened its lead a bit more with each stroke. During the last hundred yards, in the press car, Tom Bolles became agitated, then excited, and then, finally, by all accounts, "hysterical," waving his soggy old hat in the air as his freshmen—an even better crew than the previous year's, he had been saying for months—slid across the line, defeating California by four lengths.

By the time the 5:00 p.m. junior varsity race was set to go off, the rain had abated a bit, the downpour having given way to intermittent showers, but it was still windy and the water was still rough. As Joe paddled upriver toward the starting line, he, like his crewmates, had a lot to think about. Cal had not sent a JV boat to Poughkeepsie this year, but the eastern schools offered plenty of power and talent. Navy was a particular threat. The greatest danger, though, lay between the gunnels of his own shell. The defeats at the hands of the older boys had shaken his and the other boys' self-confidence. For weeks now, the whole boat had been the subject of relentless second-guessing and humiliation. Everyone from Seattle to New York seemed to want to know one thing—what the hell had happened to them? Neither he nor anybody else in the boat could begin to answer the question. All they knew was that their easy belief in themselves after the victory in California had long since shattered and given way to a mixture of despair and anxiety, as well as a fierce determination bordering on rage—an all-consuming desire to salvage some degree of respect before the season ended. As they sat at the starting line, in the *City of Seattle*, rolling with the choppy waves, waiting for the crack of the starting gun, with rainwater running down their necks and backs and dripping from their noses, the real question was whether they had the maturity and discipline to keep their minds in the boat, or whether the rage and fear and uncertainty would unhinge them. They fidgeted in their seats, subtly adjusting their grips on the oars, shifting their weight, adjusting angles, trying to keep their muscles from knotting up and freezing in place. An uncertain wind buffeted their faces, forcing their eyes to narrow.

At the gun, they got off slowly, falling behind all three other boats: Navy, Syracuse, and Cornell. For half a mile, it looked as if they might, in fact, disintegrate as a crew, as they had done so often lately. Then something kicked in—something that had been missing for a long while. Somehow determination conquered despair. They began to pull in long, sweet, precisely synchronized strokes, rowing at a composed beat of thirty-three. By the end of the first mile, they had found their swing and surged into the lead. Cornell crept up behind them and briefly threatened but then fell back. Navy made a bid, charging forward as they passed under the railroad bridge at the two-mile mark, but Wink Winslow called for more. The beat went up a notch, to thirty-four, then another notch, to thirty-five. The Navy boat hesitated and then began to fade.

For the remaining mile and a half, the sophomores settled in and rowed gorgeously—a long, sleek line of perfection—passing under the automobile bridge and finishing a comfortable two lengths ahead of Navy. A barrage of bombs went off on the bridge to signal their victory. Sitting at his radio microphone, Royal Brougham exulted at the triumph of his favorites. At the end of the three-mile race, he declared, the sophomores had looked to him just as they had at the end of the two-mile race the year before—as if they could keep on rowing right down the river to New York City and see the town without breaking a sweat.

In the press coach on the observation train, Al Ulbrickson watched silently. He remained thus, utterly impassive, as the train began to reverse course, backing four miles up the river for the beginning of the varsity race. Inside he could only have been churning. He stood now on the precipice of doing what no coach had ever done, winning all three Poughkeepsie races in eight-oared boats, fulfilling his promise to the people of Seattle, and coming home with a clean shot at going to Berlin.

As six o'clock and the start of the climactic race approached, the weather improved a bit more, though it continued to rain lightly and intermittently. More people abandoned the bars and hotel lobbies of Poughkeepsie and made their way down to the river. Rain or not, nobody in town that day wanted to miss out on seeing what sort of crew Ulbrickson had come up with that could displace his talented sophomores.

Seven varsity crews paddled to the starting line, to race for the national title, in a ghostly light mist. California had drawn the most favorable lane—lane number one, nearest the western bank of the river, where the current was least likely to affect a boat. Washington was right next door, in lane number two. Navy, Syracuse, Cornell, Columbia, and Pennsylvania stretched out across the river in lanes three through seven.

The referee called, "Ready all?" One by one, the coxswains shouted a few last-minute commands to their crews and then lowered their hands. The starting gun fired. All seven boats lurched off the line together. Rowing stroke for stroke, they remained tightly bunched up for a hundred yards. Then Washington slowly edged out to a slight lead of about four feet. In the stern of his boat, the newly built *Tamanawas*, Bobby Moch told his crew to settle in. He was happy to find that they could hold their lead with the boys rowing at thirty-two. At a half mile, Washington continued to lead by about the same margin, with Syracuse just behind them and the midshipmen of Navy, on their outside, just a few feet behind Syracuse. Cornell and California were trailing badly.

Over the next half mile, Cornell slowly moved up on the outside, clawing its way into third position. But Washington expanded its lead over Syracuse. Cal still trailed the field. In his car on the observation train, Ky Ebright was worried. He leaned forward, peering through a pair of binoculars, studying the boats intently. He did not think his boys were staying close enough to make up the ground later. At a mile and a half, Washington was out in front by open water and stretching its lead. In the press car, the Seattle sportswriters and Washington fans began hooting and hollering now, led by, of all people, John Roosevelt, who had begun to chant, "Come on, Washington. Come on . . ." Fans on the docks and yachts in Poughkeepsie began to take up variations of the same chant as the boats came into view upriver. Surprising numbers of them seemed to want to see something historic here—that elusive sweep of the Hudson—even if it was a western crew that accomplished the feat. As they crossed the two-and-a-half-mile mark, Washington remained in the lead, though its advantage had shrunk to about ten feet. Al Ulbrickson watched closely from his seat in the press car amid the storm of chanting fans. He was still a mile and a half from doing what he desperately wanted to do, and he knew it. And he could see California and Cornell finally starting to move up on both sides of his boat. Navy and Syracuse were fading. It was going to be Washington, Cornell, or California.

Inch by inch the other two boats began to gain on Washington. Bobby Moch was riding the stern of the *Tamanawas* like a jockey now, leaning forward into the rain, urging the boat on, screaming for big tens, calling on the boys to take the stroke rate higher, then higher still. In the middle of the boat, big Jim McMillin was taking huge, powerful, smooth strokes. Up front Chuck Day, the number two man, was trying to finesse it, trying to keep the boat in perfect balance stroke after stroke even as Moch kept calling for more. But they were running out of steam, and California and Cornell just kept coming. By the time the three boats passed under the railroad bridge at mile three, Cornell had nosed out in front. Then Cal came up to match them. Slowly, agonizingly, Washington fell into third. Over the final mile, Cal and Cornell battled nose to nose, so close together that nobody could tell for sure who was ahead at any given moment. But everyone could tell that Washington had fallen two lengths behind.

As the leaders crossed the line, pandemonium ensued. On the automobile bridge, Mike Bogo, the three-hundred-pound Poughkeepsie barkeep in charge of setting off explosives to signal the lane number of the winner, detonated five bombs, for Cornell. Cal fans howled in outrage. Cornell fans rushed up the hill to the town's principal bookie and demanded, and were paid, their winnings. Minutes later the official results were announced: Ky Ebright and

California had won their third consecutive national varsity title, by one-third of a second. California fans rushed up the hill and demanded their winnings from the same bookie, who again paid out. He was now thirty thousand dollars in the hole, and soon officially out of business. Mike Bogo, dejected, later commented, "I don't care who wins. I just like to bust them bombs."

Cal hadn't just won it—they'd done so in a near record time of eighteen minutes and fifty-two seconds, despite a stiff crosswind and heavy chop. The only crew ever to have turned in a faster time was Ebright's own Olympic gold medal crew of 1928.

Al Ulbrickson never betrayed a glimmer of emotion. Before leaving the press car, he dutifully congratulated Ky Ebright and then gamely fielded the barrage of questions leveled at him. Royal Brougham fired the first and potentially most lethal: Had he made a critical mistake by demoting his sophomores? "No siree!" Ulbrickson boomed out. "The sophomores rowed a great race, but they would never have finished third in that varsity event. That was one of the fastest fields in the history of the regatta . . . we didn't have the power or the poundage to beat those other fellows." But the next morning, Brougham pointed out again in his column that "those walloping sophomores of mine" had looked mighty fresh to him at the end of three miles, the varsity not so much.

For Ulbrickson, there was one overriding, and dark, fact to be confronted: he had failed again to make good on his public promises. It was very much an open question whether he was going to get another chance.

On June 21 the *Post-Intelligencer* ran a banner headline in its sports section: "$10,000 Crew Offer to Be Made for Tom Bolles." The accompanying story asserted that an unnamed eastern college had approached Bolles just hours after the freshman race. The salary—$164,000 in today's dollars—was vastly more than Washington could match, as university officials in Seattle immediately made clear. That afternoon Bolles denied that he had been approached, but likely because he had already turned the offer down. The word on the street was that, rather than going east, Bolles would replace Ulbrickson in Seattle. Bolles was working on his master's degree in history, and it seemed unlikely that he would want to leave the university until he finished it. One way or the other, it was apparent that the coaching situation at Washington was suddenly uncertain, and that while Bolles's star had suddenly ascended, Ulbrickson's had fallen just as abruptly. On June 23, Royal Brougham advised his readers to ignore the rumors, saying he had it on good authority that Bolles had promised Ulbrickson he would never take the Washington job unless Ulbrickson had moved on to greener pastures first. But nobody outside of the university's administration, including Al Ulbrickson, was really sure what was going on. Ulbrickson was sure of one thing, though: he figured he had worked too hard, brought the crew program too far, to be unceremoniously dumped. "I won't wait until they fire me," he confided to a friend. "I'll quit first."

The town of Grand Coulee, with B Street off to the right

CHAPTER ELEVEN

And the oarsman, too, when he has his mind trained at the university and his body fit, feels something. . . . I think oarsmen understand
what I'm talking about. They get that way. I've seen oarsmen—
actually I saw one man, who was so rarin' to go, so fit and bright, I
saw him try to run up a wall. Now isn't that ridiculous? But he felt
that good; he wanted to run up that wall.

—George Yeoman Pocock

Joe's old Franklin labored and coughed and wheezed, crawling up the
long, steep ascent to Blewett Pass, high in the Cascade Mountains. Snow
still lingered in the shadows of the higher peaks, and the air was cool, but the
Franklin was struggling with the steep grade and Joe was anxious, not quite
sure the car would make it to the top. It seemed as if it had been more than a
few hours since he had thrown his banjo and his clothes in the backseat,
said good-bye to Joyce for the summer, and driven out of Seattle, heading
east, looking for work.

He made it over the pass and began to drop down through dry ponderosa
pine forests to the apple and cherry orchards of Wenatchee, where magpies,
black and white, flashed among the cherry trees, seeking ripe, red plunder. He
crossed the Columbia River on a narrow steel span and climbed out of the
river's gorge to the gently rolling wheat fields of the Columbia Plateau. He
drove eastward for miles on end, the road running relentlessly arrow straight,
undulating over rolling jade-green fields of wheat.

Then he turned north and descended into the Washington scablands, a
tortured landscape shaped by a series of cataclysms between twelve and fifteen thousand years ago. As the last ice age waned, a two-thousand-foot-high
ice dam holding back a vast lake in Montana—later dubbed Lake Missoula by
geologists—gave way not once but several times, unleashing a series of floods
of unimaginable scope and ferocity. In the greatest of these, during a period of
roughly forty-eight hours, 220 cubic kilometers of water rushed over much of

what is now northern Idaho, eastern Washington, and the northern edge of Oregon, carrying more than ten times the flow of all the rivers in the world. A massive wall of water, mud, and rock—well over a thousand feet tall in places—exploded over the countryside, rumbling southwest toward the Pacific at speeds up to one hundred miles per hour, leveling whole mountains, sluicing away millions of tons of topsoil, and gouging deep scars called "coulees" in the underlying bedrock.

As Joe descended into the largest of these excavations, the Grand Coulee, he encountered a world that was in many ways alien and yet starkly beautiful—a world of broken rock, silver sagebrush, sparse desert grasses, windblown sand, and stunted pines. Under pale blue skies, he drove along the base of high, sheer basalt cliffs. Jackrabbits the size of small dogs loped awkwardly across the highway. Scrawny coyotes slunk away through the sagebrush. Blank-faced burrowing owls perched unblinking on fence posts, watching him pass. Nervous-looking ground squirrels sat on jagged rocks, one moment watching for rattlesnakes in the sagebrush below, the next moment cocking their heads to watch for hawks circling high above. Dust devils danced across the coulee floor. A stiff, dry, unrelenting wind blew up the fifty-mile length of the coulee, carrying the sweet scent of sage and the harsh, mineral smell of broken rock.

Joe drove up the coulee to the ramshackle boomtown of Grand Coulee, perched just above the Columbia River at the spot where the U.S. government had recently committed to building a dam so massive that by the time it was finished it would be the largest masonry structure built since the Great Pyramid at Giza, more than four thousand years before. He made his way down a steeply descending gravel road to the river, crossed the wide expanse of green water on a steel bridge, and parked in front of the National Reemployment Service building.

Thirty minutes later, he walked out of the office with a job. Most of the jobs remaining at the dam site, he had been told, were for common laborers, paying fifty cents an hour. But studying the application form, Joe had noticed that there were higher pay grades for certain jobs—especially for the men whose job it was to dangle from cliff faces in harnesses and pound away at the reluctant rock with jackhammers. The jackhammer job paid seventy-five cents an hour, so Joe had put a check next to that box and stepped into the examination room for his physical. Working with a jackhammer under those conditions required enough upper body strength to fight the punishing kickback of the machine, enough leg strength to keep the body pushed away from the cliff face all day, enough grace and athleticism to clamber around on the cliffs while dodging rocks falling from above, and enough self-assurance to climb over the edge of the cliff in the first place. By the time Joe had stripped down to his shorts and told the doctor that he rowed crew at the university, the job was his.

Now, in the long, lingering twilight of a late June Northwest evening, Joe sat on the hood of the Franklin, in front of the office, and studied the lay of the land before him. Across the gorge and slightly upstream, perched on a gravel bench on the west side, was the government-built town the clerk had told Joe was Engineer City—home to technical and supervisory personnel. The houses there were modest but neat, with patches of new lawn that seemed oddly green and out of place in the uniformly brown surroundings. Upstream a narrow suspension catwalk stretched fifteen hundred feet across the river, swaying slightly, like a cobweb in the evening breeze. Near it was another, sturdier, bridge built low to the water, carrying an enormous conveyor belt, which appeared to be transporting piles of rock and gravel from one side of the river to the other. A large cofferdam, made of sheets of steel, was being built on the west side of the river to divert the water away from the base of the cliffs there. The area behind the cofferdam swarmed with men and machines, all raising individual clouds of dust.

Steam shovels and electric shovels clawed at piles of loose rock; bulldozers pushed earth and rocks from one place to another; Caterpillar diesel tractors crawled back and forth, gouging out terraces; enormous Mack AP Super-Duty dump trucks labored up rough roads leading out of the canyon, carrying boulders the size of automobiles; front loaders scooped up more boulders and dropped them in side-dump trucks that carried them to conveyors; tall cranes swung steel sheets out over the water, where pile drivers emitting white puffs of steam sat on barges, pounding them into the riverbed. At the base of the cliffs, hundreds of men with sledgehammers and crowbars climbed over piles of fallen rock, loosening them for the front loaders. On the cliffs themselves, men suspended on ropes crawled and swung from one spot to another like so many black spiders. Studying them, Joe saw that they were drilling holes in the rock faces with jackhammers. A long, shrill whistle blew, and the jackhammer men scrambled quickly to the tops of their lines. The men with picks and crowbars scurried away from the base of the cliffs. The deep, hollow, concussive sound of an explosion boomed and blossomed across the canyon, reverberating against its rock walls as plumes of white rock dust shot from the face of the western cliffs, and a shower of rocks and boulders tumbled down onto the piles below.

Joe watched with deep fascination and considerable apprehension. He was not at all sure what he was getting into here. But he was dead set on finding out. On the long, undulating drive across the wheat fields up on the plateau, he had had a lot of time to think about where he was and where he was going.

Where he was, primarily, was flat broke again and more than a little discouraged. Not just about the perpetual problem of finding money but about the whole crew business. The year had taken an emotional toll on him. Demoted and promoted and demoted again, he'd started to think of himself as a kind of yo-yo in the hands of the coaches, or the Fates, he wasn't sure which—up one minute, down the next. The sense of purpose crew gave him brought with it the constant danger of failing and thereby losing the precious but fragile pride that his early successes had brought him.

And yet the notion of Olympic gold had begun to work its way into his psyche. A medal would be real and solid. Something nobody could deny or take away. It surprised him how much it had begun to mean to him. He figured maybe it had something to do with Thula. Or with his father. Certainly it had something to do with Joyce. At any rate, he felt more and more that he had to get to Berlin. Getting to Berlin, though, hinged on making the varsity crew. Making the varsity crew hinged first of all on paying for another year of school. And paying for school hinged on strapping on a harness and lowering himself over the edge of a cliff in the morning.

That same day Al Ulbrickson was licking his wounds again. Before leaving Poughkeepsie, he had agreed to meet Cal, Pennsylvania, Syracuse, Wisconsin, and UCLA in a one-off two-thousand-meter varsity matchup in Long Beach, California.

Two thousand meters was the Olympic distance, and in the wake of Poughkeepsie the national press was again asserting that California's varsity was now all but certain to represent the United States in Berlin in 1936. Ulbrickson was bent on proving them wrong. He knew full well that a two-thousand-meter race was an entirely different matter from a four-mile slog at Poughkeepsie. It was extraordinarily challenging to put a crew on the water that could prevail at both distances. In theory, a well-coached crew had to do the same basic things at both distances: get off to a good start to build up momentum, back off as much as possible to conserve energy for the finish yet remain within striking distance all the while, then throw everything they had left into a sprint to the finish line. The difference was that in a two-thousand-meter race everything came at you much faster and harder. The amount of momentum acquired at the beginning mattered more, figuring out where to position yourself in the field for the middle was more difficult and more critical, and the final sprint was inevitably much more desperate. Though all distances required enormous amounts of brawn, the two-thousand-meter race required lightning-quick thinking as well. And that's where Ulbrickson figured he had an edge at the shorter distance—he had Bobby Moch sitting in the coxswain's seat.

Beating California at that distance would offer Ulbrickson an opportunity for immediate redemption, a chance to change the prevailing assumptions about the upcoming Olympics, and, if the rumors swirling through Seattle were true, a way to save his job.

Somewhat more than six thousand fans packed into the Long Beach Marine Stadium on the day of the race, sitting in bleachers or standing on the sand along both sides of the arrow-straight saltwater course, a forest of oil derricks rising behind them. There was only a light cross-course breeze blowing in off the Pacific. A thin, acrid smell of petroleum hung in the air.

Washington and California bounded out ahead of the field. The two boats settled in, rowing in full-sprint mode, the boats streaking down the course most of the way as if locked together. With two hundred meters to go, California edged ahead of Washington by inches. With a hundred meters left, they widened the lead to a quarter of a length. Bobby Moch suddenly screamed something at his crew. He had added a new chant to his calls recently, "FERA," noting it in his scrapbook and jotting next to it, "Obscene, refers to Ebright." Perhaps that is what he called out now. He never said. Whatever it was, it had its effect. In the final fifty meters, the Washington boat surged forward again, quickly closing in on California.

But it wasn't enough. Ky Ebright's California Bears crossed the line in a sizzling 6:15.6, half a second ahead of Washington. Instead of finding redemption, Al Ulbrickson headed home with another defeat. Quite possibly his last.

The jackhammer work was brutal, but Joe came to enjoy it. For eight hours a day, he dangled on a rope in the furnacelike heat of the canyon, pounding at the wall of rock in front of him. The jackhammer weighed seventy-five pounds and seemed to have a life and a will of its own, endlessly pushing back, trying to wrest itself out of Joe's grip as he in turn tried to push it into the rock. The continual, rapid-fire *chock-chock-chock* of his machine and those of the men around him was deafening. Rock dust, gritty and irritating, swirled around him, got in his eyes, his mouth, and his nose. Sharp chips and shards of rock flew up and stung his face. Sweat dripped from his back and fell away into the void below.

Hundreds of feet of loose rock—the "overburden" as the engineers called it—had to be peeled away from the face of the cliffs in order to get down to the older granite bedrock on which the foundation of the dam would be built. Then the granite itself had to be shaped to conform to the contours of the future dam. It was hard stuff. So hard that roughly two thousand feet of steel disappeared every day from the bit ends of all the jackhammers and pneumatic drills at work in the canyon.

But tough as the work was, there was much about it that suited Joe. He learned that summer to work closely with the men dangling on either side of him, each keeping an eye out for rocks falling from above, calling out warnings to those below, searching for better places to find seams in the rock. He liked the easygoing camaraderie of it, the simple, stark maleness of it. Most days he worked without a shirt or hat. His muscles quickly grew bronzed and his hair ever blonder under the ardent desert sun. By the end of each day, he was exhausted, parched with thirst, and ravenously hungry. But—much as he sometimes had after a hard row on Lake Washington back home—he also felt cleansed by the work. He felt lithe and limber, full of youth and grace.

Three times a day, and sometimes four on weekends, he ate in the large, white clapboard company mess hall in Mason City, the hastily erected town run by MWAK, the consortium of companies building the dam. Sitting shoulder to shoulder with men arranged in rows at long tables, packed close together, he ate as he had back in his boyhood at the Gold and Ruby mine—facedown, tucking into mountains of food served on cheap crockery. The food was nothing special, but the servings were prodigious. Each morning the thirty men working in the kitchen prepared three hundred dozen eggs, twenty-five hundred pancakes, five hundred pounds of bacon and sausage, and 180 gallons of coffee. At lunch they went through three hundred two-foot loaves of bread, 150 gallons of milk, and twelve hundred cups of ice cream. At dinner they dished up fifteen hundred pounds of red meat (except on Sunday, when they served twelve hundred pounds of chicken) and 330 pies. Joe never left a scrap on his plate, or anyone else's within reach.

Every night he hiked up the hill to a place called Shack Town, where he had found a cheap room in a long, rickety shedlike building designed to house single men. Clinging to the rocky hillsides and dusty flats above the work site, Shack Town wasn't much better than a dry, dusty version of Hooverville down on the waterfront in Seattle. Most of the buildings were constructed from rough-cut lumber, some from little more than tar paper tacked over a wooden framework. Like most of the shacks, Joe's had no indoor plumbing and his room came with only enough electricity for one lightbulb overhead and a hot plate on a shelf. Each of the half-dozen gravel streets in Shack Town had a communal shower house, but Joe soon found that, eager as he was to get the rock dust off himself, taking a shower was a far from comfortable experience. Hordes of black widow spiders lurked in the rafters above the showers, and they tended to drop onto the naked men below as soon as the water was turned on and steam rose to meet them. After watching a few of his neighbors leaping out of the showers buck naked, yelping and batting at themselves, Joe finally took to carrying a broom into the shower each evening to clear the rafters of eight-legged intruders before he turned the water on.

For the first couple of weeks, Joe kept mostly to himself after work and dinner, sitting in the dark of the shack, playing his banjo, his long, thin fingers dancing up and down the neck of the instrument, and singing softly to himself. Every few nights he sat under his one lightbulb and wrote long letters to Joyce. Sometimes he'd walk out after dark and sit on a rock and look out over the canyon, just for the spectacle of it. Floodlights lit up much of the work site, and in the immense surrounding darkness of the high desert the effect was otherworldly. The scene below seemed to unfold as if it were a vast diorama in a lighted case. Veils of dust drifted under the floodlights like fog under streetlamps. The yellow headlights and red taillights of the trucks and heavy equipment moved in and out of shadows as they crawled around the uneven terrain. The welding torches of men working on the steel cofferdam flickered on and off, glowing orange and electric blue. Strings of glittering white lights defined the contours of the suspension bridges across the river. The river itself was black, invisible below them.

Two weeks into his work at Grand Coulee, Joe discovered that among the many college boys who had converged on Grand Coulee seeking work that summer there were two from the Washington shell house. He didn't know either of them very well, but that was about to change.

Johnny White was the number two man in Tom Bolles's outstanding freshman boat that year. An inch shorter than Joe, and more slightly built, he was nevertheless a fine physical specimen and striking to look at, with fine, regular features; gracefully proportioned limbs; and an open, eager face. He had warm, inviting eyes and a sunny smile. If you'd wanted a poster model for the all-American boy, Johnny would have fit the bill. He was also a thoroughly nice kid and nearly as poor as Joe Rantz.

He'd grown up in the southern part of Seattle, on the western edge of Lake Washington, south of Seward Park. Things had been fine until 1929. But with the financial crash, his father's business—exporting scrap steel to Asia—had all but evaporated. John White Sr. gave up his office in the Alaska Building downtown and set up an office upstairs in the house on the lake. For the next several years, he sat there, day after day, looking out over the lake, listening to the clock tick, waiting for the telephone to ring, hoping some business would materialize. It never did.

Finally, he got up from his chair one day, went down to the lakeshore, and began to plant a garden. His kids needed to be fed, and he was out of money, but food could be grown. Before long he had the finest garden in the neighborhood. In the rich black soil along the lakeshore, he grew tall sweet corn and large, luscious tomatoes, both perpetual challenges to Seattle gardeners. He grew loganberries, and picked apples and pears from old trees on the property. He raised chickens. Johnny's mother, Maimie, bartered the eggs for other goods, canned the tomatoes, made wine from the loganberries. She grew peonies in another garden along the side of the house and sold them to a florist in Seattle. She went to a flour mill for flour sacks, bleached them, and made them into dish towels that she sold around town. Once a week she bought a roast and served it for Sunday dinner. The rest of the week they ate leftovers. Then in 1934 the city decided to open a swimming beach along the shore in front of the house. They condemned the Whites' waterfront garden.

Johnny's father had one passion that overrode all his other interests and kept him going through those hard years—rowing. Before moving west to Seattle, he had been a first-rate sculler at the prestigious Pennsylvania Athletic Club in Philadelphia. He had brought his shell out to Seattle, and now he spent long hours rowing alone on Lake Washington, passing methodically back and forth in front of his house and the beach and what had been his garden, working out the frustration.

Johnny was the apple of his eye, and he wanted more than anything for his son to become an oarsman. Johnny, in turn, wanted nothing more than to meet his father's often very high expectations, whatever they might be. And Johnny hadn't let him down so far. He was unusually bright, accomplished, and ambitious, and he had graduated from Franklin High School two years early, at the age of sixteen.

That had created a small problem. He was far too young and too underdeveloped to row for the university, the only rowing game in town. So by mutual agreement with his father, Johnny went to work—both to make enough money to attend the university and, just as importantly, to manufacture enough muscle to row with the best of them when he got there. He chose the hardest, most physically challenging work he could find: first wrestling steel beams and heavy equipment around a shipyard on the waterfront in Seattle and then stacking lumber and manhandling massive fir and cedar logs with a peavey in a nearby sawmill. By the time he arrived at the university, two years later, he had enough cash to make it through a couple of years of school and enough brawn to quickly emerge as one of Tom Bolles's most impressive freshmen. Now, in the summer of 1935, he'd arrived at Grand Coulee looking for more—more money and more muscle.

The other Washington boy who showed up at Grand Coulee that summer was Chuck Day. Like Johnny White, he was a number two man, pure muscle, broad in the shoulders, but a bit lighter than the boys who sat in the middle of the boat. He had brown hair and a square face with a strong, broad jaw. His eyes could be mirthful one moment, flashing with rage the next. The overall effect was slightly pugnacious. He wore spectacles but managed to look tough doing it. And he almost always had a Camel or a Lucky Strike dangling from his lip, except when Al Ulbrickson was around. At any given moment, though, he was as likely to be merry as ornery. He loved to play tricks, delighted in horsing around, always seemed to have a joke at the ready. The previous year he had rowed as one of Joe's rivals in the junior-varsity-turned-varsity boat. Largely because of that, he and Joe had hardly ever exchanged two words, at least not civil words.

Irish American through and through, Day had grown up just north of the Washington campus, in the area where the fraternities were located. His father was a successful dentist, and so his family had been spared the worst effects of the Depression and lived fairly comfortably, teeth being prone to decay regardless of economic trends. At first blush it didn't seem to make sense to Joe that a kid like Day would have any reason to work in a place as dirty and dangerous as the coulee.

In point of fact, though—as Joe would soon find out—there was no place that Chuck Day was more likely to be that summer than at Grand Coulee. To understand him, you had to understand his heart. He was a ferocious competitor. If you put a challenge in front of him, he attacked it like a bulldog. And he just plain didn't know the meaning of surrender. If a river needed to be dammed, then by God just get out of the way and let him at it.

Joe and Johnny and Chuck fell into an easy and comfortable confederacy. Without a word about it, they put aside the rivalries of the shell house, forgot about the hurled insults of the past year, and ignored the contest that they all knew lay ahead the following year.

The Grand Coulee was unlike anyplace any of them had ever been. The work was crushingly hard, the sun brutal, the dirt and ceaseless din almost unbearable, but the spaces were vast, the scenery staggering, and the company fast and fascinating. Every type and variety of humanity seemed to have made it to the coulee that summer, and the most colorful of them had settled in Shack Town. Mixed in with all the college students and farm boys and out-of-work loggers, there were grizzled hard-rock miners from all over the West. There were Filipinos, Chinese, Welshmen, South Sea Islanders, African Americans, Mexicans, and Native Americans, most of the last from the adjoining Colville Reservation. Not all of Shack Town's residents worked on the dam itself. Many were there to provide various services to the men who did—doing their laundry, cooking their meals at the mess hall, selling them various sundries, disposing of their trash. And there were women too, though almost all the women practiced the same profession.

Just uphill from the main street in Grand Coulee lay B Street, a three-block stretch of dirt and gravel lined on either side with hastily contrived buildings housing every sort of distraction a young man could imagine—card rooms and bars and pool halls and brothels and fleabag hotels and dance emporiums. During the daytime, when the men were all at work down at the dam site, B Street dozed. Dogs flopped down in the middle of the street to take naps. Occasionally a car sputtered up the hill from downtown and detoured around the sleeping dogs before parking in front of Peerless Painless Dentist, its driver getting out and walking nervously into the office. Attractive young women emerged from time to time from the Red Rooster or Gracie's Model Rooms and stepped across the street to buy something at Blanche's Dress Shop or to stop in at La James Beauty Shop for a perm. Harry Wong, the cook at the Woo Dip Kitchen, usually appeared early in the afternoons, carrying crates of vegetables into the restaurant before closing and locking the door until he was ready to open for business.

But at night—especially on a Friday or Saturday night, after the men had lined up at the MWAK payroll office—B Street blossomed. Jazz and country music poured out of bars and dance halls. Men crowded into restaurants lit by flickering kerosene lamps and sat down to eat cheap steaks and drink stale beer at tables that were not more than pine planks resting on two sawhorses. Working women, "Yoo Hoo Girls" in the local vernacular, hung out the upstairs windows of cheap hotels and dance halls and even the fire department, calling out to the men on the street below. Others waited in the upstairs rooms of established brothels like the Red Rooster and Gracie's, while out in the street pimps dressed in cheap suits tried to steer customers their way. Card sharks lingered over green-felt tables in back rooms, smoking cigars, waiting for victims. At the Grand Coulee Club and the Silver Dollar, small orchestras played dance tunes for taxi dancers. For ten cents, a lonely fellow could dance one dance with a pretty woman. As the evening wore on and the liquor flowed, the orchestra played faster and faster, the intervals between dances grew shorter and shorter, and the men emptied their pockets at an ever-faster pace, desperate to keep dancing in silky arms, their faces nestled in perfumed hair.

In the wee hours, men eventually began to stagger back toward their bunks in Mason City or Engineer City or Shack Town. Those bound for Mason City faced a challenge waiting for them on the way home. The most direct way across the canyon was on the narrow fifteen-hundred-foot suspension catwalk swaying over the river. Nobody ever seemed to have trouble with it when heading up to B Street early in the evening, but returning home full of liquor at 3:00 a.m. was another matter. With a couple of dozen drunken men at a time lurching across it, the catwalk bucked and heaved and swayed like a tormented snake. Almost every weekend night someone went over the edge. So many, in fact, plunged off the catwalk that MWAK had taken to stationing a man in a boat downstream from it on Friday and Saturday nights to pluck the survivors from the water.

Joe and Johnny and Chuck walked B Street on Saturday nights, taking it all in with wide eyes. None of them had ever seen anything quite like it, and they weren't quite sure how to behave in this new world. Al Ulbrickson's "no smoking, no drinking, no chewing, no cussing" dictum always rang like a bell in the backs of their minds. As athletes they prided themselves on their self-discipline. But the temptations were many. So they nervously prowled the bars and card rooms and dance halls, drinking beer and taking occasional shots of whiskey and singing along with ragtag cowboy bands. Occasionally Chuck or Johnny shelled out a dime for a dance, but to Joe the price seemed extravagant. For a dime, you could buy a loaf of bread or a dozen eggs at Carsten's Grocery just down the street. And he had Joyce back home to think about. They stood staring sheepishly up at the Yoo Hoo Girls who beckoned to them from windows, but they stayed out of their lairs. In the card rooms, they gathered around felt-top tables, but Joe kept his wallet in his pocket. His money came too hard to risk it on a hand of cards, even in the unlikely event that it was honestly dealt. When Chuck Day sat down at the tables, Joe and Johnny both stood by, keeping a close eye on him, ready to extricate him from any trouble. Disputes here, they had noticed, generally led to fistfights that poured out into B Street, and it wasn't unheard-of for knives and guns to come into the mix.

The Grand Coulee Theater showed first-run movies every weekend. Joe and Johnny and Chuck found that it was a good place to pass a Saturday afternoon out of the sun and the dust, eating popcorn, drinking cold root beer, and mingling with the other patrons, many of whom were the taxi dancers and Yoo Hoo Girls dressed in ordinary street clothes. Chatting with them before the show and during intermissions, the boys found many of them to be friendly, simple, honest young women, not terribly different, really, from the kinds of girls they had grown up with back in their hometowns, except that the hard times had driven them to desperate measures.

Food also drew them to B Street: chow mein at the Woo Dip Kitchen; homemade tamales from the Hot Tamale Man's shack; mountainous sundaes at the soda fountain in Atwater's Drugstore; fresh-baked cherry pie at the Doghouse Café. And the Best Little Store by a Dam Site was a good place to shop for treats and small luxuries, everything from cheap cigars to Oh Henry! candy bars.

When they wanted to escape the clamor of B Street and Grand Coulee, the boys sometimes drove to Spokane and explored Joe's old haunts or traveled down the coulee to swim in Soap Lake, a geological oddity where brisk, warm winds piled the mineral suds that gave the lake its name into creamy white drifts two or three feet deep along the beach.

For the most part, though, they stayed in Grand Coulee, where they could toss a football around in the sagebrush, chuck rocks off the edges of the cliffs, bask shirtless on stone ledges in the warm morning sun, sit bleary-eyed in the smoke around a campfire at night telling ghost stories as coyotes yelped in the distance, and generally act like the teenagers they actually were—free and easy boys, cut loose in the wide expanse of the western desert.

George Pocock's shop

CHAPTER TWELVE

Just as a skilled rider is said to become part of his horse, the skilled oarsman must become part of his boat.

—George Yeoman Pocock

As Joe Rantz, Johnny White, Chuck Day, and thousands of other young American men labored down in the hot, stony recesses of the Grand Coulee in the summer of 1935, thousands of young German men swarmed over the site of another great public works project, this one in Berlin. Since Adolf Hitler had visited it in the fall of 1933, the sprawling 325-acre site of the Reichssportfeld had been dramatically transformed. The adjoining racetrack had been torn down, and now more than five hundred companies contracted by the Nazi state were at work preparing the site for the Olympic Games. In order to put the maximum number of men to work, Hitler had decreed that virtually all the labor was to be done by hand, even that which machines could do more efficiently. All the men, however, were required to be "complying, nonunion workers of German citizenship and Aryan race."

Everything about the project was massive. The great bowl of the Olympic Stadium, its floor forty-two feet below ground level, had been excavated and leveled, its central field sown with grass that was already lush and green. One hundred thirty-six evenly spaced square pillars had been erected around the perimeter of what would become the two-story colonnade. Forms for seventy-two tiers of seating had been built, enough to accommodate 110,000 people. Seventeen thousand tons of concrete were in the process of being poured into those forms. Seven thousand three hundred tons of sheet metal were being welded together. Over thirty-nine thousand cubic yards of natural stone had arrived on the site, and hundreds of stonemasons were at work, with hammers and chisels, covering the exterior of the stadium with blocks of fine, ivory-colored Franconian limestone. A hockey stadium, a swimming stadium, an equestrian stadium, an enormous and monolithic exhibition hall, a gymnasium, a Greek amphitheater, tennis courts, restaurants, and sprawling administrative buildings were all in various stages of completion. Like the stadium, most were being clad with natural stone, all of it German—more limestone from Franconia, basalt from the Eifel hills, granite and marble from Silesia, travertine from Thuringia, porphyry from Saxony.

West of the stadium, a vast, flat assembly area, the Maifeld, had been leveled and a great limestone bell tower was being erected. The tower would eventually stand just over 248 feet tall. The great bell it would house would bear around its bottom edge an inscription sandwiched between two swastikas, "Ich rufe die Jugend der Welt!" ("I summon the youth of the world!"). And the youth would indeed come. First for the Olympics and then for something else. A little less than ten years in the future, in the last few desperate days of the Third Reich, scores of Hitler Youth—boys as young as ten or eleven—would crouch below the bell tower among blocks of fine Franconian limestone, the rubble of the buildings now being erected, shooting at advancing Russian boys, many of them not a great deal older than they. And in those last few days, as Berlin burned all around them, some of those German boys—those who cried or refused to shoot or tried to surrender—would be lined up against these limestone slabs by their officers and shot.

Fifteen miles to the southeast, in the leafy and pleasant lakeside community of Grünau, preparations for the Olympic rowing, canoeing, and kayaking events were also well under way. Grünau was located on the west bank of the long, narrow Langer See, one of several lakes fed by the Dahme River, just where suburbs began to give way to open meadows and tracts of dark forest southeast of Berlin. The Langer See, with its deep blue water, had long been the center of water sports in Berlin. Rowing and sailing regattas had been held there since the 1870s. Kaiser Wilhelm II had built a sprawling summer pavilion in Grünau so the imperial family could reside in splendor while watching the competitions or taking to the water themselves. By 1925 dozens of rowing clubs were headquartered in and around Grünau—among them some whose members were exclusively Jewish, some whose members were exclusively Nordic, and many whose members were congenially mixed. Since 1912 women as well as men had rowed in these clubs, though the dress code for women required outfits that were distinctly uncomfortable for rowing: high-laced boots, long skirts, and long-sleeved tops secured tightly at the neck.

For the occasion of the 1935 European Rowing Championships, engineers had recently completed a large covered grandstand with a seating capacity of seventy-five hundred. An expansive grassy area had been laid out along the water to the east of the grandstand to accommodate another ten thousand standing spectators. Now with the Olympics approaching, officials were planning to add a massive set of wooden grandstands built out over the water on the other side of the lake. Meanwhile masons and carpenters were at work building a large and stately new boathouse, Haus West, just east of the permanent grandstands, supplementing two large existing boathouses, Haus Mitte and Haus Ost. Not one of these was anything like the shell houses Joe and his crewmates had known—the old seaplane hangar in Seattle or the rickety shell houses of Poughkeepsie. These were impressive, modern, limestone buildings with red tile roofs. Among them they sported twenty separate dressing rooms, four shower rooms, twenty hot-water showers, storage on the ground level for ninety-seven racing shells, and rooms full of massage tables for bone-weary oarsmen. For the duration of the Olympics, Haus West, nearest the finish line, was to be largely devoted to administrative services, with rooms set aside for news writers, radio-transmitting equipment, Teletypes, telephones, rapid film-developing labs, and a customs office to aid the international press with immigration and customs issues. Haus West would also feature a sweeping terrace on its second story. With its unobstructed view of the racecourse, the terrace would serve as a viewing point from which the most powerful men in Germany could watch the Olympic races, and as a stage on which the world could watch them doing so.

In mid-September, Joe returned from the Grand Coulee with enough money to make it through another year if he was thrifty. He visited Sequim briefly, to catch up with the McDonalds and Joyce's parents, and then quickly returned to Seattle to be near Joyce herself. Joyce had abruptly left her job in Laurelhurst that summer, after the judge had chased her around the dining table one afternoon, in pursuit of services not generally required of maids. She had promptly found work with another family nearby, but things had gotten off to a rocky start. On Joyce's first day of work, Mrs. Tellwright, the lady of the house, had casually asked her to prepare duck à l'orange for dinner. Joyce was horrified. She knew what a duck was, and she knew what an orange was, but what the two had to do with each other was beyond her. As far as cooking went, she was pretty much a country girl. Fried chicken and meat loaf were more up her alley. But she wanted to impress, so she gave it her best try. The results were apparently unpalatable, if not inedible. Mrs. Tellwright took one bite, made a slight grimace, put her fork down, and said, chirpily, "Well, dear, perhaps a cooking class would be in order." It turned out to be the beginning of a long and happy friendship. Mrs. Tellwright did, in fact, pay for cooking classes for Joyce, and she took them herself, right alongside the younger woman. Over the next several years, they spent many enjoyable hours in the kitchen together.

Joe and Joyce were increasingly worried about something more serious than duck *à l'orange*, though. When Joe resumed visiting his father at the bakery, sitting in the Franklin and sharing his lunch, Harry mentioned that he and Thula had spent much of the summer making long excursions—"picnics," they called them—to various places around the state, mostly to their old haunts in eastern Washington, and planned on making similar jaunts that autumn. At first this suited Joe just fine. It meant he could visit his half siblings without worrying about Thula throwing him out of the house. But the first time he and Joyce stopped by Bagley Avenue on one of these occasions, they found that Harry and Thula had been gone for three days. They'd left Harry Junior, Mike, Rose, and Polly alone, without supervision and largely without food. Harry Junior, the oldest, at thirteen, said his parents had packed a pressure cooker full of stewed beef, potatoes, and vegetables, taken a loaf of bread and some canned goods, and gone on a jaunt to Medical Lake, where they had first courted. He wasn't sure when they would return. In the meantime, he and his siblings had pretty much cleaned out the cabinets trying to find enough to eat.

Joe and Joyce took the four children out for ice cream and then stopped by a grocery store and bought some basic provisions before dropping them off back at the house. By the next day, when Joe checked, Harry and Thula had returned. But Joe couldn't fathom what his father and Thula had been thinking. Apparently this had been going on all summer long.

Thula Rantz was having quite a summer. Her star had begun to ascend at last. Since Harry had secured the job at the Golden Rule, she had finally had the leisure to pursue her violin career full-time, and now years of grimly determined practice back in the cabin in Idaho and the half-finished house in Sequim had finally begun to pay off. She had managed to land an audition in Los Angeles with no less a light than Fritz Kreisler.

Kreisler was among the greatest violinists of the twentieth century. An

Austrian, the son of Sigmund Freud's family physician, he had been, at age seven, the youngest student ever admitted to the Vienna Conservatory. At age ten, he won the conservatory's prestigious gold medal before going on to the Paris Conservatory, where he studied under Joseph Massart and Léo Delibes. From there he had gone on to true greatness, performing to packed houses for decades in all the most hallowed concert halls in the world—in Berlin, Vienna, Paris, London, New York—and recording on major record labels in both Europe and the United States. Gravely wounded in World War I, he had survived and returned an even greater maestro. But when the Nazis had come to power in 1933, he refused ever to play again in Germany, became a French citizen, and moved to the United States.

Thula returned to Seattle from her audition jubilant. Kreisler had called her, by her own account, "the greatest female violinist I have heard." It had not yet led to a seat with a major orchestra, but it raised that possibility, and it stood as the highlight of Thula's life thus far, validation of what she and her parents had believed all along. And it did lead to a degree of celebrity, at least locally. That spring and summer KOMO Radio in Seattle aired a series of live performances by Thula, and for the first time thousands of people heard what she was capable of. Now, with that to build on for the future, and a steady income from Harry's job, she was bent on getting out of the house and celebrating—living life, for a change, as it was meant to be lived.

Joe was now back at that shell house every day, getting in shape for what was to come. Johnny White and Chuck Day showed up too, dusty and tanned from the Grand Coulee, wearing wide grins and drawing lots of questions from the other fellows whenever they and Joe talked about a mysterious place called B Street.

Al Ulbrickson was back as well. As Royal Brougham had predicted back in June, rumors of his demise had proved premature, much to the relief of Joe and the other boys. Whatever inclination there might have been to replace him after Poughkeepsie and Long Beach had evaporated in the off-season, or at least been suspended. The fact was that the administration didn't believe they could do better, not for the pittance they were paying Ulbrickson. It remained unclear, though, how long they were going to pay him anything at all.

Early one morning that September his wife, Hazel, arose to find Ulbrickson already awake, sitting in his pajamas at an old typewriter, assiduously pecking at the keys. His face was grim, determined. He ripped the paper from the typewriter, wheeled around in his seat, and handed it to Hazel. It was a statement for the *Seattle Times*. The gist of it was a simple, bold assertion—the University of Washington's eight-oared crew was going to win gold at the Berlin Olympics in 1936. Hazel raised her eyes from the document and stared at him, flabbergasted. She thought he'd lost his mind. The Al Ulbrickson she knew never made proclamations like that, seldom said anything even remotely suggesting what his hopes and dreams were, even at home, let alone in the newspapers. But Ulbrickson rose and folded the document and put it in an envelope addressed to the *Times*. He had crossed some kind of Rubicon. If he was going to stay in the rowing game, he told Hazel, there wouldn't be any second-place finishes this year. Not at Poughkeepsie or anywhere else. He was going all out. He'd likely never again have boys of the caliber he had returning in the fall, he told his wife. If he couldn't win with them, if he couldn't find the right combination this time, if he didn't, in fact, go all the way and fetch gold in Berlin in 1936, he would quit coaching at the end of the season.

On September 10, Ulbrickson met with reporters at the shell house. He didn't share the pledge he had made to Hazel, but he made clear what he felt the stakes were going into the new year. Calmly, in measured tones, with no sense of hyperbole, he said that he and his boys would face "the stiffest competition this country has ever known to win the right to wear the Stars and Stripes in Berlin. . . . We have ambitions, and from the very start of fall turnout the Washington oarsmen will have in mind the Olympic trials." He said he was aware that it would be a long shot. Everyone knew Cal had the inside track. But, he concluded, "Certainly we cannot be arrested for trying."

Ulbrickson knew that saying it was one thing; doing it was another. Pulling it off was going to mean marshaling all his resources and making some very tough decisions. He was going to have to overlook boys he liked personally and work with boys he didn't necessarily like. He was going to have to outwit Ky Ebright—no small challenge. He was going to have to find funding in what was shaping up to be yet another lean year. And he was going to have to make better use of perhaps his greatest resource, George Pocock.

Al and Hazel Ulbrickson often shared dinner with George and Frances Pocock at one couple's or the other's home. After dinner, the two men reveled in talking about rowing for hours on end. They discussed boat design and rigging techniques, debated racing strategy, recounted past victories and defeats, and analyzed the strengths and weaknesses of other crews and coaches. It was a chance for the reticent Ulbrickson to relax, to open up and confide in the Englishman, to joke about shell house events, to smoke a cigarette out of sight of the boys. Most of all, it was a chance to do what Washington coaches had been doing since 1913—to learn something from Pocock, whether it was an apt quote from Shakespeare, a better way to sequence a race, or how to understand the inner workings of an oarsman's mind. Going into the Olympic year, their talk inevitably centered on the strengths and weaknesses of the boys at Ulbrickson's disposal.

A successful quest for Olympic gold would require finding nine young men of exceptional strength, grace, endurance, and most of all mental toughness. They would have to row almost flawlessly in long races and short, under all kinds of conditions. They would have to live well together in close quarters for weeks at a time—traveling, eating, sleeping, and racing without internal friction among them. They would have to perform under immense psychological pressure on the most prominent stage in the sport, in full view of the whole world.

At some point that fall, the subject of Joe Rantz came up. Ulbrickson had been studying Joe for a year now, ever since Tom Bolles had first warned him that the boy was touchy and uneven, that there were days when he could row like quicksilver—so smooth and fluid and powerful that he seemed a part of the boat and his oar and the water all at once—and days when he was downright lousy. Since then, Ulbrickson had tried everything—he'd scolded Joe, he'd encouraged him, he'd demoted him, he'd repromoted him. But he wasn't any closer to understanding the mystery of him. Now Ulbrickson turned to Pocock for some help. He asked the Englishman to take a look at Rantz—to talk to him, to try to figure him out, and, if possible, to fix him.

On a bright, crisp September morning, as Pocock started up the steps to his loft in the shell house, he noticed Joe doing sit-ups on a bench at the back of the room. He motioned Joe to come over, said he'd noticed him peering up at the shop occasionally, and asked him if he'd like to look around. Joe all but bounded up the stairs.

The loft was bright and airy, with morning light pouring in from several large windows in the back wall. The air was thick with the sweet-sharp scent of marine varnish. Drifts of sawdust and curls of wood shavings lay on the floor. A long I beam stretched nearly the full length of the loft, and on it lay the framework of an eight-oared shell under construction.

Pocock started off by explaining the various tools he used. He showed Joe wood planes, their wooden handles burnished by decades of use, their blades so sharp and precise they could shave off curls of wood as thin and transparent as tissue paper. He handed him different old rasps and augers and chisels and files and mallets he'd brought over from England. Some of them, he said, were a century old. He explained how each kind of tool had many variations, how each file, for instance, was subtly different from another, how each served a different function but all were indispensable in the making of a fine shell. He guided Joe to a lumber rack and pulled out samples of the different woods he used—soft, malleable sugar pine, hard yellow spruce, fragrant cedar, and clear white ash. He held each piece up and inspected it, turning it over and over in his hands, and talked about the unique properties of each and how it took all of them contributing their individual qualities to make a shell that would come to life in the water. He pulled a long cedar plank from a rack and pointed out the annual growth rings. Joe already knew a good deal about the qualities of cedar and about growth rings from his time splitting shakes with Charlie McDonald, but he was drawn in as Pocock began to talk about what they meant to him.

Joe crouched next to the older man and studied the wood and listened intently. Pocock said the rings told more than a tree's age; they told the whole story of the tree's life over as much as two thousand years. Their thickness and thinness spoke of hard years of bitter struggle intermingled with rich years of sudden growth. The different colors spoke of the various soils and minerals that the tree's roots encountered, some harsh and stunting, some rich and nourishing. Flaws and irregularities told how the trees endured fires and lightning strikes and windstorms and infestations and yet continued to grow.

As Pocock talked, Joe grew mesmerized. It wasn't just what the Englishman was saying, or the soft, earthy cadence of his voice, it was the calm reverence with which he talked about the wood—as if there was something holy and sacred about it—that drew Joe in. The wood, Pocock murmured, taught us about survival, about overcoming difficulty, about prevailing over adversity, but it also taught us something about the underlying reason for surviving in the first place. Something about infinite beauty, about undying grace, about things larger and greater than ourselves. About the reasons we were all here.

"Sure, I can make a boat," he said, and then added, quoting the poet Joyce Kilmer, "'But only God can make a tree.'"

Pocock pulled out a thin sheet of cedar, one that had been milled down to three-eighths of an inch for the skin of a shell. He flexed the wood and had Joe do the same. He talked about camber and the life it imparted to a shell when wood was put under tension. He talked about the underlying strength of the individual fibers in cedar and how, coupled with their resilience, they gave the wood its ability to bounce back and resume its shape, whole and intact, or how, under steam and pressure, they could take a new form and hold it forever. The ability to yield, to bend, to give way, to accommodate, he said, was sometimes a source of strength in men as well as in wood, so long as it was helmed by inner resolve and by principle.

He took Joe to one end of the long I beam on which he was constructing the frame for a new shell. Pocock sighted along the pine keel and invited Joe to do the same. It had to be precisely straight, he said, for the whole sixty-two-foot length of the boat, not a centimeter of variance from one end to the other or the boat would never run true. And in the end that trueness could only come from its builder, from the care with which he exercised his craft, from the amount of heart he put into it.

Pocock paused and stepped back from the frame of the shell and put his hands on his hips, carefully studying the work he had so far done. He said for him the craft of building a boat was like religion. It wasn't enough to master the technical details of it. You had to give yourself up to it spiritually; you had to surrender yourself absolutely to it. When you were done and walked away from the boat, you had to feel that you had left a piece of yourself behind in it forever, a bit of your heart. He turned to Joe. "Rowing," he said, "is like that. And a lot of life is like that too, the parts that really matter anyway. Do you know what I mean, Joe?" Joe, a bit nervous, not at all certain that he did, nodded tentatively, went back downstairs, and resumed his sit-ups, trying to work it out.

That month the Nazi Party staged its seventh annual rally at Nuremberg, themed, with staggering irony, the Rally for Freedom. Again the storm troopers and the Blackshirts came in the hundreds of thousands. Again Leni Riefenstahl—now thirty-three and firmly established as Hitler's favorite filmmaker—was there to document the spectacle, though the only footage that would ever emerge was a short film documenting the war games Hitler staged at the rally to dramatize Germany's defiance of the Treaty of Versailles's ban on German rearmament. Years later, after the war, Riefenstahl would speak as little as possible about her participation in the Rally for Freedom. By then it was remembered, not primarily for the war games, but for what happened on the evening of September 15.

The rally reached its climax that night when Adolf Hitler stepped before the German parliament, the Reichstag, to introduce three new laws. The Reichstag had been assembled in Nuremberg for the first time since 1543 in order to pass—and to make a public spectacle of passing—a law making the Nazi Party emblem, the swastika, the official flag of Germany. But Hitler now introduced two more laws, and it was these second and third laws for which the 1935 rally would forever be remembered, and from which Riefenstahl would later try to distance herself.

The Reich Citizenship Law defined citizens to be any German national "of German or related blood" who "proves by his conduct that he is willing and fit to faithfully serve the German people and Reich." By omission, any national not of "German or related blood" was thereby relegated to the status of a subject of the state. The effect was to strip German Jews of their citizenship and all associated rights beginning in January of 1936. The Blood Law—formally, the Law for the Protection of German Blood and German Honor—forbade the marriage of Jews and non-Jews; nullified any such marriages made in defiance of the law, even if carried out in a foreign nation; forbade extramarital sexual relations between Jews and non-Jews; forbade Jews from employing female Germans under the age of forty-five in their homes; and forbade Jews from displaying the newly anointed national flag. And that, as it would turn out, was just for starters. In the next few months and years, the Reichstag would add dozens of additional laws restricting every aspect of the lives of German Jews, until, in effect, simply being Jewish was outlawed.

Even before the advent of the Nuremberg Laws, life had become all but intolerable for German Jews. Since the Nazi Party's assumption of power in 1933, Jews had been—by law, by intimidation, and by outright violence—excluded from working in the civil service or holding public office; from practicing professions like medicine, law, and journalism; from participating in the stock exchanges; and from entering a wide variety of public and private places. In every German town and city, signs proclaiming "Juden unerwünscht" ("Jews not welcome") had appeared over the entrances to hotels, pharmacies, restaurants, public swimming pools, and shops of all sorts. Jewish-owned businesses had been the targets of massive state-sponsored boycotts. Near the town of Ludwigshafen a road sign read "Drive carefully! Sharp curve! Jews

75 miles per hour." By 1935 perhaps half of German Jews had lost their means of livelihood.

All this was evident everywhere one went in Germany, even in the most peaceful and pastoral of places. As the linden and birch trees fringing the Langer See at Grünau began to turn yellow and red that fall, men and women belonging to the area's many rowing clubs continued to meet early in the mornings or on the weekends, sliding their shells out onto the clear blue lake water and rowing up and down the regatta course as they had done for decades. After a good row, they still gathered in local *Gaststätten* for beer and pretzels or sprawled on the lawns in front of the boathouses, keeping an eye on the progress of the new Olympic facilities under construction.

But beneath the surface, things had changed in Grünau. Much of the old conviviality of rowing was gone. The large Jewish Helvetia Rowing Club had already been banned outright in 1933. Now the many clubs with mixed Jewish and non-Jewish membership were threatened with dissolution if they did not purge their rolls. Some smaller, discreet, all-Jewish clubs continued to exist. But now that Jews were no longer citizens, these clubs and their members were subject to the whims of the local Nazi Party officials—they could be raided and closed down, their equipment confiscated, at any time.

Men who had rowed with one another for a lifetime had begun to turn their backs on their former crewmates and neighbors. Names had been scratched off lists. Forbidding signs had gone up over the doors of shell houses. Doors had been locked, keys changed. In the pretty countryside surrounding Grünau, large, comfortable houses belonging to Jewish merchants and professionals had been boarded up or rented out to German families for a fraction of their value, their owners among those who were wealthy enough and prescient enough to find a way out of Germany.

In the United States, talk of boycotting the 1936 Olympics had been simmering since the Nazis had come to power in 1933. Now, in parts of the country, it began to boil.

In Seattle, Al Ulbrickson deferred the varsity turnout until October 21. He needed further time to study the pieces on the chessboard, to figure out a strategy for his Olympic endgame before he even began to move pieces around.

That gave Joe a few weeks in which to settle into his engineering classes and spend more time with Joyce when she could get a day or a half day off. On long, lazy weekend afternoons, afternoons when the air was translucent and still and full of the smell of burning leaves, they rented canoes again and paddled around in Portage Bay. They went to football games and the dances that always followed the games. They stopped by the house on Bagley when Harry and Thula were away, piled Joe's half siblings into the Franklin, bought bologna and day-old bread and milk at a corner store, and had quick picnics at Green Lake. Then they rushed the kids back home before Harry and Thula could return. On crisp, black, starry nights they went downtown and window-shopped—peering into the window displays at the Bon Marché, and Frederick & Nelson, and Nordstrom's Shoe Store—talking about their future wedding and the days to come when they would actually be able to shop at such places. On Sunday afternoons, when they could get into the theaters for fifteen cents, they went to the movies: *Here Comes Cookie*, with George Burns and Gracie Allen, at the Paramount; *She Married Her Boss*, with Claudette Colbert, at the Liberty; *Top Hat*, with Fred Astaire and Ginger Rogers, at the Orpheum.

When Joyce couldn't get away, Joe spent much of his free time at the shell house. With the competition for seats still a few weeks off, the tensions of the year before had eased some, and he enjoyed hanging around with Johnny White, Chuck Day, Roger Morris, and Shorty Hunt. They did calisthenics together, tossed a football around, took shells out for impromptu rows, and did whatever they could to avoid talking about the upcoming season.

At the end of the day, after the others had drifted off to their homes or their part-time jobs, Joe often lingered at the shell house well into the evening, as he had the previous spring. On one of those evenings, he came out of the steam room wrapped in a towel and found the big, gangly number five man from last year's jayvee boat, Stub McMillin, pushing a broom around and emptying trash cans. Joe realized that McMillin must have taken a job as the shell house janitor. With all the hard feelings between the two boats, Joe had never had much to do with McMillin, but now, watching him at work, he felt a surge of affinity for the boy. He sauntered over, stuck out his hand, struck up a conversation, and finally confided what he had long kept secret from the other fellows—that he himself worked a late-night shift as janitor at the YMCA.

Joe quickly found that he liked Stub McMillin a good deal. He'd grown up in Seattle, on Queen Anne Hill, and was nearly as poor as Joe. He was putting himself through college by working at anything and everything that came his way—mowing lawns, delivering newspapers, sweeping floors. When he wasn't rowing, studying, or sleeping, he was working, and just barely keeping himself clothed and fed doing it. Joe found it comfortable to be around Mc-Millin. He felt as if he could let his guard down a little when it came to talking about his own financial circumstances. Before long, Joe was staying late almost every day, pushing a broom alongside McMillin, helping him get through his work quickly so he could go home and study.

Sometimes, late in the day, instead of helping McMillin, Joe would climb the stairs at the back of the shell house and see if George Pocock had time for a chat. If the Englishman was still working, Joe would perch on a bench, his long legs bent in front of him, and just watch the Englishman, not saying much, studying the way the boatbuilder shaped the wood. If Pocock was done for the day, Joe would help him put tools and lumber away or sweep the saw-dust and wood shavings from the floor for him. Pocock didn't deliver any more long discourses on wood or rowing or life, as he had the first time they'd talked. Instead he seemed interested in learning more about Joe.

One afternoon he asked Joe how he came to be there, at the shell house. It was a big question asked in a small way, Joe realized. He answered hesitantly, cautiously, unused to unveiling himself. But Pocock persisted, gently and deftly probing him about his family, about where he'd come from and where he hoped to go. Joe talked in fits and starts, circling nervously around stories about his mother and father and Thula, about Spokane and the Gold and Ruby mine and Sequim. Pocock asked him about his likes and dislikes, the things that made him get up in the morning, the things he feared. Slowly he zeroed in on what he most wanted to know: "Why do you row?" "What do you hope to get out of it, Joe?" And the more he enticed Joe to talk, the more Pocock began to plumb the inner workings of this enigma of a boy.

It helped that Pocock's own mother had died six months after his birth. His father's second wife had died a few years later, before George's remembering. He knew something about growing up in a motherless home, and about the hole it left in a boy's heart. He knew about the ceaseless drive to make oneself whole, and about the endless yearning. Slowly he began to close in on the essence of Joe Rantz.

When varsity turnout commenced on the afternoon of October 21, four boatloads of boys showed up, all veteran oarsmen. Right from the outset, the previous season's rivalries and hard feelings and insecurities erupted again.

A palpable tension filled the vast interior of the shell house as the oarsmen changed into their rowing togs. Ulbrickson made no effort to allay it.

There was no fiery speech this time. There was no need for it. Everyone knew exactly what the stakes were this year. He gathered all the boys on the ramp, straightened his tie, and made a series of flat pronouncements: Except for a period leading up to the Class Day Races in the spring, there wouldn't necessarily be a sophomore or junior or senior boat this year, or any boats made up exclusively of men from any one class. He might sometimes race them in their old configurations, but for the most part he would mix and match to his heart's content, experimenting until he found one boat that was clearly superior to the others. Until the ideal mix was found, it was going to be every man for himself. And right from the start they would row two-thousand-meter sprints as well as longer races. To win at Poughkeepsie and Berlin, he needed a boat that had both the speed for a sprint and the endurance for a four-mile slog—the improbable kind of boat that Ky Ebright had taken to Poughkeepsie and Long Beach the previous spring and would no doubt be back with next spring.

Ulbrickson had magical, almost alchemical, materials to work with—Tom Bolles's outstanding freshman champions from last year, now sophomores; the boys in Joe's boat, all juniors now and still undefeated; and some outstanding boys from last season's JV boat, now a mix of juniors and seniors. And the ruminations that Ulbrickson had given the matter in September seemed to pay dividends right from the start. He had devoted a lot of thought to his initial boat assignments, and in the first few days of rowing two of the new crews seemed to show particular promise. The first was built largely around a core of last year's freshmen: Don Hume, the big powerful stroke; Gordy Adam at number seven; William Seaman at number six; and Johnny White at number four. The only member of Joe's old crew in that first boat was Shorty Hunt, at number two. The second boat that showed particular promise had three of Joe's old crewmates: Bob Green at number six, Charles Hartman at number two, and Roger Morris in the bow. But Joe Rantz hadn't made either of those boats. For the next few weeks, he bumped back and forth between two other boats, rowing hard but his spirits starting to flag again as he realized just how stiff the competition was going to be this year.

It wasn't just the boat assignments that ate at Joe that fall, or the growing realization that getting to Berlin was going to be harder than anything he had ever done. Like most competitive rowers, he was drawn to difficult things. A good challenge had always interested him, appealed to him. That was, in many ways, why he rowed.

What was eating at him now wasn't so much a fear of failing as a creeping sense of loss. He missed the low-key camaraderie that had grown among his sophomore classmates after two years of rowing—and winning—together. He missed Shorty Hunt sitting behind him, whispering, "Don't worry, Joe. I've got your back," whenever Ulbrickson barked at him. He missed the easy if largely wordless comradeship he'd had with gruff, sardonic old Roger Morris right from the first day of freshman turnout. He hadn't really thought before about the fact that it mattered to him that those two fellows were in the boat with him, but it turned out that it did matter, a lot. It came now as a startling and painful realization that he'd had something and lost it without fully understanding that he'd had it in the first place. He had the same feeling every time he watched his new Grand Coulee buddy Johnny White and Shorty sweep by him in another boat, part of something else now, a crew of boys dead set on beating the boat in which Joe sat. When he was abandoned in Sequim, he promised himself he'd never depend on anyone else, not even on Joyce, for his happiness or his sense of who he was. He began to see that he'd allowed himself to do exactly that, with the usual painful results. He hadn't expected it, hadn't prepared for it, and now the ground seemed to be shifting under him in an unpredictable way.

Then, just a few days into the season, the ground under Joe positively lurched. On October 25, when he arrived back at the shell house after a long, cold, wet workout, his brother Fred was waiting for him, standing in the rain on the floating dock, peering grimly out from under the brim of his fedora, white faced. He'd gotten a call from Harry at the hospital, then gone by the house on Bagley to tell the kids. Thula was dead. Septicemia caused by an obstructed bowel.

Joe was numb. He didn't know what to think or to feel about Thula. Pathetic as it was, she had been the closest thing to a mother that he had known since he was three. There had been some good times back in Spokane when they had sat together on the swing out in the backyard in the sweet night air, when they had all gathered around the piano in the parlor to sing. Over the years he had pondered what he might have done to make things better between them later, when the trouble had started. How he might have tried harder to get along with her, to sympathize with her own cramped circumstances, maybe even to see at least some of what his father had seen in her. Now he would never have a chance to show her what he could become. But he also found that there were limits to his regret, and beyond a certain point he simply couldn't feel much of anything for her. Mostly he worried about his father, and even more about his half siblings. If there was one thing Joe knew, it was what it was like for a child to be motherless.

The next morning Joe went by the house on Bagley. He rapped lightly on the front door. When no one answered his knock, Joe followed a brick path through some hydrangeas and around behind the house to try the back door. He found his father and the kids sitting at a picnic table on a soggy lawn. Harry was mixing up a pitcher of cherry Kool-Aid, the kids' favorite. Without saying anything, Joe sat down at the table with them and scanned their faces. Rose and Polly were red about their eyes. So was Mike. Harry Junior had a distracted, weary look, as if he had not had much sleep. Joe's father looked deeply hurt, and suddenly a good deal older.

Joe told his father how sorry he was. Harry thanked him, poured the Kool-Aid into Dixie cups, and sat down wearily.

They talked for a while about Thula's life. Joe, conscious of the kids watching him over the rims of their Dixie cups, found himself elaborating on the things he remembered fondly. Harry began to talk about a trip they had recently taken to Medical Lake, but then choked up and had to stop. All in all, though, he seemed to Joe to be relatively composed for a man who had now twice lost a young wife. He showed no inclination to run away to Canada or anyplace else this time. Instead he seemed to be working on some kind of inner resolve.

Finally he turned to Joe and said, "Son, I've got a plan. I'm going to build a house where we can all live together. As soon as it's done, I want you to come home."

At this last pronouncement, Joe sat at the table staring at his father as if struck dumb. He did not know what to make of it, did not know if he could trust the man. He stammered out a noncommittal answer. He and his father talked some more about Thula. Joe told the kids that he would be coming by to keep them company from now on. But he drove back to the YMCA that night not sure what to do, confusion morphing into resentment, resentment merging into silent anger, and anger giving way again to confusion, all of it washing over him in waves.

If Joe was emotionally numb on the inside, he was physically numb on the outside. For a third consecutive year, unusually cold and stormy weather descended on Seattle shortly after crew practice got under way. On October 29 fifty-mile-per-hour gale winds raked the outer coast of Washington; thirty-mile-per-hour winds tossed boats about on Lake Washington. That night the mercury plummeted into the twenties and a heavy snow began to fall. Nine houses in Seattle burned down as a result of chimneys clogged by snow. For the next seven days, each day was colder than the one before.

Al Ulbrickson sent his four potential varsity boats out onto Lake Washington nonetheless. This was serious cold-weather rowing. The boys rowed with white knuckles and chattering teeth, their hands so cold they could hardly feel the oars, their feet throbbing with pain. Icicles dangled from the bow, the stern, and the riggers that held the oarlocks. Layer upon layer of clear, hard ice grew on the shafts of the oars themselves as they dipped in and out of the water, weighing them down. Lumps of ice formed wherever water splashed on the boys' sweatshirts and the stocking hats they wore pulled down over their ears.

They practiced rowing from half-slide and quarter-slide positions. They sprinted one day and rowed long, punishing ten- or twelve-mile marathons the next. Ulbrickson seemed oblivious to the cold. He followed them up and down the lake in his launch, wrapped in an overcoat and muffler, bellowing at them through his megaphone. When they finally stopped rowing in the iron-cold dark of late afternoon and returned to the dock, they had to chip ice off the oarlocks to get the oars out. Then, with their shells inverted over their heads, the icicles on the riggers standing oddly upright, their leg and arm muscles cramping in the cold air, they slid and slipped along the ice-slick dock and hobbled up the ramp to the shell house. Inside, they stretched out on benches and yelped in pain as they tried to regain the use of their limbs in the steam room.

By mid-November the weather had moderated, which is to say that it had become cold and rainy as it always is in Seattle in November. To the boys, it felt almost tropical compared with what they had just been through. Ulbrickson announced that he would wrap up fall training on November 25 with a two-thousand-meter competition under full racing conditions. The results would let everyone know where they stood going into the longer, harder push after the Christmas break.

On the twenty-fifth, another cold snap arrived. Ulbrickson told the coxswains of all four boats to go no higher than a beat of twenty-six. He wanted to see where the power lay, and a lower stroke was likely to reveal that. The results pleased Ulbrickson a good deal. He was, by his standards, buoyant when he met with reporters after the event. "We have," he said, "a stronger lineup than in the spring of 1935, and we figure to have three good fast boats in contention in January." The same boat that had been dominant all fall—the boat built around four of last year's freshmen—had won by an impressive three lengths in a time of 6:43. That was well off what he would consider a fast two thousand meters, but for low-stroke work the time was good. In second place was the boat that had been second best all fall—the boat with big Stub McMillin in the middle and Roger Morris in the bow. Joe's boat came in third.

Joe had been struggling with his rowing for weeks, especially since Thula had died. Then he got a letter from Sequim. Charlie McDonald was dead too, killed in an automobile crash on Highway 101. It was a stunning blow. Charlie had been an adviser and a teacher, the one adult who had stood by him and given him a chance when no one else had. Now he was gone, and Joe found himself unable to focus on anything other than the losses back home.

As the fall season wound down, his mind was almost never in the boat, and it showed in his rowing. He took some consolation from the fact that Ulbrickson had told the press that the third boat was still in contention. But he could not help but wonder whether Ulbrickson really meant it. As far as Joe could tell, nobody in the coaching launch was even watching him anymore.

But, in fact, someone was watching him very closely. Joe had noticed that George Pocock had been riding along in the coaching launch frequently that fall, but he hadn't noticed where Pocock had been training his binoculars.

On December 2, a little more than a month after Thula died, Harry Rantz put some money down on a two-thousand-dollar piece of lakefront property right next door to the house in which Fred and Thelma lived, near the north end of Lake Washington. Then he got out a pencil and paper and set about designing a new house—a house he would again build with his own hands, and in which he would finally reunite Joe with his family.

A few days later, on December 8, at the Commodore Hotel in New York, the Amateur Athletic Union of the United States voted on a resolution to send a three-man committee to Germany to investigate claims of Nazi maltreatment of Jews there. When all the votes—including fractional votes—had been tallied, the resolution had failed, 58.25 to 55.75. And with that—after several years of struggle—the last serious American effort to boycott the Berlin Olympics was effectively dead. In many ways it was a victory for the thousands of young Americans who were then competing for a chance to participate in the Olympics. It was also a victory for Avery Brundage, president of the American Olympic Committee, and his allies who had fought tooth and nail to ensure that there was no boycott. Most of all it was a victory for Adolf Hitler, who was rapidly learning just how ready the world was to be deceived.

As recently as late November, the boycott movement had been very much alive. On November 21 ten thousand anti-Nazi demonstrators under police escort had marched peacefully through New York rush-hour traffic. Carrying placards and following a banner reading "The Anti-Nazi Federation Calls on All Americans to Boycott the Olympic Games in Nazi Germany," the marchers had moved somberly down Eighth Avenue and then east on Twenty-Third Street to mass in Madison Square Park. There the crowd—mostly concerned Jews, labor leaders, university professors, and Catholics—had listened to more than twenty speakers detailing what was happening in Germany, how the Nazis were concealing it, and why it would be unconscionable for the United States to participate in the games.

Avery Brundage and his allies on the AOC had fought back vehemently. Brundage believed strongly in the Olympic spirit, and particularly in the principle that politics should play no role in sports. He argued, reasonably, that it would be unfair to American athletes to let German politics deprive them of their chance to compete on a world stage. But as the situation in Germany darkened and the fight over a possible boycott intensified, many of his arguments began to take a different turn. In September of 1934, Brundage had toured Germany. He had been given a quick and closely supervised tour of German athletic facilities and been assured by his Nazi handlers that Jewish athletes were being treated fairly. He had returned to the United States reporting confidently and loudly that the Jewish outcry was much ado about nothing.

The Nazis had not had to work very hard at deceiving Brundage, though. The fact was that Brundage's views—like those of many Americans of his class—appear to have been tainted by his own anti-Semitic prejudices. He had written, in chilling terms in 1929, about the probable coming of a master race, "a race physically strong, mentally alert and morally sound; a race not to be imposed upon." Now, in fighting the boycott movement, he advanced a

226 • The Boys in the Boat

number of disturbing arguments. He pointed out that Jews were not admitted to the clubs he belonged to either, as if one wrong justified another. Like the Nazis, he consistently lumped Jews and communists together, and frequently threw all supporters of the boycott movement into the same general category. He and his allies, even speaking publicly, regularly drew a distinction between "Americans" and Jews, as if the two could not be one and the same. Perhaps the most important of those allies, Charles H. Sherrill, formerly U.S. ambassador to Turkey, had often proclaimed himself a friend to American Jews. But like Brundage he had recently toured Germany. He had, in fact, attended the Nuremberg Rally of 1935 as Hitler's personal guest. There, and in a private meeting with Hitler, he had been mesmerized, as many visiting Americans were, by Hitler's force of personality and by his undeniable accomplishments in resurrecting Germany's economy. Returning home with the same empty assurances as Brundage, Sherrill began to systematically deny the increasingly obvious evidence of what was happening to Jews in Germany. He also took to mixing threats into his "pro-Jewish" remarks: "I shall go right on being pro-Jewish, and for that reason I have a warning for American Jewry. There is a great danger in this Olympic agitation. . . . We are almost certain to have a wave of anti-Semitism among those who never before gave it a thought and who may consider that 5,000,000 Jews in this country are using 120,000,000 Americans to pull their chestnuts out of the fire." It was Brundage himself, however, who came up with perhaps the most twisted bit of logic to advance the antiboycott cause: "The sportsmen of this country will not tolerate the use of clean American sport as a vehicle to transplant Old World hatreds to the United States." The trouble—the "Old World hatreds"—in other words, came not from the Nazis but from the Jews and their allies who dared to speak out against what was happening in Germany. By late 1935, deliberately or not, Brundage had crossed the line between deceived and deceiver.

Nevertheless, the issue was settled. America was going to the Berlin Olympics. What remained was to select the athletes worthy of carrying the American flag into the heart of the Nazi state.

PART FOUR

1936

Touching the Divine

The 1936 varsity crew

Left to right: Don Hume, Joe Rantz, Shorty Hunt, Stub McMillin,
Johnny White, Gordy Adam, Chuck Day, Roger Morris. *Kneeling:* Bobby Moch

CHAPTER THIRTEEN

When you get the rhythm in an eight, it's pure pleasure to be in it. It's not hard work when the rhythm comes—that "swing" as they call it. I've heard men shriek out with delight when that swing came in an eight; it's a thing they'll never forget as long as they live.

—George Yeoman Pocock

On the evening of January 9, Al Ulbrickson gathered the boys at the shell house and issued a stark warning: anyone who showed up for varsity turnout the following Monday, he said, "must be ready to take part in Washington's greatest and most grueling crew season." After months of talking about the Olympic year, it was finally here. Ulbrickson didn't want anyone to underestimate the stakes or the brutal price of participation.

When Joe reported to the shell house that Monday and glanced at the chalkboard, he was surprised to find that his name was listed among those in the number one varsity boat, as were Shorty Hunt's and Roger Morris's. After rowing in the number three and four shells all fall, Joe couldn't fathom why he had suddenly been promoted. As it turned out, it wasn't really much of a promotion. Ulbrickson had partially reconstituted some of the old boat assignments from 1935, purely on a temporary basis. He wanted to spend the first few weeks working on fundamentals. "As a general rule," he said, "men are in a more receptive mood for pointers when working with familiar teammates." As soon as they started rowing at a racing beat, though, he would bust the boatings up, and it would once again be every man for himself. The boat assignments really didn't amount to a hill of beans for now.

And so they all took to the water again. Through the rest of January and into February, rowing six days a week now, rowing from quarter slides and half slides, taking shorter strokes to focus on technique. They practiced racing starts. They worked on individual weaknesses. Every few days snow flurries descended on Lake Washington. When it wasn't snowing, it was clear, bitter cold, and windy. They rowed anyway, some of them attired in ragged sweat suits, some, incongruously, in shorts and stocking caps. Universal Pictures came and shot newsreel footage of them, just in case it was needed for the Olympics. Occasionally they staged short races against one another. The nominal first boat, Joe's, kept coming in third. The third boat kept coming in first. Ulbrickson noted that the boys in Joe's boat would get going, then lose their swing, then regain it, then lose it again, as many as three times in a single race. Their catching was the worst of the top three boats.

One gray day in February, Ulbrickson was out in the launch, struggling to correct the problems in boat number one and growing frustrated with the effort, when he noticed George Pocock sculling by himself in the distance. He hollered, "Way enough!" at the boys and slipped the launch into idle, still watching Pocock.

The boys noticed Ulbrickson's faraway stare and turned in their seats to see what he was looking at. Pocock was ghosting over the water as if effortlessly, his boat ethereal looking in a light mist that had settled on the water. His lean, upright body slid forward and backward in the boat fluidly, without hesitation or check. His oars entered and left the water noiselessly, broad, smooth puddles blooming in the dark water alongside his boat.

Ulbrickson grabbed his megaphone, motioned the boatbuilder over to the shell, and said, "George, tell them what I'm trying to teach them. Tell them what we try to accomplish around here." Pocock circled the shell slowly in his own boat, talking softly to each boy in turn, leaning ever so slightly toward the long cedar shell. Then he waved at Ulbrickson and rowed away. No more than three minutes had passed.

When Ulbrickson barked, "Row!" the boys pulled their shell smartly ahead, their catching and their rowing suddenly crisp and clean. From that point on, George Pocock rode along in the coaching launch most days, bundled up in an overcoat and neck scarf, a fedora pulled down over his ears, taking notes, pointing things out to Ulbrickson.

In general Ulbrickson was pleased. Despite the difficult weather and the erratic performance of boat number one, things were progressing very well; the time trials were promising for so early in the season. With the infusion of new blood from the previous year's exceptional freshman boat, he was again faced with the dilemma of having almost too much talent out on the water. It made it hard sometimes to separate good from great, great from greater. Nevertheless by late February he was starting to form solid ideas about what a first varsity boat—a boat for Berlin—would look like, though he wasn't ready to talk to the press or to the boys themselves about it. As long as they were competing with one another on even terms, they were likely to keep improving. At least one thing was obvious, though. If a Washington boat did go on to ply the waters of the Langer See in Berlin later that year, Bobby Moch was going to be sitting in the stern with a megaphone strapped to his face.

At five foot seven and 119 pounds, Moch was almost the perfect size for a coxswain. George Pocock, in fact, designed his shells to perform optimally with a 120-pound coxswain. Even less weight was generally desirable, but only provided that the man had the strength to steer the boat. Like jockeys, coxswains often went to extraordinary lengths to keep their weight down—they starved themselves, they purged, they exercised compulsively, they spent long hours in the steam room trying to sweat off an extra pound or two. Sometimes oarsmen who thought their cox was weighing them down took matters into their own hands and locked their diminutive captains in the steam room for a few hours. "Typical coxswain abuse," one Washington cox later said, laughing. In Bobby Moch's case, staying small had never been much of a problem. And at any rate, even if he had carried an extra pound here or there, the roughly three pounds devoted to his brain would have more than made up for it.

The first task of a coxswain is to steer the shell on a straight course for the duration of a race. In a Pocock shell in the 1930s, the cox controlled the rudder by pulling a pair of ropes in the stern, at the end of which were a pair of wooden dowels, called "knockers" because they were sometimes used to raise the stroke rate by beating them on an ironbark "knocker-board" fastened to the side of the boat. When eight very large men are in constant motion in a twenty-four-inch-wide vessel and the wind is blowing and the tide or current is relentlessly trying to push them off course, steering is no small challenge. But it's the least of what a coxswain must worry about.

From the moment the shell is launched, the coxswain is the captain of the boat. He or she must exert control, both physical and psychological, over everything that goes on in the shell. Good coxes know their oarsmen inside and out—their individual strengths and vulnerabilities—and they know how to get the most out of each man at any given moment. They have the force of character to inspire exhausted rowers to dig deeper and try harder, even when all seems lost. They have an encyclopedic understanding of their opponents:

how they like to race, when they are likely to start sprinting, when they like to lie in wait. Before a regatta, the cox receives a race plan from the coach, and he or she is responsible for carrying it out faithfully. But in a situation as fluid and dynamic as a crew race, circumstances often change abruptly and race plans must be thrown overboard. The cox is the only person in the shell who is facing forward and can see how the field is shaping up throughout a race, and he or she must be prepared to react quickly to unforeseen developments. When a race plan is failing to yield results, it is up to the cox to come up with a new one, often in a split second, and to communicate it quickly and forcefully to the crew. Often this involves a lot of shouting and a lot of emotion. In Cal's Olympic gold medal race in Amsterdam in 1928, Don Blessing put on what the *New York Times* called "one of the greatest performances of demonical howling ever heard on a terrestrial planet. . . . But such language and what a vocabulary! One closed one's eyes and waited for the crack of a final cruel whip across the backs of the galley slaves." In short, a good coxswain is a quarterback, a cheerleader, and a coach all in one. He or she is a deep thinker, canny like a fox, inspirational, and in many cases the toughest person in the boat.

Little Bobby Moch was all of that and more. He had grown up in Montesano, a foggy little logging town on the Chehalis River in southwestern Washington. It was a wet, dusky world; a world dominated by big trees, big trucks, and big men. Massive Douglas firs and cedars grew in the misty hills outside town. Ponderous logging trucks rumbled through town on Highway 41 night and day on their way to the mills in Aberdeen. Beefy lumberjacks in thick flannel shirts and hobnailed boots strutted up and down the main street, shot pool at the Star Pool Hall on Saturday nights, and sat in the Montesano Cafe drinking coffee by the gallon on Sunday mornings.

Bobby's father, Gaston—a Swiss watchmaker and jeweler—was not a large man. But he was a prominent member of the citizenry, a proud member of the all-volunteer fire department, and was celebrated for having driven the first automobile twelve miles from Aberdeen to Montesano, a journey that he had accomplished in a jaw-dropping hour and a half. When Bobby was five, a botched operation on his appendix nearly killed him. The recovery left him short, skinny, and sickly—afflicted with severe asthma—throughout his grade-school years and beyond. Determined not to let his frailty and his stature stand in his way, in high school he went out for every sport he could think of, mastering none but playing all of them tenaciously. When he couldn't make it onto the school football team, he and other boys who weren't large enough to make the cut gathered on a vacant lot just down Broad Street from his home, playing rough-and-tumble scrub football without benefit of helmets or pads. The smallest of the small boys on the lot, Bobby was always chosen last, and though he spent much of each game with his face planted in the dirt, he later credited the experience for much of his subsequent success in life. "It doesn't matter how many times you get knocked down," he told his daughter, Marilynn. "What matters is how many times you get up." In his senior year in high school, by sheer force of will, he lettered in—of all things—basketball. And the three pounds of gray matter he carried around in his skull served him well in the classroom. He wound up at the top of his class, honored as Montesano High's class valedictorian in 1932.

When he enrolled at the University of Washington, he set his sights on coxing. As with everything else he attempted, he had to fight tooth and nail to win a seat in the stern of one of Al Ulbrickson's boats. But once he was in that seat, his tenacity quickly made a believer out of Al Ulbrickson. Like everyone else in the shell house, Ulbrickson soon discovered that the only time Moch didn't seem entirely happy and comfortable in the coxswain's seat was when he was in the lead. As long as he could see another boat out ahead of him, as long as he had something to overcome, someone to beat, the boy was on fire. By 1935 Moch wielded the megaphone in the JV boat that contended with Joe and the other sophomores for varsity status that season. He wasn't a popular choice. He had displaced a well-regarded boy his new crewmates had been rowing with for two years, and they initially refused to give Moch the respect a coxswain absolutely depends on. That just made Moch push them harder. "That was a tough year. I wasn't liked at all," he later said. "I demanded they do better, so I made a lot of enemies." Moch drove those boys like Simon Legree with a whip. He had a deep baritone voice that was surprising in a man so small, and he used it to good effect, bellowing out commands with absolute authority. But he was also canny enough to know when to let up on the crew, when to flatter them, when to implore them, when to joke around with them. Slowly he won his new crewmates over.

The bottom line was that Bobby Moch was smart and he knew how to use his smarts. In fact, by the end of the 1936 season he'd have a Phi Beta Kappa key of his own to twirl on his finger, just like Al Ulbrickson.

———

In late February, as he sorted through the boys, Ulbrickson began attaching more significance to which boats he labeled number one, number two, and number three. Joe had dropped from the number one to the number two boat. On February 20, rowing hard in a heavy snow and a steady east wind, number two and number one came in about even. Joe's hopes rose. But a week later Ulbrickson moved him down to the number three boat.

The weather continued to be atrocious. Mostly the boys rowed anyway. Cold, rain, sleet, hail, and snow they simply ignored. But there were days when the wind ripped up the surface of Lake Washington so badly that nobody could row on it without being swamped. Despite the weather, the time trials turned in by the top boats were still good, but they weren't improving as rapidly as Ulbrickson had been hoping for at this point. He hadn't yet found a boat that would walk away from the others. And with all the cold-weather rowing interspersed with days when they couldn't row at all, the boys' morale began to erode. "Too many gripers," Ulbrickson scrawled in the logbook on February 29.

One exceptionally stormy afternoon in early March, when the boys were lounging morosely about the shell house, George Pocock tapped Joe on the shoulder and asked him to come up into the loft. He had a few thoughts he wanted to share with him. In the shop Pocock leaned over one side of a new shell and began to apply varnish to its upturned hull. Joe pulled a sawhorse to the other side of the shell and sat down on it, facing the older man.

Pocock began by saying he'd been watching Joe row for a while now, that he was a fine oarsman. He'd noted a few technical faults—that Joe was breaking his arms at the elbows a little too early in the stroke and not catching the water as cleanly as he would if he kept his hands moving at the same speed that the water was moving under the boat. But that wasn't what he wanted to talk about.

He told Joe that there were times when he seemed to think he was the only fellow in the boat, as if it was up to him to row the boat across the finish line all by himself. When a man rowed like that, he said, he was bound to attack the water rather than to work with it, and worse, he was bound not to let his crew help him row.

He suggested that Joe think of a well-rowed race as a symphony, and himself as just one player in the orchestra. If one fellow in an orchestra was playing out of tune, or playing at a different tempo, the whole piece would naturally be ruined. That's the way it was with rowing. What mattered more than how hard a man rowed was how well everything he did in the boat harmonized with what the other fellows were doing. And a man couldn't harmonize with his crewmates unless he opened his heart to them. He had to care about his crew. It wasn't just the rowing but his crewmates that he had to give himself up to, even if it meant getting his feelings hurt.

Pocock paused and looked up at Joe. "If you don't like some fellow in the boat, Joe, you have to learn to like him. It has to matter to you whether he wins the race, not just whether you do."

He told Joe to be careful not to miss his chance. He reminded him that he'd already learned to row past pain, past exhaustion, past the voice that told him it couldn't be done. That meant he had an opportunity to do things most men would never have a chance to do. And he concluded with a remark that Joe would never forget. "Joe, when you really start trusting those other boys, you will feel a power at work within you that is far beyond anything you've ever imagined. Sometimes, you will feel as if you have rowed right off the planet and are rowing among the stars."

The next day was a Sunday, and as he had every weekend for weeks, Joe took Joyce and drove over to the lot on Lake Washington where his father was building his new house. The basement portion was nearly complete, and with the upstairs portion under way Harry had moved into the basement with his children. It was more like a cave than a house, with one large garage-style door for an entrance and only one small window facing the lake. But Harry had lugged in a woodstove, and it was at least warm and dry inside.

Joe and his father spent the morning hauling lumber from the road down to the construction site in a driving rain, then hoisting it up to the level of what would become the main floor of the house. Joyce entertained the kids inside, playing card games and making fudge and cocoa on the woodstove. She and Joe were worried about all four of them—they were still having a hard time adjusting to the loss of their mother. With Harry working on the house full-time, they weren't receiving much in the way of attention. They were frequently assaulted by terrifying dreams, Rose and Polly often cried when left alone, and although they had all remained in school, their grades were suffering. Joe had promised each of them a dime for every A they brought home. Now Joyce was trying to think of motherly things she could do with them.

Joe at Harry's new house on Lake Washington

Playing mother to Thula's children was easy and natural to Joyce in almost all regards. She saw grief-stricken children in desperate need, and every instinct within her impelled her to sweep them into her arms and nurture them. That's what she had done from the first time she had seen them after Thula's death. The resentment and anger she still felt toward Thula she kept locked away deep down inside, safely out of view of the children. What was harder for Joyce, though, was to know what to do and what to feel about Joe's father. They got along well enough on the surface. Harry treated her pleasantly, even warmly, and she tried to reciprocate. But inside, Joyce still seethed. She could not forget or forgive Harry for his failure to stand behind Joe for all those years, for his weakness, for letting Thula cast Joe aside as if he were nothing more than a stray dog. And the more she brooded on it the more it made her angry.

By late that afternoon, Joe and his father had moved all the lumber into position, and with the rain falling harder than ever, Harry started to retreat into the house. Joe shouted after him, "I'll be inside soon, Pop," and walked out onto the dock at Fred's house next door, looking out over the heaving gray-and-white folds of the lake, pondering the near future.

The finish line for the Pacific Coast Regatta in April was a little less than a mile up the lake from there. Would he be in the varsity boat when it passed this dock? He figured he probably wouldn't. Gusts of wind buffeted him; rainwater poured down his face. He didn't care. He stared at the water, pondering what Pocock had imparted the day before, running the boatbuilder's words over in his mind.

For Joe, who had spent the last six years doggedly making his own way in the world, who had forged his identity on stoic self-reliance, nothing was more frightening than allowing himself to depend on others. People let you down. People leave you behind. Depending on people, trusting them—it's what gets you hurt. But trust seemed to be at the heart of what Pocock was asking. Harmonize with the other fellows, Pocock said. There was a kind of absolute truth in that, something he needed to come to terms with.

He stood on the dock for a long time, gazing at the lake, oblivious to the rain, thoughts assembling themselves, connecting with other thoughts and drawing together in new ways. Harmony was something he understood as a musician. He and Harry Secor had worked together to stalk the giant chinook salmon of the Dungeness River. He had watched and marveled at Charlie Mc-Donald's horses, Fritz and Dick, squatting and pulling together, moving enormous cottonwood trees as if they were matchsticks, the animals heaving and pulling in unison, like one creature. Charlie had told him that they would pull until their harnesses broke or their hearts burst. On the cliff face of the Grand Coulee, Joe and the men he had worked with had looked out for each other as they dodged rocks falling from above. In the evenings and on weekends, he and Johnny White and Chuck Day prowled B Street together, seeking adventure instead of advantage over one another.

Joe turned and peered through a curtain of rain at the house his father was building. Just behind the house, a freight train lumbered past on the railroad tracks that the observation train would follow during the California race. Inside, the kids and Joyce and his father were all under one roof, sitting in front of the fire right now, waiting for him to come in out of the rain. And as he stood in the rain, Joe's feelings began to shift—moving around like notes on a musical staff, bits and pieces of new themes starting to fall into place.

When he returned to the warm cave his father had constructed, Joe toweled his hair dry, unpacked his banjo, and pulled a chair up in front of the woodstove. He gathered the kids around him. He tuned the banjo carefully, fiddling with knobs and plucking at steel strings. Then he cleared his throat, cracked open a big white smile, and began to sing. One by one, the kids and Joyce and Harry all joined in.

By March 19, Al Ulbrickson figured he had found his best bet for an Olympic boat. He still had it pegged as the second boat on his chalkboard, but the boys in it were beginning to edge the first boat consistently, and Ulbrickson was quietly putting his final selections into this boat.

At bow he had Roger Morris. At number two, Chuck Day. At number three was one of Tom Bolles's freshmen from the previous year, Gordy Adam, the dairy-farm kid from up on the Nooksack River near the Canadian border. Gordy had attended a two-room country schoolhouse, then Mount Baker High in the small town of Deming. Then he'd spent five brutal months fishing for salmon on the Bering Sea, up in Alaska, to put together enough money to start at the university. He was a quiet young man. So quiet that in the previous year's race against California he'd rowed the whole two miles with his thumb cut to the bone and never mentioned it to anyone. In honor of that, Royal Brougham had begun to refer to him now as Gordy "Courage" Adam.

At number four Ulbrickson had lithe, good-looking Johnny White. Big, rangy Stub McMillin was at number five. Shorty Hunt was at number six. At number seven was another of Tom Bolles's former freshmen, Merton Hatch. At the stroke position was a fourth member of last year's freshman crew: poker-faced Don Hume.

It was an unusual move to put a nineteen-year-old sophomore at the critical stroke position, but Hume had proven so sensational as a freshman that many were already saying he might turn out to be Washington's best stroke since Ulbrickson himself had rowed at that position, maybe even better. He hailed from Anacortes, then a gritty lumber and fish-canning port fifty miles north of Seattle. In high school he'd been the consummate all-around athlete—a star in football, basketball, and track—and an honor student. He was also an accomplished pianist, a devotee of Fats Waller, and capable of pulling off anything from swing tunes to Mendelssohn. When he sat down at a piano, he always drew a crowd. After the crash, his father lost his job at a pulp mill and moved to Olympia in search of work. Don stayed behind in Anacortes, lodging with family friends and eventually finding work in a lumber mill.

Walking the cobbled beach on the channel between Anacortes and Guemes Island one day, he came across an abandoned and dilapidated thirteen-foot clinker-built rowboat. He refurbished it, took it down to the water, and discovered that he loved rowing. Loved it, in fact, more than anything he had ever done. For a year following his graduation from high school, he rowed obsessively—up and down the channel on foggy days and on long voyages out among the San Juan Islands on sunny days. When the job at the lumber mill gave out and he decided to join his parents in Olympia, he rowed all the way there—a six-day voyage that covered nearly a hundred miles of water. That fall he moved to Seattle, registered as a geology major at the university, and then made a beeline for the shell house, where Tom Bolles and Al Ulbrickson quickly discovered that they had an extraordinary athlete on their hands.

Hume pulled as smooth as silk, and with the precise, mechanical regularity of a metronome. He seemed to have an innate, deep-seated sense of rhythm. But more than that, his mastery of his oar, his steady reliability, and his rock-solid sureness were so apparent that every other boy in the boat could sense them immediately and thus easily fall into synch with Hume regardless of water conditions or the state of a race. He was key.

In the stern of Ulbrickson's star boat, wearing the megaphone, was, inevitably, Bobby Moch.

Joe was in the third boat. And it looked as if he'd be staying there. So far he hadn't even made the presumed JV boat, and so it looked as if he would not be rowing in the Cal race or beyond. But then, on March 21, he walked into the shell house and found his name on the chalkboard, sitting at seat number seven in boat number two, the boat everyone was talking about as the best bet for the varsity slot. He couldn't believe it. He didn't know if Pocock had talked to Ulbrickson, or if Merton Hatch had simply messed up in some spectacular way, or if Ulbrickson simply needed someone else at number seven for the day. Whatever the reason, this was his chance.

Joe knew what he had to do, and he found doing it surprisingly easy. From the moment he stepped into the shell that afternoon, he felt at home. He liked these boys. He didn't know Gordy Adam and Don Hume well, but both made a point of welcoming him aboard. His oldest, most reliable shell house friend, Roger Morris, sitting up front in the bow, gave him a wave and shouted the length of the boat, "Hey, Joe, I see you finally found the right boat!" His buddies from Grand Coulee, Chuck Day and Johnny White, were sitting up near the front too. As he strapped his shoes to the footboard and began to lace his feet into the shoes, Stub McMillin, his face alight, said, "OK, this boat is going to fly now, boys." Shorty Hunt slapped him on the back and whispered, "Got your back, Joe."

Joe rowed that day as he had never been able to row before—as Pocock had told him to row, giving himself up to the crew's effort entirely, rowing as if he were an extension of the man in front of him and the man behind him, following Hume's stroke flawlessly, transmitting it back to Shorty behind him in one continuous flow of muscle and wood. It felt to Joe like a transformation, as if some kind of magic had come over him. The nearest thing to it he could remember was the night as a freshman when he had found himself out on Lake Union with the lights of Seattle twinkling on the water and the breaths of his crewmates synchronized with his in white plumes in the dark, cold air. Now, as he climbed out of the boat in the twilight, he realized that the transformation wasn't so much that he was trying to do what Pocock had said as that this was a bunch of boys with whom he *could* do it. He just trusted them. In the end, it was that simple. Ulbrickson wrote in the logbook, "Changed Rantz and Hatch and it helped a lot."

That turned out to be an understatement of considerable magnitude. It was the last change Ulbrickson had to make. Over the next few days, the boat began to fly, just as Stub McMillin had said it would.

On March 22 it led all the other boats from start to finish. On March 23 it won by an astonishing seven lengths in one race and a commanding three or four in a second. On the morning of March 27, in a heavy late spring snowstorm, it came in three lengths ahead. That afternoon, rowing a two-thousand-meter sprint, Don Hume took the stroke rate up to a punishing forty, the boys fell in behind him flawlessly, and the boat flashed across the finish line well ahead of the others again. On March 28, with light snow still falling, Ulbrickson officially elevated the boat to varsity status. He wouldn't announce it to the press for a few more days, but the man had made the decision of his career. This was the crew with which he would attempt to go to the Berlin Olympics.

That afternoon George Pocock personally christened the new shell in which the boys would row in the trials. As Joe and his crewmates held the shell aloft, Pocock poured a jarful of mysterious fluid over its bow and pronounced, "I christen this boat *Husky Clipper*. May it have success in all the waters it speeds over. Especially in Berlin." As the boys began to carry the boat down the ramp to the water, some of them crinkled their noses, trying to make out the odd scent of the fluid on the bow. Pocock chuckled. "Sauerkraut juice. To get it used to Germany." He grinned.

On April 4, Ulbrickson held one final three-mile time trial before officially announcing the boatings for the Pacific Coast Regatta. Two miles into the trial, Bobby Moch kicked the beat up to thirty-two and settled in there. The three-mile course record was then 16:33.4, set by the Washington varsity that Joe had watched from the ferry in 1934. Now Joe and his crewmates came in at 16:20, and they did it sitting upright at the end of the race, breathing easy, feeling good. Every time they climbed into the *Husky Clipper* together, they just seemed to get better.

There was a straightforward reason for what was happening. The boys in the *Clipper* had been winnowed down by punishing competition, and in the winnowing a kind of common character had issued forth: they were all skilled, they were all tough, they were all fiercely determined, but they were also all good-hearted. Every one of them had come from humble origins or been humbled by the ravages of the hard times in which they had grown up. Each in his own way, they had all learned that nothing could be taken for granted in life, that for all their strength and good looks and youth, forces were at work in the world that were greater than they. The challenges they had faced together had taught them humility—the need to subsume their individual egos for the sake of the boat as a whole—and humility was the common gateway through which they were able now to come together and begin to do what they had not been able to do before.

But before the Olympic trials at Princeton, Al Ulbrickson faced another daunting series of challenges: First the Pacific Coast Regatta with California on Lake Washington. Win all three races there and, Ulbrickson figured, he might just convince the people of Seattle to again finance sending all three boats to Poughkeepsie for the national championships in June. Then—win or lose in Poughkeepsie—he would take the varsity to Princeton in July. Prevail there and it would mean a trip to Berlin, another qualifying race or two, and finally the gold medal race against the best crews in the world. It was a tall order, but every time Al Ulbrickson watched his new varsity crew take to the water his confidence that he could pull it off grew.

In Berkeley, Ky Ebright was, if anything, probably even more confident than Al Ulbrickson, both about the upcoming regatta in Seattle and about his

Olympic prospects. He had almost certainly read about the 16:20 three-mile time trial Ulbrickson's varsity had turned in, but the news couldn't have fazed him. His boys had already turned in a stunning three-mile time of 15:34 on the estuary. The shell had been running with the tide, but, still, the difference was nearly a minute. On April 8 he ran another time trial in slack water. His varsity came in at 16:15, still five seconds better than Ulbrickson's crew. Guarding against complacency, Ebright allowed himself, when his crew reached the dock, only a gruff "You looked good out there for a change." The fact of the matter, though, was that Ebright had every reason to feel good about how things were shaping up for 1936, and he hadn't seen anything coming out of Seattle that would change his mind.

He wasn't taking any chances, though. In fact he was throwing everything he had into starting the Olympic year off right by beating Washington in Seattle. He'd begun the season by writing the names of each of his oarsmen on scraps of paper and throwing them into a hat—the Poughkeepsie champions right along with all the other sophomore, junior, and senior contenders. Then he'd pulled names out one at a time to determine his initial boatings. The point was that none of his boys could rely on past performance to gain a seat in the varsity boat. Each of them would have to earn it all over again.

Things had shaped up nicely since then. The endless California sun had allowed him to work his boys at his own pace, culminating in a series of three-mile pulls on the estuary that had left them well conditioned and in top form. When he'd tried them at the shorter distance, they'd done just as well. Given that, and his shellacking of Washington in both Poughkeepsie and Long Beach the previous summer, he figured he was well positioned to take the longer races at Washington and Poughkeepsie and then move on to dominate the shorter races at the Olympic trials and Berlin.

In the last few weeks, he'd reinstituted a tradition he'd employed before big races since his 1932 Olympic triumph—the varsity training table. Any boy who had worked his way into the top two varsity boats was entitled to sit down with his crewmates for a free dinner at Stephens Union on the Berkeley campus. Given the hard times, it gave his boys a powerful incentive to make it into one of those top boats. It also gave Ebright the ability to control the nutritional value of what his boys were tucking into. The training-table fare was hearty—rich in protein and calcium in particular. Most nights that meant a large, juicy steak and as much milk as a boy could drink.

There was no budget for a training table in Seattle. But Al Ulbrickson was just as concerned as Ebright that his boys be well nourished going into racing season. Ulbrickson's prescription was considerably less enjoyable than a steak. Every afternoon the Washington boys were compelled to choke down first a glass of a chalky-tasting pink calcium solution, then a glass of Knox Sparkling Gelatine. The gelatin sometimes proved tricky, depending on how and when it had been mixed. A fellow had to get it down his gullet quickly before it began to solidify, or he would gag on it. Later that year, after reading an article about Ulbrickson's nutritional regimen, and contemplating his boys' success, a horse trainer named Tom Smith would go in search of hay with a high calcium content for a racehorse named Seabiscuit.

Ky Ebright and his boys arrived in Seattle late on the afternoon of Tuesday, April 14, and checked into the Edmond Meany Hotel. Earlier in the day, Ulbrickson had sent his boys out in water so rough that they had not rowed in its like since the day in 1932 when Cal had defeated Washington by eighteen lengths and Washington had barely made it across the finish line before sinking.

But when the Cal boys showed up at the Montlake Cut on Wednesday morning, the sun was out in full force and the water was glass smooth. As they carried their shells down the ramp to the water, the national champion California boys were an intimidating sight. Seattle reporters marveled at how sun-bronzed they looked when seen side by side with the pallid boys from Washington. And if any of the writers assembled on the ramp that day harbored any doubt that Ky Ebright was taking the Washington threat seriously, those doubts were put to rest directly. Ebright himself promptly strapped on a megaphone, climbed into the coxswain's seat of his varsity boat, the *California Clipper*, and began barking commands as he took the boat out for an eight-mile pull far down Lake Washington, well out of sight of the Washington coaching staff.

For the next two days, neither Ulbrickson nor Ebright staged time trials, or if they did, they kept the results to themselves. Both coaches continued to issue the customary gloomy assessments of their boys' chances. Ebright yawned that his varsity was nothing to write home about—"a good average outfit," he called them. Ulbrickson summoned up a deeper level of despair, calling the Bears the clear favorites before lamenting, "We have been handicapped this year by inclement weather." Then he flat out lied: "The boys are not exceptional."

———

Saturday, April 18, was a lovely day on which to watch a crew race, a hard day on which to row one. The skies were flawlessly blue. Temperatures promised to climb into the low seventies by race time. By midmorning, a steady flow of warm air from the south had ruffled the blue surface of Lake Washington. With weather like this, the regatta promised to draw throngs of people to the beaches at the north end of the lake.

Joe had come up with a scheme for profiting from the arrival of these throngs in his father's new neighborhood. He and Harry had bought a hundred pounds of unshelled peanuts in two burlap sacks. The night before, Joyce, Harry, Rose, Mike, Polly, and Harry Junior had stayed up late, transferring the peanuts to paper sacks, planning to sell them to the race fans. Now they had hundreds of sacks ready to go, and as soon as people began to show up, in the early afternoon, Joyce and the kids fanned out along the beaches, hawking peanuts for ten cents a sack.

As in 1934, at 1:00 p.m. a ferry—this year the MV *Chippewa*—departed the University of Washington's Oceanographic Dock with a full load of students and the school's marching band. The *Chippewa* was elegantly appointed for a ferryboat. Many of her passengers, in fact, said that boarding her felt like boarding a North Atlantic liner, with Philippine mahogany paneling throughout the main cabin, a men's smoking room, a ladies' lounge, a full-service galley, red-leather padded seats, and a glassed-in observation room up front. She was often chartered for special moonlight cruises, during which an elaborate loudspeaker system piped live music from the observation room throughout the ship. The Washington marching band now took up a position in the observation room, switched on the microphones, and began to play dance music. As they had two years before, young men in slacks and shirt-sleeves and young women in flouncy summer dresses danced out of the cabin and onto the decks.

As the *Chippewa* headed north, up the lake toward the finish line at Sheridan Beach, a navy cruiser and nearly four hundred other vessels flying purple and gold pennants joined her. By now the wind out of the south had stiffened considerably. Black smoke and white steam pouring from the larger vessels' stacks streamed briskly northward, and whitecaps began to dance at the north end of the lake, where the wind was piling the water up against the shore.

At 2:15 p.m. an observation train left University Station and made its way to 125th Street for the start of the two-mile freshman race. By now, the largest crowd ever to witness a crew race in the Northwest had assembled along the racecourse.

Tom Bolles followed his freshman crew out to the starting line in his launch. Once again he believed he had an outstanding bunch in his shell, but as is always the case for freshman coaches, he had no reliable way to assess his boys' true capabilities until he saw them racing against a major rival.

They did not disappoint. When the freshman race went off promptly at 3:00 p.m., it looked as if it would be a close race. Cal leapt out into the lead, but the conditions made for tough rowing. Waves were quartering across the racecourse now, constantly threatening to throw the boats off keel. It was treacherously easy to catch nothing but air between waves or to dig too deeply into a wave and catch a crab. At the quarter-mile mark the number seven man in the Cal boat did just that, and all four oars on the starboard side came almost to a halt while they reset. When they got going again, the number three man caught another crab. In the meantime Washington had quickly grabbed a substantial lead, and then settled down to build on it. When they crossed the finish line four and a half lengths ahead, their official time was recorded as 10:11.2. That would have eclipsed the 11:24.8 course record set by Joe and his freshmen crewmates in 1934 by well more than a minute. Four other, unofficial, timekeepers reported a more reasonable time of 10:42, and the figure was revised. But it was still a new course record by a wide margin, and Tom Bolles remained undefeated on Lake Washington. Before the day was out the East Coast schools, particularly Harvard, would take note of that. Bolles's days at Washington were numbered.

The JV race began at 3:45 p.m., and for all intents and purposes it was over a hundred yards down the line. Four of the boys in the Washington boat were veterans of Joe's all-sophomore crew of the year before: Bud Schacht, George Lund, Delos Schoch, and Chuck Hartman. These were boys who knew how to row in rough water, and how to win. They took the lead easily at the start, widened it at each quarter-mile buoy, and crossed the line almost six lengths ahead of California. Their time, 16:14.2, beat the record set by Cal by almost a full minute.

On the dock at Fred Rantz's house, Harry and his kids and Joyce sat eating peanuts and tossing the shells into the lake. The sales that morning had been disappointing. They were going to be eating peanuts for a long while. Harry peered down the lake toward Sand Point with a pair of binoculars. The Philco

radio in the house—a luxury he had bought secondhand for the occasion—
was turned all the way up so they would be able to hear the NBC broadcast of
the varsity race on KOMO when it began.

Joyce dangled her legs over the edge of the dock. At the north end of the
lake, a silver airplane circled the area of the finish line. She peered down into
the water, past the floating peanut shells. She felt unsettled.

Early that morning she had cut Joe's hair as he sat perched on a chair in his
little room at the YMCA, a towel fastened around his neck with a clothespin.
It was a ritual Joyce performed once a month, and she always looked forward
to it. It offered her a chance to be close to Joe, to chat with him privately,
away from the eyes and ears of others, and it always seemed to please Joe, to
relax him.

That morning, though, as she worked methodically, combing his blond
hair up, measuring it carefully by eye, using the comb as a cutting guide and
snipping the hair at just the right length to create the crew cut he favored, Joe
had been fidgety in the chair. Finally she asked him what was wrong. He'd hesitated, struggling for words, but as she remembered later, the gist of it was
that there was something about this race, this boat, that was different. He
couldn't really explain it; he just knew he didn't want to let this bunch of boys
down.

At 4:15 p.m., as the two varsity crews paddled out to the starting line, the NBC
Red Network went on the air with coast-to-coast prerace coverage. The tail-
wind had stiffened further, slicing up the length of the lake now, piling more
rough water into heaps of whitecaps at the north end. So far all four boats on
the course that day had come in well ahead of the previous course records,
even the losing boats. The long, upright bodies of the oarsmen were catching
the wind, acting essentially as sails, hurrying the shells down the course. It
was clear now that, absent an unforeseen disaster, somebody was about to set
a new varsity record as well.

At the start line, the *Husky Clipper* bobbed in the swells. Roger Morris and
Gordy Adam, up front, struggled to keep the bow of the boat pointed due
north under the relentless push of the quartering waves. Bobby Moch lowered his hand to indicate his crew was ready to row. Over in the Cal boat,
coxswain Tommy Maxwell did the same.

In the coaching launches idling in the water behind the shells, Al Ulbrickson and Ky Ebright were decidedly nervous. The fact was that neither of them knew quite what they were facing in the other boat. Both coaches had excellent crews and knew it; neither was quite sure about the other man's crew. The boys in the California boat weighed a total of 1,557 pounds; the boys in the Washington boat weighed 1,561, just four pounds heavier. Both boats had savvy coxswains and powerful, experienced oarsmen. Both boats were state-of-the-art shells—Pocock's latest and greatest, sleek splinters of cedar, the *Husky Clipper* and the *California Clipper*. Both boats were sixty-two feet long and, within a pound or two, weighed the same. Both featured sleek cedar skins, five thirty-seconds of an inch thick. Both had elegant yellow cedar washboards, ash frames, Sitka-spruce gunnels, fore and after decking made of silk impregnated with varnish. Most important, both featured Pocock's trademark camber, the slight curvature that gave them compression, spring, and liveliness in the water. It was hard to see a clear advantage. It would simply come down to watermanship, and guts.

When the starter shouted, "Row!" both boats bolted off the line like nervous racehorses held too long in the starting gate. Both crews started off rowing hard and high, at thirty-five or thirty-six. In the Cal boat, the big stroke, Gene Berkenkamp, who had mowed Washington down in Poughkeepsie and Long Beach the year before, quickly powered his crew to a short lead. For three-quarters of a mile, the two crews rowed in lockstep, both furiously hacking at the choppy water. In the Washington boat, Don Hume was matching Berkenkamp's stroke rate but making no progress in pulling even with him.

Then Bobby Moch began to make use of those three pounds of brains. He did what was counterintuitive but smart—what was manifestly hard to do but he knew was the right thing to do. With his opponent out in front of him, rowing in the midthirties and maintaining a lead, he told Hume to lower the stroke count. Hume dropped it to twenty-nine.

Almost immediately the boys in the Washington boat found their swing. Don Hume set the model, taking huge, smooth, deep pulls. Joe and the rest of the boys fell in behind him. Very slowly, seat by seat, the *Husky Clipper* began to regain water on the *California Clipper*. By the one-mile mark, the two boats were even and Washington was starting to edge out ahead.

In the Cal boat, Tommy Maxwell, shocked, glanced over at Washington and immediately called out, "Give me ten big ones!" Bobby Moch heard him, glanced back at him, but refused to take the bait. Gene Berkenkamp and the rest of the Cal boys leaned into their oars and took the prescribed ten extra-hard pulls. Bobby Moch hunched down in the stern, looked Don Hume in the eyes, and growled at him to keep it steady at twenty-nine. When Cal had finished their big ten, they had not appreciably narrowed Washington's small lead.

With the wind in their faces, both crews were fairly flying down the course now, with spray breaking over the bow of their shells as they skipped from wave to wave, the blades of their oars slicing in and out of the chop. Cal had dropped its rate to thirty-two and then thirty-one after the big ten, but at twenty-nine the Washington boat continued to inch ahead. Tommy Maxwell called for another big ten. Again Moch held his fire and let the challenge go unanswered, and again Washington held her position, the *Husky Clipper's* bow perhaps eight feet ahead of Cal's bow now.

In Washington's number seven seat, a realization flickered through Joe's awareness—the boat was drawing abreast of his father's house on the west side of the lake. He was tempted to sneak a peek over his shoulder, to see if he could catch a glimpse of Joyce. But he didn't. He kept his mind in the boat.

The observation train was, at that moment, just rumbling behind Harry Rantz's house, the smoke from its diesel engines streaming out ahead of it in the brisk wind. Next door, on Fred's dock, Joyce and the kids were on their feet, jumping up and down and waving as they saw the nose of Joe's boat out ahead. Harry stood beside them, his old binoculars locked on the boat, a grin on his weathered face.

Coming up to the two-mile buoy, the California shell rolled slightly off keel; a moment later it happened again. Twice a pair of boys on the starboard side failed to make clean releases from the water, and each time it happened it broke their rhythm and slowed them down. Washington moved out to a three-quarter-length lead. Tommy Maxwell, in trouble now, called on his boys to give him more. Berkenkamp took the rate back up to thirty-five, then thirty-six. Bobby Moch continued to ignore him.

Finally, with a half mile to go, Moch bellowed at Hume to pick it up. Hume took the crew up to thirty-two, as high as he dared to go in the choppy water, and as high as he needed to go. The *Husky Clipper* surged forward, as George Varnell reported in the *Seattle Times* the next day, "like a thing alive." The boys now had open water between them and the *California Clipper*, and in the last half mile they accelerated in a way that no shell had ever accelerated on Lake Washington. As they flew down the last few hundred yards, their eight taut bodies rocked back and forth like pendulums, in perfect synchronicity. Their white blades flashed above the water like the wings of seabirds flying in formation. With every perfectly executed stroke, the expanse between them and the now exhausted Cal boys widened. In airplanes circling overhead, press photographers struggled to keep both boats in the frame of a single shot. Hundreds of boat whistles shrieked. The locomotive on the observation train wailed. Students on the *Chippewa* screamed. And a long, sustained roar went up from the tens of thousands standing along Sheridan Beach as the *Husky Clipper* crossed the line three lengths ahead of the *California Clipper*.

The California crew valiantly rowed on as hard as they could nevertheless. Once again both boats beat the previous course record, but Washington beat it by a good deal more, coming in at 15:56.4, a commanding 37 seconds ahead of the mark.

Al Ulbrickson sat quietly in the launch at the finish line, listening to the band on the *Chippewa* play "Bow Down to Washington." Watching his boys paddle over to the Cal boat to collect their jerseys, he had much to take stock of. His varsity had beaten a very good California crew, the defending national champions, and they had done it in difficult circumstances. They had rowed, as he would himself remark to reporters later that afternoon, "better than they had ever rowed." It was clear that they were, in fact, something far out of the ordinary, but it was too early to say whether the magic would hold. Two years running now, his varsity had beaten Ebright's in the Pacific Coast Regatta only to turn around and lose in Poughkeepsie. Who was to say that this bunch wouldn't do the same? And this year the Olympic trials loomed just beyond Poughkeepsie, not to mention what lay beyond that.

Ulbrickson remained steadfastly and resolutely dour. The Sunday papers in Seattle the next morning, though, were full of excited talk of Berlin. Many who had watched events on the lake closely thought they had seen something beyond merely a good crew race. Clarence Dirks, writing for the *Seattle Times*, mixing his metaphors with abandon, was the first to put his finger on it: "It would be useless to try to segregate outstanding members of Washington's varsity shell, just as it would be impossible to try to pick a certain note in a beautifully composed song. All were merged into one smoothly working machine; they were, in fact, a poem of motion, a symphony of swinging blades."

Poughkeepsie at night

CHAPTER FOURTEEN

To be of championship caliber, a crew must have total confidence in each other, able to drive with abandon, confident that no man will get the full weight of the pull. . . . The 1936 crew, with Hume at stroke, rowed with abandon, beautifully timed. Having complete confidence in one another they would bound on the stroke with one powerful cut; then ghost forward to the next stroke with the boat running true and hardly a perceptible slowdown. They were a classic example of eight-oar rowing at its very best.

—George Yeoman Pocock

Two days later, on April 20, Adolf Hitler turned forty-seven. In Berlin thousands of celebrants gathered to watch and to cheer as Hitler reviewed a procession of more than fifteen hundred tanks, armored vehicles, and artillery pieces rumbling through the city's massive park, the Tiergarten. The crowds along Charlottenburger Chaussee were so thick that people in the back rows had to use rented periscopes to see what was happening up front. Joseph Goebbels's little girls, wearing long white dresses and white headbands, presented Hitler with a bouquet of flowers. The Reich League of German Officials gave Hitler a copy of *Mein Kampf* that had been transcribed by hand onto parchment in a medieval script. With its iron bindings, the tome weighed seventy-five pounds.

But a month earlier, Hitler had already received an even greater gift, and it had been given him by those who would soon become his mortal foes. On the morning of March 7, thirty thousand German troops had rolled into the demilitarized Rhineland, in open defiance of both the Treaty of Versailles and the Locarno Pact to which Germany was a signatory. It was by far the most brazen thing Hitler had yet attempted, his biggest gamble, and a major step toward the catastrophe that was soon to envelop the world. For the next two days, Hitler, Goebbels, and the rest of the Nazi leadership waited anxiously for the world to react. They knew that Germany did not yet have sufficient military strength to survive a war with either France or Britain, let alone the two of them combined. The next forty-eight hours, Hitler later confessed, were the tensest of his life.

He needn't have worried. In England, foreign secretary Anthony Eden said he "deeply regretted" the news, and then set about pressuring the French not to overreact. They didn't. They did nothing at all. A relieved Joseph Goebbels sat down and wrote, "The Fuehrer is immensely happy . . . England remains passive. France won't act alone. Italy is disappointed and America is uninterested."

Hitler now understood with absolute clarity the feeble resolve of the powers to his west. However, the reoccupation of the Rhineland had not come without some cost. Though there had been no military reaction, there had been a public relations uproar in many foreign capitals. Increasing numbers of people in Europe and the United States were beginning to talk again about Germany, as they had during the First World War, when it had generally been seen as a nation of "Huns," of lawless barbarians. Hitler knew it would be much easier for the West to mobilize against a nation of barbarians than a civilized nation. He needed a PR win—not at home, where the reoccupation of the Rhineland had been immensely popular—but in London and Paris and New York.

The Nazi leadership was now convinced that the upcoming Olympic Games, in August, would provide the perfect opportunity for a masquerade. Germany would present herself to the world as an unusually clean, efficient, modern, technologically savvy, cultured, vigorous, reasonable, and hospitable nation. From street sweepers to hoteliers to government clerks, thousands of Germans now went ardently to work to make sure that, come August, the world would see Germany's best face.

In the Ministry of Propaganda, Joseph Goebbels set about constructing an alternate reality in the German press, temporarily sanitizing it of anti-Semitic references, spinning out elaborate fictions about Germany's peaceful intentions, promoting Germany in glowing terms as welcoming to all the peoples of the world. In plush new offices at the Geyer printing labs in southern Berlin, Leni Riefenstahl began putting to work the 2.8 million reichsmarks the Nazi government had secretly funneled to her through the Ministry of Propaganda for the purpose of producing her film about the upcoming games: *Olympia*. The secrecy, dating back to the previous October, was designed to conceal from the International Olympic Committee the political and ideological source of the film's funding. Indeed for the rest of her life Riefenstahl would continue to insist that the film was merely an artistic sports documentary. But in fact, from its genesis *Olympia* was a political and ideological production.

By deliberately conflating wholesome images of grace and beauty and youthful vigor with the iconography and ideology of the Nazis, Riefenstahl would cunningly portray the new German state as something ideal—the perfect end product of a highly refined civilization descended directly from the ancient Greeks. The film would not just reflect but in many ways define the still nascent but increasingly twisted Nazi mythos.

Following the sweep of California on Lake Washington, Al Ulbrickson gave the varsity boys two weeks off to attend to their coursework and get their personal affairs in order before beginning the final push for Berlin. Once they left for Poughkeepsie, Ulbrickson reminded them, they might not—if all went well—be returning to Seattle until September. There was much to do.

When they returned to the shell house on May 4, he set them to low-stroke work, still trying to smooth out the last few technical glitches. They rowed raggedly for the first few days back on the water, until they found their swing again. But find it they did, and they promptly began to power past the other shells on the lake. But on May 18, the shadow of academic disaster fell over the crew. Ulbrickson learned that despite the break, four of his varsity boys still had incompletes and were just days away from being declared ineligible. He was furious. Back in January he had warned the boys, "We can't tarry with scholastic laggards . . . any who fall behind are just out, that's all." Now he dragged Chuck Day, Stub McMillin, Don Hume, and Shorty Hunt into his office, slammed the door shut, and gave them hell. "You can be the best individual oarsmen in the country, but you will be of no service or use to this squad unless you whip up your class efforts. . . . That means study!" Ulbrickson was still fuming as the boys trooped out of the office. Everything was suddenly at risk. The worst of it was that while most of them just had to turn in some overdue work, Don Hume had to flat out ace a final examination to remain eligible. If there was one boy Ulbrickson couldn't afford to lose, it was Don Hume.

The boys, though, were having the times of their lives. On or off the water, they were almost always together now. They ate together, studied together, and played together. Most of them had joined the Varsity Boat Club and lived in the club's rented house on Seventeenth Avenue, a block north of the campus, though Joe remained in the basement of the YMCA. On weekend evenings they gathered around the old upright piano in the club's parlor and sang for hours as Don Hume tore through jazz tunes, show tunes, blues, and ragtime. Sometimes Roger Morris pulled out his saxophone and joined in. Sometimes Johnny White got out his violin and played along fiddle-style. And almost always Joe got out his banjo or his guitar and joined in as well. Nobody laughed at him anymore; nobody dreamed of laughing at him.

Don Hume aced his exam. The others finished their incompletes. And by the end of May, the boys were again turning in phenomenal times on the water. On June 6, Ulbrickson took the varsity and JV out for one final four-mile trial. He told Bobby Moch to hold the varsity back behind the JV for the first two miles. But as they moved down the lake, even rowing at a leisurely twenty-six, the varsity could not manage to stay behind their very good counterparts in the JV boat. They kept edging out in front simply on the power of their long, slow strokes. When Moch finally turned them loose in the final mile, they exploded into a seven-length lead, and they were still pulling away as they crossed the finish line.

That was all Al Ulbrickson needed to see. Training was essentially over until they got onto the Hudson. He told the boys to start packing their things and to pack as if they were going to Berlin.

That same evening, in Berkeley, Ky Ebright and the California boys climbed aboard an eastbound train, heading for Poughkeepsie. Ebright was radiating pessimism. Asked if he had been brushing up on his German, Ebright shot back, "I don't expect to have to have any knowledge of the language." When he was reminded that he had been just as sour about his prospects before both the 1928 and 1932 Olympics, he replied curtly, "This time it's different." But once again the doom and gloom was mostly pro forma. Ebright had made some lineup changes since his boys' loss on Lake Washington, and the new outfit had turned in outstanding time trials on the estuary. He knew his loss in the three-mile race on Lake Washington didn't necessarily tell him anything about the four-mile race on the Hudson, not any more than it had last year. At the very least, Ebright must have believed his boys would be in the thick of things in Poughkeepsie. Washington would likely fade at the end, as they had the year before. And even if Washington somehow prevailed, the

Olympic trials to follow in Princeton would reset the stage. Washington had yet to show they could win a two-thousand-meter sprint. With any luck, Ebright would be coming home by way of Berlin with both a national title and a third consecutive gold medal. So said the Bay Area press, so said much of the national press, and, one has to believe, so thought Ky Ebright.

Four days later, at eight o'clock on the evening of June 10, with red lights flashing and sirens wailing, a police escort led a convoy of cars carrying the Washington crews and coaches down Greek Row, past cheering students, then through downtown Seattle, en route to Union Station. The boys were flying high, and so were the coaches. As instructed, they had prepared for the trip with the assumption that they would not be returning until September. Some of them had even begun to make plans to tour Europe after the Olympics—a heady proposition for boys from Seattle—though none of them was quite sure what he was going to do for money if that happened. Johnny White had a grand total of fourteen dollars in his pocket. George Pocock had written to his father, Aaron, saying that he might be stopping by to pay him a visit in London. Bobby Moch had asked his father for the addresses of his relatives in Switzerland and Alsace-Lorraine, so he could visit them. His father, Gaston, had hesitated, looking suddenly stricken for reasons Bobby could not fathom, but finally said he would send him the addresses later, if the crew really went to Europe.

At the station, as they had in previous years, the marching band played fight songs, cheerleaders danced, the coaches made brief speeches, flashbulbs popped, and newsreel cameras whirred as the boys climbed onto the train. This year the station was packed, not just with students and newsmen, but also with parents, siblings, uncles, aunts, grandparents, cousins, next-door neighbors, and utter strangers. Maybe the city was finally about to be put on the map. If so, everyone wanted to bear witness to the coronation. As Royal Brougham climbed onto the train, he noted that he had never seen a crew leave town "with as much cheerful determination and optimism. These lads feel it in their bones. . . . They're practically shaking hands with Hitler right now."

But Brougham was worried. He had seen all this before, and he had seen the sad consequences of dashed hopes in Seattle the previous year. He sat down at a typewriter in his coach and pounded out the concluding lines for his morning column. Don't forget, he warned his readers, about "the haunting specter of that last mile." For now, he left unstated his even deeper concern about the two-thousand-meter sprint at the Olympic trials.

As the train coughed, lurched, and began to pull away, boys hanging from the windows shouted farewells: "Good-bye, Mom!" "I'll write from Berlin." Joe hung out a window as well, searching. Then, in a far corner, he found her. Joyce was standing with his father and the kids, jumping up and down, holding high over her head a sign on which she had painted a large, green four-leaf clover.

As the train rolled eastward, the boys kicked back, feeling free and easy. The weather was warm but not stifling, and they lolled in their berths for as long as they wanted, played blackjack and poker, and revived their old tradition of lobbing water balloons at random cows and sleeping dogs along the way. The first morning out, Al Ulbrickson gave them happy news. He announced that he wanted each of them to put on three or four pounds before they reached Poughkeepsie. The dining car was all theirs—no restrictions. The boys all but stampeded forward. Joe could hardly believe it. He ordered a steak, then another, this time with a side of ice cream.

As the boys ate, Al Ulbrickson, Tom Bolles, and George Pocock convened a strategy session in their coach. They were well aware of what Ky Ebright was thinking, what Royal Brougham was fretting about, and what many in the eastern press were saying: Washington would come up short again in the last few hundred feet of the four-mile varsity race. Whatever else happened, they were determined that they would not lose the race in that way this year. So they came up with a race plan. Ulbrickson had always liked to come from behind, to save something for the end of the race, but in the past he'd always tried to get a strong start, stay close to the leaders throughout, and then defeat them with a killing sprint at the end. The new plan stuck close to that basic strategy, but with a twist. They would leave the starting line with just enough of a surge to get some momentum behind the boat but then drop immediately to a low stroke rate of twenty-eight or twenty-nine. What's more, they'd keep it low no matter what the other boats were doing, so long as they stayed within roughly two lengths of the field. Ideally, they would stay low for a full mile and a half, then take it up to thirty-one until they got to the two-mile mark. At two miles Bobby Moch would tell Don Hume to gun it and start taking down the leaders, who would by now be starting to tire. The deliberately slow start was risky. It meant they'd likely have to pass every boat on the river on their way to the finish line, but at the very least they'd still be rowing hard at the end. When they were all in agreement, Al Ulbrickson went to tell Bobby Moch the plan.

The Washington boys arrived in Poughkeepsie early in the morning on June 14, in the midst of a summer thunderstorm. Drenched to the skin by torrential rain, they unloaded the shells from a baggage car, lifted them over their heads, and hustled down to the river to stow the boats and inspect their new quarters. They were not using the rickety old shack on the Highland side of the river this year. Al Ulbrickson had arranged for them to move into Cornell's former house, a much more substantial structure on the east side of the river, right next door to the California house. As they shed their wet coats and tromped through the building, they marveled at the luxuries the new quarters afforded. There were hot showers, exercise facilities, electric lights, and a spacious dormitory, complete with extra-long beds. There was even a radio on which the boys would be able to listen to everything from baseball games to *Fibber McGee and Molly* to live broadcasts of the New York Philharmonic direct from Carnegie Hall or, if Joe got his hands on the dial, to *The National Barn Dance* from Chicago. There was a wide screened-in porch where they could sleep if the weather turned hot. And as the rain thundered down outside, it was no small thing that the roof didn't leak.

By the time they had finished settling in, they could smell food cooking. Led by their noses, and by Joe Rantz's nose in particular, they quickly discovered the best feature of the new place—a cookhouse on the beach, just twenty-five feet from their front door. In command of the cookhouse was the imposing figure of Evanda May Calimar, a lady of color and, as it would turn out, an awe-inspiring cook. Working for her were her son Oliver, her mother, and her brother-in-law, all busily preparing fried chicken for the Washington boys' lunch. The boys quickly found that they had just landed smack-dab in the heart of hog heaven. Royal Brougham, amused, watched them go at their first meal and then wired home a story about it. The *Post-Intelligencer* ran it under a picture of Joe captioned "Joe Rantz, The Eating Champion."

Over the next few days, George Pocock went from boathouse to boathouse, tending to the shells of Washington's competitors. Seventeen of the eighteen boats on the river this year had again come out of his shop. Pocock enjoyed working on them, adjusting the riggers, revarnishing hulls, making minor repairs. He didn't want to see shabby or derelict boats with his name on them out on the river. And this kind of service made for excellent customer relations. The first place he went was right next door to the California boat-house to tend to Ky Ebright's boats.

The Washington boys, though, declined to speak to the California boys, and vice versa. On the float they shared, the two crews passed each other silently, with eyes averted, only taking the occasional sidelong glance, like dogs circling before a fight. And a fight was a real possibility. Not long after they arrived, a reporter sauntered up to Shorty Hunt and mentioned that the impression in the California shell house was that the Washington boys seemed to think they were awfully tough, that they seemed always to be spoiling for a fight, that if they couldn't pick a fight with someone else they'd pick a fight with themselves, but that California would be happy to save them the trouble. Shorty replied, "If those lobs want a fight we'll fight, but we aren't looking for any."

Meanwhile Ulbrickson and Bolles began to work their boys hard, rowing at a low rate but for long distances, trying to take right back off the three or four pounds they had deliberately encouraged them to put on during the train trip. The theory was that they would thus arrive at a perfect racing weight and in perfect condition by race day, on June 22, neither too light nor too heavy. Mrs. Calimar's cooking, however, was soon countering the coaches' best efforts.

Then news leaked out that the California varsity had turned in a blazing 19:31 over four miles. It was by far the year's fastest time on the river. The Cornell boys had also begun to turn in impressive times. On the evening of June 17, Al Ulbrickson kicked things up a notch and staged a time trial of his own. Rowing at nine in the evening, under the cover of darkness and in rough water, Joe and his crewmates streaked down the four-mile course in what Al Ulbrickson told writers was a time just a fraction of a second over 19:39, significantly off Cal's impressive 19:31. Johnny White recorded the true time in his journal that night: 19:25.

The next day rumors began to circulate that California had held yet another time trial. Ebright wouldn't reveal the time, but observers reported that his varsity had come in with the phenomenal time of 18:46. The *Poughkeepsie Eagle-News* had it at 18:37. Royal Brougham wired a grim report back to the *Post-Intelligencer*: "The sun-browned oarsmen of California will again rule as the favorites. . . . That's not rowing, it's flying."

But Ulbrickson remained unruffled. He wanted well-rested boys in the race, and he'd seen enough. He told his boys to relax. From now until race day on the twenty-second there would be only light workouts, to keep in shape. That was fine with the boys. They already knew something that nobody else knew, not even Ulbrickson.

Late on the night of the final time trial, after the wind had died down and the waters had calmed, they had begun to row back up the river, in the dark, side by side with the freshman and JV boats. Soon the red and green running lights of the coaches' launch disappeared upriver. The shells passed under the two bridges draped with shimmering necklaces of amber lights. Along the shore and up on the palisades, warm yellow light poured from the windows of homes and shell houses. It was a moonless night. The water was ink black.

Bobby Moch set the varsity boys to rowing at a leisurely twenty-two or twenty-three. Joe and his crewmates chatted softly with the boys in the other two boats. But they soon found that they had pulled out ahead without meaning to, just pulling soft and steady. Soon, in fact, they had pulled so far ahead that they could not even hear the boys in the other boats. And then, one by one, they realized that they couldn't hear anything at all except for the gentle murmur of their blades dipping into and out of the water. They were rowing in utter darkness now. They were alone together in a realm of silence and darkness. Years later, as old men, they all remembered the moment. Bobby Moch recalled, "You couldn't hear anything except for the oars going in the water . . . it'd be a 'zep' and that's all you could hear . . . the oarlocks didn't even rattle on the release." They were rowing perfectly, fluidly, mindlessly. They were rowing as if on another plane, as if in a black void among the stars, just as Pocock had said they might. And it was beautiful.

In the final days before the Poughkeepsie Regatta, another big sports story dominated the headlines on sports pages and sometimes on front pages around the country—the story of a heavyweight boxing match. Max Schmeling of Germany had been the heavyweight champion of the world from 1930 to 1932, and he was set on reclaiming the title from James Braddock. But a twenty-two-year-old African American boxer from Detroit, named Joe Louis, stood in Schmeling's way. Louis had battled his way through twenty-seven professional matches with twenty-three knockouts and no defeats to reach his current status as the number one challenger in the world. In doing so he had gradually begun to erode the racial attitudes of many—though far from all—white Americans. He was on his way, in fact, to becoming one of the first

African Americans to be widely viewed as a hero by ordinary white Americans. Louis's rise to prominence had been so spectacular that few American sportswriters or bookies gave Schmeling much of a chance.

In Germany, though, the view was very different. Although Schmeling was not a Nazi Party member, Joseph Goebbels and the Nazi elite had enthusiastically latched onto him and promoted him as a symbol of German and Aryan supremacy. The German press, under the careful direction of the minister of propaganda, had made much of the upcoming fight.

Everyone on both sides of the Atlantic had an opinion about what would happen. Even the crew coaches in Poughkeepsie took time out to comment on the fight. "Schmeling might go four rounds," opined Al Ulbrickson. Ky Ebright was blunter: "Louis will murder him."

When the fight began, in a sold-out Yankee Stadium on the evening of June 19, Louis was, at eight to one, the overwhelming favorite in New York. In Germany, though interest in the fight was at a fever pitch, there was almost no betting on the fight. The odds were so low on Schmeling that few wanted to risk their cash, and no one wanted to be caught betting on a black American.

In a small square of white light in the vast, dark void of the stadium, Louis stalked Schmeling around the ring like a predator for three rounds, lacing him with hard left jabs to the face. It looked as if it would be a short evening. But in the fourth round, out of nowhere, Schmeling landed a hard right to the temple that knocked Louis to a sitting position on the floor. Louis took a count of two and then rose to his feet, covering his face and retreating until the bell sounded. Through the fifth round, Louis seemed dazed and ineffective. And then, at the end of the fifth, following the bell—which neither fighter heard over the crowd noise—Schmeling landed a particularly devastating right to the left side of Louis's head. For the next six rounds, Louis staggered about the ring, punished by a relentless barrage of rights to the jaw, somehow staying on his feet but scoring few if any points and inflicting little damage on the German boxer. Many in the overwhelmingly white crowd had by now turned suddenly and savagely against Louis. "Delirious with joy," by the *New York Times* account, they screamed for Schmeling to end it. Finally, in the twelfth, Schmeling went in for the kill. With Louis now careening almost aimlessly around the ring, the German leaned into Louis's body and launched a rapid-fire flurry of hard rights to his head and face, followed by one final crushing blow to the jaw. Louis sank to his knees, then toppled forward on his face. Referee Arthur Donovan counted him out. In the dressing room afterward, Louis said he couldn't remember anything about the fight beyond the fifth round.

That night in Harlem, grown men wept openly in the streets. Younger men threw rocks at cars full of white fans returning from the match. In German American sections of New York, people danced in the streets. In Berlin, Adolf Hitler wired his congratulations to Schmeling and sent his wife flowers. But no one in Germany was happier with the evening's developments than Joseph Goebbels. He had spent the night at his posh summerhouse at Schwanenwerder, sitting with Magda and Schmeling's wife, Anny, listening to the fight on the radio into the wee hours. He sent Schmeling a congratulatory telegram of his own: "We are proud of you. With best wishes and Heil Hitler." Then he ordered the state-controlled Reuters News Agency to issue a statement: "Inexorably and not without justification we demand Braddock shall defend the title on German soil." The next day, still excited, Goebbels sat down and made an entry in his journal: "We were on tenterhooks the whole evening with Schmeling's wife. We told each other stories, laughed, and cheered. In round twelve, Schmeling knocked out the Negro. Fantastic. A dramatic, thrilling fight. Schmeling fought for Germany and won. The white man prevailed over the black, and the white man was German. I didn't go to bed until five."

In the end, though, Joe Louis would have the last laugh. He would indeed fight Max Schmeling again, two years later, and Schmeling would last all of two minutes and four seconds before his corner threw in the towel. Joe Louis would reign as heavyweight champion of the world from 1937 to 1949, long after Joseph Goebbels's charred body had been pulled out of the smoldering rubble of the Reich Chancellery in Berlin and laid next to those of Magda and their children.

On Saturday evening Ulbrickson told the varsity they could take the coaching launch out for a spin if they wanted. They were bored with the amusement park just up the hill, and Ulbrickson didn't want them lounging around the house all evening getting restless and nervous about the race on Monday.

The boys recruited one of the crew's student managers as pilot and navigator, and piled into the boat. Not sure where to go, they decided they'd pay a visit to the president of the United States, whom they understood to live somewhere upriver. They goosed the throttle, and the boat swung out into the river, heading north past the Navy and Columbia shell houses. They roared northwest through the bend at Krum Elbow and continued another two miles alongside forest and cliff until they came to a dock marked "Hyde Park Station." There they asked someone how to get to the president's house and were directed to a cove a mile back down the river.

When they found the cove, they left the manager in charge of the boat, crossed some railroad tracks, walked gingerly across a narrow trestle, and headed uphill through the woods. For the next half hour, they wandered up bridle paths and overgrown roads, hurrying across broad lawns, and trooping past an abandoned gristmill and a stable the size of a cathedral, until they finally came across some greenhouses and a gardener's cottage that appeared to be occupied. They knocked on the door and an elderly couple appeared. When the boys asked whether they were anywhere near the president's estate, the couple nodded enthusiastically and announced that they were standing on it, then pointed out the way to the main house. Walking through the adjoining nursery and up another path, they finally arrived on a wide gravel drive leading up to a large expanse of lawn on which stood Springwood, the Roosevelts' stately three-story brick-and-masonry mansion, complete with a semicircular portico supported by white Grecian columns. It was by far the most magnificent house any of them had ever seen.

Nervous, but too far along to back down now, they shuffled deferentially up onto the portico and peered inside. It was coming up on nine o'clock, and growing dark. Inside they could see a young man about their age, leaning against the end of a long table and reading a book. They knocked on the door. The young man appeared to call for a servant, but then put the book down and came to the door himself. When he opened the door, the boys announced who they were, mentioned that they had met John Roosevelt the previous year, and asked if the president was in. He was not, the young man said, but he invited them in eagerly. He was, he said, Franklin Roosevelt Jr., but they should call him Frank. He grinned slightly and announced that he rowed in the number six seat in the Harvard JV boat and had just returned from New London, Connecticut, where, though the Crimson's varsity had won their annual race against Yale, the JV had not. Just before the race, he said, Harvard's coach, Charlie Whiteside, had been fired, and there was a great deal of talk now that the next head coach at Harvard would be a fellow named Tom Bolles, particularly if Bolles pulled off another freshman victory at Poughkeepsie. Roosevelt couldn't wait to talk to the boys from Washington.

He ushered them into the president's library and sat them down and began talking rapidly about rowing and about coaches. As he talked, the boys gaped at the room. Most of the walls were lined from the floor to the high ceiling with shelves of books. Any spots on the walls not taken up by books were covered with pictures of American presidents and various Roosevelts. An ornate fireplace dominated the end of the room where they were seated. In front of the fireplace was a fifteen-foot-long library table stacked with new editions of books on every conceivable topic. Nearly every other table in the room had a vase of fresh flowers or a porcelain figurine on it. Shorty Hunt, starting to relax, settled into a comfortable upholstered chair near the fireplace, and then nearly jumped out of it when Frank told him it was the president's favorite, and that he occasionally delivered his famous fireside chats on the radio from that very chair.

They talked for an hour. Later that night, back at the shell house, Johnny White got out his diary and wrote, as if he had just stopped in at a neighbor's house back in Seattle, "Visited the President's home at Hyde Park tonight. They sure have a fine place."

By the morning of the regatta, the consensus in the eastern press, at least, was that California and Cornell were the boats to beat in the varsity race, with Washington expected to come in perhaps just a beat or two behind the leaders. Cornell, after all, had come within four-tenths of a second of beating California the year before. The Seattle papers gave the odds, narrowly, to Washington. Royal Brougham, despite his earlier gloomy assessment, had already announced his personal prognostication: Washington to win, Cornell in second, California third. Writing for the Post-Intelligencer that morning, though, he said he thought Cal would probably go off as the slight favorite among the bookmakers. Actually, the bookies in the cigar shops in Poughkeepsie had Cal and Washington at even money, with Cornell lagging just behind at eight to five. The bottom line seemed to be that any one of the three schools might win the varsity honors.

Now Brougham was poking around town. He wanted to gather as much color as he could before it was time to sit down and pound out his story after the final race. Because of tidal conditions, the race would not go off until after 8:00 p.m., just after sundown. So Brougham took his time, looking for tidbits. It was, he noted, a fine, clear day in Poughkeepsie. A few cottony white clouds drifted across a pale blue sky, moved along by just enough of a breeze to keep things pleasantly cool.

At midafternoon he hiked down the steep descent to the waterfront, where a U.S. Navy destroyer and two coast guard cutters had taken up positions among the usual flotilla of yachts, sailboats, launches, dinghies, and canoes assembling near the finish line. At the California shell house, Ky Ebright sat on the upstairs porch, wearing dark glasses, nodding and smiling at people as they streamed by below, saying nothing. Next door Al Ulbrickson, wearing an unusually colorful outfit—a white cloth cap, a yellow-striped sweater, and the lucky purple tie given to him by Loyal Shoudy back in 1926—sat on the dock in front of the Washington shell house. When pressed for a comment by a gaggle of reporters, Ulbrickson spat into the water, chewed a piece of grass, and looked at the wind-ruffled river for a long while before finally saying, "Going to be fast if she flattens out a little." Royal Brougham moved on. He knew that was about all the press boys were going to get out of Ulbrickson.

By late afternoon the Main Street wharf was crowded with people waiting for ferries to get them across the river to the observation train. Brougham sat watching as dozens of lesser boats—everything from outboard speedboats to rowboats—also ferried more people of all sorts across: tipsy women in fashionable Fifth Avenue hats, fat men with cigar stubs in their mouths, old men wearing raccoon coats and clutching college pennants.

One by one the freshman crews boarded their shells and began to paddle upriver to the starting line near the Columbia shell house—an elegant structure that looked as if it could double as the clubhouse at any of the East's fine country clubs. A little before 6:00 p.m., Royal Brougham climbed aboard the observation train on the west side of the river just as it was about to start backing up toward the two-mile freshman starting line, pulling a press car and twenty-three flatcars with bleachers full of fans sitting under white canvas canopies. As many as ninety thousand people now lined both sides of the Hudson—the largest crowd in years. The earlier breeze had died down, and the water was placid, smooth and glassy, tinged with bronze in the slanting late afternoon light. Ulbrickson was right. It was going to be fast.

As the train began to back up, Tom Bolles, wearing his battered lucky fedora, had much to ponder. He had heard what had happened to Charlie Whiteside. Harvard had made clear to the world that they were prepared to pay handsomely to get what they wanted in the way of a new head coach. And Bolles knew he was again at the top of their list. If his boys came through for him yet again this year, he'd be getting an offer, and he figured this time he'd probably take it.

His boys did come through for him. And they made short, sweet work of it. When the race went off, exactly at 6:00 p.m., Navy and California moved out to early leads. Washington settled in at a relatively low beat of thirty-two but stayed close. Pulling gracefully and efficiently, they gradually overpowered Navy and settled in behind Cal. At the one-mile mark, going under the railroad bridge, they crept ahead of Cal. California challenged several times but Washington repeatedly moved back in front, still holding at thirty-two. Finally, a quarter of a mile from the finish, California began its sprint, charging up from behind, one more time, to nose out ahead of Bolles's boys. Washington's coxswain, Fred Colbert, turned his crew loose. Washington exploded forward, rowing at thirty-nine and pulling away from Cal by a full length at the line. And with that, Washington won the race but lost Tom Bolles.

An hour later the JV race began, and once again Washington made short work of their opponents, rowing a remarkably similar race. Early on, Navy and Cornell pulled out ahead of Washington by a quarter of a length, but, finding that he could hold his bow in that position with his crew rowing at a relaxed thirty or thirty-one, Washington's cox, Winslow Brooks, was content to sit back and watch the two leaders burn themselves out. He sat there, in fact, for a mile and a half, then found that he was slowly pulling even with the boys from Annapolis and Berkeley without having asked his men to raise the beat. A mile above the finish line, he finally called on them to take up the stroke rate. The beat went to thirty-seven, and Washington simply got up and walked away from the field. The boys in the Navy and Cornell boats suddenly looked as if they were rowing in glue. Every stroke Washington took in the last mile widened the distance. They crossed the line three lengths ahead of Navy, still pulling away at the head of a long, strung-out parade of boats far to their rear.

Even as the last boats crossed the line and the cheering began to die down, an audible murmur began to ripple through the crowd along the shore as a number of realizations clicked into place. Washington, for the second time in two years, now stood again on the brink of sweeping the regatta. California, on the other hand, could become only the second school ever to win the varsity race four years in a row, as well as the first to ever go on to win three consecutive Olympic berths. But there was still hope for eastern fans. Cornell looked as if they could finally redeem their cause this year. Or maybe Navy.

As the observation train drew back upriver again for the start of the varsity race, the atmosphere grew electric, the dusky sky crackling with static. The crowd began to buzz. Boat whistles shrilled. Alumni draped arms over one another's shoulders and sang fight songs. Somebody was about to win big; somebody was about to lose big.

Four miles up the river, just below Krum Elbow, Joe Rantz, sitting in the *Husky Clipper* near the eastern shore, heard five bombs go off downstream and knew that the Washington JV, in the number five lane, had won their race. He lifted his fist silently in the air. So did Shorty Hunt and Roger Morris. Half the boys in the JV boat had been members of their all-sophomore crew in 1935. Every one of them had been disappointed not to be sitting where Joe and Shorty and Roger were sitting, waiting for the varsity race to begin at 8:00 p.m.

The sun had already slipped behind the palisades, on the west side of the river. The tips of church spires up in Poughkeepsie, on the east side, were just catching the last rays of sunlight. Down on the river, twilight was settling over the water like gray gauze. The river itself had turned a rich and lustrous shade of violet, reflecting the sky overhead. A line of gray stake boats stretched across the river, marking the starting line. Far downstream, twinkling lights began to appear at the portholes of some of the larger yachts anchored near the finish line. On the east side of the river, a passenger train flashed by, trailing clouds of swirling smoke. On the west side, the observation train jolted to a stop adjacent to the line of stake boats. Just above the line, a telegraph operator sat perilously on the steep riverbank, his keypad in hand and a strand of copper wire running up the hill behind him to a pole where he had made a connection with the main line, ready to tell the world when the race began. Joe and his crewmates began to paddle out to the line of stake boats to take their position. In the stern, Bobby Moch began quietly talking them through the race plan one more time. Out in Seattle, Hazel Ulbrickson locked the front door to her home so as not to be disturbed during the race. Joyce got permission from Mrs. Tellwright to switch on the large cabinet radio in her parlor.

On the observation train, in a press car full of Washington coaches, alumni, and sportswriters, George Pocock and Tom Bolles paced up and down the aisle. Al Ulbrickson sat alone in silence, methodically chewing a piece of gum, looking out intently from under the brim of his white cloth cap toward the spot where Joe sat. Washington had drawn the worst lane, number seven, far out in the middle of the river, where any hint of wind or current would be strongest and where, in the failing light, it would be hard even to see the boat. As in 1935, California had drawn lane number one, the most protected lane, snug up against the railroad embankment, sitting right under Ulbrickson's nose.

Ten years ago Ulbrickson himself had stroked Washington's varsity to a national championship here. No Washington varsity crew had won one since. Ulbrickson remembered his oath to his wife, and his failed promise to Seattle the year before. The Olympics loomed. Nearly everything Al Ulbrickson wanted out of life was going to be determined in the next twenty minutes.

At 8:00 p.m. the starter called out, "Are you ready?" Two coxswains lowered their hands. The starter waited a minute or two, then called out again, "Are you all ready?" This time three coxswains lowered their hands. Exasperated, the starter waited again while the different crews made a few final adjustments. He called out a third time, "Are you *all* ready?" This time all seven hands went down.

The starting gun popped, the boats lurched away from the line, and the telegrapher clinging to the riverbank tapped at his key to let the world know that the thirty-eighth annual varsity crew race at Poughkeepsie was finally under way.

For five full strokes, all seven boats stayed absolutely abreast of one another, their crews digging hard. Then Washington suddenly eased up. The entire field surged out in front of them. That was OK with Bobby Moch. That was just what he wanted. He settled his crew in, rowing at a steady twenty-eight, and began to watch the backs of his rival coxswains disappear down the river into the dusk. To steady the boys, Moch began to chant their newest rowing mantra in time with the stroke—"Save, Save, Save"—reminding them that this was all about conserving power.

Pennsylvania, Navy, and California quickly moved out in front of the pack, rowing high at first, then gradually dropping their stroke rates into the low thirties. After half a mile, Washington was seventh in a field of seven—almost five lengths behind the leaders. Syracuse and, surprisingly, mighty Cornell—the Big Red hope of the East—continued to hang back with Washington, perhaps playing their game.

Bobby Moch began to fudge his shell over toward the Syracuse lane. He was thinking ahead. Far down the course, his assigned lane was going to carry the *Husky Clipper* under the railroad bridge right at the point where water swirled around behind an abutment and flowed back upriver. If they ran into the swirl, the boat would all but stop momentarily. The only way he was going to avoid it was by running right down the line between his lane and Syracuse's. The *Clipper* slid over to the line until the Orange's blades were all but clicking up against the Huskies'. Furious, the Syracuse coxswain began bellowing, cussing at Moch. As Washington pulled even, Moch leaned over toward the Syracuse boat, smiled, and said, rather softly but in his deep baritone voice, "Go to hell, Syracuse." As the Syracuse coxswain resumed cussing, his boys' timing began to falter and his boat began to fall back.

A mile into the race, to the astonishment of the crowd on the observation train, Columbia had crept up to third place, passing California and settling in behind Navy and Penn. As the boys from New York City stroked past the boys from Berkeley, New Yorkers on the train began to cheer. But by the mile-and-a-half mark, California had answered the move and powered back past Columbia and Penn into second again. Navy, California, and Penn now formed a cluster, far out in front, exchanging leads, cutting each other up. Washington remained four full lengths behind the leaders. Cornell seemed unable to get anything going and lingered back near Washington. Syracuse had fallen well to the rear.

In the press car, a hush had gradually fallen over the Washington contingent of writers and coaches as they had taken in just how far behind the *Husky Clipper* was. People began to murmur, "Come on, Bobby, take it up, take it up." Al Ulbrickson was silent, calm, sphinxlike, slowly working the gum in his mouth. Any moment now, he figured, Bobby Moch would make his move, just as they'd planned. He stared ever more intently across the river as the growing darkness began to envelop the shell. All one could really see of Washington were the white tips of their blades appearing and disappearing rhythmically in the water, still at a nice, steady, leisurely twenty-eight.

At two miles Penn had begun to fade, falling behind Columbia. Cal and Navy were duking it out for the lead. Cornell had fallen behind Washington, which had moved into fifth place. But Bobby Moch still hadn't altered the beat at all. He was still four lengths back. In the press car, Al Ulbrickson began to grow uneasy. Moch had been told not to let the leaders get more than two lengths ahead. He was twice that far behind. And he was supposed to have started moving by now. This was most definitely not the race plan Moch had been given. Tom Bolles and George Pocock sat down, looking morose. It was starting to look like a case of suicide. But out on the water, Bobby Moch told Don Hume, "Take your time. We can catch those boys anytime we want."

As they passed the two-and-a-half-mile mark it was essentially the same story. California and Navy were far out in front, with Columbia trailing them; Washington had eased past a weakening Penn crew but remained a devastating four lengths back. Ulbrickson still didn't flinch; he just continued to stare out the window at the flickering white blades on the water, chewing his gum. But he had begun to slump in his seat. He couldn't believe what was happening. What on earth was Moch doing? Why in God's name didn't he turn them loose?

In the boat Bobby Moch took a look at the four lengths between his bow and California's stern, and hollered to his crew, "OK, you lugs! We're one length behind."

Downriver, the thousands of fans packing the shoreline and yachts and other vessels in Poughkeepsie could not yet see the oncoming shells, but they could hear the coxswains barking like so many seals out in the river's darkness. Slowly the barking grew closer. Then the bows of three boats began to materialize out of the gloaming, just beyond the railroad bridge. A roar went up as the crowd began to discern the state of play. Navy was neck and neck with Cal, and the two of them seemed to be running away with it, though Columbia, astonishingly, appeared to be in third place. Cornell, also astonishingly, was nowhere to be seen, but at least the East had one boat in the race after all, maybe two. Almost nobody even noticed the Washington shell apparently limping along out in the middle of the river, so far back one could barely see it in the gathering darkness.

As the Washington boat swept under the black skeleton of the railroad bridge at the three-mile mark, it was still nearly three lengths back with a mile to go. The leaders had slowed just a bit, and that had narrowed the gap, but if Moch had raised the rate at all, it was imperceptible.

The Washington boys were rowing as if in a kind of trance now, somehow detached from themselves yet keenly aware of one another's every minute motion. There was little sound out in the middle of the river, except for Moch's chanting, the rattle of oars in oarlocks, their own deep rhythmic breathing, and their pulses pounding in their ears. There was almost no pain. In the number five seat, Stub McMillin realized with astonishment that he was still breathing through his nose after three full miles of rowing.

On the train Al Ulbrickson had all but given up. "They're too far behind," he muttered. "They're overplaying their hand. We'll be lucky to finish third." Ulbrickson's face was ashen. It seemed to have turned entirely to stone. He'd even stopped chewing his gum. In the lane nearest to him, California had powered back out in front, rowing beautifully. With a tiring field behind them and less than a mile to go Cal was in a commanding position to win. Ky Ebright, it seemed, had somehow outwitted him again.

But if anybody had outwitted Al Ulbrickson, it was his own coxswain—the short kid with his own Phi Beta Kappa key. And now he would show his hand. Suddenly he leaned into Don Hume's face and bellowed, "Give me ten hard ones for Ulbrickson!" Eight long spruce oars bowed in the water ten times. Then Moch bellowed again, "Give me ten more for Pocock!" Another ten enormous strokes. Then another lie: "Here's California! We're on them! Ten more big ones for Mom and Dad!" Very slowly the *Husky Clipper* slipped past Columbia and began to creep up on Navy in second.

Someone on the train idly remarked, "Well, Washington is picking up." A minute later someone else called out, much more urgently, "Look at Washington! Look at Washington! Here comes Washington!" On the train and onshore, all eyes shifted from the leaders to the eight white blades barely visible out in the middle of the river. Another deep guttural roar began to rise from the crowd. It seemed impossible for Washington to close the gap. They were a half mile from the finish now, still in third place, still two lengths back. But they were moving, and the way they were moving compelled immediate and absolute attention.

In the boat Moch was incandescent. "OK! Now! Now! Now!" he barked. Don Hume took the stroke up to thirty-five, then to thirty-six, then to thirty-seven. On the starboard side, Joe Rantz fell in behind him, just as smooth as silk. The boat began to swing. The bow began to rise out of the water. Washington slid past the middies as if the Navy boat were pinned to the water.

Cal's coxswain, Grover Clark, glanced across the river and, for the first time since he'd left it behind at the starting line, he saw the Washington boat, sweeping up on his stern. Stunned, he bellowed at his crew to pick it up, and Cal's rate climbed quickly to thirty-eight. Moch hollered at Hume to take it up another notch, and Washington went to forty. The rhythm of the California boat seemed to waver, then grow erratic.

California and Washington careened into the last five hundred yards, storming down the corridor of open water between the spectators' boats. People in rowboats were standing up now, risking a dunking to see what was happening. Some of the large excursion steamers began to list toward the center of the river as people crowded their rails. The roar of the crowd began to engulf the oarsmen. Boat whistles shrieked. On the float in front of Washington's shell house, Evanda May Calimar, the crew's cook, waved a frying pan over her head, whooping and urging the boys on. In Washington's press car, pandemonium broke out. George Varnell of the *Seattle Times* shoved his press credentials into his mouth and began to devour them. Tom Bolles commenced beating a stranger on the back with his lucky old fedora. Royal Brougham was shouting, "Come on, Washington! Come on!" Only Al Ulbrickson remained motionless and silent, still riveted to his seat, his eyes cold gray stones locked on the white blades out in the river. Joe Williams of the *World-Telegram* stole a glance at him and thought, "This guy has ice water in his veins."

With the finish line looming ahead of him in the gathering dark, Bobby Moch screamed something inarticulate. Johnny White, in the number three seat, suddenly had the sensation that they were flying now, not rowing. Stub McMillin desperately wanted to peek, to glance over toward lane one where he knew California would be, but he didn't dare. In number six, over the crowd noise, Shorty Hunt could hear someone on a radio, yelling frantically. He tried to make out the words, but all he could tell was that something terribly exciting was happening. He had no idea how things stood except that he still hadn't seen the California boat fall into his field of view. He kept his eyes locked on the back of Joe Rantz's neck and pulled with his whole heart. Joe had boiled everything down to one action, one continuous movement, one thought: the crew's old mantra running on through his mind like a river, hearing it over and over, not in his own voice but in George Pocock's crisp Oxford accent, "M-I-B, M-I-B, M-I-B."

Then, in the last two hundred yards, thinking itself fell away, and pain suddenly came shrieking back into the boat, descending on all of them at once, searing their legs, their arms, their shoulders, clawing at their backs, tearing at their hearts and lungs as they desperately gulped at the air. And in those last two hundred yards, in an extraordinary burst of speed, rowing at forty strokes per minute, pounding the water into a froth, Washington passed California. With each stroke the boys took their rivals down by the length of another seat. By the time the two boats crossed the line, in the last vestiges of twilight, a glimmer of open water showed between the stern of the *Husky Clipper* and the bow of the *California Clipper*.

In the press car, the corners of Al Ulbrickson's mouth twitched reluctantly into something vaguely resembling a smile. He resumed chewing his gum, slowly and methodically. Standing next to him, George Pocock threw back his head and howled like a banshee. Tom Bolles continued to flog the back of the fellow in front of him with his old fedora. George Varnell removed the well-masticated remains of his press credentials from his mouth. In Seattle, Hazel Ulbrickson and her son Al pounded the glass top of their coffee table until it shattered into dozens of pieces. Up on the automobile bridge, Mike Bogo had the distinct pleasure of setting off seven bombs in rapid succession. In the boat the boys pumped their fists in the dark night air.

For a long while, Ulbrickson just sat there staring into the darkness as fans came rushing through the car congratulating him and slapping him on the back. When he finally stood up, reporters crowded around him and he said, simply, "Well, they made it close. But they won." Then he elaborated. "I guess that little runt knew what he was doing."

Washington had become the national champions and swept the Hudson. The varsity's astounding come-from-behind victory that day was historic in its scope and drama. In the press center at the Poughkeepsie railroad station, the nation's sportswriters sat down to typewriters and began to pound out superlatives. Robert Kelley of the New York Times called it "a high mark in the history of Poughkeepsie." Herbert Allan of the New York Post called it "spectacular and unprecedented." George Timpson of the Christian Science Monitor called it "brilliant." James Burchard of the World-Telegram found more original phrasing: "It was a story of psychology, pure nerve, and rowing intelligence. Moch's noodle was the best oar in the Washington boat." Royal Brougham thought long and hard about how to characterize what Bobby Moch had pulled off. Finally he settled on: "It was positively cold blooded."

Al Ulbrickson went down to the water and followed the boys back upriver to the shell house in his launch. As they rowed upstream in the warm summer dark, Ulbrickson saw that they were pulling flawlessly, with the exceptional grace and precision that was quickly becoming their norm. He grabbed a megaphone and bellowed over the wet growling of the boat's engine, "Now that's it! Why didn't you row like that in the race?" The boys glanced at one another, grinning nervously. Nobody quite knew whether he was kidding or not.

He was, but the comment had purpose. To reach his goal, Ulbrickson was going to have to beat Ebright one more time. In a little less than two weeks, they were going to have to race again, twice, in a pair of two-thousand-meter sprints, to earn the right to represent the United States in Berlin. In one of those races, California would be sitting in an adjoining lane, with one last chance to finally get even and send themselves to Germany. Ulbrickson didn't want his boys getting all swell-headed again. And, thrilled as he was with the result, he wasn't entirely pleased with Moch's insubordination. At any rate, he needed to remind them who was in charge.

But, Dour Dane or not, Ulbrickson also felt the need to say something commensurate with the occasion. When they got to the shell house, they found hundreds of exuberant fans jockeying for space on the wobbly float and milling around in front of the building, hooting and hollering. The boys climbed out of the boat and threw Bobby Moch into the Hudson to the delight of the spectators. Then, after retrieving him from the water, they formed a phalanx, forced their way into the building, and slid the doors closed behind themselves, letting in only a few Seattle pressmen. Ulbrickson climbed up onto a bench and the boys, clutching jerseys they'd collected from the losing crews, sat on the floor around him. "You made history today, you freshmen, junior varsity, and varsity oarsmen and coxswains. I am proud of you. Every son and daughter of Washington is proud of you. . . . Never in history has a crew given a more gallant, game fight to win the most coveted rowing honor at stake in this country than the varsity did today. And I can only say to you that I am proud and very happy." He paused and looked around the room and then concluded, "I never expect to see a better rowed race." Then he stepped down. Nobody cheered. Nobody stood up and applauded. Everyone just sat, silently soaking in the moment. On the stormy night in January 1935, when Ulbrickson had first started talking openly about going to the Olympics, everyone had stood and cheered. But then it had seemed like a dream. Now they were on the verge of actually making it happen. Cheering somehow seemed dangerous.

Bobby Moch

CHAPTER FIFTEEN

Therein lies the secret of successful crews: Their "swing," that fourth dimension of rowing, which can only be appreciated by an oarsman who has rowed in a swinging crew, where the run is uncanny and the work of propelling the shell a delight.

—George Yeoman Pocock

"For four straight years now, coarse outlanders from the Far West have dominated the Hudson," Joe Williams of the *New York World-Telegram* spat out the day following the Poughkeepsie races. "The regatta has lost all its original form and pattern. It is no longer an eastern show. . . . When one western team doesn't win, the other does. . . . Washington took everything there was to be taken on the river yesterday. The townspeople were relieved that the visitors had the decency to leave the bridges and the fat-bodied ferries." Williams then went on, presumably in jest, to call upon President Roosevelt to do something about the "very disturbing situation."

The tone may have been tongue-in-cheek, but the substance of Williams's piece was no joke for thousands of eastern crew fans—their schools seemed to be falling out of contention in a regatta they had designed to test and demonstrate their own rowing prowess.

And it wasn't just eastern sports scribes and fans who found themselves facing a new reality after the 1936 regatta. Ky Ebright knew exactly what he had seen in the varsity race, and he was smart enough and diplomatic enough to acknowledge it straight out. Packing up his own boys for their trip to Princeton and the Olympic trials, where he would take one more stab at defeating Washington, he pointed to Joe and his crewmates and said, "There's the best crew in America. That's the boat that should go to Berlin, and the rest of the world will have to produce something pretty hot to beat them in the Olympics." This wasn't the usual prerace "downplay your chances" banter that both he and Al Ulbrickson regularly engaged in. Ebright was dead serious, and he needed to tamp down expectations in Berkeley. He'd go to Princeton and compete and try to win the Olympic berth, but when Bobby Moch engineered that cold, calculating, come-out-of-nowhere victory, Ebright quickly saw the demoralizing effect it had on his own crew. The deliberate way Washington rowed that race had seemed partly a challenge, partly a dare, but mostly it had seemed a warning. As he made his way down the course, Moch might as well have raised over his stern a flag emblazoned with the words "Don't Tread on Me" and the figure of a coiled rattlesnake.

On July 1, after a week of working out and relaxing in Poughkeepsie, the boys packed up their possessions, loaded the *Husky Clipper* onto a baggage car, and headed for the 1936 U.S. Olympic trials. By six that evening, they had arrived at Princeton and entered the world of the Ivy League, a world of status and tradition, of refined tastes and unstated assumptions about social class, a world inhabited by the sons of bankers and lawyers and senators. For boys who were the sons of working-class parents, this was uncertain but intriguing terrain.

They moved into the stately Princeton Inn, perched majestically on the edge of the Springdale Golf Club's manicured fairways, a building that made even the president's home at Hyde Park look a bit cramped and shabby. From their rooms, the boys watched Princeton alumni stroll around the golf course wearing their knickerbockers, high argyle socks, and tweed caps. The boys explored Lake Carnegie and stopped by the Princeton Boathouse to check the facilities. It was a large stone structure, complete with Gothic arches over the entrances to the boat bays—a structure far more elegant than the clapboard homes most of them had come from. It was a far cry from their old airplane hangar; it looked more like the new Suzzallo Library back in Seattle. Even Lake Carnegie itself was an emblem of wealth and privilege. Until early in the twentieth century, Princeton crews had rowed in the Delaware and Raritan Canal, which ran directly along the south side of the campus. The Princeton boys, though, found it inconvenient to row among the coal barges and recreational vessels that also made use of the canal, so they got Andrew Carnegie to build them a private lake. For roughly one hundred thousand dollars, about two and a half million in today's dollars, Carnegie quietly bought up all the properties along a three-mile stretch of the Millstone River, dammed it, and produced a first-class rowing course—shallow, straight, protected, lovely to look at, and quite free of coal barges.

For the first few days at Princeton, the boys kicked back and luxuriated in the posh surroundings of the hotel and country club. Don Hume tried to throw off the effects of a nasty cold. Twice a day they took light workouts in the shell. Mostly, they practiced rowing high-stroke-rate sprints and racing starts. Starts were among the most critical components of a two-thousand-meter race, and something they were having trouble with lately.

Six crews were competing for the right to go to Berlin: Washington, California, Penn, Navy, Princeton, and the New York Athletic Club. The field would be divided into two groups of three for a preliminary elimination heat on July 4. The top two boats in each heat would advance to a final contest of four boats the next day.

As the elimination heats approached, the weather grew oppressively warm—the first intimations of what was about to become a lethal heat wave all across the East. By the night of July 3, the boys had grown nervous and unsettled, the magnitude of what was at stake starting to sink in. They had trouble sleeping in the damp heat. Al Ulbrickson went from room to room telling them to settle down, but there was an edge to his voice that betrayed his own anxiety. That night, long after lights-out, Joe and Roger sat up in the dark, joking, telling stories, trying to talk themselves down from an emotional cliff. Now and then the darkness was punctuated by an orange glow as Chuck Day took another drag on a forbidden cigarette.

It wasn't that they were seriously concerned about their preliminary heat. They would race against Princeton and the Winged Footers of the New York Athletic Club. Neither was a real contender. California, on the other hand, would have to face Penn and Navy, both excellent sprinting crews. The worry came from what would happen after the preliminaries. Penn had swapped out three of its eight Poughkeepsie oarsmen, replacing them with recent graduates not eligible to race in the intercollegiate regatta but perfectly legal in Olympic trials. Navy had inserted Lieutenant Vic Krulak of the marine corps as its coxswain. California had also moved recent alumni into its boat. Washington, in fact, was the only crew that would be made up entirely of undergraduates. Assuming the boys qualified in their own preliminary, whichever crews they met in the final would, to some extent, be made up of unknowns—unknowns who were presumably superior to the boys they had just defeated in Poughkeepsie.

On Saturday, the Fourth of July, the boys left the Princeton shell house for their race a little before six thirty. It was a buggy, sultry evening. Several thousand people had gathered along the shores of the lake for the qualifying heats, most of them climbing into the newly constructed grandstands at the finish line. The boys backed the *Husky Clipper* into their starting stall, on a floating platform that had been specially built for the Olympic trials, and waited.

At the gun, Washington charged out of the stall at a high beat of thirty-eight. The *Husky Clipper* began to move out in front almost immediately. After about a minute, Moch told Don Hume to drop the rate. Hume went down to thirty-four. In the third minute, Hume dropped it to thirty-two, and even as the boys dropped the rate, the boat stayed out in front and began to widen its lead. The New York Athletic Club's Winged Footers and the Princeton boys were both rowing at thirty-five. By the halfway mark, Washington had open water on both boats. As they began to approach the finish line, the Winged Footers made a move, sprinting past Princeton and challenging Washington. Moch told Hume to ease the stroke rate back up to thirty-eight. The *Husky Clipper* pulled briskly ahead and sliced across the line two and a half lengths ahead of the Winged Footers.

Confident as they had been, the Washington boys were nevertheless surprised at just how easily they had won. Even in the muggy evening air, they'd hardly broken a sweat. They paddled out of the racing lanes and took up a position along the bank at about the fifteen-hundred-meter mark. The real question of the day was how California would do in their qualifying heat, and the boys wanted to see the answer for themselves.

At 7:00 p.m. Navy, Penn, and California left the mark, all rowing hard and high. For the first thousand meters, the three boats settled in and contended more or less evenly for the lead. At that point, Penn picked up its pace and began to move slowly out in front. As they entered the final five hundred meters, though, it was Cal that brought the fans in the grandstands to their feet. The boys from Berkeley executed a tremendous surge, suddenly blowing past both Navy and Penn, seizing the lead and winning by a quarter of a boat length. It was an impressive show, and it reinforced the long-standing belief— shared by many of the coaches and writers present that day—that despite Washington's wins in the long races at Poughkeepsie and in Seattle, California remained the superior sprinting crew. It was hard to argue otherwise. California had won its heat in 6:07.8; Washington had taken 10 full seconds longer, 6:17.8, to cover the same distance. "An almost insurmountable handicap for the Huskies," declared the *New York Sun's* Malcolm Roy.

As the Washington boys retreated to the Princeton Inn that night, anxiety cascaded down on them again. Al Ulbrickson once more spent much of the evening going from room to room, sitting on the ends of bunks, reassuring his boys, reminding them that they had in effect won a sprint in the last two thousand meters at Poughkeepsie, telling them what they already knew in their hearts but needed to hear one more time—that they could beat any crew in America, at any distance, including California. All they had to do, he told them, was to continue to believe in one another.

They nodded and agreed with him. The spring campaign—the instant fellowship they had all felt when they took to the water together for the first time, their commanding victory over Cal on Lake Washington, their stunning come-from-behind triumph at Poughkeepsie, and their almost effortless qualifying race earlier that day—had more than convinced them that together they were capable of greatness. None of them doubted anyone else in the boat. But believing in one another was not really at issue anymore. What was more difficult was being sure about one's self. The caustic chemicals of fear continued to surge in their brains and in their guts.

Late that night, after Ulbrickson had finally retired to his quarters, the boys stole out of the hotel singly or in pairs and walked along the shore of Lake Carnegie. The moon was full, the lake silver and glimmering. Crickets sang in the grass at their feet; cicadas buzzed in the trees overhead. They gazed into the moon-washed stars above, talking quietly, reminding themselves of who they were and what they had done. For some of them, that was enough. Joe remembered years later that a sense of calm had come over him that evening. Resolve had begun to flow into him, at first like a freshet, then like a river. Eventually, in the wee hours, they returned to their rooms and slept—some peacefully, some fitfully.

In the morning Chuck Day got up and wrote in his journal, "Final Olympic trials, very nervous but confident." Johnny White wrote, "We woke up all scared and having frequent visits with Alvin."

Alvin Ulbrickson couldn't have been exactly relaxed himself. This was his day of judgment. Many of his peers would be on hand to watch the race that evening—not just Ebright, but old Jim Ten Eyck from Syracuse, Ed Leader from Yale, Jim Wray from Cornell, and Constance Titus, an Olympic bronze sculler from 1904. More than that, though, Royal Brougham was there, getting set to broadcast the race live to fifty stations around the country on the CBS network. All of Seattle—and much of the rest of the country—would be listening. There would be no place to hide if the boys didn't come through for him.

Thunderstorms rumbled over New Jersey that morning, and rain pounded the roof of the Princeton Inn. By noon, though, the clouds had scudded off to the horizon and the day had grown hot and muggy but clear. Lake Carnegie lay mirror smooth, reflecting a translucent blue sky. The final Olympic trial was not scheduled to begin until 5:00 p.m., so the boys spent most of the day lounging in the Princeton shell house, trying to stay cool. Late in the afternoon, black sedans and coupes full of crew fans began to arrive at Lake Carnegie. Their drivers eased their vehicles under shade trees along the last few hundred meters of the racecourse, then spread picnic blankets on the grass and opened hampers full of sandwiches and cold drinks. The grandstands at the finish line slowly filled with people fanning themselves with their programs—men in fedoras and Panama hats, women in flat-brimmed hats perched on their heads at jaunty angles. All told, perhaps ten thousand people braved the heat to witness just six minutes of racing—six minutes that would shatter the dreams of all but nine of the boys about to take to the water.

At 4:45 the first- and second-place crews from the previous day's trials—California, Pennsylvania, Washington, and the New York Athletic Club—paddled from the Princeton shell house out onto Lake Carnegie. They made their way under the graceful arches of a stone bridge, around a long, sweeping bend in the lake, and up the straightaway to the starting stalls. The Winged Footers swung their boat around and backed it into its stall first, then Penn did the same. As Washington tried to back into its stall, a large and recalcitrant white swan blocked the way until Bobby Moch, yelling at it with his megaphone and waving his arms furiously, finally persuaded it to move slowly aside. Then California backed in.

In the late afternoon sun, tall trees growing along the bank cast long shadows over the starting stalls and the boats, but the heat had not abated appreciably. The Washington boys were bare chested, having stripped off their jerseys just before climbing into their boat. They sat now with their oars in the water ready for the first hard pull, each staring straight ahead at the neck of the man in front of him, trying to breathe slow and easy, settling their hearts and minds into the boat. Bobby Moch reached under his seat and touched Tom Bolles's lucky fedora, a few extra ounces of weight in exchange for a lot of luck.

A little after five, the starter called out, "Are you all ready?" All four coxswains dropped their hands, and the starting gun flashed immediately.

Washington got off to a poor start. Four or five strokes into the race, Gordy

Adam and Stub McMillin "washed out," their oars popping out of the water before they had completed their pulls. The effect was to throw the boat momentarily out of balance and to abruptly check the crucial momentum that the crew was trying to build up. The other three boats surged ahead. On the next stroke, all eight of the Washington oars caught the water cleanly, perfectly, at once.

The New York Athletic Club went briefly to the head of the pack, but Penn, pounding the water at a high cadence of forty strokes per minute, quickly snatched the lead back. California, rowing at thirty-eight, settled into third place, ten feet in front of Washington's bow. Bobby Moch and Don Hume took the rate up to thirty-nine to regain momentum, but once that was accomplished they immediately began to lower it again, to thirty-eight, then to thirty-seven, then to thirty-six, then to thirty-five. As the rate dropped, the *Husky Clipper* continued to hold its position just off of California's stern. Out front, Penn was still thrashing the lake white at thirty-nine. A quarter of the way down the course, Bobby Moch found himself creeping up on California. He told Hume to drop the rate yet again, and Hume settled at a surprisingly low thirty-four. As they approached the halfway mark, the New York Athletic Club suddenly began to fade and quickly fell away behind Washington. Penn remained out in front by three-quarters of a length, and even continued to slowly draw farther ahead of California. The *Husky Clipper* remained stuck on California's tail. The boys continued to row at thirty-four.

But what a thirty-four it was. Don Hume on the port side and Joe Rantz on the starboard were setting the pace with long, slow, sweet, fluid strokes, and the boys on each side were falling in behind them flawlessly. From the banks of Lake Carnegie, the boys, their oars, and the *Husky Clipper* looked like a single thing, gracefully and powerfully coiling and uncoiling itself, propelling itself forward over the surface of the water. Eight bare backs swung forward and backward in perfect unison. Eight white blades dipped in and out of the mirrorlike water at precisely the same instant. Each time the blades entered the lake, they disappeared almost without a splash or ripple. Each time the blades rose from it, the boat ghosted forward without check or hesitation.

Just before the fifteen-hundred-meter mark, Bobby Moch leaned into Don Hume and shouted, "Here's California! Here's where we take California!" Hume knocked the stroke rate up just a bit, to thirty-six, and Washington swiftly walked past Cal seat by seat. They began to creep up on Penn's stern. Penn's stroke man, Lloyd Saxton, watching the bow of the *Husky Clipper* coming up behind him, raised his beat to a killing forty-one. But as Penn's strokes grew more frequent, they began inevitably to grow shorter. Glancing at the "puddles" Washington's blades left behind in the water, Saxton was shocked at the distance between them. "They were spacing five feet to our three. It was unbelievable," he said after the race. Washington pulled abreast of Penn.

But Bobby Moch still hadn't really turned the boys loose. Coming inside five hundred meters, he finally did so. He barked at Hume to pick up the tempo. The rate surged to thirty-nine and then immediately to forty. For five or six strokes, the bows of the two boats contested for the lead, back and forth like the heads of racehorses coming down the stretch. Finally Washington's bow swung decisively out in front by a few feet. From there on, it was, as Gordy Adam would later say, "duck soup." With four hundred meters to go, Washington simply blew past the exhausted boys from Penn, like an express train passing the morning milk train, swinging into the last few hundred meters with extraordinary grace and power. The last twenty strokes, Shorty Hunt wrote his parents the next day, were "the best I ever felt in any boat." At the finish they were a full length ahead and still widening the lead. As they crossed the line, Bobby Moch, defying the laws of physics and common sense, suddenly stood bolt upright in the stern of his twenty-four-inch-wide shell, triumphantly thrusting one fist into the air.

Penn came in second; California, third. The New York Athletic Club's shell finally more or less drifted across the finish line, three and three-quarter lengths behind the Washington boat, half her crew lying prone across their oars, having collapsed in the heat.

All over Washington State—in smoky little mill towns out on the Olympic Peninsula, on soggy dairy farms nestled up against the Cascades, in posh Victorian homes on Seattle's Capitol Hill, and in the Huskies' drafty shell house down on the Montlake Cut—people stood and cheered. Mothers and fathers rushed off to Western Union offices to send congratulations to their sons back east. Newspapermen frantically scrambled to compose headlines. Bartenders served rounds on the house. What had been a dream was a reality. Their boys were going to the Olympics. For the first time ever, Seattle was going to play on the world stage.

Sitting by the radio at Harry Rantz's unfinished home on Lake Washington, Joyce and the kids cheered too. Harry said nothing but suddenly, beaming, he began rummaging around in a box, pulled out a large American flag, tacked it on the wall above the radio, and stood back to admire it. The kids ran off to tell their friends in the neighborhood the good news. Joyce, quietly jubilant, set about cleaning up the peanut shells the kids had let drop on the floor as they listened nervously to the race. A small sadness niggled at the back of her mind: this meant Joe would not be coming home until the end of the summer. But that was a trifle, she knew, and it was swept away by sheer joy as she began to contemplate the prospect of Joe, dressed in an Olympic uniform, climbing off a train in Seattle when he did finally come home in the fall.

Flashing broad, white grins, Joe and his crewmates paddled back to the Princeton shell house, tossed Bobby Moch in the water, fished him out, and then lined up for the press and newsreel photographers waiting for them on the float. Henry Penn Burke, chairman of the U.S. Olympic Rowing Committee, positioned himself next to Bobby Moch and extended a silver cup to him. As the newsreel cameras whirred, Moch, dripping wet and bare chested, held one of the cup's handles and Burke, in a suit and tie, held the other. Then Burke began to speak. He spoke and he spoke and he spoke. The boys were tired, and it was blazing hot out on the float, and they wanted to hit the showers and start celebrating. Still Burke continued to talk. Finally Moch gave a little tug on the cup and it popped free from Burke's hand. Burke kept right on talking. Eventually, with Moch clutching the cup, the boys just drifted away, leaving Burke alone on the float, still talking as the newsreel cameras continued to roll.

Al Ulbrickson also made a few, much briefer, remarks to the press. When asked how he accounted for his varsity's success this year, he went straight to the heart of the matter: "Every man in the boat had absolute confidence in every one of his mates. . . . Why they won cannot be attributed to individuals, not even to stroke Don Hume. Heartfelt cooperation all spring was responsible for the victory."

Ulbrickson was no poet. That was Pocock's territory. But the comment was as close as he could come to capturing what was in his heart. He must have known, with a kind of certitude that he felt in his gut, that he finally had in his grasp what had eluded him for years. Everything had converged: the right oarsmen, with the right attitudes, the right personalities, the right skills; a perfect boat, sleek, balanced, and wickedly fast; a winning strategy at both long and short distances; a coxswain with the guts and smarts to make hard decisions and make them fast. It all added up to more than he could really put into words, maybe more than even a poet could—something beyond the sum of its parts, something mysterious and ineffable and gorgeous to behold. And he knew whom to thank for much of it.

Walking back to the Princeton Inn that evening with George Pocock, the two men holding their suit coats over their shoulders in the warm, humid twilight, Ulbrickson stopped suddenly, turned abruptly to Pocock, and extended his right hand. "Thanks, George, for your help," he said. Pocock later remembered the moment: "Coming from Al," he mused, "that was the equivalent of fireworks and a brass band."

Later that night the boys were treated to the annual Loyal Shoudy banquet, where they found the traditional purple necktie and a five-dollar bill waiting at each place setting. But even as they dined and celebrated, disturbing rumors began to circulate in the hallways of the Princeton Inn.

By eight o'clock, the rumors were confirmed. After his windy speech on the float in front of the Princeton shell house, Henry Penn Burke had taken Al Ulbrickson, George Pocock, and Ray Eckman, the athletic director at Washington, into a room and given them, in effect, an ultimatum. If Washington wanted to go to Berlin, the boys were going to have to pay their own way. "You'll have to pay your own freight, or else," Burke said. "We just haven't got the dough." Burke, who was also, coincidentally, the chairman of and a major fundraiser for the Pennsylvania Athletic Club in Philadelphia, went on to say that he understood that Penn had plenty of money and as the second-place finisher they would naturally be glad to take Washington's place in Berlin.

Similar dramas were playing out across America that week. The American Olympic Committee had come up short of funds. Swimmers, fencers, and dozens of other teams were being asked to finance or partially finance their fare to Berlin. But until this moment, neither the AOC nor the Olympic Rowing Committee had hinted that they would be unable to send the winning crew to the games. Caught unawares, Ulbrickson was stunned and livid. The university had already had to beg and scrape every dime it could from alumni and the citizens of Seattle just to send the boys east to Poughkeepsie and Princeton. And there was no chance any of these boys could contribute their own funds. These weren't the heirs and scions of industry; these were working-class Americans. The whole thing stank. The Washingtonians were ready to storm out of the room, but Burke kept on talking. He pointed out that California had paid its own way in 1928, as well as 1932. Yale, he said, had no problem raising "private funds" in 1924. Surely somebody in Seattle could come up with the money.

Ulbrickson knew full well that money more or less grew on the trees at Yale, and that funds had been vastly easier to come by in 1928, before the Depression, than in 1936. In 1932, Ebright had been faced only with transporting his crew 350 miles, from Berkeley to Los Angeles. Icily Ulbrickson asked Burke how much he needed to come up with and how soon. Five thousand dollars by the end of the week, Burke replied. Otherwise, Penn would go.

After the meeting, Ulbrickson huddled with Royal Brougham and George Varnell, and within minutes they were composing headlines and writing special columns to be wired to the *Post-Intelligencer* and the *Times* for the next day's editions. In Seattle, a few minutes later, phones began to ring. Ray Eckman called his assistant, Carl Kilgore, who in turn started making local calls. By 10:00 p.m. Seattle time, Kilgore had enlisted dozens of civic leaders and put a rough plan in place. In the morning they would open their headquarters at the Washington Athletic Club, name a chairman, and set up teams. In the meantime everyone began placing more calls. Al Ulbrickson tried not to alarm his athletes. This was exactly the kind of nonsense he didn't want them fretting about. He told them as little as possible about the funding shortage, and they went to bed that night believing all would be well.

The next morning Shorty Hunt jotted off a short letter to his parents: "A dream come true! Oh boy, what lucky kids we are! Nobody can tell me we didn't have Old Dame Luck perched on our shoulders." Then he and the rest of the crew chowed down on cantaloupe and ice cream for breakfast before turning out to row in front of Fox Movietone's newsreel cameras.

A few hours later, Seattleites awoke to alarming headlines and radio news bulletins. The entire town went to work. Coeds on summer break grabbed tin cans and began going door-to-door in their neighborhoods. Paul Coughlin, president of the alumni association, started placing calls to some of the university's more prominent graduates. Thousands of lapel tags were quickly printed up, and students on campus for summer session began to sell them for fifty cents apiece in the hallways. Radio announcers broke into their morning programming to appeal for funds. Downtown, I. F. Dix, the general manager of Pacific Telephone and Telegraph, signed on as chairman of the campaign. In short order, telegrams began to rattle out of Dix's office to the chambers of commerce of every city, town, and hamlet in the state. More than a thousand letters were mailed out to American Legion posts and other civic and fraternal organizations.

By afternoon the money and pledges had begun to pour in: a hefty $500 from the *Seattle Times* to get things started; $5 from the Hide-Away Beer Parlor; $50 from mighty Standard Oil; $1 from a donor who wished to remain anonymous; $5 from Cecil Blogg of Tacoma, one of Hiram Conibear's coxswains. Money began to come in as well from the boys' hometowns, where their accomplishments had been making local headlines for weeks: $50 from Bobby Moch's Montesano; $50 from Bellingham, the nearest town of any size to the dairy farm on which Gordy Adam had grown up; $299.25 from Don Hume's Olympia; $75 from Joe Rantz's Sequim. By the end of the first day of the drive, volunteers had sold $1,523 worth of fifty-cent tags. At the end of the second day, T. F. Davies, chairman of the Seattle Chamber of Commerce, put a $5,000 certified check in an envelope and airmailed it to Al Ulbrickson.

By then Ulbrickson and the boys were blithely getting ready to sail for Germany on the SS *Manhattan* on July 14. Just hours after the meeting with Henry Penn Burke and his brief conversations with Royal Brougham and George Varnell that evening, Ulbrickson had put on his best poker face—which is to say his natural face—gone back to Burke and the AOC, and declared that as a matter of fact Washington did have the funds to pay its way to Berlin. Then, before anyone could raise any awkward questions about just how he'd managed to get his hands on five thousand dollars so quickly, he'd speedily accepted the invitation of the New York Athletic Club to use its training facilities, in a nearby suburb on Long Island Sound, and quickly slipped out of Princeton.

As the boys—now officially the U.S. eight-oared Olympic rowing team—settled in at Travers Island they were, largely unbeknownst to them, beginning to become national celebrities. Back home in Seattle, they were already full-blown superstars. Eastern coaches and sportswriters had been following them with increasing interest ever since their freshman victory at Poughkeepsie in 1934. And now, after watching those last twenty strokes at Princeton, newspapermen from across the country were starting to put down in print what many of them had first begun to think when they saw Joe and his crewmates emerge suddenly out of the twilight that evening in Poughkeepsie two weeks before. These young men just might be the greatest collegiate crew of all time.

Travers Island sat on Long Island Sound, just south of New Rochelle. The New York Athletic Club's facility there, completed in 1888, sprawled over thirty neatly manicured acres at the center of which stood a posh, sprawling clubhouse. With a formal dining room and an oyster bar, a billiards room, a full-featured gymnasium, a boathouse, every conceivable sort of athletic training equipment, trap-shooting facilities, a baseball diamond, a bowling alley, a boxing ring, tennis courts, squash courts, a cinder running track, Turkish baths, a swimming pool, a barbershop, valet services, and wide, sweeping lawns, it was, for all practical purposes, a country club for amateur athletes, as well as a prominent venue for Westchester County society events. It afforded easy access to excellent rowing water on the sound. And, best of all, for boys from the fields, forests, and small towns of the Pacific Northwest, it was just a few miles from all the manifold mysteries and wonders of New York City.

The sweltering heat continued to build over the East Coast and over much of America that week, but the boys weren't going to let a little heat keep them from taking a bite of the Big Apple. They visited Grant's Tomb, tried to board the *Queen Mary* but were turned away, inspected Columbia's campus, toured Rockefeller Center, walked up and down Broadway, and ate at Jack Dempsey's. They trooped into Minsky's Burlesque and came out with wide eyes and sheepish grins, though Johnny White confided his personal opinion in his journal: "It was foul." They walked around Wall Street, recalling the hushed tones in which their parents had talked about the place in 1929.

They rode the subway out to Coney Island and found that hundreds of thousands of New Yorkers had beaten them there, fleeing the stifling heat of Manhattan even in the middle of the workweek. From the crowded board-walk, as far as they could see up and down the shoreline, the beaches were a dark, seething mass of bodies packed together on the sand. They made their way through the throng, fascinated by the thousand voices of New York—Italian-speaking mothers and Spanish-speaking Puerto Rican boys, Yiddish-speaking grandfathers and Polish-speaking girls, giddy children calling out to one another in dozens of tongues and all varieties of English, their voices tinged with the inflections of the Bronx and Brooklyn and New Jersey. They shoveled down five-cent hot dogs at Nathan's, ate cotton candy, guzzled ice-cold Coca-Colas. They rode on the 150-foot Wonder Wheel and the hair-raising Cyclone roller coaster. They wandered through the spires and turrets of Luna Park, rode more rides, gobbled peanuts, and guzzled more Cokes. By the time they headed back to the city, they were exhausted and not entirely impressed by Coney Island. "What a hole," Chuck Day confided in his journal. "Dirty, crowded, gyp joints." And he wasn't much impressed by the hot, sweltering citizens of Greater New York either: "People in New York are all very tired looking, pale, & soft. The people seldom smile & don't look healthy & full of vigor as out west."

As they explored New York, they began to come, one by one, to a new realization about how things stood for them. In Times Square one afternoon, a tall, somewhat heavy man rushed up to Shorty, took a good look, and said, "You're Shorty Hunt!" He looked at the other boys. "You fellows are the Washington crew, aren't you?" When they assured him they were, he gushed that he had recognized Shorty from a picture in the newspaper. He was a former Columbia oarsman himself, he said, and after watching their recent exploits he had decided to send his son west for college so he too might become a great crewman. It was the first time any of them really began to understand that they were now America's crew, not the University of Washington's—that the W on their jerseys was about to be replaced with "USA."

For Joe, the moment of epiphany came on the eighty-sixth floor of the new Empire State Building. None of the boys had ever ridden an elevator more than a few floors in a hotel, and the rapid ascent both thrilled and frightened them. "Ears popped, eyes bulged," Shorty Hunt wrote home breathlessly that night.

Joe had never flown in an airplane, never seen a city from any higher vantage point than that afforded by his own six-foot-three frame. Now, standing on the observation deck, he looked out at the many spires of New York rising through a pall of smoke and steam and heat haze and did not know whether he found it beautiful or frightening.

He leaned over the low stone parapet and peered down at miniature cars and buses and swarms of tiny people scurrying along the streets. The city below him, Joe realized, murmured. The cacophony of honking horns and wailing sirens and rumbling streetcars that had assaulted his ears at street level were reduced up here to something gentler and more soothing, like the sonorous breathing of an enormous living thing. It was a much bigger, more connected, world than he had ever thought possible.

He dropped a nickel in a telescope for a better view of the Brooklyn Bridge, then swept across Lower Manhattan and out to the distant Statue of Liberty. In a few days, he would be sailing under her on his way to a place where as he understood it, liberty was not a given, where it seemed to be under some kind of assault. The realization that was settling on all the boys settled on Joe.

They were now representatives of something much larger than themselves—a way of life, a shared set of values. Liberty was perhaps the most fundamental of those values. But the things that held them together—trust in one another, mutual respect, humility, fair play, watching out for one another—those were also part of what America meant to all of them. And right along with a passion for liberty, those were the things they were about to take to Berlin and lay before the world when they took to the water at Grünau.

Sudden revelation paid Bobby Moch a visit as well. His came as he sat, in the shade under a tree in a wide-open field on Travers Island, opening an envelope. The envelope contained a letter from his father, the letter Bobby had requested, listing the addresses of the relatives he hoped to visit in Europe. But the envelope also contained a second, sealed envelope labeled, "Read this in a private place." Now, alarmed, sitting under the tree, Moch opened the second envelope and read its contents. By the time he had finished reading, tears were running down his face.

The news was innocuous enough by twenty-first-century standards, but in the context of social attitudes in America in the 1930s it came as a profound shock. When he met his relatives in Europe, Gaston Moch told his son, he was going to learn for the first time that he and his family were Jewish.

Bobby sat under the tree, brooding for a long while, not because he suddenly found himself a member of what was then still a much discriminated against minority, but because as he absorbed the news he realized for the first time the terrible pain his father must have carried silently within him for so many years. For decades, his father had felt that in order to make it in America it was necessary to conceal an essential element of his identity from his friends, his neighbors, and even his own children. Bobby had been brought up to believe that everyone should be treated according to his actions and his character, not according to stereotypes. It was his father himself who had taught him that. Now it came as a searing revelation that his father had not felt safe enough to live by that same simple proposition, that he had kept his heritage hidden painfully away, a secret to be ashamed of, even in America, even from his own beloved son.

By July 9, New York City was baking in the greatest heat wave in American history. For a month, unheard-of temperatures had been searing the West and Midwest. Even the terrible summer of 1934 hadn't been this bad. Now the dome of heat extended from coast to coast and far north into Canada. Three thousand Americans would die of the heat that week, forty of them in New York City.

The U.S. Olympic eight-oared crew was as cool as could be, though. Every afternoon they boarded a boat and made their way out to the New York Athletic Club's private retreat, Huckleberry Island, a mile off Travers Island, out in the cool waters of Long Island Sound. The island was twelve acres of paradise, and the boys fell in love with it the moment they stepped out of their launch and onto a beach in one of its many small granite coves, wearing the Indian headbands with turkey feathers that club members donned whenever they visited the island. They leapt off stone ledges, plunged into the cool green water of the sound, swam, horsed around, then stretched out on warm flat slabs of granite, toasting themselves brown before plunging back into the water again.

Chuck Day smoked Lucky Strikes and cracked jokes. Roger Morris lay about looking sleepy, making gruff observations about Day's smoking habit. Gordy Adam was content to bask quietly in the sun wearing his Indian headband. Joe wandered off to study the geology of the island, discovering glacial striations etched in the granite. Bobby Moch tried to organize activities, hustled the boys about, and got unceremoniously tackled and tossed in the water three or four times for his trouble. All of them were at their ease there, comfortable in their skins. With the sea and woods at hand, they were in their element in a way they could never be in Manhattan for all its glitter and glamour.

On the third day, Al Ulbrickson put the kibosh on their swimming. He was firmly of a mind that any kind of exercise other than rowing was bad for rowers—it developed the wrong sets of muscles.

Finally, it came time to pack and prepare for Germany. On July 13, Pocock supervised the boys as they carefully loaded the sixty-two-foot *Husky Clipper* onto a long truck and—with a police escort—drove it through the heart of New York City to Pier 60 on the Hudson River, where the SS *Manhattan* was being readied for its departure two days later. Pocock had spent his days at Travers Island carefully sanding down the shell's hull and then applying coat after coat of marine varnish, buffing each coat until the shell glistened. It wasn't just a matter of aesthetics. Pocock wanted the shell to have the fastest possible racing bottom he could impart to it. Fractions of a second might well tell the story in Berlin.

When they pulled up alongside the *Manhattan*, Pocock found that the dock was a jumble of offices, storage sheds, stacks of cargo, and canopied gangways for passengers. He and the boys were responsible for loading the boat onto the ship themselves, and they quickly discovered that there wasn't any place where they could maneuver the long shell into a position to get her aboard. They were all wearing ties, for a reception to be followed by dinner at the Lincoln Hotel later that day. Carrying the shell over their heads in the stifling, humid heat, they walked carefully but wearily up and down the dock for nearly an hour, staring up at the great red hull of the ship, trying everything they could think of.

Finally, far up the dock, someone spotted a baggage chute descending at a sixty-degree angle to street level. Gingerly, they inserted the prow end of the shell into the chute. Then, crawling on hands and knees, they snaked it up the chute to the promenade deck. From there, holding it high over their heads again, they angled it all the way up to the boat deck, tied it down, covered it with a tarp, and hoped and prayed that no one would mistake it for a bench and sit on it. Then they hurried off to their reception, massively late and soaked in sweat.

At the Lincoln Hotel, they signed in officially with the AOC, then mingled for the first time with their fellow Olympians in the lobby. Glenn Cunningham was there, dressed in a sharp gray suit and a bright yellow tie. In a corner of the room, photographers had cornered Jesse Owens, dressed in an ice-cream-white suit, and talked him into posing with a saxophone. "When I give the word," said one of the photographers, "blow on that thing." On command, Jesse blew. The instrument emitted a long, wheezing sigh. "Better look at your tires, Jesse, that sounded like a puncture," someone joked.

Walking around the room, the Washington boys figured they might not be the most famous people there, or the fastest afoot, or even the strongest, but—with the exception of Bobby Moch—they were probably the tallest. Then they met six-foot-eight Joe Fortenberry and six-foot-nine Willard

Schmidt from the first-ever U.S. Olympic basketball team. When he went to shake their hands and tried to look Schmidt in the eye, even Stub McMillin found that he risked getting a crick in his neck. Bobby Moch didn't even try. He figured he would have needed a ladder.

The next day was a whirl of activity—picking up their Olympic credentials and their German visas, stocking up on a few last-minute sundries, buying travelers' checks. Johnny White didn't know what he was going to do for money in Europe. He still had most of the fourteen dollars he'd left home with, but that wasn't going to last long. Then, at the last minute, an envelope with a hundred dollars arrived from Seattle. His sister, Mary Helen, had sent it—nearly all her savings—saying she'd take his old violin in exchange. Johnny knew full well she had no interest at all in the violin.

They capped off their tour of New York that evening with a trip to Loew's State Theatre, where Duke Ellington and his orchestra were finishing up a weeklong engagement. For Joe and Roger especially, it was the highlight of

Joe's Olympic passport

the stay in New York. Under the theater's huge Czech-crystal chandelier, sitting in red-plush theater seats and surrounded by gilded woodwork, they listened entranced as Ellington and his orchestra lilted through "Mood Indigo," "Accent on Youth," "In a Sentimental Mood," "Uptown Downbeat," and a dozen and a half more tunes. Joe basked in the bright, brassy music, soaking it in as it washed over him, feeling it swing him.

Late that night they settled in at the Alpha Delta Phi Club for one last night's sleep before their even grander adventure commenced the following morning. As they turned out the lights, fifty miles to the south of them, the zeppelin *Hindenburg* cast off from its mooring place in Lakehurst, New Jersey, and lumbered out over the Atlantic on its way home to Germany and its own small role in the 1936 Olympics, looming dark against the night sky, large black swastikas emblazoned on its tail fins.

With newsreel cameras rolling and flashbulbs popping, the boys bounded up the gangplank and onto the *Manhattan* at ten thirty the next morning. Like the 325 other members of the U.S. Olympic team boarding this ship, they were giddy, charged with earnest excitement. None of them had ever been on a boat any larger than the ferries back in Seattle, and the SS *Manhattan*—668 feet long, weighing in at 24,289 tons, with eight passenger decks, and able to accommodate 1,239 passengers—was no ferry. She was in fact a full-fledged luxury liner. Just five years old, she and her sister ship, the SS *Washington*, were the first large North Atlantic liners to be built in America since 1905 and the largest that Americans had ever built.

Lying at berth on the Hudson that morning, the *Manhattan* was about as all-American a sight as one could imagine, her red hull and gleaming white superstructure topped by twin funnels, each swept jauntily back and painted with red, white, and blue horizontal stripes. As the athletes piled gleefully on board, each was given a small American flag, and soon the rails were crowded with bright-faced young people waving the flags and calling out to family and well-wishers gathered on the dock below.

The boys found their quarters down in tourist class and stowed their gear. They met and shook hands with the other oarsmen who would represent the United States in Berlin: Dan Barrow, a single sculler from the Pennsylvania Athletic Club; two pairs, one with and one without a coxswain, also from the Pennsylvania Athletic Club; a double sculls crew from the Undine Barge Club in Philadelphia; and two four-oared crews, one made up of Harvard boys from the Riverside Boat Club in Massachusetts, with a coxswain, and one from the West Side Rowing Club in Buffalo, New York, without a coxswain.

Then, with the formalities over, they joined the flag wavers up on deck. As the noon sailing time approached, more than ten thousand spectators crowded onto Pier 60. Blimps and airplanes circled overhead. Newsreel photographers shot a few more feet of film on deck and then scampered off the ship to set up their cameras for shots of it leaving. Black smoke began to billow out of the red, white, and blue funnels. Nautical pennants fluttered from rigging on the fore and after masts in a light, hot breeze.

Just before noon the athletes assembled on the sundeck, gathering around Avery Brundage and other AOC officials as they unfurled an enormous white flag with the five interlocking Olympic rings and began to raise it on the after mast. The crowd on the dock, doffing their hats and waving them over their heads, began a thunderous chant: "Ray! Ray! Ray! For the USA!" A band struck up a martial tune, the lines were cast off, and the *Manhattan* began to back slowly out into the Hudson.

Joe and the other boys rushed back to the rails, waving their flags now, unabashedly taking up the chant: "Ray! Ray! Ray! For the USA!" On the dock people shouted, "Bon voyage!" The whistles on tugs and ferries and nearby ships began to shriek. Out on the river, fireboats let loose with their sirens and shot white plumes of water high into the air. The planes overhead tipped to one side and circled in tight loops as photographers snapped aerial views.

Tugs pushed the bow of the *Manhattan* until she pointed down the river, and the ship began to power majestically down the west side of Manhattan. As she made her way past the Battery, Joe felt the first cooling breeze in days. When she passed Ellis Island and then the Statue of Liberty, he, like everyone, dashed to the starboard rail to watch her pass. He stayed on deck as the ship made her way through the narrows, with Staten Island on one side and Brooklyn on the other, and then progressed through the lower bay and out finally into the Atlantic, where she began to roll slightly as she made a long, slow, sweeping turn to port.

Still Joe stayed on deck, leaning on the rail, enjoying the cool air, watching Long Island pass by, trying to absorb everything, to remember everything, so he could tell Joyce all about it when he returned home. It was only hours later, when the sun had begun to decline in the west and Joe had finally grown downright chilly on deck, that he retreated into the bowels of the ship, starting to get his sea legs, looking for the rest of the boys and food.

As the *Manhattan* sailed northeast that night and darkness enveloped her, she was ablaze with lights and loud with music, alive with the laughter of young people at play, having the time of their lives, venturing out onto the black void of the North Atlantic, on their way to Hitler's Germany.

The SS *Manhattan*

CHAPTER SIXTEEN

Good thoughts have much to do with good rowing. It isn't enough for the muscles of a crew to work in unison; their hearts and minds must also be as one.

—George Yeoman Pocock

As Joe drifted into sleep aboard the *Manhattan*, the first light of dawn crept over Berlin, revealing small groups of men, women, and children being marched through the streets at gunpoint. The arrests had begun hours earlier, under the veil of night, when police and SA storm troopers broke into the shanties and wagons that were home to Roma and Sinti families—Gypsies—and rousted them from their beds. Now they were on their way to a sewage-disposal site in the Berlin suburb of Marzahn, where they would be kept in a detention camp, well away from the eyes of foreigners arriving in Berlin for the Olympics. In time they would be sent east to death camps and murdered.

Their removal was just one more step in a process that had been unfolding for months as the Nazis transformed Berlin into something resembling a vast movie set—a place where illusion could be perfected, where the unreal could be made to seem real and the real could be hidden away. Already the signs prohibiting Jews from entering public facilities had been taken down and stored for later use. The fiercely anti-Semitic *Der Stürmer* newspaper—with its grotesque caricatures of Jews and its slogan, "The Jews Are Our Misfortune"—had been temporarily removed from newsstands. In *Der Angriff*, his principal propaganda publication, Joseph Goebbels had handed Berliners the script for their part in the performance, detailing how they should conduct themselves toward Jews and how they should welcome the foreigners when they arrived: "We must be more charming than the Parisians, more easygoing than the Viennese, more vivacious than the Romans, more cosmopolitan than London, more practical than New York."

When the foreigners arrived, all would be pleasant. Berlin would become a sort of benign amusement park for adults. Strict controls would limit what visitors could be charged for everything—from rooms at luxury hotels like the Adlon to the bratwurst sold by street vendors all over town. To improve the scenery, not only the Gypsies but more than fourteen hundred homeless people had been collected and removed from the streets. Hundreds of prostitutes had been seized, forcibly examined for venereal disease, and then turned loose to ply their trade for the carnal satisfaction of the visitors.

Visiting journalists, who would convey their impressions of the new Germany to the rest of the world, would be given special accommodations, the finest equipment, the best vantage points for viewing the games, free secretarial services. There was one contingency, though, that would have to be handled delicately, should it arise. If foreign journalists attempted to interview German Jews or investigate "the Jewish question," they were to be politely directed to the nearest gestapo office, so that they could be questioned as to their intentions, and then trailed secretly.

Along the railroad tracks on which the visitors would travel into Berlin, grimy buildings had been whitewashed, vacant apartment buildings had been rented out inexpensively, and identical window boxes full of red geraniums had been placed beneath windowsills of even the apartments that remained vacant. Virtually every home along the tracks now displayed the red, white, and black swastika flag. Many also flew the white Olympic flag. A few—mostly Jewish homes—flew only the Olympic banner. Thousands more swastika flags hung in railroad stations. Indeed all of Berlin was draped with swastikas. Along the central promenade on Unter den Linden, Berlin's wide central boulevard, the hundreds of linden trees that had given the street its name had been replaced with regimented colonnades of flagpoles bearing enormous forty-five-foot red banners with swastikas. Equally tall banners hung from the Brandenburg Gate. At Adolf-Hitler-Platz, concentric rings of tall masts flying Olympic flags surrounded a central tower, sixty-two feet high, draped with twenty swastika flags, forming a dramatic, bloodred cylinder in the middle of the grassy square. On the pleasant, shady streets leading to the rowing course out in Grünau, strands of smaller flags with swastikas were strung from tree to tree.

The streets had been swept and reswept. Shop windows polished. Trains freshly painted. Broken windows replaced. Dozens of new courtesy Mercedes limousines had been parked in neat rows outside the Olympic Stadium, awaiting VIPs. Nearly everyone from taxi drivers to sanitation workers had

Berlin decked out for the Olympics

been outfitted in some kind of smart new uniform. Foreign books, banned books, books that had escaped the bonfires of 1933, suddenly reappeared in bookshop windows.

With the set fully decorated, Leni Riefenstahl was busily at work mobilizing dozens of cameramen and sound technicians, putting scores of cameras in place. In the Olympic Stadium, out at the Reichssportfeld, she set up thirty cameras for the opening ceremony alone. She dug pits for low-angle shots and erected steel towers for high-angle shots. She constructed rails on which camera dollies could run alongside the red-clay track. She immersed cameras in waterproof housings in the Olympic swimming and diving pools. She attached cameras to saddles for equestrian events and floated them on pontoon boats for swimming events. In central Berlin she set cameras on strategic buildings, mounted them on the tops of trucks, suspended them from blimps, and dug more pits—all to capture ground-level footage of the marathon runners and the torch-relay runners as they made their way through the city. Out at the rowing course at Grünau, she constructed a jetty in the Langer See, running parallel to the racecourse, and installed rails along which a dolly with a camera could follow the shells for the final hundred meters of the races. She borrowed an antiaircraft balloon from the Luftwaffe and tethered it near the finish so a cameraman could dangle from it for aerial shots.

Everywhere she set up cameras, Riefenstahl made sure she had the most flattering angles, generally cast upward, for filming the ultimate stars of the show, Adolf Hitler and his entourage. Then, with the cameras mostly in place, she and all of Berlin waited for the rest of the cast to arrive.

Don Hume and Roger Morris lay retching in their berths aboard the *Manhattan* that morning. Al Ulbrickson felt fine, but he was worried about Hume and Morris, laid low by seasickness. They were already the two lightest oarsmen in the boat, and he had planned to make sure they put on some weight during the voyage.

Joe Rantz woke up feeling great. He made his way up to the promenade deck, where he found a riot of athleticism unfolding. Lithe gymnasts twirled on parallel bars and uneven bars and took long running leaps at vaulting horses, trying to time their precise movements to coincide with the slow roll of the ship. Stout weight lifters hoisted enormous hunks of iron over their heads, quivering and swaying slightly beneath their loads. Boxers sparred in a makeshift ring, dancing to keep their feet under them. Fencers lunged. Sprinters jogged by, running slow laps, taking care not to turn an ankle. In the ship's small saltwater swimming pool, coaches had tied rubber ropes to their swimmers, keeping them in place as they swam, and making sure they didn't get sloshed onto the deck when particularly large waves rolled the boat. Pistol shots cracked from the stern as pentathletes fired their weapons out over the empty ocean.

When the gong sounded for men's breakfast, Joe went to his assigned table and was disappointed to find that athletes were permitted to order only from a special restricted menu, designed, apparently, to feed canaries or coxswains. He ate everything he could order and tried to order seconds but was denied. He left the room nearly as hungry as he had entered it. He resolved to talk to Ulbrickson about it.

On the boat to Berlin

Meanwhile he had a look around. Belowdecks he found a gymnasium full of exercise apparatus, a children's playroom, barbershops, a manicure shop, and a beauty salon. He discovered a comfortable lounge in tourist class, complete with a screen for what were then still often called "talking pictures." All of it seemed pretty swell to Joe. But when he ventured up on the first-class decks he found another world entirely.

The cabins there, paneled in exotic woods, were spacious, with built-in vanities, plush upholstered furniture, Persian rugs, bedside telephones, and private bathrooms with hot and cold freshwater showers. Joe wandered quietly on plush carpeting through a maze of corridors, leading to a full cocktail bar, then a cigar shop, then a writing room, and then a library with oak paneling and heavy beams. He found a smoking lounge with a wood-burning fireplace that stretched the width of the room and murals and carvings meant to suggest that the smoker had entered an Aztec temple. He found the Veranda Café, its walls painted with Venetian scenes and featuring a large elliptical dance floor. He found the Chinese Palm Court, complete with not only live palm trees but high white-plastered rococo ceilings, marble columns, delicate hand-painted Asian wall murals, and Chippendale furniture. He found the first-class dining room, with its own orchestra balcony, cove lighting behind recessed windows to create the illusion of perpetual daylight, and round dining tables, each draped with an elegant tablecloth and carrying its own Louis Seize–style brass lamp, all arranged under a domed ceiling painted with murals of mythological scenes like the feast of the Bacchanalia. And finally he found the Grand Salon, featuring its own theatrical stage and talking-picture screen, with more Persian rugs, formal divans and armchairs, fluted walnut pilasters, hand-carved molding, wide windows hung with velvet curtains, and another high, domed rococo plaster ceiling.

Joe tried to look inconspicuous, or as inconspicuous as a six-foot-three boy could look. He wasn't, technically speaking, supposed to be wandering around in such places. The athletes were expected to remain in the tourist-class areas, except when exercising on the promenade deck during daylight hours. This was intended to be the province of the sort of people Joe had seen on the golf course at Princeton or on the manicured lawns of estates he had glimpsed up the Hudson. But Joe lingered, mesmerized by his peek at how the other half still lived.

When he returned to his cabin, he found something waiting for him that made him feel pretty classy himself. In New York the boys had been measured for their Olympic outfits, and now Joe found a double-breasted blue serge sports coat and matching blue slacks spread out on his bunk. The coat had the U.S. Olympic shield emblazoned on the breast and bright brass buttons, each with a miniature shield. There was a pair of white flannel slacks; a white straw boater with a blue hatband; a crisp white dress shirt; white socks with red, white, and blue edging; white leather shoes; and a blue-striped necktie. There was a blue sweat suit, with "USA" printed boldly across the chest. And there was a rowing uniform—white shorts and an elegant white jersey with a U.S. Olympic shield on the left breast and red, white, and blue ribbons stitched around the neck and down the front. For a boy who had worn the same rumpled sweater to rowing practice for a year, this was an astonishing collection of sartorial treasure.

The fabric of the jersey was smooth, almost like silk, and it shimmered in the afternoon light streaming in through his porthole when he held it up for a better look. He had never yet been beaten, had never been obliged to surrender a jersey to a rival oarsman. He had no intention of letting this jersey be the first. He was taking this one home.

Over the next few days, Don Hume and Roger Morris slowly recovered from their seasickness, and the boys began to roam the boat together. They found a rowing machine on deck and tried it out, posing on it for news photographers. Al Ulbrickson posed with them, but when the photographers were done he quickly chased the boys off the apparatus, saying, as he often did, that the only proper way to develop rowing muscles was by rowing in a real shell. As they wandered away, Roger Morris gave him a grin over his shoulder and said, "Heck, if you want us to row in a shell just lower the *Clipper* over the side and we'll row the rest of the way over."

When Ulbrickson wasn't watching, they ran laps around the deck, worked out in the gym, played shuffleboard and Ping-Pong with other athletes, and got on a first-name basis with a few who already were or would soon be household names, among them Ralph Metcalfe, Jesse Owens, and Glenn Cunningham. Johnny White went prowling for girls and returned unhappy with the prospects. And, except for Don Hume, all of them began to put on weight.

Al Ulbrickson had talked to someone in the galley and someone on the AOC, making the case that a menu suitable for a thirteen-year-old gymnast might not be appropriate for a six-four oarsman, explaining that a boatload of skeletons was not likely to win any medals. The strict menu restrictions had promptly been lifted, and the boys began more or less living in the tourist-class dining salon. Free now to order anything from the menu as often as they wanted, except for sugary desserts or items excessively high in fat, they did just that, eating helping after helping of the main courses, just as they had on the train to Poughkeepsie. They were the first of the athletes to sit down and the last to get up. And no one—with the possible exception of Louis Zamperini, the long-distance runner from Torrance, California—out-ate Joe Rantz. Stub McMillin gave it a try, though. One morning he sneaked into the dining salon ahead of the rest of the crew. He ordered two stacks of hotcakes, slathered them with butter, drowned them with syrup, and was just about to dig in when Al Ulbrickson entered the room. Ulbrickson sat down, cocked an eye at the plate, slid it to his side of the table, and said, "Thanks a million, Jim, for fixing those for me," and slowly devoured both stacks as McMillin glowered at him over a plate of dry toast.

After dinner each evening, there were more formal entertainments—a variety show, an amateur hour, mock trials and mock weddings, bingo games, checkers and chess tournaments, and a casino night during which the athletes wagered stage money. There were raucous sing-alongs and a captain's ball, for which everyone was given balloons and noisemakers and party hats. There was a formal debate on the always contentious proposition that "the

East is a better place to live than the West." Talking pictures were shown in the tourist lounge for the athletes and in the Grand Salon for first-class passengers. The Washington boys didn't think much of the class business, though, and they flouted it. They soon discovered that when five or six big oarsmen sat down in the Grand Salon, and they just happened to be Olympic athletes representing the United States of America, there wasn't much anybody was going to do about it. So they took to visiting the upper decks for their movie viewing, stopping each evening on their way into the Grand Salon to swipe one of the large platters of hors d'oeuvres and then passing it around as they watched the show.

It soon became clear that there were limits beyond which one could not transgress on the *Manhattan*. Eleanor Holm was twenty-two years old, beautiful, married, and a minor celebrity, having performed bit parts in several Warner Brothers movies. She was somewhat notorious for having sung "I'm an Old Cowhand" in a cabaret while wearing only a white cowboy hat, a white swimsuit, and high heels. She was also a very good swimmer and had won a gold medal at the 1932 Olympics in Los Angeles. Now she was widely favored to win the hundred-meter backstroke in Berlin. On the second day out of New York, a group of journalists invited her up to the first-class decks for what turned out to be an all-night party, during which she drank a good deal of champagne, ate caviar, and entranced many of the writers, among them William Randolph Hearst Jr. By six o'clock the next morning, she was dead drunk and had to be carried back to her cabin in tourist class. When she came to, she was summoned into the presence of Avery Brundage, who read her the riot act and told her he would throw her off the team if she continued drinking. She did. Several nights later she again attended a party held by the hard-drinking news writers. This time the swim team's chaperone, Ada Sackett, caught her in the act.

In the morning Sackett and the ship's surgeon awoke a badly hungover Holm in her cabin. The surgeon took one look at her and pronounced her an alcoholic. Dee Boeckmann, coach of the women's team, then marched a number of Holm's teammates through the cabin, pointed at the pale, disheveled, and retching Holm, and expounded on the diabolical effects of alcohol. Later that day, Avery Brundage expelled Holm from the U.S. Olympic team.

Holm was devastated, and many of her fellow athletes were outraged. Some felt that Holm had been deliberately set up by the journalists in order to manufacture a story. Others felt that she had been dropped not so much for drinking as for defying Brundage. Although the athlete's handbook prohibited drinking, Brundage had convened a meeting of the entire U.S. team on the first day out of New York and told them that the matter of "eating, smoking, and drinking" was one of individual judgment. And indeed Brundage later wrote that Holm had been removed partly for "insubordination." More than two hundred of Holm's fellow athletes signed a petition asking that she be reinstated. All of them knew that in fact alcohol was widely available and widely used belowdecks. In fact even as Holm and the writers were partying up in first class, Chuck Day and some of his mates were holding their own all-nighters down in tourist class, merrily mixing milk, Ovaltine, and alcohol. But discipline was sacrosanct for Brundage.

The Eleanor Holm story, as at least some of the journalists had calculated, made headlines for days back in the United States, and in the long run it did wonders for her career. In the wake of Prohibition, many Americans were sick and tired of hearing about the dangers of Demon Rum, and the press coverage was largely sympathetic to Holm. Alan Gould of the Associated Press promptly hired her to cover the Berlin Olympics as a reporter, though in fact her pieces would be ghostwritten. Within a few years, she would land roles in major feature films and appear on the cover of *Time* magazine. The story made headlines in Europe as well, and it caught the eye of Joseph Goebbels, who found himself decidedly in accord with Brundage's thinking. "It wasn't herself who mattered. It was the others—and discipline. For that, no sacrifice is too great, no matter how many tears are shed," proclaimed a statement from the Ministry of Propaganda.

By the night of July 21, the boys could see the glimmer of lighthouses on the southwest coast of Ireland. At three the next morning, the *Manhattan* put into the small port of Cobh. From there she proceeded around the Cornish coast to Plymouth and then across the channel to Le Havre, where she arrived early on the morning of July 22. The boys were not allowed off the ship, but they spent much of the day at the railings on deck, watching French longshoremen load and unload cargo. This was the first good look at Europe any of them had ever had, and they were intrigued by simple details—the crumbling old buildings, Frenchwomen on bicycles carrying loaves of bread as long as their arms, boys in jaunty berets, men at work on the docks stopping periodically to drink some wine, in no apparent hurry to complete their tasks.

The U.S. Olympic team arrives in Berlin

That night they sailed up the channel with the lights of Calais blazing brightly to the east. By dinnertime on July 23, they were finally in Germany. At Cuxhaven a motor launch flying Nazi flags pulled alongside the ship to take off German news writers and photographers who had boarded at Le Havre. The *Manhattan* started up the Elbe River toward Hamburg just at dusk. The boys crowded onto the deck along with everyone else. They were edgy, anxious to get off the boat. Except for Don Hume, who seemed to again be fighting some kind of cold, they had put on five or six pounds each. They were starting to feel flabby, decidedly unathletic. They wanted to stretch their legs and arms and climb into a racing shell. They wanted to get a look at this Nazi state.

What they saw surprised them. Years later nearly all of them remembered the voyage up the Elbe that night as one of the highlights of the trip. The *Manhattan*'s crew had trained floodlights on the enormous white Olympic flag flying from the after mast, on the American flag on the foremast, and on the ship's red, white, and blue funnels. As the ship made its way up the river, throngs of Germans rushed to docks and quays along the way to watch her pass. They waved, they shouted bits of broken English, and they cheered. The boys waved back and gave Indian whoops. The big liner passed smaller ships and pleasure craft flying swastikas from their sterns. Almost every boat they passed blinked its lights on and off or sounded its whistle or horn in greeting. They made their way past beer gardens illuminated by bright strings of electric lights, full of people singing gaily, dancing polkas, and hoisting steins of beer in their direction. Up on the sundeck, the first-class passengers drank champagne and sang as well. Everyone was starting to feel pretty good about being in Germany.

The next morning, in Hamburg, the boys awoke at five and struggled to unload the *Husky Clipper* from the *Manhattan* in a hard, driving rain. Dressed in their formal Olympic uniforms, they maneuvered the shell from one deck down to the next, trying to stay clear of lifeboat davits and guylines. George Pocock and Al Ulbrickson looked on anxiously. Eager German longshoremen tried to help, but Pocock chased them off, employing nearly the full extent of his German vocabulary, shouting, "*Nein!* No thanks! *Danke!*" afraid the longshoremen would put a hand or foot through the delicate skin of the shell. When they finally got the shell onto the dock, the boys trooped back onto the *Manhattan*, their serge coats soggy and their straw hats starting to droop, and waited for the formal disembarking.

When they marched back off the ship with the rest of the U.S. Olympic team an hour later, they made their way through a shed full of barrels and shipping crates into a high-ceilinged reception hall where hundreds of cheering Germans and an oompah band playing Sousa marches greeted them. They waved and smiled and climbed aboard buses and were driven through narrow streets to Hamburg's Rathaus, its old city hall. There the city's *Bürgermeister*, a staunch Nazi by the name of Carl Vincent Krogmann, delivered a long welcoming oration in German. Not understanding a word of it, the boys, as Shorty Hunt put it, "just sat and took it." They perked up, though, when city officials began passing out free cigars, wine, beer, and orange juice.

By noon they were on a train to Berlin. When they arrived in the city's palatial old Lehrter Station, just north of the Tiergarten, that afternoon, they were stunned by the reception that greeted them. As they clambered down from the train and formed columns with their teammates, another brass band struck up another Sousa march. Avery Brundage and Duke Adolf Friedrich Albrecht Heinrich of Mecklenburg exchanged kisses on the cheeks. Then the American athletes marched down the platform, past a looming black locomotive with swastikas emblazoned on its sides. They entered another reception area, where thousands of Germans had packed the station to get a glimpse of them. Shorty Hunt was immediately taken aback at the scene: "It made you feel very much like a freak in a sideshow—pointing at you with their mouths open and saying something about *zwei meter*, meaning, of course, that we were two meters tall—over six feet." Statuesque young men dressed in white led them through the crowd and onto open-top, mud-colored military buses flying American flags.

The bus procession made its way past the Reichstag building, through the Brandenburg Gate, and then eastward down the flag-draped Unter den Linden. Here tens of thousands of Germans—perhaps as many as a hundred thousand by some estimates—lined the route, cheering and waving Olympic, Nazi, and occasionally American flags, shouting greetings in German and English. With the roof of their bus rolled back, the Washington boys stood waist-high above the top, more or less gaping in astonishment but waving back enthusiastically as they began to absorb just how friendly the Berliners seemed to be. At the redbrick city hall, the Rotes Rathaus, Avery Brundage accepted the keys to the city and made a brief speech. After the long battle over the boycott issue, Brundage was clearly thrilled to be here. Basking in the applause of his German hosts, he exulted: "No nation since ancient Greece has captured the true Olympic spirit as has Germany."

As Brundage spoke, Joe and his crewmates warily eyed the large number of sober German dignitaries lined up behind him. The boys were exhausted. They'd begun the day at five that morning on the *Manhattan*. They didn't really want to hear any more speeches they couldn't understand. Mercifully, when Brundage stopped speaking the athletes were ushered back outside, where a light rain was falling and the crowds had begun to disperse. Most of the athletes boarded buses heading west to the new Olympic village in Charlottenburg, but the American oarsmen climbed onto two buses bound for the little village of Köpenick southeast of Berlin.

That same day, back in the States, a New Yorker named Richard Wingate sat down and penned what would turn out to be a prophetic letter to the sports editor of the *New York Times*. "Mr. Brundage," he began, "has reached his destination, the Utopia of sportsmanship and good-will, where Nazi beer and Jewish blood flow freely—where Hitler-made robots torment and persecute the living dead. . . . For two months the dead will be buried. But with the conclusion of the Olympics in September, their graves will be desecrated . . . and dead men once more will walk the streets of Germany."

Later that afternoon, the boys arrived at what would be their home for the next several weeks, a police cadet training academy in Köpenick, just a few miles down the Langer See from the Olympic rowing course at Grünau. The building—all glass, steel, and concrete—was brand-new and so modern in design that to latter-day eyes it would look as if it had been built in the 1970s or 1980s rather than the 1930s. Most of the police cadets who ordinarily inhabited it had been moved out to make room for the American rowers as well as oarsmen from several other nations. The only thing the cadets had left behind was a stable full of police horses on the ground floor. As the boys explored the building, they found it to be squeaky-clean, well lit, and efficient but perpetually cold and equipped only with cold-water showers—an unwelcome reminder of their old shell house in Poughkeepsie.

After visiting the dining room, where caterers from the North German Lloyd company served up hearty helpings of American-style food, most of the boys stretched out on their bunks to read or write letters home. Joe decided to take a walk and see where he was. He quickly felt as if he had wandered into a German fairy tale. To Joe, Köpenick felt medieval, though in fact much of what he saw was eighteenth century in origin. On narrow cobblestone streets, he walked past bakeries and cheese shops and butcher shops, each with a hand-carved or painted sign hanging outside and proclaiming its function in Gothic script: *Bäckerei, Käserei, Fleischerei*. He passed the town's Rathaus with its tall clock tower, slender side towers, and Gothic arches. Music and laughter and the sweet smell of German beer poured from the rathskeller in the building's basement. He passed a quaint old synagogue on Freiheit street, a bright Star of David rising above its peaked roof. At the southern end of town, he crossed a bridge over a moat and came to a castle built by a Prussian prince in 1690. Behind the castle he found formal gardens. There he sat down on a bench and looked down the length of the Langer See, toward the regatta course at Grünau where his Olympic hopes would be realized or crushed in a little more than two weeks. The sun had all but set, the skies had cleared, and the lake spread out before him like a polished stone, glowing in the last reflected light of day. It was, he thought, one of the most peaceful things he had ever seen.

He had no way of knowing about the bloody secret that Köpenick and its placid waters concealed.

The next morning, the boys awoke early, eager to get out on the water. After breakfast a gray German army bus transported them three miles down the Langer See to the regatta course at Grünau, where they discovered that they were to share a fine new brick and stucco shell house with the German national rowing team. Over the entrance, an American flag and a Nazi flag faced each other. The German oarsmen were courteous but hardly gushing with enthusiasm to see them. George Pocock found them to be a bit arrogant. Products of Berlin's Viking Rowing Club, where they rowed as the Glider crew, they seemed, on average, to be a bit older than the Washington boys. They had excellent equipment. They were also exceptionally fit and disciplined, almost military in their bearing. Unlike every other German crew at Grünau that summer, they had not been individually selected by the Nazi state. Instead they had emerged as the German national team through their obvious prowess as a unit. George Pocock and Al Ulbrickson strongly suspected, though, that the Nazi government had heavily subsidized their extensive training.

As the boys prepared to take the *Husky Clipper* out on the Langer See for the first time, a photographer who had crawled under her to take a shot stood up too abruptly and hit his head on the shell, ripping open a long, thin crack in her hull. She was out of commission until George Pocock could repair her. Frustrated, Al Ulbrickson turned the boys loose until Pocock could work his magic on the *Clipper*. The boys returned to the police academy, stole lumps of sugar from the kitchen to feed the police horses in the stables, quickly grew bored, and then wandered around Köpenick in the rain, drawing crowds of curious villagers wherever they went.

When Pocock had repaired the shell, and the boys took to the water again, the results were spectacularly disappointing. Their timing was all off, their pulls weak and inefficient. The Canadian and Australian crews, practicing sprints, blew past them with smirks on their faces. "We went lousy," Johnny White wrote in his journal that night. Al Ulbrickson agreed. Since he had first put them together in a boat in March, he had never seen them row so badly. There was a lot of work to do, and for most of them there was a lot of weight to burn off. To make matters worse, almost all of them had colds to some extent, and Don Hume's seemed to be settling into his chest, becoming something more worrisome than a case of the sniffles. It didn't help that a steady rain driven by a chilling wind continued to blow across the Langer See almost continuously, and that the police barracks soon proved cold and drafty.

Over the next few days, the boys fell into a routine: rowing badly in the morning and then heading into Berlin to play in the afternoon. Their Olympic passports gave them free access to nearly everything in the city. They went to a vaudeville stage show, visited the tomb of an unknown soldier from the Great War, and took in a light opera. They went to the Reichssportfeld and came away impressed by the immensity and modernity of the stadium. They rode the S-Bahn into the center of the city, where everyone except Joe, who could not afford the twenty-two-dollar price tag, bought or ordered a Kodak Retina camera. They made their way up and down Unter den Linden, where the sidewalks were jammed with foreign visitors and provincial Germans, more than a million of whom had poured into the city in recent days. They bought bratwurst from street vendors, flirted with German girls, and gawked at black-shirted SS officers rushing by in sleek Mercedes limousines. Over and over again, ordinary Germans greeted them by extending their right hands palms down and shouting, "Heil Hitler!" The boys took to responding by extending their own hands and shouting, "Heil Roosevelt!" The Germans, for the most part, pretended not to notice.

In the evenings they returned to Köpenick, where the town fathers seemed bent on providing nightly entertainment whether the athletes wanted it or not. One night it was an exhibition of trained police dogs at the castle. Another night it was a concert. "It was a lousy orchestra. All out of tune," Roger Morris grumbled in his journal. Johnny White concurred, employing what was rapidly becoming his favorite term of displeasure: "It was foul." Wherever they went, townspeople surrounded them, asking for autographs as if they were movie stars. At first it was amusing, but it soon grew tiresome. Finally the boys took to renting boats in the evenings and rowing around the castle in the rain, keeping company with the white swans that plied the same waters, just to get some peace and quiet.

They weren't entirely averse to attention, though. On July 27 they amused themselves by wearing their Indian headbands and feathers from Huckleberry Island to practice in Grünau. The result was what Johnny White called "a small riot," as German fans crowded around them trying to get a glimpse of what they half believed to be members of some pale northwestern tribe. It was mostly for fun, but also an effort to improve slumping morale in the shell house.

The boat still wasn't going as well as it should, and though most of the boys

Left to right: Joe Rantz, Stub McMillin, Bobby Moch, Chuck Day, Shorty Hunt

were recovering from their colds, Gordy Adam and Don Hume were still sick. By July 29, Hume was too ill to row. Too ill, in fact, to get out of bed. Ulbrickson put Don Coy, one of two substitute oarsmen who had made the trip, in at the critical stroke position. But the boys were as unfamiliar with Coy's stroke as he was with rowing at that position. The boat just didn't feel right.

Al Ulbrickson was starting to get concerned. As crews from other nations arrived at Grünau, he and George Pocock were spending a lot of time down by the water, quietly studying the competition. After seeing just how well-disciplined the Germans were, he was beginning to take them very seriously. The Italians—four of them veterans of the crew from Livorno that had come within two-tenths of a second of beating California at the 1932 Olympics— also looked like a threat. They were big, tough, working-class young men, considerably older than his boys. Their average age was twenty-eight, and some of them were in their midthirties, but they looked to be in terrific condition. They rowed with tremendous heart, though with a tendency to throw their heads dramatically back and forth with each stroke. Ulbrickson figured they, like the German boys, had likely been subsidized by the fascist government that had sent them to the games. He wasn't seriously concerned about the Japanese crew, from Tokyo Imperial University. They rowed in a much smaller shell, just fifty-two feet long, with short oars and small blades, all designed to accommodate their smaller bodies. They averaged just 145 pounds per oarsman. But they had startled everyone at Grünau their first day out when they suddenly demonstrated the one advantage of their smaller sweeps, raising their beat from twenty-seven to an absurd fifty-six in just fifteen seconds, suddenly flogging the water white and accelerating so rapidly that they looked, as Ulbrickson put it, "like ducks trying to rise off the water." The Australian crew was entirely made up of big, beefy policemen from New South Wales, and although their technique didn't look like much, they had fire in their somewhat ample bellies as well as a good dose of Australian attitude, particularly in regard to the British crew.

Earlier in the month, the Australians had arrived in England to row in the most prestigious and tradition-bound of all crew races, the Grand Challenge Cup at the Henley Royal Regatta. At Henley they had been politely but firmly informed that the rules of the regatta, in place since 1879, prohibited the participation of anyone "who is or has been by trade or employment for wages a mechanic, artisan, or labourer." Policemen, it seemed, were deemed to be "labourers." They could not, regrettably, row in the regatta. Men who worked for their livings, it was felt, would have an unfair advantage over young men of "sedentary occupations." Enraged, the Aussies had left Britain and headed for Berlin, where they were determined, against all odds, to defeat what they called "the damned limeys."

But above all, the British were, in the eyes of many—including Al Ulbrickson and George Pocock—the boat to beat in Berlin. Rowing was, after all, a quintessentially British sport, and the 1936 British Olympic eight-man crew hailed from the venerable old Leander Club. Its oarsmen and its coxswain were the best of the British best, carefully selected from the ranks of many fine oarsmen at Oxford and Cambridge, where the boys wore tweed suits and ties to class, where they sometimes sported silk ascots around their boathouses, where they were apt to climb into their shells wearing white shorts, dark knee-high socks, and neck scarves, but where they rowed nevertheless as if they had been born for it.

Ulbrickson could hardly wait to get a good look at them up close. Neither could the Aussies.

By midafternoon on August 1, Joe and the rest of the American Olympic team had been standing in neatly ordered ranks for more than two hours on the vast green expanse of the Maifeld at the Reichssportfeld. They were awaiting the arrival of Adolf Hitler and the beginning of perhaps the most spectacular public ceremony the world had yet seen—the opening of the Eleventh Olympiad. Nothing on the scale of what was planned for the day had ever been attempted, but then, as Albion Ross had written in the *New York Times* a few days before, no Olympics before had ever been orchestrated "by a political regime that owes its triumph to a new realization of the possibilities of propaganda, publicity, and pageantry. Staging the Olympics in the past has been in the hands of amateurs. Here the work has been done by professionals, and by the most talented, resourceful, and successful professionals in history."

Light rain had been spattering on the boys' straw hats on and off since their arrival, but now the clouds were beginning to burn off, and in their blue blazers, neckties, and white flannel trousers, they were, along with the rest of the American athletes, beginning to get uncomfortable. Off in the distance, the *Hindenburg*, trailing an Olympic flag, droned over central Berlin in a lazy loop, then turned and slowly began to approach the stadium. Young German women dressed in uniforms walked among the ranks of athletes, smiling, handing out cookies and orangeade, trying to keep everyone peppy. But the Americans were tired of standing and waiting.

While the athletes of the other nations remained more or less at attention, the Americans began to meander about, checking things out—peering down the barrels of some field artillery pieces that had been arrayed facing them point-blank, studying the monolithic stone sculptures at the entrance to the stadium, or simply stretching out on the damp grass and pulling their straw hats over their faces for a nap. Joe and his crewmates wandered through a gateway to an area under the looming bell tower and came across a detachment of Hitler's military honor guard marching back and forth, goose-stepping across stone pavement with such gusto that granite dust flew up from under their black hobnailed boots. Even the horses, Shorty Hunt noticed, were goose-stepping.

Inside the stadium, Leni Riefenstahl and Joseph Goebbels were screaming at each other. Riefenstahl had been there since 6:00 a.m., rushing about, deploying some thirty cameras and sixty cameramen, setting up sound equipment, alternately hectoring and tearfully beseeching IOC officials to allow her to place equipment where she wanted, ordering international newsreel camera crews out of her way, relentlessly seeking and ruthlessly claiming the best possible positions from which to film the day's events. Prime among these was a narrow strip of concrete on which she had affixed a camera to the railing of the platform where Nazi officials would preside over the ceremony. The platform was to be so crowded with members of the top echelons of the party that Riefenstahl had been compelled to station her cameraman outside the railing, tying him and the camera to the railing for safety's sake. It was an awkward arrangement, but it would allow Riefenstahl to do what she was always driven to do—to capture the perfect shot, the ideal shot. In this case, it was to be a close-up shot of Adolf Hitler gazing out over the massed multitudes as they hailed him.

But earlier in the afternoon, Riefenstahl had discovered SS officers untying both her camera and her cameraman from the railing. Enraged, she demanded to know what they were doing and was informed that Goebbels had ordered them to remove the camera and cameraman. Riefenstahl, furious, screamed at the officers that Hitler himself had given her permission to locate the camera there. The SS men, taken aback, hesitated. Riefenstahl climbed over the railing, tied herself to the camera, and said she would remain there until the games began. High-ranking guests began to arrive and take their seats around the rostrum, staring at Riefenstahl, who was, by her own account, now in tears and shaking with anger as she clung tenaciously to the edge of the balcony.

Goebbels himself arrived. "Have you gone mad?" he screamed when he saw Riefenstahl. "You can't stay here. You're destroying the whole ceremonial tableau. Get yourself and your cameras out of here immediately!"

Riefenstahl hissed back at him, "I asked the Führer for permission way ahead of time—and I received it."

"Why didn't you build a tower next to the rostrum?" Goebbels bellowed.

"They wouldn't let me!" Riefenstahl hurled back at him.

Goebbels was now "incandescent with rage," as Riefenstahl later put it. But she was not about to relinquish the spot. Nothing, not even the enormously powerful minister of propaganda, was going to stand between her and her vision for this film.

At this juncture, the imposing figure of Hermann Göring strode onto the platform, outfitted in a spectacular white military uniform. Seeing Göring, Goebbels began to scream at Riefenstahl even more loudly. But Göring raised his hand abruptly and Goebbels fell suddenly silent. Göring turned to Riefenstahl and cooed, "C'mon, my girl. There's room here even for my belly." Riefenstahl climbed over the railing, and the camera remained in place.

Goebbels quietly seethed. But his battle with Riefenstahl—ultimately and ironically a battle over a shared goal, glorifying the ideals of the Nazis—raged on throughout the remainder of the games and beyond. A few days hence he would sit down and write in his diary, "I gave Riefenstahl, who is behaving indescribably, a dressing down. A hysterical woman. Simply not a man!"

At 3:18 p.m., Adolf Hitler left the chancellery in central Berlin, standing upright in his Mercedes limousine, his right arm lifted in the Nazi salute. Tens of thousands of Hitler Youth, storm troopers, and helmeted military guards lined his route from the Brandenburg Gate through the Tiergarten and out to the Reichssportfeld. Hundreds of thousands of ordinary German citizens had massed along the way, leaning from windows and waving flags or standing twelve or more deep along the street, again using periscopes to get a glimpse of Hitler. Now, as his limousine passed, they extended their right arms in the Nazi salute, their faces upturned, ecstatic, screaming in pulsing waves as he rode by, "Heil! Heil! Heil!"

At the Maifeld, the boys began to hear the distant sound of crowds cheering, the noise slowly swelling and growing nearer, then loudspeakers blaring, "He is coming! He is coming!" The boys ambled back toward the rough formation of Americans. At 3:30 officials from the International Olympic Committee, draped in gold cords and wearing tall silk top hats and coats with long tails, walked out onto the Maifeld and formed a double cordon. At 3:50 Hitler arrived at the bell tower. He reviewed the honor guard as they marched past him, and then strode onto the Maifeld. For a few moments, he was a small figure in a khaki uniform and high black boots, alone in the great expanse of grass. Then he strode through the cordon of officials and began to pass the athletes, separated from them by a rope line. For the most part, the athletes held their formations, except for the Americans, a good number of whom rushed up to the ropes to get a better look at Hitler. The boys from Washington simply sat on the grass and gave him a wave as he passed.

At exactly 4:00 p.m., Hitler entered the western end of the stadium. A massive orchestra—the Berlin Philharmonic merged with the national orchestra and supplemented by half a dozen military bands—launched into Wagner's *Huldigungsmarsch*, the *March of Homage*. As they saw Hitler descending the Marathon steps toward field level, 110,000 people rose to their feet, thrust out their right hands, and began to roar rhythmically, "Sieg Heil! Sieg Heil! Sieg Heil!"

Flanked now by gray-uniformed Nazi officers and trailed by the Olympic officials in silk hats, Hitler made his way along the red-clay running track, the *Heils* pulsating through the stadium. A five-year-old girl, Gudrun Diem, dressed in a light blue frock and wearing a flower chaplet in her hair, stepped forward, said, "Heil, mein Führer!" and presented him with a small, delicate bouquet of flowers. Hitler beamed at her, took the flowers, and then climbed the steps to his wide viewing platform, where he strode to his place of honor and gazed out over the crowd as the massed orchestra, conducted by Richard Strauss, began to play the "Deutschlandlied," with its refrain of "Deutschland, Deutschland über alles," followed immediately by the Nazi Party anthem, the "Horst-Wessel-Lied."

As the last strident strains of the latter song faded away, there was a moment of silence. Then the enormous bell out beyond the Maifeld began to toll, slowly and softly at first, then growing louder, more insistent, and more sonorous as the athletes began to parade into the stadium, led, as always, by the Greek national team. As each team passed Hitler, it dipped its flag. Most also rendered some form of salute to him. Some offered the Olympic salute, which bore an unfortunate resemblance to the Nazi salute—the right arm extended, palm down, but held off to the right side of the body rather than straight ahead as in the Nazi version. Some offered the straightforward Nazi version. Many, including the French, offered various ambiguous versions somewhere between the two. A few offered no salute at all. In response to each of them, the crowd responded by applauding enthusiastically or unenthusiastically, depending on how closely the gesture matched the Nazi salute.

Out on the Maifeld, the Americans finally mustered themselves into proper columns, straightened their ties or smoothed their skirts, adjusted their hats, and began to stroll toward the tunnel through which they were to enter the stadium. Marching was not their strong suit, certainly not compared to the Germans. But as they entered the tunnel, hearing a flurry of *Heils* inside the stadium, they threw back their shoulders, picked up the pace, and started to sing spontaneously, belting it out:

Hail, hail, the gang's all here
What the deuce do we care?
What the deuce do we care?
Hail, hail, we're full of cheer
What the heck do we care . . . ?

Led by gymnast Alfred Joachim, the American flag bearer, they emerged singing from the darkness of the tunnel and marched out into the vast interior of the stadium. It was a world of sights and sounds that few of them would ever forget, even when they were old men and women. As the orchestra played a light, airy tune, they marched eight abreast out onto the track. Coming even with Hitler, they turned their heads to the right, gazed expressionless up at him on his high platform, removed their straw hats, placed them over their hearts, and walked on by as Joachim held the Stars and Stripes defiantly aloft. For the most part, the crowd applauded politely. Mixed in with the applause, though, was a spattering of whistles and the stamping of feet, the European equivalents of catcalls and boos.

But the sounds of dissent were quickly drowned out. Even as the last Americans were still passing Hitler, the first German athletes began to emerge from the tunnel, dressed in crisp white linen suits and sporting white yachting caps. Immediately, an enormous, rumbling roar went up from the crowd. Virtually all of the 110,000 spectators again leapt to their feet and raised their right arms in the Nazi salute. The orchestra shifted abruptly from the light march tune it had been playing to another swelling rendition of the "Deutschlandlied." The crowd, frozen in place, their thousands of arms outstretched, sang along lustily. On the dais, Hitler's eyes glistened. As the German flag bearer carried the swastika past him, he saluted and then touched his heart with his right hand, as Riefenstahl's cameras rolled. The Americans marched awkwardly on around the track and onto the infield to the strains of the "Deutschlandlied." George Pocock would later say that when they heard the strains of the German anthem they began to march deliberately out of step with the music.

When all the athletes were assembled in ranks on the infield, Theodor Lewald, president of the German Olympic Organizing Committee, stepped to a bank of microphones on the dais and launched into what soon turned into an interminable speech. As it went on and on, a British radio announcer broadcasting it back home struggled to keep his audience entertained: "We'll have Herr Hitler in just a moment. . . . There's the cheering. I believe Dr. Lewald has finished. No, he's going on again." Lewald's voice echoed in the background as the announcer labored to fill the air, describing the uniforms of various teams, the platform on which the speakers stood, the *Hindenburg* circling overhead like a near moon.

Finally Lewald broke off. Hitler, who had been chatting with Leni Riefenstahl, stepped to the microphone and pronounced the games open in one brief sentence. The British announcer, caught unawares, broke back in, excited and relieved, "That was Herr Hitler! The games are open!"

The ceremony rose to a crescendo. Ranks of trumpeters on the Marathon Gate sounded a fanfare. The Olympic flag was hoisted. Richard Strauss conducted the enormous orchestra in the debut of his *Olympic Hymn*. The artillery outside the stadium thundered. Thousands of white pigeons suddenly rose from cages on the field, swirling through the stadium in a white whirlwind. Another fanfare sounded and a slender, blond young man dressed in white and holding aloft a torch appeared at the eastern gate of the stadium. A hush fell over the crowd as he loped gracefully down the eastern steps, around the red-clay track, and up the western steps, where he paused again, silhouetted against the sky, holding the torch high over his head. Then, with the Olympic bell tolling in the background, he turned, rose on his toes, and touched the torch to an enormous bronze cauldron on a tripod. Flames leapt from the cauldron. Finally, with the sun beginning to decline behind the Olympic flame, a choir of thousands dressed in white rose en masse and began to sing the "Hallelujah Chorus" from Handel's *Messiah*. The spectators stood and joined in. The music and the voices rose and melded and surged through the vast interior of the stadium, filling it with light and love and joy.

As the athletes began to march out of the stadium that evening, nearly everyone on the field and off felt more or less stunned. Nobody had ever witnessed anything quite like what had just transpired. International journalists rushed to their Teletypes and flooded the wires, and by the next morning newspapers around the world carried rapturous headlines. The boys from Washington were impressed too. It was "the most impressive sight I have ever seen," said Roger Morris. Johnny White said, "It gave you a grand feeling." And that was precisely what it had been carefully crafted to do—give you a grand feeling. It had begun the process of determining the world's opinion about the new Germany. It had hung out a sign for all to see: "Welcome to the Third Reich. We are not what they say we are."

Ulbrickson's final advice

CHAPTER SEVENTEEN

To see a winning crew in action is to witness a perfect harmony in which everything is right. . . . That is the formula for endurance and success: rowing with the heart and head as well as physical strength.

—George Yeoman Pocock

The weather on the Langer See turned positively wintry in early August. A cold, cutting wind blew relentlessly down the racecourse at Grünau. The boys rowed into the wind dressed in sweatshirts, their legs slathered in goose grease. With the preliminary races less than two weeks away, they still hadn't regained their form. The boat checked on the catches and bounced in the rough water rather than slicing efficiently through it. Their timing was off. They caught crabs. Their bodies were still not in condition. They littered their journals with self-deprecating commentary. "We went lousy," Johnny White noted simply.

All the boys were worried, but off the water they continued to exult in the heady atmosphere that enveloped Berlin that summer, and to revel in one another's company, meandering through the city, eating schnitzel, drinking beer, hoisting steins, and singing "Bow Down to Washington." When the athletic director from Stanford, Jack Rice, invited them to dinner at the posh Adlon hotel, they jumped at the chance. Wearing everyday trousers and their crew sweaters with big Ws on the front, they made their way through a police cordon and into the hotel's ornate lobby, where the scents of leather and malt whiskey mingled with gales of laughter, the clinking of glasses, and the tinkling of soft, slow piano music. In the high-ceilinged dining room, a waiter in coattails led them to a table with ivory candles and a white linen tablecloth. They sat wide-eyed, gazing around the room at the other diners—international Olympic officials; well-heeled Americans and Brits; elegant German women in flowing evening gowns of silk or chiffon, sleek lamé, or satin studded with sequins. Here and there SS officers sat apart, at their own tables, chatting, laughing, drinking French wine, and attacking beefsteaks or sauerbraten with knives and forks. In their gray-and-black dress uniforms, their peaked hats adorned with silver skulls and crossbones sitting on their tables, they stood out from the rest of the crowd—neat, severe, and ominous. But no one seemed to mind their presence.

On August 6, Al Ulbrickson grounded the boys. There would be no more trips into Berlin or anywhere else until after the games. With just six days to go now until their preliminary race, Ulbrickson wasn't at all happy with their progress. He wasn't happy, in fact, with any number of things. The cold, wet weather and the lack of heating in the police barracks were making it hard for Don Hume to throw off the cold—or whatever it was that was lingering in his chest. Since he'd first gotten sick at Princeton in early July, Hume had never really stopped coughing and dragging around. "Hume means everything to us. Unless he recovers quickly and regains condition we won't have much chance," Ulbrickson had griped to the Associated Press a week before. Hume was still at least as sick as he had been then.

And then there was the matter of the racecourse. On August 5, Ulbrickson had gotten in an argument—loud, multilingual, and largely incomprehensible to all involved—with officials from the Fédération Internationale des Sociétés d'Aviron and German Olympic officials. The course at Grünau was six lanes wide, but the outermost two lanes—lanes five and six—were so exposed to the prevailing winds on the Langer See that they were at times all but unrowable. Earlier that day, in fact, Ulbrickson had canceled a workout rather than have his boys risk drowning out in the far lanes. Lanes one through three, on the other hand, came in so close to the southern shore of the lake that they were almost entirely protected through much of the course. The disparity made for a very uneven playing field. If the wind was blowing on race day, whoever was assigned lanes five and six would likely start off with about a two-length handicap to overcome relative to the inside lanes. Ulbrickson wanted the two outside lanes ruled out of commission. In all previous Olympic rowing competitions, he pointed out, preliminary heats as well as finals had been limited to four boats. But after a long, heated exchange Ulbrickson lost the argument. All six lanes would be used.

Ulbrickson's concern ratcheted up another level when he started taking a good look at the British crew. At the heart of the outfit were two Cambridge men in the rear of the boat: John Noel Duckworth, the coxswain, and William

George Ranald Mundell Laurie, the stroke. Duckworth was, as someone would later say about him, "Short of stature, great of heart." The stature part was obvious just by looking at him. The heart part he showed every time he took to the water. He would also show it a few years later in the South Pacific when, against orders, he stayed behind with wounded British soldiers as Japanese troops surrounded them. When the Japanese arrived and prepared to execute the wounded, Duckworth berated them so roundly that they beat him severely but spared his companions. They sent him to the infamous Changi POW camp in Singapore. Then they marched him and 1,679 other prisoners 220 miles through the jungle to the Songkurai No. 2 Camp in Thailand and put them to work as slave labor on the Thailand-Burma Railway. There, as they began to die of beriberi, diphtheria, smallpox, cholera, and torture, Duckworth ministered to them as chaplain even as he worked side by side with them. In the end, only 250 survived, and Duckworth was one of them.

Laurie, who went by Ran, was perhaps the best British stroke of his generation—188 pounds of power, grace, and keen intelligence. His son, Hugh, the actor, would also eventually row for Cambridge. Ran was, by all accounts, an unusually gracious young man. Together, Duckworth and Laurie had piloted Cambridge to three consecutive victories—adding on to a string of seven previous wins—over Oxford in the annual Boat Race, despite the fact that the Oxonians had recently switched from beer to milk at their training table in a desperate bid to reverse the trend. Ulbrickson figured that experience alone—racing in front of the half million to million fans who crowded the banks of the Thames for the Boat Race each year—had to give the British boys an edge in the confidence department.

What most concerned Al Ulbrickson, though, as he watched the British crew working out at Grünau, was how much they reminded him of his own boys. Not that any of them particularly resembled his boys physically—they didn't. And it wasn't that their rowing styles were similar. In fact the British boys still rowed with the long layback that English prep schools and universities had taught for generations. Washington, of course, used the shorter, more upright stroke that George Pocock had adapted from the Thames watermen's style and taught Hiram Conibear twenty years earlier.

Where the British boys resembled Ulbrickson's was in strategy. They liked to do exactly what the Washington boys did so well. They excelled at sitting back but staying close, rowing hard but slow, pressuring their opponents into raising their stroke rates too high too soon, and then, when the other crews were good and fagged out, suddenly sprinting past them, catching them un-awares, unnerving them, mowing them down. Except for the cricket cap and neck scarf that Duckworth wore in the coxswain's seat, he coxed an awful lot like Bobby Moch. And Ran Laurie handled the stroke oar an awful lot like Don Hume. It was going to be interesting to see what happened when two crews playing the same game met on the Langer See.

As the Olympic preliminary heats approached and the gravity of what was coming settled on them, Ulbrickson's boys began to get tense and fidgety again. Those who were keeping journals or writing letters home began to confide in them about nervousness as they had before the Olympic trials at Princeton. Chuck Day began to seek out Al Ulbrickson for confidence-building sessions. Between them, he chain-smoked Lucky Strikes and Camels, laughing off the other boys as they tried to get him to cut back.

The Americans weren't alone in feeling edgy. Twenty-four international teams shared the same rowing and dining facilities in Grünau and Köpenick. All were composed of large, healthy, and highly competitive young men, each of whom was about to face a defining moment in his life. For the most part, the Olympic spirit prevailed among them, and many new friendships had emerged during the three weeks that they had lived and competed in Germany. The boys from Washington, in particular, fell into an easy comrade-ship with the all-police crew from Australia, with whom they shared not only a more or less common language but also a kind of easy, confident, and swaggering approach to life. They also hit it off well with the Swiss crew. They were "big devils," Johnny White noted, but full of mirth and goodwill, and the boys got a kick out of riding with them in the bus between Köpenick and Grünau as the Swiss belted out full-throated yodeling songs.

But with the preliminaries approaching, nerves began to grow raw among all the crews in Grünau and Köpenick. The Aussies made no effort to conceal their contempt for the Brits. The Brits could not look at the Germans without remembering the last war and worrying about a future one. And the boys from Washington were having a hard time sleeping. Almost every night there was some kind of disturbance in the cobblestoned street below their windows. One night it was brown-shirted storm troopers singing and parading past in hobnailed boots. Another it was military night maneuvers—roaring motorcycles with sidecars, trucks with glowing green night-lights in their cabs, caissons carrying field artillery—all rattling past under the streetlamps. Then it was police cadets drilling at odd hours. Then German oarsmen singing. Then a contingent of canoeists who had finished their races, and been badly beaten, and were bent on holding a consolation party downstairs.

Exasperated, the boys decided to do something about it. Six of them were engineering students, so they took an engineer's approach to the problem. They contrived a device whereby they could, while lying in their bunks, yank on some strings, dump buckets of water on whoever happened to be down in the street annoying them, and retrieve and conceal the buckets quickly and without getting out of their beds. They got an opportunity to put it to use that night when the Yugoslavian team decided to raise a ruckus down in the street. The boys yanked their strings and water cascaded down, not only on the Yugoslavians but also on some German police cadets who were trying to quiet them down. Drenched, outraged athletes and police cadets stormed into the building hollering. More athletes poured from their rooms and into the stairwell. Everyone was yelling in a different language. Finally the boys from Washington emerged, looking sleepy, confused, and decidedly innocent. When someone demanded to know where the water had come from, they shrugged their shoulders and pointed meekly upstairs toward the Canadians.

The next day, at lunchtime, things erupted again. It had become a tradition for different crews to sing national songs during meals. When it came time for the Yugoslavian crew to rise and sing, they launched into an odd rendition of "Yankee Doodle." Nobody could quite tell what the point was. It wasn't even entirely clear if they were singing in English or one of the several languages of Yugoslavia. But the American boys knew the tune, and something about the way certain lines were delivered convinced Chuck Day that the Yugoslavians had figured out the previous night's shenanigans and now were directing a mortal insult at the United States of America. Day bolted out of his seat and plowed into the Yugoslavians, fists flying. Bobby Moch charged in right behind him, going not for the Yugoslavian coxswain but for the biggest man on the crew. Right behind Moch came the rest of the Washington boys, and behind them, just for the hell of it, the entire Australian team. The German crew rushed to the side of the Yugoslavians. Chairs flew. Insults were hurled. Chests bumped into chests. Boys shoved other boys. A few more fists flew. Everyone was yelling again, and again nobody could understand what anybody else was saying. Finally the Dutch national crew dove into the melee, separating boys, pulling them back to their tables, smoothing out their feelings in crisp, perfect, diplomatic English.

Yet even as they fretted and fumed, something else was quietly at work among Ulbrickson's boys. As they began to see traces of tension and nervousness in one another, they began instinctively to draw closer together. They took to huddling on the float before and after workouts, talking about what, precisely, they could do to make each row better than the one before, looking one another in the eye, speaking earnestly. Joking and horseplay fell by the wayside. They began to grow serious in a way they had never been before. Each of them knew that a defining moment in his life was nearly at hand; none wanted to waste it. And none wanted to waste it for the others.

All along Joe Rantz had figured that he was the weak link in the crew. He'd been added to the boat last, he'd often struggled to master the technical side of the sport, and he still tended to row erratically. But what Joe didn't yet know—what he wouldn't, in fact, fully realize until much later, when he and the other boys were becoming old men—was that every boy in the boat felt exactly the same that summer. Every one of them believed he was simply lucky to be rowing in the boat, that he didn't really measure up to the obvious greatness of the other boys, and that he might fail the others at any moment. Every one of them was fiercely determined not to let that happen.

Slowly, in those last few days, the boys—each in his own way—centered and calmed themselves. Huddled on the dock, they draped arms over one another's shoulders and talked through their race plan, speaking softly but with more assurance, accelerating their advance along the rough road from boyhood to manhood. They quoted Pocock to one another. Roger and Joe took walks along the shores of the Langer See, skipping stones, clearing their minds. Johnny White took some time to lie shirtless in the sun on the lawn in front of Haus West, working on a tan to complement his Pepsodent-white smile but also thinking through how he was going to row. Shorty Hunt wrote long letters home, purging his anxiety by leaving it behind on pieces of paper. And finally the boat beneath them began to come to life again. Rowing twice a day, they began to release what was latent in their bodies and to find their swing. Everything began to feel right again, so long as Don Hume was in at stroke. And Hume seemed to be key. As soon as Hume returned, the tentativeness, awkwardness, and uncertainty they had felt when Ulbrickson had taken him out evaporated. George Pocock had seen the difference at a glance.

They were back. All they needed now, Pocock told them on August 10, was a little competition. The next day a British reporter watching them warned readers back home that the boys from the Leander Club might just meet their match in the American crew: "The Washington University [*sic*] eight is the finest eight here, and it is as perfect as a crew can be."

By the rules devised for the 1936 Olympic rowing regatta, each of the fourteen eight-oared crews was to have two chances to make it into the medal race on August 14. If a given crew won its preliminary race on August 12, it would proceed directly to the medal round, and have a precious day off. Each of the losing crews would have to race in a repechage, a re-rowing, on August 13 and would need to win that heat to advance to the medal race the following day. For their preliminary, the boys from Washington were assigned to race against France, Japan, Czechoslovakia, and the crew they were most concerned about, Great Britain.

With the boat finally performing as it should, Al Ulbrickson did what he always did before big races: he backed off the training and, except for some

View from the grandstands at Grünau

light paddling, he told the boys to rest up for their first race. On August 11 they sat in the Grünau grandstands and watched the preliminaries in all the rowing events except their own eight-oared contest, scheduled for the following day. The entire American rowing team had arrived in Berlin with high hopes and expectations. "Rowing experts and critics were unanimous today in predicting the United States will carry off its share of the Olympic crew races," one sportswriter had proclaimed boldly back on July 28, under a confident headline, "Experts Figure U.S. to Sweep Rowing Events." George Pocock wasn't so sure about that. He had examined the equipment of the other American crews and found it heavy, shoddy, old, and decrepit.

In the six events held that day, the United States finished second to last in three and dead last in the other three. To the great delight of the crowd surrounding the boys in the grandstands, Germany came in first in all six heats. "A very rotten performance," Chuck Day wrote that night. "The rowing started today but the old USA seemed to forget to start," Roger Morris said. "I guess it is up to us to come through," said Johnny White.

By August 12, the day of the eight-oar preliminaries, Don Hume had lost a worrisome 14 pounds from his normal weight, the 172 pounds he had carried in Poughkeepsie. At 158 pounds, his six-foot-two frame was down to skin and bones. His chest was still congested, and he was running a low fever on and off. But he insisted that he was ready to row. Al Ulbrickson kept him in bed in Köpenick for as long as he could. Then, late that afternoon, he rousted him out and put him on the bus, with the rest of the boys, headed for the regatta course.

Conditions were almost ideal for rowing. The skies were lightly overcast, but the temperatures were in the low seventies. Only a hint of a wind out on the Langer See ruffled the slate-gray water, and what wind there was came from the stern of the boats. The boys had been assigned to row in the first heat, at 5:15 p.m., and in lane one, the most protected lane on the course, though with such calm water it hardly mattered.

By the time the boys arrived in Grünau, festive crowds clutching binoculars and cameras had begun to line up at the ticket windows in front of the regatta course. As they made their way into the grounds, spectators with pricier tickets headed for the permanent, covered grandstand on the near side of the water; those with less expensive tickets trundled across a pontoon bridge to the massive wooden bleachers on the far side, where the national flags of the various nations entered in the rowing events fluttered along the broad back side of the structure. On the flagpole in front of Haus West, a large white Olympic flag stirred lazily.

Two thousand meters up the course, on the far side of the lake, a gangway had been constructed to the starting line, 325 feet out into the Langer See. Young men in uniforms stood ready there to grab hold of the sterns of the boats when they arrived for the start. Well behind the gangway, and oddly out of sight of the coxswains, the starter stood on a platform constructed atop the super-structure of a flat-bottomed boat. Hundreds of international reporters with notepads and cameras crowded the opposite bank; a short distance away fleets of automobiles stood ready to rush them to the finish line so they could wit-ness both the start and the finish of each heat. A boat carrying an announcer and a shortwave-radio transmitter idled behind the line, ready to trail the shells down the course, broadcasting a stroke-by-stroke account of each heat directly to loudspeakers at the finish line, so spectators and reporters could be apprised of the progress of each boat before any of them came into view.

Waiting to go for gold

By the time Joe and the boys had limbered up and paddled to the starting line, at a little before 5:15, perhaps twenty-five thousand people had entered the regatta grounds. The boys backed the *Husky Clipper* up to the gangway and waited. Right next door, in lane two, Ran Laurie, Noel Duckworth, and the rest of the British crew did the same. Duckworth nodded at Bobby Moch, and Moch returned the gesture.

The race started at 5:15 exactly. The American boys got away badly again. Just as at Princeton, someone in the middle of the boat washed out on the first or second stroke. In lane four the Japanese fluttered rapidly out into the lead, whipping the water at nearly fifty strokes per minute with their short oars and short slides. Noel Duckworth and Ran Laurie took the British boat out hard but then eased up and settled into second place behind the Japanese, followed by Czechoslovakia, France, and the United States, dead last, rowing at thirty-eight.

Moch and Hume kept the rate up until they passed the Czechs at three hundred meters. Then they eased the throttle back to thirty-four. Out in front, the Japanese, still rowing like demons possessed, stretched their lead over the British to a full length. But neither Moch nor Duckworth was thinking about the Japanese. They were thinking about each other. For another seven hundred meters, the boats held their relative positions. As they approached the halfway mark, the exhausted Japanese suddenly and predictably began to fade and fall away behind the field, along with the Czechs. So did the French. That left the Americans and the Brits right where they had expected to be, alone with each other at the front of the pack as the grandstands and the boathouses began to come into view down the course. Now it was a game of cat and mouse.

Moch told Hume to edge the rate up, to see what would happen. Hume kicked it up to thirty-six. The U.S. boat crept up to within a half length of the British boat's stern. Duckworth glanced over his shoulder. He and Laurie took the British boys up to thirty-eight. That checked the Americans' advance. The British boat held its lead. The boys in both boats could now hear the roar of the crowd down the lake. Both coxswains could see the grandstands and the large black-and-white sign, "Ziel," demarking the finish line up ahead, but neither was ready to make his move yet. Both were holding back. The British boys were taking long, sweeping strokes, all but lying on their backs at the end of each pull. The Americans were taking somewhat shorter strokes and spending a lot less time recovering between them.

Finally, with 250 meters to go, Moch shouted, "Now, boys. Now! Give me ten!" The boys dug hard and the American flag snapping on the foredeck of the *Husky Clipper* began to move past Duckworth, creeping halfway up the length of the British boat. Duckworth and Laurie went up to forty strokes per minute. For a moment, they held their position, the white blades of the U.S. shell flashing furiously alongside the crimson blades of the British. Then Bobby Moch yelped at Hume to up the rate again, and the *Clipper* resumed advancing.

In the British boat, Ran Laurie dug furiously at the water. He was still relatively fresh. He wanted to do more. But like many British strokes in those days, he was wielding an oar with a smaller, narrower blade than the rest of his crew—the idea being that the stroke's job was to set the pace, not to power the boat. With the small blade, he avoided the risk of burning himself out and losing his form. But it also meant he wasn't getting a full purchase on the water. Now he was in danger of finishing the most important race he'd rowed without having come close to exhausting himself—the last thing any oarsman wants.

Still, the British bow remained out in front of the American bow with 150 meters to go. But the American boys had found their swing and they were holding on to it. They were rowing as hard as they had ever rowed, taking huge sweeping cuts at the water, over and over again, rocking into the beat as if they were forged together, approaching forty strokes per minute. Every muscle, tendon, and ligament in their bodies was burning with pain, but they were rowing beyond pain, rowing in perfect, flawless harmony. Nothing was going to stop them. In the last twenty strokes, and particularly in the final twelve gorgeous strokes, they simply powered past the British boat, decisively and unambiguously. The twenty-five thousand international fans in the stands—a good portion of them Americans—rose and cheered them as their bow knifed across the line a full twenty feet ahead of the British shell. A moment later, Don Hume pitched forward and collapsed across his oar.

It took Moch a full minute of splashing water on Hume's face before he was able to sit upright again and help paddle the shell over to the float. When they got there, though, the boys got sweet news. Their time, 6:00.8, was a new course record. And, sweeter yet, it was a new world and Olympic record, eclipsing California's 1928 time of 6:03.2. When Al Ulbrickson arrived on the float, he crouched down next to the boat and, with a cryptic smile, quietly said, "Well done, boys."

Joe had never heard his coach speak in quite that tone of voice. There seemed to be a hint of hushed respect in it. Almost deference.

As the boys tucked into their dinners at the police academy in Köpenick that night, they were jubilant. The British would now have to row and win in a repechage the next day if they were to be one of the final six boats in the medal race. The American boys would have a day off. Al Ulbrickson, though, was anything but jubilant. He was deeply concerned. After dinner he ordered Don Hume back to his sickbed. The boy looked like death risen. Whatever he had, it was clearly more than a cold—perhaps a bronchial infection or walking pneumonia. Either way, Ulbrickson had to figure out who was going to stroke the boat when the boys raced for gold in forty-eight hours.

After lunch the next day, the boys wandered through town, joshing one another, poking into shops, taking pictures with their new cameras, buying a few souvenirs, exploring corners of Köpenick they hadn't yet seen. Like most of the Americans in Berlin that summer, they had concluded that the new Germany was a pretty nice place. It was clean, the people were friendly almost to a fault, everything worked neatly and efficiently, and the girls were pretty. Köpenick was charmingly quaint; Grünau green, leafy, and pastoral. Both towns were about as pleasant and peaceful as anything back home in Washington.

But there was a Germany the boys could not see, a Germany that was hidden from them, either by design or by time. It wasn't just that the signs— "Für Juden verboten," "Juden sind hier unerwünscht"—had been removed, or that the Gypsies had been rounded up and taken away, or that the vicious *Stürmer* newspaper had been withdrawn from the racks in the tobacco shops in Köpenick. There were larger, darker, more enveloping secrets all around them.

They knew nothing of the tendrils of blood that had billowed in the waters of the river Spree and the Langer See in June of 1933, when SA storm troopers rounded up hundreds of Köpenick's Jews, Social Democrats, and Catholics and tortured ninety-one of them to death—beating some until their kidneys ruptured or their skin split open, and then pouring hot tar into the wounds before dumping the mutilated bodies into the town's tranquil waterways. They could not see the sprawling Sachsenhausen concentration camp under construction that summer just north of Berlin, where before long more than two hundred thousand Jews, homosexuals, Jehovah's Witnesses, Gypsies, and eventually Soviet prisoners of war, Polish civilians, and Czech university students would be held, and where tens of thousands of them would die.

And there was much more just over the horizon of time. They could see the sprawling yellow clinker-brick complex of the AEG Kabelwerk factory just outside town, but they could not see the thousands of slave laborers that would soon be put to work there, manufacturing electric cables, laboring twelve hours a day, living in squalid camps nearby until they died of typhus or malnutrition. When the boys walked past the pretty synagogue at 8 Freiheit, or "Freedom," street, they could not see the mob with torches that would loot it and burn it to the ground on the night of November 9, 1938—Kristallnacht.

If they peered into Richard Hirschhahn's clothing shop, they might have seen Richard and his wife, Hedwig, at work on sewing machines in the back of the shop as their daughters—eighteen-year-old Eva and nine-year-old Ruth—waited on customers up front. The Hirschhahns were Jewish, members of the congregation on Freiheit street, and they were deeply concerned about how things were going in Germany. But Richard had fought and been wounded in the Great War, and he did not think any harm would come to him or his family in the long run. "I've bled for Germany. Germany won't let me down," he liked to tell his wife and daughters. Still, Hedwig had returned recently from a trip to Wisconsin, and the Hirschhahns had begun to think about trying to move there. They had, in fact, some American friends staying with them in Köpenick that week, in town to see the Olympics.

The boys might have peeked into the shop and seen all of them, but what they couldn't have seen was the night when the SS men would come for Ruth, the littlest of them. Ruth they would take to her death first, because she had asthma and was too weak to work. The rest of the family they would leave in Köpenick to work as slaves—Eva in a Siemens munitions factory, her parents in a sweatshop, manufacturing German military uniforms—until it was time to come back for them too, in March 1943. Then the SS men would put Richard and Hedwig on a train to Auschwitz. Eva would evade them, escape into Berlin, hide there, and miraculously survive the war. But she would be the only one, the rarest of exceptions.

Like the Hirschhahns, many of the Köpenickers the boys passed on the street that afternoon were doomed: people who waited on the boys in shops, old women strolling around the castle grounds, mothers pushing baby carriages on cobblestone streets, children shrieking gleefully on playgrounds, old men walking dogs—loved and loving and destined for cattle cars and death.

That evening the boys went down to the water in Grünau to watch the repechage boats and learn who would join them, Hungary, and Switzerland in the medal race. Surprisingly, neither Germany nor Italy—the two crews, other than the British, about whom Ulbrickson was most concerned—had won their preliminary heats. Now, though, rowing under gray skies, Germany easily cruised past the Czechs and the Australian police officers. Italy crushed the high-stroking Japanese crew, Yugoslavia, and Brazil. Both winners seemed to ease up at the end, conserving energy and turning in relatively slow times, doing just enough to qualify. Great Britain, on the other hand, had its hands full with the Canadians and French, and the crew had to turn in the fastest time of the day to win their heat, but win they did.

Al Ulbrickson knew now which crews he was going to race against for the gold medal on the following day: Italy, Germany, Great Britain, Hungary, and Switzerland. But when he went to find out his lane assignment, he got a rude surprise. The German Olympic Committee and Fédération Internationale des Sociétés d'Aviron—headed, respectively, by Heinrich Pauli, chairman of the rowing committee for the Reich Association for Physical Training, and Rico Fioroni, an Italian Swiss—had implemented new rules for lane selection, rules never used before in Olympic competition. Ulbrickson didn't understand the formula, and to this day it is unclear how it worked or whether there even was really a formula at all. The net effect was the opposite of the usual procedure, in which the fastest qualifiers earned the favored lanes and the slower finishers had to make do with the least favored lanes. In this case, as everyone at Grünau was by now painfully aware, the best lanes were the protected ones closest to shore: lanes one, two, and three; the least desirable were lanes five and six, out in the widest part of the Langer See. Ulbrickson was horrified and furious when he saw the assignments—lane one: Germany; lane two: Italy; lane three: Switzerland; lane four: Hungary; lane five: Great Britain; and lane six: the United States of America. It was the almost perfect inverse of the order he had expected based on the qualifying times. It handicapped the most talented and fastest boats, and gave every advantage to the slower boats. It gave the protected lanes to the host country and her closest ally, the worst lanes to her prospective enemies. It was deeply suspicious, and just what he had feared since first seeing the course at Grünau. If there was any kind of headwind or crosswind the next day, his boys were going to have to make up as much as a solid two lengths just to get back to even with the field.

The next morning a cold, steady rain was falling in Grünau, and a blustery wind was whipping down the racecourse. At the police academy in Köpenick, the jubilation had evaporated. Don Hume was still in bed, his fever spiking once again, and Al Ulbrickson had decided he could not row. Don Coy would have to step into the shell again at the stroke position. Ulbrickson broke the news to Hume, then to the others as they got up that morning.

At the breakfast table, the boys ate scrambled eggs and steak, sitting silently, their eyes seeing nothing and no one. This was the day they had worked for all year—three years for most of them—and it was inconceivable to them that they would not all be together in the boat in the last race. They began to talk it over, and the more they talked the more certain they were—it just wasn't right. Hume had to be there with them, come what may. They weren't just nine guys in a boat; they were a crew. They got up en masse and went to Ulbrickson. Stub McMillin was the team captain now, so he cleared his throat and stepped forward as their spokesman. Hume was absolutely vital to the rhythm of the boat, he told his coach. Nobody else could respond as quickly and smoothly to the moment-by-moment adjustments that a crew had to make during a competitive race. Bobby Moch piped up. Nobody else but Hume could look him in the eye and know what he was thinking even as he was thinking it, he said. He just had to have Hume sitting in front of him. Then Joe stepped forward: "If you put him in the boat, Coach, we will pull him across the line. Just strap him in. He can just go along for the ride."

Ulbrickson told them to go upstairs and get their gear and get on the German army bus waiting outside to take them down to Grünau for the race. The boys began to troop upstairs. After a long few moments, Ulbrickson shouted up the stairwell after them, "And bring Hume along with you!"

By early afternoon the rain had still not let up in Grünau. Low clouds wreathed the peaks of the Müggelberg above the racecourse, and fog filtered through the woods down closer to the water. The Langer See was rough, the wind still brisk out on the water, the scene dark and gloomy.

But tens of thousands of spectators, most of them German, began to flood into the regatta grounds, huddled under black umbrellas or wearing rain

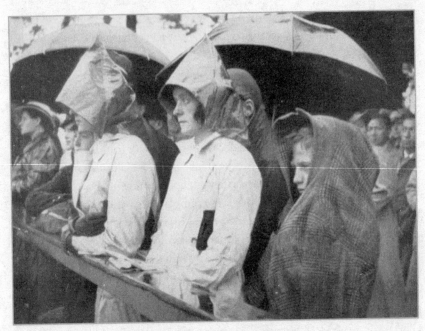

German fans waiting in the rain

slickers and hats. Despite the weather, they were in high spirits. In the 1930s rowing was the second most popular Olympic event—after track and field—and in the preliminaries Germany had shown every sign of being highly competitive, if not dominant, in this year's medal round. A stream of fans crossed the pontoon bridge at the western end of the course and began to fill the massive wooden bleachers on the far side of the water. Thousands more jammed themselves into the grass enclosures at the water's edge, pressed shoulder to shoulder in the rain. Three thousand of the luckiest took refuge under the cover of the massive permanent grandstand, right in front of the finish line. By the time the first race approached, somewhat more than seventy-five thousand fans had packed the regatta grounds, the largest crowd ever to witness an Olympic rowing event.

Leni Riefenstahl's cameramen scurried about, chasing spectators out of the way of their shots, trying to keep their equipment dry. In the elaborate press headquarters inside Haus West, hundreds of journalists from all over the world tested their telewriters and their shortwave and standard radio-transmission equipment. Bill Slater, NBC's commentator, opened his hookup to New York. Olympic judges tested the electronic timing apparatus at the finish line. The shortwave-broadcasting boat took up its position behind the starting line. In the elaborate shell houses along the Langer See, oarsmen stowed their street clothes in lockers and began to don their national uniforms. Some of them stretched out on massage tables and let masseurs work the prerace tension out of their back and shoulder muscles. The American boys found a free massage table and laid Don Hume out on it, like a corpse bundled in overcoats, keeping him warm and dry and rested for as long as they could. George Pocock, meanwhile, began applying a coat of sperm whale oil to the underside of the *Husky Clipper*.

At 2:30 p.m., as the boys continued to prepare in their shell house, the first race of the day—the four-man with coxswains—got under way at the starting line. The Swiss jumped out to an early lead but were soon overtaken by the German boat. As the boats began to approach the finish line, the American boys could hear the roar of the crowd swelling outside, beginning to chant, "Deutschland! Deutschland! Deutschland!," the sound rising to a crescendo as Germany sliced across the finish line a full eight seconds ahead of the Swiss. Then the strains of the "Deutschlandlied" joined by tens of thousands of voices. Then another, deeper, more guttural roar from the crowd, and a different chant: "Sieg Heil! Sieg Heil! Sieg Heil!"

Adolf Hitler had entered the regatta grounds, followed by a large entourage of Nazi officials. Wearing a dark uniform and a full-length rain cape, he stood for a few moments gripping the hand of FISA's Italian Swiss president, Rico Fioroni, as the two smiled and carried on an animated conversation. Then he made his way up a staircase to the wide balcony in front of Haus West and took his place of honor, looking out over the crowd and the Langer See, holding his right hand up. As his entourage arranged itself on either side of him, the crowd and the international press saw that he had brought nearly the entire top tier of the Nazi hierarchy with him. Just to his right was Joseph Goebbels. The crowd continued to thunder "Sieg Heil!" until Hitler finally lowered his hand and the racing resumed.

The crowd soon had plenty of opportunity to make more noise. In event after event that afternoon, German oarsmen charged down the course ahead of their competition, winning gold medals in the first five races. Each time, the Nazi flag was raised in front of Haus West at the end of the race, and each time the crowd sang "Deutschland über alles" a little more loudly. On the balcony Goebbels, dressed in a light-colored trench coat and a fedora, applauded theatrically, almost clownishly, as each German boat crossed the line. Hermann Göring, in a dark uniform and cape like Hitler's, bent over and slapped his knee with each German victory and then turned and beamed at Hitler. Hitler, peering through his binoculars, simply nodded enthusiastically each time a German boat crossed the line in first place. By five thirty the rain had tapered off, the skies had lightened, and the crowd was in a frenzy as it began to look as if Germany, despite all expectations to the contrary, would sweep the day.

In the sixth race, the double sculls, the German boat led all the way down the course to the final 250 meters, but the two Britons Jack Beresford and Dick Southwood staged a terrific rally and won by almost six seconds. For the first time all day, a queer hush fell over the regatta course at Grünau. In the shell house, where he was checking the rigging on the *Husky Clipper* one final time, George Pocock paused for a moment and realized with sudden pride that, out of old habit, he was standing bolt upright, listening to "God Save the King."

As the final and most prestigious event of the day—the eight-oared race—grew near, the crowd began to grow noisy once more. This was the rowing event that nations boasted about more than any other, the ultimate test of young men's ability to pull together, the greatest display of power, grace, and guts on water.

A little before six, Don Hume got up from the massage table where he had been resting and joined the rest of the boys as they hoisted the *Husky Clipper* to their shoulders and began to amble down to the water. The German boys and the Italian boys were already in their boats. The Italians were wearing silky light blue uniforms, and they had tied white bandanas rakishly around their heads, pirate-style. The Germans were resplendent in white shorts and crisp white jerseys, each emblazoned with a black eagle and swastika. The American boys were wearing mismatched track shorts and tattered old sweatshirts. They didn't want to get their new uniforms dirty.

Bobby Moch tucked Tom Bolles's lucky fedora beneath his seat in the stern of the shell. Just offshore, a German naval officer stood on the bow of a launch, his arm extended in a Nazi salute in the direction of Hitler. The boys huddled briefly with Ulbrickson as he went over the race plan one last time. Then they stepped into the shell, sat down and laced their feet into the stretchers, pushed off from the float, and started to paddle up the lake toward the starting line. Ulbrickson, Pocock, and Royal Brougham, clutching binoculars, made their way through the crowd and climbed up to a balcony of one of the shell houses near the finish line. All of them were grim faced. Good as their boys were, they figured their chances of taking the gold were slim to none—not out in lane six and not with Don Hume looking like a dead man.

In Seattle it was early morning. For days, department stores, electrical appliance stores, the Sherman Clay piano store, even the jewelry store Weisfield & Goldberg had been doing a land-office business selling new Philco 61F Olympic Special cabinet radios. Despite the $49.95 price tag, Seattleites had been snatching them up. Each came with a shortwave tuner and a special "high-efficiency aerial" kit to ensure clear reception of both the standard radio broadcast on NBC and shortwave broadcasts in a variety of languages direct from Berlin. Now, as race time approached, sales representatives were trundling the last few radios ordered the night before into Seattle homes and setting them up.

At Harry Rantz's now nearly finished house on Lake Washington, there was no money for a fancy new international radio, but Harry figured the older Philco he had bought back in April for the California race would pull in the NBC broadcast on KOMO just fine. He had gotten up before dawn and made coffee and turned the radio on, just to make sure it was working. Joyce had come over a bit later and gotten the kids up, and now they were all in the kitchen, eating oatmeal, smiling awkwardly at one another, and trying to steady their nerves.

All over America millions of people—people who had hardly heard of Seattle before the Poughkeepsie Regatta, people who had to go to work later that Friday morning, if they were lucky enough to have a job, people who had to tend to the farm chores, if they were lucky enough to still have a farm—were also starting to fiddle with the dials on their radios. The Jesse Owens story had already galvanized much of the nation, driving home what exactly was at stake in these Olympic Games. Now America waited to see if the rough-and-tumble western boys from Washington State would write another chapter in the story.

At 9:15 a.m., the voice of NBC's commentator, Bill Slater, began to crackle over KOMO's airwaves in Seattle, relayed from Berlin. Joyce rummaged in her purse and pulled out a small book. She flipped through its pages and carefully extracted a delicate green four-leaf clover that Joe had given her and she had pressed between the book's pages. She laid it atop the radio, pulled up a chair, and started to listen.

As the boys rowed up the course toward the starting line, it became clear just how challenging the weather and their lane assignment were going to be. Rain showers had begun to slant down out of the sky again, but the rain wasn't the problem. They were from Seattle, after all. The wind, however, was gusting erratically out of the west, quartering across the racecourse at roughly a forty-five-degree angle, pushing in bursts and fits at the starboard side of the shell. Up front, Roger Morris and Chuck Day were having a hard time keeping the boat on an even keel. In the stern, Bobby Moch was clutching the wooden knockers on the tiller ropes, tugging this way one moment and that way the next, manipulating the rudder, trying to keep the boat on a straight course.

The boys had rowed through plenty of wind in Seattle as well as Pough-keepsie, but this gusty, nearly sideways stuff was going to cause problems. Moch would have preferred a steady, straight-on headwind. Directly in front of him, facing him, Don Hume was trying to conserve energy, setting a nice, methodical paddling pace for the boys behind him but not putting much into his own strokes. Moch didn't like the looks of him.

Joe Rantz felt pretty good, though. As the noise of the crowd fell away behind them, the world in the shell had grown quiet and calm. It seemed to be past time for words. Joe and the boys in the middle of the boat were just rocking gently back and forth, rowing slow and low, limbering up, enjoying the in and out of their breathing, the synchronized flexing and relaxing of their muscles. The boat felt easy under them, sleek and lithe.

Anxiety had bubbled in Joe's belly all morning, but it started now to give way to a tenuous sense of calm, more determined than nervous. Just before they'd left the shell house, the boys had huddled briefly. If Don Hume had the guts to row this race, they'd agreed, the rest of them just flat out weren't going to let him down.

They pulled the shell up in front of the starting line, pivoted the *Husky Clipper* 180 degrees, and backed her up against the gangway. A delicate young man in what looked like a Boy Scout uniform crouched down, reached out his arm, and laid hold of the stern. They were out in the middle of the Langer See here. Ahead of them lay a wide-open and exposed gulf formed by the curvature of the northern shore. The wind was worse than it had been down in front of the grandstands, pushing relentlessly now at their bow, slapping small, choppy waves against the port side. Roger Morris and Gordy Adam were struggling, stroking in place on the starboard side, trying to lever the boat back against the wind and keep the bow pointed more or less down the middle of the lane. In the next lane over, the British boat backed into position. Noel Duckworth was hunkered down in the stern, his cricket cap pulled tight on his head to keep it from blowing away.

They waited for the start. Bobby Moch flipped the megaphone down in front of his face. Every few moments he hollered instructions up front to Roger and Gordy, then glanced anxiously over his shoulder to see whether the starter had emerged yet from the canvas shelter on top of the starting boat. Duckworth was doing the same next door. But both of them were primarily focused on their bows. It was critical that the boat be lined up straight at the start. Behind them, and out of sight, the official starter suddenly emerged from his shelter, holding a flag aloft. The flag snapped wildly over his head for a moment. Almost immediately, he turned slightly in the direction of lanes one and two, shouted into the wind in one continuous, unbroken utterance, "Êtes-vous prêts? Partez!" and dropped the flag.

Bobby Moch never heard him. Never saw the flag. Neither, apparently, did Noel Duckworth. Four boats surged forward. The British boat and the *Husky Clipper*, for a horrific moment, sat motionless at the line, dead in the water.

Nazis at Grünau

CHAPTER EIGHTEEN

Men as fit as you, when your everyday strength is gone, can draw on a mysterious reservoir of power far greater. Then it is that you can reach for the stars. That is the way champions are made.

—George Yeoman Pocock

Out of the corner of his eye, Joe saw the Hungarian boat, two lanes over, leap forward, its oarsmen already in midpull. A split second later, he saw the British boat do the same. He bellowed, "Let's get out of here!" Bobby Moch barked, "Row!" All eight American oars dug into the water. For another fraction of a second, the *Husky Clipper* sagged slightly under the boys as nearly a ton of deadweight resisted being put into motion. Then the boat sprang forward, and the boys were away—already a stroke and a half behind in the race of their lives.

As he realized what had happened, Chuck Day's confidence slipped a notch. He felt it in his gut, a sharp, sinking feeling. An unnerving thought shot through Roger Morris's mind: "We and the English are screwed." Bobby Moch had the same thought, but it was his job to think things through, not to panic. He'd planned to come from behind anyway, as always. But the spectacularly bad start meant that the two-length handicap he faced by virtue of his lane assignment was even greater now. He needed to build up some momentum, and he needed to do it quickly. It was going to be a titanic struggle to gain headway against the wind. He shouted at Hume to hit it hard. Hume set the pace high at thirty-eight. The boys dug hard and fast.

Across the racecourse, in lanes one and two, the Germans and Italians pulled off the line cleanly and moved briskly to the front of the field. The British boat, once it got going, also went out hard, charging furiously back up into contention. At the rear of the field, the American boat began to claw its way more slowly back into position. As the first boats crossed the hundred-meter mark, an announcer aboard the shortwave-radio boat broadcast the standings to the loudspeakers down at the finish line. The crowd roared when

The German eight

it learned that Germany was in first place. It wasn't a commanding lead, though, and it didn't mean much so early in the race. All six boats were loosely bunched up, roughly a length and a half separating the German bow in first place from the American bow in last place. Bobby Moch told Hume to ease off on the rate a bit, and Hume backed it down toward thirty-five. It was still higher than Moch wanted to row, nearly a sprinting pace, but it was what he needed to stay in contention. He ran some quick calculations in his mind. If he could manage to hang in at the back of the field, rowing in the midthirties, he figured, maybe he'd still have some gas in the tank for the inevitable sprint at the end. The boys began to settle in and swing with the boat.

As they moved out into the widest part of the Langer See, the winds grew even stronger. White, frothy waves began splashing over the small American flag that was flapping wildly out on the foredeck. With gusts pummeling his bow on the port side now, Bobby Moch began to wrestle with the tiller lines in his hands. In buffeting winds like these, the only way to keep the boat from meandering down the course in a series of S curves was to use the rudder to crab the boat slightly to port, proceeding down the course in a straight line, but with the bow slightly out of alignment with the stern. It meant there would be more resistance from the water, increased drag on the boat, and

The Italian eight

therefore more work for the boys with oars in their hands. And it was fiend-ishly tricky. Too much rudder and Moch ran the risk of careening into the lane to his left, too little and he might get blown to his right and off the course entirely.

Two hundred meters out, Noel Duckworth and Ran Laurie made a play for the early lead, surging quickly past Germany and into second place behind Switzerland, pressing them hard. Bobby Moch glanced over at them but didn't take the bait. It was fine with him if the Brits wanted to burn themselves out in the first half of the race. But then, three hundred meters out, Moch saw something that chilled him to his core. Right in front of him, Don Hume sud-denly went white in the face and all but closed his eyes. His mouth fell open. He was still rowing, still holding a steady rhythm, but Moch wasn't sure Hume was fully aware of what he was doing. Moch yelled at him, "Don! Are you OK?" Hume didn't respond. Moch couldn't tell if he was about to pass out or just in some kind of zone. He decided just to hold things as they were for now, but he was starting to seriously doubt that Hume could finish the race, let alone sprint when the time for sprinting came.

The boats were approaching the five-hundred-meter mark now, a quarter of the way down the racecourse, with Switzerland, Britain, and Germany es-sentially tied for the lead, the U.S. and the Italian shells behind them. Hungary was last. Except for the British, the leaders were all moving into the lee of the southern shore, where the water was nearly flat. The American boys were only a length off the pace but still out in the widest part of the lake, bucking the relentless, punishing winds, spray flying from their oars with every release. A slow, burning pain started to pulse up their arms and legs and dance across their backs. Very slowly they began to fall farther back. By six hundred meters, they were a length and a half back. By eight hundred meters, they were dead last again. Their heart rates began climbing toward 160 or 170 beats per minute.

Over in the sheltered water of lane two, Italy suddenly came up from the rear and worked its way into a narrow lead over Germany. As the bow of the Italian boat sliced across the halfway point at the thousand-meter mark, a bell began to toll, signaling the spectators down at the finish line that the competitors were approaching. Seventy-five thousand people rose to their feet and for the first time started to get a look at the boats edging toward them, down the gray expanse of the Langer See, like so many long, narrow spiders. On the balcony of Haus West, Hitler, Goebbels, and Göring pressed their binoculars to their eyes. On the balcony of the boathouse next door, Al Ulbrickson saw the *Husky Clipper* coming down the outside lane alongside the British boat. Trees and buildings blocked his view of the near lanes and the boats in them. For a moment, from his vantage point, it looked as if maybe his boys and the Brits were all alone out front, duking it out. Then he heard the PA announcer call out the thousand-meter-split times. The crowd roared. Italy was in first place, but just one second ahead of Germany, in second place. Switzerland was another second behind Germany, in third. Hungary was fourth. Great Britain had faded to the rear of the field, essentially tied with the United States for last place. Ulbrickson's boys were nearly five full seconds behind the leaders now.

In the stern of the *Husky Clipper*, Bobby Moch couldn't afford to wait any longer. He hunched forward and bellowed for Hume to take the stroke rate up. "Higher!" he shouted into Hume's face. "Higher!" Nothing happened. "Higher, Don! Higher!" he screamed, pleading now. Hume's head rocked back and forth with the rhythm of the boat, as if he were about to nod off. He seemed to be staring at something on the floor of the boat. Moch couldn't even make eye contact with him. The boys kept rowing at thirty-five, losing their battle with the wind, and nearly every other boat on the water. Bobby Moch tried to fight off panic.

At the eleven-hundred-meter mark, Germany retook the lead from Italy. Another enormous roar went up from the crowd, just down the lake now. Then the roaring resolved itself into chanting—"Deutsch-land! Deutsch-land!

Deutsch-land!"—in time with the stroke of the German boat. On his balcony Hitler peered out from under the visor of his hat and rocked back and forth in time with the chant. Al Ulbrickson could finally see the German and Italian boats now, forging up the near side of the lake, clearly in the lead, but he ignored them and locked his gray eyes onto the American boat, over on the far side of the water, trying to read Bobby Moch's mind. This was starting to look like Poughkeepsie all over again. Ulbrickson didn't know if that was a good thing or a bad thing. In Seattle a hush fell over Harry Rantz's living room. It was hard to tell exactly what was going on in Berlin, but the announcement of the split times was alarming.

In the boat, Joe had no idea how things stood, except that he was vaguely aware that he hadn't seen any boats falling away behind him—nothing but the flotilla of motor launches trailing the field, carrying officials and Riefenstahl's cameramen. He had been rowing hard against the wind all the way, and his arms and legs were starting to feel as if they were encased in cement. There had been no real opportunity to conserve energy. It was too early for the sprint, but he was starting to wonder what would happen when Moch called for it. How much would he have left? How much would any of them have left? All he could do was trust Moch's judgment.

Two seats in front of him, Bobby Moch was still desperately trying to figure out what to do. Hume still wasn't responding, and as they approached the twelve-hundred-meter mark, the situation was becoming critical. The only option Moch had left, the only thing he could think of, was to hand the stroke off to Joe. It would be a dangerous move—unheard-of really—more likely than not to confuse everyone with an oar in his hand, to throw the rhythm of the boat into utter chaos. But Moch had lost his ability to regulate the pace of his boat, and that spelled certain doom. If he could get Joe to set the rhythm, maybe Hume would sense the change and pick it up. At any rate, he had to do something, and he had to do it now.

As Moch leaned forward to tell Joe to set the stroke and raise the rate, Don Hume's head snapped up, his eyes popped open, he clamped his mouth shut, and he looked Bobby Moch straight in the eyes. Moch, startled, locked eyes with him and yelled, "Pick 'er up! Pick 'er up!" Hume picked up the pace. Moch yelled again, "One length to make up—six hundred meters!" The boys leaned into their oars. The stroke rate jumped to thirty-six, then thirty-seven. By the time the field charged past the fifteen-hundred-meter mark, the *Husky Clipper* had eased from fifth to third place. On the shell house balcony, down the course, Al Ulbrickson's hopes silently soared when he saw the boat move, but the move seemed to peter out with the boys still well short of the lead.

With five hundred meters to go, they were still nearly a full length behind Germany and Italy, over in lanes one and two. The Swiss and the Hungarians were fading badly. The British were coming back, but once again Ran Laurie, with his narrow-bladed oar, was having a difficult time getting enough of a catch to help power his shell through the wind and waves. Moch commanded Hume to take the beat up another notch. Across the way, Wilhelm Mahlow, the cox in the German boat, told Gerd Völs, his stroke, the same thing. Thirty-year-old Cesare Milani in the Italian boat shouted the same directive to his stroke, Enrico Garzelli. Italy crept a few feet farther ahead of the field.

As the Langer See narrowed down into the home stretch, the *Husky Clipper* at last entered water that was more sheltered from the wind, protected on both sides by tall trees and buildings. The game was on now. Bobby Moch eased the rudder back parallel with the hull of the boat and the *Clipper* finally began to run free. With the playing field more even, and Don Hume back among the living, the boys suddenly started to move again at 350 meters, reeling the leaders in seat by seat. With 300 meters to go, the bow of the American boat pulled roughly even with the German and Italian bows. Approaching the final 200 meters, the boys pulled ahead by a third of a length. A ripple of apprehension shuddered through the crowd.

Bobby Moch glanced up at the huge black-and-white "Ziel" sign at the finish. He began to calculate just what he needed to get out of the boys to make sure he got there ahead of the boats off to his left. It was time to start lying.

Moch barked, "Twenty more strokes!" He started counting them down, "Nineteen, eighteen, seventeen, sixteen, fifteen . . . Twenty, nineteen . . ." Each time he hit fifteen he reset back to twenty. In a daze, believing they were finally bearing down on the line, the boys threw their long bodies into each stroke, rowing furiously, flawlessly, and with uncanny elegance. Their oars were bending like bows, the blades entering and leaving the water cleanly, smoothly, efficiently, the shell's whale-oil-slick hull ghosting forward between pulls, its sharp cedar prow slicing through dark water, boat and men forged together, bounding fiercely forward like a living thing.

Then they rowed into a world of confusion. They were in full-sprint mode, ratcheting the stroke rate up toward forty, when they hit a wall of sound. They were suddenly right up alongside the enormous wooden bleachers on the north side of the course, not more than ten feet from thousands of spectators screaming in unison, "Deutsch-land! Deutsch-land! Deutsch-land!" The sound of it cascaded down on them, reverberated from one shore to the other, and utterly drowned out Bobby Moch's voice. Even Don Hume, sitting just eighteen inches in front of him, couldn't make out what Moch was shouting. The noise assaulted them, bewildered them. Across the way, the Italian boat began another surge. So did the German boat, both rowing at over forty now. Both clawed their way back to even with the American boat. Bobby Moch saw them and screamed into Hume's face, "Higher! Higher! Give her all you've got!" Nobody could hear him. Stub McMillin didn't know what was happening, but he didn't like whatever it was. He flung the F word into the wind. Joe didn't know what was happening either, except that he hurt as he'd never hurt in a boat before—hot knives slipped into the sinews of his arms and legs and sliced across his broad back with each stroke; every desperate breath seared his lungs. He fixed his eyes on the back of Hume's neck and focused his mind on the simple, cruel necessity of taking the next stroke.

On the balcony of Haus West, Hitler dropped his binoculars to his side. He continued to rock back and forth with the chanting of the crowd, rubbing his right knee each time he leaned forward. Goebbels held his hands over his head applauding wildly. Göring began thumping Werner von Blomberg's back. On the balcony next door, Al Ulbrickson, the Deadpan Kid, stood motionless, expressionless, a cigarette in his mouth. He fully expected to see Don Hume pitch forward over his oar at any moment. NBC's Bill Slater was screaming over KOMO's airwaves in Seattle. Harry and Joyce and the kids couldn't make out what was happening, but they were all on their feet. They thought maybe the boys were ahead.

Moch glanced left, saw the German and Italian boats surging again, and knew that somehow the boys had to go even higher, give even more than they were giving, even as he knew they were already giving everything they had. He could see it in their faces—in Joe's contorted grimace, in Don Hume's wide-open, astonished eyes, eyes that seemed to stare past him into some unfathomable void. He grabbed the wooden knockers on the tiller lines and began to bang them against the ironbark knocker-boards fastened to either side of the hull. Even if the boys couldn't hear it, maybe they could feel the vibrations.

They did. And they immediately understood it for what it was—a signal that they needed to do what was impossible, to go even higher. Somewhere, deep down inside, each of them grasped at shreds of will and strength they did not know they possessed. Their hearts were pumping at nearly two hundred beats per minute now. They were utterly beyond exhaustion, beyond what their bodies should be able to endure. The slightest miscue by any one of them would mean catching a crab, and catastrophe. In the gray gloom below the grandstands full of screaming faces, their white blades flickered in and out of the water.

It was neck and neck now. On the balcony, Al Ulbrickson bit the cigarette in his mouth in half, spat it out, jumped onto a chair, and began to bellow at Moch: "Now! Now! Now!" Somewhere a voice squealed hysterically on a loudspeaker, "Italien! Deutschland! Italien! Achh . . . Amerika! Italien!" The three boats stormed toward the finish line, the lead going back and forth. Moch pounded on the ironwood as hard and as fast as he could, the *snap-snap-snap* of it firing almost like a machine gun in the stern of the boat. Hume took the beat higher and higher until the boys hit forty-four. They had never rowed this high before—never even conceived of it as possible. They edged narrowly ahead, but the Italians began to close again. The Germans were right beside them. "Deutsch-land! Deutsch-land! Deutsch-land!" thundered in the boys' ears. Bobby Moch sat astride the stern, hunched forward, pounding the wood, screaming words no one could hear. The boys took one last mighty stroke and hurled the boat across the line. In the span of a single second, the German, Italian, and American boats all crossed the line.

On the balcony Hitler raised a clenched fist shoulder high. Goebbels leapt up and down. Hermann Göring slapped his knee again, a maniacal grin on his face.

In the American boat, Don Hume bowed his head as if in prayer. In the German boat, Gerd Völs toppled backward into the lap of the number seven man, Herbert Schmidt, who had raised a triumphant fist high over his head. In the Italian boat, somebody leaned forward and vomited overboard. The crowd continued to roar, "Deutsch-land! Deutsch-land! Deutsch-land!"

Nobody knew who had won.

The American boat drifted on down the lake, beyond the grandstands, into a quieter world, the boys leaning over their oars, gasping for breath, their faces still shattered by pain. Shorty Hunt realized he couldn't get his eyes to track. Someone whispered, "Who won?" Roger Morris croaked, "Well . . . we did . . . I think."

Finally the loudspeakers crackled back to life with the official results. The

The gold medal finish, USA in the far lane

bow of the American boat had touched the line in 6:25.4, six-tenths of a second ahead of the Italian boat, exactly a second ahead of the German boat. The chanting of the crowd faded suddenly, as if turned off by a spigot.

On the balcony of Haus West, Hitler turned and strode back into the building, unspeaking. Goebbels and Göring and the rest of the Nazi officials scurried in behind him. In the American boat, it took a moment for the boys to understand the German announcement. But when they did, their grimaces of pain turned suddenly to broad white smiles, smiles that decades later would flicker across old newsreels, illuminating the greatest moment of their lives.

In Seattle, Joe's half siblings whooped and hollered and cheered and tumbled about the house, tossing seat cushions and pillows in the air. Harry stood, in the middle of the chaos, applauding. Joyce sat in an easy chair, crying unabashedly, rapturously. Eventually, with tears still streaming down her face, she rose to turn off the radio. She carefully returned the clover to her book, hugged her father-in-law-to-be for the first time ever, and started making sandwiches.

The medal ceremony, Bobby Moch on the podium

CHAPTER NINETEEN

Where is the spiritual value of rowing? . . . The losing of self entirely
to the cooperative effort of the crew as a whole.

—George Yeoman Pocock

When they were sure that they had won, the boys rowed slowly past
the grandstands to polite applause. Al Ulbrickson and George Pocock scrambled down from their balcony and began to shove their way
through the crowds on the lawn in front of Haus West, desperately trying to
get to their boys. Royal Brougham bolted for the press room and began to
pound out the sports story of his career, pouring his heart into it, searching
his soul for language that could begin to do justice to what he had just seen,
unaware that the news writers' guild back in Seattle had just thrown picket
lines up around the *Seattle Post-Intelligencer's* offices. There would be no edition
of the *Post-Intelligencer* in the morning, and his story would never see print. As
Leni Riefenstahl's cameras continued to capture it all, the boys pulled up to
the float in front of Haus West. A few Nazi officers watched idly as an Olympic
official reached down and shook Bobby Moch's hand and presented Don
Hume with an enormous laurel wreath, so large it looked as if it was designed
to be worn by a horse rather than a man. Hume, embarrassed and not quite
sure what he was supposed to do with it, lowered the wreath momentarily
over his head, smiled sheepishly, and then handed it back to Joe, who did the
same and handed it back to Shorty Hunt, and so on, all the way to Roger
Morris in the bow. Al Ulbrickson arrived on the float breathless, crouched
down by the boat, and found himself characteristically unable to find words.
Finally, feigning indifference, he pointed to the wreath and grumbled to
Roger Morris, "Where'd you get the hay?" Roger motioned over his shoulder
with his thumb and said, "Picked it up downstream."

The boys climbed out of the shell and stood at attention while a German
band played "The Star-Spangled Banner." Then they shook some hands,
hoisted the *Husky Clipper* onto their shoulders, and carried it back to the shell

house, looking for all the world, in their dirty sweatshirts and mismatched shorts, as if they'd just come in from a workout on Lake Washington. A reporter from United Press buttonholed Al Ulbrickson on the way into the shell house and asked him what he thought of his boys. This time Ulbrickson found his voice. They were, he said unambiguously, "the finest I ever saw seated in a shell. And I've seen some corking boatloads."

Early the next morning, they returned to Grünau, where Leni Riefenstahl's crew and international newsreel photographers were clamoring to film them. Riefenstahl had already captured good footage of the gold medal race, both from boats and from shore, but she wanted close-ups from the points of view of the victorious coxswain and the stroke. The boys agreed to row with a cameraman sitting first in Hume's seat, then in Bobby Moch's seat. The Italian and German crews made similar accommodations for her. The results were spectacular. The eight-oared rowing sequence is still among the most dramatic action scenes in *Olympia*. Riefenstahl cleverly intercut long shots of the progress of the boats with close-ups of Bobby Moch and the other coxswains barking commands point-blank into the camera. These, in turn, are intercut with close-ups of the stroke oarsmen grimacing with effort as they rock rhythmically back and forth, leaning into the camera and then back away again.

When the filming was over, the boys prepared the *Husky Clipper* for shipment back to Seattle, put on their Olympic dress uniforms again, and headed to the Reichssportfeld one more time, where they watched the gold medal soccer match between Austria and Italy. After the match, the boys took to the field themselves, to receive their medals. As they lined up next to the German and Italian crews, Olympic officials went down the American line, hanging gold medals around the boys' necks and placing small laurel wreaths on their heads. Then Bobby Moch, the shortest among them, stepped up onto the highest platform on the podium. One of the boys behind him wisecracked, "You just wanted to win this thing so you could be taller than us for once, didn't you?" Someone handed Moch a sapling oak tree in a pot. Their names suddenly appeared on the enormous, forty-three-foot-wide announcement board at the eastern end of the stadium. "The Star-Spangled Banner" began to play, and the American flag slowly ascended a flagstaff behind the announcement board. As Joe watched the flag rise with his hand over his heart, he was surprised to find that tears had crept into the corners of his eyes. On the podium Moch choked up too. So did Stub McMillin. By the time it was over, they were all fighting back tears.

That night the boys went out on the town, all except for Joe. At some point they got themselves into some kind of trouble, documented only obscurely in Chuck Day's journal: "Talked ourselves out of a coupla places ... cops, etc." By four thirty that morning, they were stumbling through central Berlin, singing "Bow Down to Washington," their arms draped over one another's shoulders. It was ten thirty in the morning before they finally returned to Köpenick, nursing massive hangovers.

At the police academy, they found that Joe had been lying awake there all night. He had spent much of the night simply staring at his gold medal, contemplating it as it hung on the end of his bunk. As much as he had wanted it, and as much as he understood what it would mean to everyone back home and to the rest of the world, during the night he had come to realize that the medal wasn't the most important thing he would take home from Germany.

Immediately after the race, even as he sat gasping for air in the *Husky Clipper* while it drifted down the Langer See beyond the finish line, an expansive sense of calm had enveloped him. In the last desperate few hundred meters of the race, in the searing pain and bewildering noise of that final furious sprint, there had come a singular moment when Joe realized with startling clarity that there was nothing more he could do to win the race, beyond what he was already doing. Except for one thing. He could finally abandon all doubt, trust absolutely without reservation that he and the boy in front of him and the boys behind him would all do precisely what they needed to do at precisely the instant they needed to do it. He had known in that instant that there could be no hesitation, no shred of indecision. He had had no choice but to throw himself into each stroke as if he were throwing himself off of a cliff into a void, with unquestioned faith that the others would be there to save him from catching the whole weight of the shell on his blade. And he had done it. Over and over, forty-four times per minute, he had hurled himself blindly into his future, not just believing but knowing that the other boys would be there for him, all of them, moment by precious moment.

In the white-hot emotional furnace of those final meters at Grünau, Joe and the boys had finally forged the prize they had sought all season, the prize Joe had sought nearly all his life.

Now he felt whole. He was ready to go home.

Joe with his young family

EPILOGUE

Harmony, balance, and rhythm. They're the three things that stay with you your whole life. Without them civilization is out of whack. And that's why an oarsman, when he goes out in life, he can fight it, he can handle life. That's what he gets from rowing.

—George Yeoman Pocock

All over Seattle—in cozy restaurants downtown, in smoky neighborhood bars in Wallingford, in clattering coffee shops out in Ballard, in grocery store lines from Everett to Tacoma—people just couldn't stop talking about it. For the next few weeks, crowds packed into movie theaters to witness for themselves, on newsreels, what their boys had done in Berlin.

On their way home, the boys stopped in New York, where they rode through the city's canyons in open-top cars as swirls of paper—ticker tape, pages torn from old phone books, shreds of newspaper—spiraled down from skyscrapers. Joe Rantz, from Sequim, Washington, stood blond, lithe, and grinning, holding high over his head a rowing jersey—on its front, a black eagle and a swastika, and running around the back, a slash of bloodred.

By the middle of September, Joe was home, living at the new house on Lake Washington, sleeping in the bedroom his father had built for him right next to his own. Joe delivered the oak sapling that the boys had been awarded in Berlin to the university, and a groundskeeper planted it near the shell house. Then Joe set about trying to make a few dollars before school began.

Don Hume, finally over his respiratory infection, also hurried quickly home, worried, like Joe, about making enough money to stay in school for another year. Stub McMillin visited Mount Vernon, New York, for a few days, where relatives prepared a shoe box full of sandwiches and fruit to tide him over on the long train ride home. Johnny White and Gordy Adam went first to Philadelphia, to visit Johnny's relatives, then on to Detroit to pick up a new Plymouth Johnny's father had ordered and drive it home. Shorty Hunt returned in time to be honored in a ceremony at the annual Puyallup Fair in his hometown. Roger Morris, Chuck Day, and Bobby Moch didn't arrive back in Seattle until early October, after a six-week grand tour of Europe.

George and Frances Pocock and Al and Hazel Ulbrickson stopped in England on the way home. Pocock was able to check up on his father—now much reduced in circumstances and ravaged by old age—for the first time in twenty-three years. At Eton College, Pocock had found two of the men with whom he had worked as a boy—Froggy Windsor and Bosh Barrett—still at work in the old boat shop. The two embraced him heartily and then brought out the first shell that Pocock had ever built—the Norwegian pine and mahogany single in which he had won fifty pounds at Putney twenty-seven years before—still in fine shape and now a favorite of the Eton boys. Pocock promptly took to the Thames in it, proudly sculling back and forth in the shadow of Windsor Castle as Frances recorded the scene on a home movie camera.

By mid-October, everyone was back in Seattle and it was time to turn out for the 1936–37 crew season. Bobby Moch had graduated magna cum laude and signed on as an assistant crew coach under Al Ulbrickson. Everybody else was back in the boat.

The following spring, on the morning of April 17, 1937, the *San Francisco Chronicle* featured dueling headlines: "Seabiscuit Goes Today!" and "California Faces Washington Crew Today." That afternoon, Seabiscuit won the ten-thousand-dollar added Marchbank Handicap race at Tanforan Racetrack in San Bruno by three lengths. Just across the bay, the boys from Washington defeated California on the Oakland Estuary by a commanding five lengths. Seabiscuit was near the beginning of his career; many of the boys were nearing the end of theirs. But not before leaving one more mark on rowing history. On June 22 they rowed again for the national title in Poughkeepsie. The Washington freshmen had already won their race. So had the junior varsity. When the gun went off, the boys stormed down the river, blowing past Navy at the two-mile mark, leaving them and five other crews in their wake, winning by four lengths, setting a new course record, and accomplishing what eastern sportswriters a few hours before had been proclaiming impossible—a second consecutive sweep of the Poughkeepsie Regatta.

After the race, the sagest and most ancient among Al Ulbrickson's peers, old Jim Ten Eyck of Syracuse, finally said flat out what he'd been thinking about the Washington varsity boat for some time: "It's the greatest eight I ever saw, and I never expect to see another like it." Coming from a man who had watched crews come and go since 1861, it was quite a statement.

Poughkeepsie was the last race for Roger Morris, Shorty Hunt, and Joe Rantz. By Royal Brougham's calculations, done that night on a bar napkin, in four years of college rowing, each of them had rowed approximately 4,344 miles, far enough to take him from Seattle to Japan. Along the way, each had taken roughly 469,000 strokes with his oar, all in preparation for only 28 miles of actual collegiate racing. In those four years, and over the course of those 28 miles, the three of them—Joe, Shorty, and Roger—had never once been defeated.

Royal Brougham watched the boys from a distance as they left their shell house in Poughkeepsie the next day and wrote, "The eight oarsmen quietly shook hands, departed on different paths, and the crew that is hailed as the finest rowing combination of all time passed into history."

Within days of the closing ceremony of the 1936 Olympics, the Nazis renewed their persecution of German Jews and others to whom they believed they were superior, with a savage and unrelenting vengeance. The anti-Semitic signs were rehung; the brutality and terror resumed and intensified. In December, Hermann Göring met secretly with a number of German industrialists in Berlin and said privately what he could not yet say in public: "We are already on the threshold of mobilization, and we are already at war. All that is lacking is the actual shooting."

The larger world knew nothing of this. The illusion surrounding the Olympic Games was complete, the deception masterful. Joseph Goebbels had artfully accomplished what all good propagandists must, convincing the world that their version of reality was reasonable and their opponents' version biased. In doing that, Goebbels had not only created a compelling vision of the new Germany but also undercut the Nazis' opponents in the West— whether they were American Jews in New York City or members of Parliament in London or anxious Parisians—making all of them seem shrill, hysterical, and misinformed. As thousands of Americans returned home from the games that fall, many of them felt as one quoted in a German propaganda publication did: "As for this man Hitler. . . . Well I believe we should all

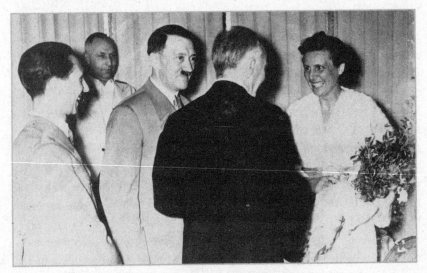

Hitler and Goebbels congratulate Leni Riefenstahl
at the premiere of *Olympia*

like to take him back to America with us and have him organize there just as
he has done in Germany."

Leni Riefenstahl's *Olympia* premiered in Berlin on April 20, 1938, in a lavish
extravaganza at the UFA-Palast am Zoo. Hitler and the entire Nazi elite were
there, along with ambassadors and envoys from more than forty nations,
including the United States and Great Britain. Military leaders and film stars
and athletes were there, among the latter, Max Schmeling. The Berlin Philharmonic provided the music. Riefenstahl entered the room to wild applause and
was cheered roundly after the screening of the film. Berlin adored it. It would
go on to win plaudits around the world as Riefenstahl launched herself into a
giddy European tour, followed by an American tour that took her all the way
to Hollywood.

The day after the premiere, Joseph Goebbels awarded Riefenstahl a hundred-
thousand-reichsmark bonus. That same day Hitler met with General Wilhelm
Keitel to discuss preliminary plans for seizing and occupying the Sudetenland
in Czechoslovakia.

By September 1939, the illusion of a civilized Nazi state had utterly fallen
away. Hitler had rolled into Poland, and the most catastrophic war in world

history was under way. In the next five years, it would take the lives of between fifty and sixty million people—so many that the exact number would never be known. The war did not reach America until the end of 1941, but when it did it swept up the boys who had rowed in Berlin, as it did the whole nation. All of them would survive the war—some were too tall to serve and many of them had recently earned engineering degrees. Those degrees made them too valuable to the Boeing Airplane Company and other companies essential to the war effort to put them in tanks or foxholes.

Joe graduated from Washington in 1939, after making up two years' worth of chemistry labs that he had missed during his rowing career. Joyce graduated Phi Beta Kappa the same day as Joe, and they were married at eight o'clock that evening. With his degree in chemical engineering, Joe went to work first for the Union Oil Company in Rodeo, California, and then returned to Seattle to work for Boeing in 1941. At Boeing he soon found himself helping to design elements of the B-17 for the war effort and later worked on the laminar flow "clean room" technology that NASA would use in the space program. With a steady job, Joe bought a house in Lake Forest Park, not far from the finish line of the Washington-California crew races. He and Joyce would live there for the rest of their lives.

Over the years, Joe and Joyce raised five children—Fred, Judy, Jerry, Barb, and Jenny. In all those years, Joyce never forgot what Joe had gone through in his early years, and she never wavered from a vow she had made to herself early in their relationship: come what may, she would make sure he never went through anything like it again, would never again be abandoned, would always have a warm and loving home.

In his later years, after he retired from Boeing, Joe immersed himself in his old passion for working with cedar. He hiked deep into the northwest woods, climbed up steep mountain inclines, and scrambled over jumbles of fallen trees, hauling with him a chainsaw, a peavey, a splitting maul, and assorted iron wedges jammed into his pockets, in search of salvageable wood. When he found what he was looking for, he thrilled as he had as a boy at finding things others had overlooked or left behind, things with essential value. He wrestled the logs down from the mountains and brought them back to his workshop, where he crafted them by hand into shakes and posts and rails and other useful items, and established a small and successful business fulfilling orders for his

Joe and Joyce on their graduation and wedding day

cedar products. As he moved into his ninth decade, his daughter Judy, and occasionally other family members, went along with him to lend a hand, and to
watch out for him.

Bobby Moch entered law school, got married, and continued to serve as an
assistant coach at Washington until he was offered the head coach position at
MIT in 1940. Displaying his congenital tenacity, he accepted the position, engineered a transfer to Harvard Law, and for the next three years managed to
hold down the coaching job while simultaneously earning the most prestigious JD in America. By 1945 he had passed both the Massachusetts and the
Washington bar exams and was back in Seattle practicing law. He would go
on to a highly successful legal career, arguing and winning many cases and
becoming one of Seattle's most prominent attorneys.

Stub McMillin returned from Germany broke and would have had to drop
out of school but for the generosity of Seattle's Rainier Club, which raised
$350 to get him through the remainder of his studies. Disqualified for military
service by virtue of his height, he took over Bobby Moch's job at MIT, where

he both coached and worked on classified research as a lab engineer for twelve years. Eventually he returned to Seattle, settled on Bainbridge Island, went to work for Boeing, and married.

Chuck Day earned his medical degree and entered the navy at the outbreak of the war. After serving as a naval doctor in the South Pacific, he returned to Seattle and established a successful practice as a gynecologist. But he continued to smoke his Lucky Strikes and Camels, a habit that would soon exact a terrible price.

Shorty Hunt married his girlfriend, Eleanor, graduated, went to work for a construction firm, and then spent the war years putting his engineering expertise to good use as a Seabee in the South Pacific. When he returned to Seattle after the war, he cofounded a construction company and settled down with Eleanor to raise his two daughters.

Don Hume spent the war years serving in the merchant marine, sailing out of San Francisco. Following the war, he began to build a career in oil and gas exploration, a job that kept him on the road much of the time, taking him sometimes to places as far away as Borneo. In time he became president of the West Coast Mining Association. He married but divorced soon after.

Johnny White graduated in 1938 with a degree in metallurgical engineering and married in 1940. Johnny followed his father into the steel business, going to work for Bethlehem Steel, where he eventually became general manager of sales. In 1946 his sister Mary Helen gave him back the violin he had sold her for a hundred dollars.

Gordy Adam ran out of money before he could graduate and so took a part-time night job with Boeing in his senior year. He remained there for the next thirty-eight years, working on the B-17, the B-29, the 707, and the 727. He married in 1939.

Roger Morris graduated in mechanical engineering, married, spent the war doing military construction in the San Francisco Bay Area, and then returned to the Seattle area to work for the Manson Construction Company, where he specialized in large-scale dredging projects.

Al Ulbrickson coached at Washington for another twenty-three years. Along the way he had many stirring victories and a few crushing defeats. His varsity crews won six IRA titles; his junior varsity won ten. He was inducted into the National Rowing Hall of Fame in 1956, the same year as Tom Bolles, Ky Ebright, and Hiram Conibear. During most of his reign, Washington remained—as it remains today—at or near the top of collegiate rowing in the

United States and the world. When Ulbrickson met with reporters in 1959, to talk about his retirement, and began to tick off the highlights of his career, among the first things he recalled was the day in 1936 that he put Joe Rantz in his Olympic boat for the first time, and watched the boat take off.

Ky Ebright went on to win his long-sought-after third Olympic gold medal in London in 1948. Like Ulbrickson, he retired in 1959, but not before establishing himself as one of the great crew coaches of all time, bringing home seven national varsity and two junior varsity championships. The rowing program he created, like the program at Washington, has remained a perpetual contender for top honors nationally and internationally ever since.

By the time the war ended, George Pocock had already long since realized his dream of becoming the best shell builder in the world, but he went on to further perfect his craft for the next twenty-five years. Generations of American oarsmen and coaches continued to buy and row in Pocock shells and also to seek him out and learn from him whenever and wherever he talked rowing. Through it all, Pocock's overriding passion remained the simple pleasure of shaping cedar, crafting his exquisite and delicate shells. One of his greatest personal triumphs came on the day when an order arrived in his shop for a western red cedar shell to be delivered to Oxford University for use in the upcoming Boat Race against Cambridge.

In 1969, at the Biltmore Hotel in New York, Pocock was inducted into the Helms Rowing Hall of Fame. By then Stan, his son, was mostly running the boatbuilding shop. Over the next ten years, synthetics such as fiberglass and carbon-fiber composites began to replace wood as the primary material from which competitive racing shells were manufactured, and the Pocock company, under Stan's guidance, slowly made the transition. George, perhaps mercifully, never lived to see the day when the elegance of cedar shells finally all but disappeared from American rowing regattas. He died on March 19, 1976.

If the boys went off on their separate paths after the Poughkeepsie Regatta in 1937, they made sure those paths crossed often. For the rest of their lives they remained close, bonded by their memories and by deep mutual respect. They met at least once a year, usually twice. Sometimes it was just the nine of them, but as time went on more and more often the get-togethers included their spouses and their growing families. They gathered around grills at backyard barbecues or around dining tables at informal potlucks. They played badminton and Ping-Pong and threw footballs and horsed around in swimming pools.

They also staged more formal ten-year anniversaries. At the first of these, in the summer of 1946, they carefully removed the *Husky Clipper* from its rack, donned shorts and sweatshirts, and pulled briskly out onto Lake Washington as if they hadn't missed a turnout in ten years. Bobby Moch took them up to a respectable twenty-six, and they cruised back and forth in front of news cameras. In 1956 they all rowed together again. But by the time the 1966 anniversary came along, Chuck Day had succumbed to lung cancer, dying in the hospital where he had practiced medicine. When he was gone, the nurses and doctors he had worked with wept in the hallways.

In 1971 the entire crew was inducted into the Helms Rowing Hall of Fame at a banquet in New York. In 1976 the eight of them still remaining reconvened for the fortieth-anniversary row. They lined up at the Conibear Shellhouse for photographs, bare chested and clutching their oars. By then shoulders were sagging and bellies were bulging and the hair of most of those who still had any had gone gray. But as TV cameras shot video of them for the evening news, they clambered into the *Husky Clipper* and rowed. And they rowed well, if a bit slowly—crisp, clean, and efficient even yet.

Ten more years went by, and in 1986, fifty years after their victory in Berlin,

The 1956 reunion row

they rowed one last time. Wearing matching white shorts and rowing shirts, they pushed the *Husky Clipper* down to Lake Washington on a wheeled cart and boarded her gingerly as photographers crowded around them, ready to offer helping hands. Bobby Moch strapped on his old megaphone and croaked "Row!" With troubled joints and aching backs, they dipped white blades into the water and glided out onto Lake Washington. Still pulling together as one, they crept across water burnished to bronze by a late afternoon sun. Then, with evening coming on, they hobbled back up the ramp to the shell house, waved to photographers, and placed their oars in the racks for the final time.

They and their families continued to get together off the water, celebrating birthdays and other special occasions. But in the 1990s those occasions began to include funerals. Gordy Adam died in 1992, Johnny White in 1997, but not before the crew was honored by a military band concert in Washington's capital city of Olympia to commemorate the sixtieth anniversary in 1996. Shorty Hunt died in 1999. Five days after the 9/11 attacks in 2001, Don Hume passed away.

A year later, in September 2002, Joe lost Joyce. He and she were sharing a room at a skilled nursing facility at the time—he recovering from a fractured pelvis and she dying from congestive heart failure and kidney failure. The staff had, with uncommon compassion, pushed their beds together so they could hold hands, and that's how Joyce died. A few days later, Joe went to the memorial service. Then he returned to the room, alone again for the first time in sixty-three years.

Bobby Moch died in January of 2005, and Stub McMillin followed him in August of that year. That left only Joe and Roger.

In the aftermath of Joyce's death, even as his own health began to decline, Joe's family helped him to realize many lifelong dreams. Although he had become wheelchair bound, he traveled with them on a cruise to Alaska, ventured up the Columbia River on a paddle-wheel steamer, rode the Snow Train to the village of Leavenworth in the Cascade Mountains, revisited the site of the Gold and Ruby mine in Idaho, flew to Hawaii, took another paddle-wheel steamer up the Mississippi, went to Los Angeles to visit Rose, Polly, and Barb, went twice to Milwaukee to visit his daughter Jenny and her family, attended the Grand Ole Opry in Nashville, and cruised through the Panama Canal.

By early 2007, Joe was on hospice care and living at Judy's house. In March he wore his purple "Husky Hall of Fame" jacket to a Varsity Boat Club banquet in Seattle. Four hundred fifty people stood and cheered him. In May he watched from his wheelchair on the shore of the Cut as Washington's crews held their opening day races. But by August he'd come up on the finish line one last time. He died peacefully at Judy's home on September 10, months after I first met him and began to interview him for this book. His ashes were interred in Sequim, next to Joyce's.

Somewhere along the way, the oak tree that Joe brought home from the Olympics died after being transplanted several times on the university campus. That had bothered Joe in his last years. So on a winter day in 2008 a small group gathered near Conibear Shellhouse. At Judy's urging, the university had secured a new oak tree. Bob Ernst, director of rowing at Washington, made a brief speech, and then Judy slowly and reverently placed nine shovelfuls of soil at the base of the tree—one for each of the boys.

Roger Morris, the first of Joe's friends on crew, was the last man standing. Roger died on July 22, 2009. At his memorial service, Judy rose and recalled how in their last few years Joe and Roger would often get together—in person or on the phone—and do nothing at all, hardly speaking, just sitting quietly, needing only to be in each other's company.

And so they passed away, loved and remembered for all that they were—not just Olympic oarsmen but good men, one and all.

In August of 2011, I traveled to Berlin to see the place where the boys had won gold seventy-five years earlier. I visited the Olympic Stadium and then took the S-Bahn out to Köpenick, in what used to be Soviet-occupied East Berlin. There I wandered through cobblestone streets, among ancient buildings left mostly undamaged by the war, except for occasional brick facades scarred by shrapnel. I walked past the vacant lot on Freiheit where Köpenick's synagogue stood until the night of November 9, 1938, and I thought of the Hirschhahn family.

In Grünau I found the regatta grounds little changed from 1936. A large electronic readerboard now dominates the area near the finish line, but otherwise the place looks much as it does in the old newsreels and photographs. The neighborhood is still lovely—green and leafy. The covered grandstands still rise near the finish line. The Langer See is still placid and tranquil. Earnest young men and women in racing shells still ply its waters in racing lanes laid out just as they were in 1936.

I visited the Wassersportmuseum in Grünau, where late in the afternoon Werner Phillip, the director, kindly led me up a set of stairs to the balcony of Haus West. I stood there for a long, quiet minute, near where Hitler stood seventy-five years before, gazing out over the Langer See, seeing it much as he saw it.

Down below me young men were unloading a shell from a truck, singing something softly in German, and preparing for an evening row. Out on the water, a single sculler, his blades glinting, worked his way down one of the lanes toward the large "Ziel" sign at the end of the course. Closer to me, swallows flew low over the water on silent wings, silhouetted against the declining sun, touching the water from time to time, dimpling the silver surface.

Standing there, watching them, it occurred to me that when Hitler watched Joe and the boys fight their way back from the rear of the field to sweep ahead of Italy and Germany seventy-five years ago, he saw, but did not recognize, heralds of his doom. He could not have known that one day hundreds of thousands of boys just like them, boys who shared their essential natures—decent and unassuming, not privileged or favored by anything in particular, just loyal, committed, and perseverant—would return to Germany dressed in olive drab, hunting him down.

They are almost all gone now—the legions of young men who saved the world in the years just before I was born. But that afternoon, standing on the balcony of Haus West, I was swept with gratitude for their goodness and their grace, their humility and their honor, their simple civility and all the things they taught us before they flitted across the evening water and finally vanished into the night.

One survivor of the 1936 gold medal race is still with us today, though—the *Husky Clipper.* For many years, she resided at the old shell house, mostly unused except on the occasions of the boys' ten-year anniversary rows. For a number of years in the 1960s, she was on loan to Pacific Lutheran University in Tacoma. In 1967, Washington asked for her return, restored her, and put her on display in the student union. Later she was displayed at the George Pocock Memorial Rowing Center in Seattle.

Today she is in Washington's Conibear Shellhouse, a spacious open building built in 1949 and recently renovated. She hangs in the light, airy dining commons, suspended from the ceiling, a graceful needle of cedar and spruce, her red and yellow woodwork gleaming under small spotlights. Be-

Joe in the woods

yond her, on the eastern side of the building, Lake Washington spreads out behind a wall of glass. From time to time, people wander in and admire her. They snap photos of her and tell one another what they know about her and the boys who rowed her in Berlin.

But she is there for more than decoration and admiration. She is there for inspiration. Every fall several hundred freshmen—men one day, women another day, most of them tall, a few of them notably short—assemble beneath her on early October afternoons. They fill out registration cards and anxiously look around the room, sizing one another up and chatting nervously until the freshman coach steps in front of them and calls for quiet in a loud, no-nonsense voice. As they settle down, he begins to talk to them about what they can expect if they seek a spot on his crew. Mostly, at first, he talks about how hard it will be, how long the hours will be, how cold and wet and miserable it will be. He points out that Washington's crew typically has the highest GPA of any athletic team on campus, and that that's no accident. They will be expected to perform in the classroom as well as in the boats. Then he shifts his tone a bit and begins to talk about the glory of earning a chance to pull one of the white blades of Washington. He talks about recent regional victories, about the now age-old rivalry with California, about the

Royal Brougham's Olympic press badge

AUTHOR'S NOTE

If books can be said to have hearts and souls—and I believe they can—this book owes its heart and soul to one person above all others: Joe Rantz's daughter Judy Willman. I could not have begun to tell Joe's story, and the larger story of the 1936 Olympic crew, if it had not been for Judy's deep collaboration with me at every stage of the project. Her contributions are too many to catalog here, but they range from sharing her vast collection of documents and photographs, to connecting me to members of the crew and their families, to reviewing and commenting on many drafts of the book at all stages of development. All of this, however, pales in comparison with one contribution in particular: the countless hours she spent sitting with me in her living room, telling me her father's story, sometimes tearfully, sometimes joyfully, but always with unbounded pride and love.

Judy grew up absorbing the details of her father's accomplishments as well as the hardships he endured and the psychological impact that both had on him. She spent untold hours listening to his stories. She learned about her mother's role in Joe's early life as she worked side by side with her in the kitchen. Over the years and at frequent get-togethers, she came to know the other eight oarsmen well and to regard them almost as members of the family. She heard Joe's father—by then reconciled with family and known affectionately as "Pop"—tell his version of the story. She learned Thula's side of things from her uncle—Thula's son Harry Junior. And over nearly sixty years she asked countless questions, collected clippings and memorabilia, and documented every detail. In essence, she became the keeper of her family's story.

In several places in this book I quote bits of conversation or delve into the thinking to which only Joe or Joyce were privy. Though no one was there to record these conversations, and no one made transcripts of Joe's and Joyce's thoughts, Joe and Joyce were the key witnesses to their own lives, and they are the ultimate sources of these pieces of the story. In the several months during which I was able to interview Joe before he passed away, he shared not only the fundamental facts of their story but also, sometimes in exquisite detail, many of his specific feelings and thoughts at key junctures of the tale. He was able, for instance, to recount his shell house conversations with George Pocock, his emotional devastation upon being abandoned in Sequim, his journey out to Grand Coulee, and his troubled relationship with his father and Thula. Later, after Joe was gone, as Judy and I sat together for all those many hours poring over photographs and letters and scrapbooks, she was able to help me fill in the gaps, particularly at those key points in the story, many of which her father or her mother had narrated to her over and over again during the course of a lifetime. These conversations and recollections are documented most fully in the complete notes for this book online.

Few things offer so much opportunity for common effort as the making of a book. With that in mind, I want to convey my very deep appreciation to the following people in addition to Judy who contributed to the making of this one.

First, Ray Willman, "Mr. Judy," who has been indispensable to the project in countless ways, large and small, from day one.

In the publishing world: At WME, my stunningly brilliant and delightfully gutsy agent, Dorian Karchmar, the wonderfully capable Anna DeRoy, Raffaella De Angelis, Rayhané Sanders, and Simone Blaser. At the Viking Press, my sterling editor, Wendy Wolf, who wields the scalpel so expertly that one hardly feels the pain and is ever so grateful for the cure. Also Josh Kendall, who acquired the book and edited the initial draft, assistant editor Maggie Riggs, and the whole team of clever, resourceful professionals at Viking. And far from Manhattan, Jennifer Pooley, who has helped me along the road in so many ways.

Among those who call the 1936 crew family or close friends, many of whom generously shared their recollections and made their private collections of documents and memorabilia—scrapbooks, letters, and journals—available to me: Kristin Cheney, Jeff Day, Kris Day, Kathleen Grogan, Susan Hanshaw, Tim Hume, Jennifer Huffman, Josh Huffman, Rose Kennebeck, Marilynn Moch, Michael Moch, Pearlie Moulden, Joan Mullen, Jenny Murdaugh, Pat Sabin, Paul Simdars, Ken Tarbox, Mary Helen Tarbox, Harry Rantz Jr., Polly Rantz, Jerry Rantz, Heather White, and Sally White.

At the University of Washington's shell house: Eric Cohen, Bob Ernst, and Luke McGee, all of whom reviewed the manuscript and offered many fine suggestions and essential corrections. Also Michael Callahan and Katie Gardner for help tracking down photographs. I'd like to call particular attention to Eric's excellent website, www.huskycrew.com. It is by far the single best source for anyone who wants to know more about the long, illustrious history of rowing at Washington.

In the wider world of rowers and crew coaches: Bob Gotshall, John Halberg, Al Mackenize, Jim Ojala, and Stan Pocock.

In the world of libraries and dusty archives: Bruce Brown, Greg Lange, Eleanor Toews, and Suz Babayan.

For help with things German: Werner Phillip at the Wassersportmuseum in Grünau and, closer to home, Isabell Schober.

For lending his technical expertise and his fine eye to the production of original photographs: Joshua Huffman.

For her astonishing generosity: Cathi Soriano, Royal Brougham's granddaughter, who presented me with Royal's press badge from the 1936 Olympics, pictured on page 372. This is the badge that he wore the day the boys won gold, and I will treasure it forever.

Finally, this is, in many ways, a book about a young man's long journey back to a place he can call home. Writing his story has reminded me again and again that no one is more blessed by his home life than I am. I want to thank the three lovely and intelligent women who make it so: my daughters, Emi and Bobi—each of whom has lent her own unique talents to the making of this book—and my wife, Sharon. Her thoughtful reading of the manuscript, her many conversations with me about it, and her deeply insightful comments and suggestions have vastly improved it on every conceivable level. Her love, her confidence, and her continual support have made writing it possible in the first place. Without her, there would be no books.

NOTES

The original manuscript for this book contained well over a thousand endnotes. What follows is a much condensed and incomplete version of those notes. In this condensed version, I use the following abbreviations: *ST* (*Seattle Times*), *PI* (*Seattle Post-Intelligencer*), *WD* (*University of Washington Daily*), *NYT* (*New York Times*), *DH* (*New York Daily Herald*), *HT* (*New York Herald Tribune*), and *NYP* (*New York Post*).

FRONT MATTER AND PROLOGUE

The Pocock quote is from Gordon Newell's excellent biography, *Ready All!: George Yeoman Pocock and Crew Racing* (Seattle: University of Washington Press, 1987), 159. The Pocock quotes taken from Newell, throughout the book, are used with permission of the University of Washington Press. The Greek epigraph is from Homer's *Odyssey*, 5.219–20 and 5.223–24. The translation is by Emi C. Brown.

The Pocock quote serving as an epigraph to the prologue is from Newell (154).

CHAPTER ONE

The chapter epigraph here is from a letter Pocock wrote to C. Leverich Brett, printed in the National Association of Amateur Oarsmen's *Rowing News Bulletin*, no. 3 (Season 1944), printed in Philadelphia, June 15, 1944. My descriptions of weather conditions in the Seattle area, throughout the book, are drawn from daily Cooperative Observers meteorological records taken at various stations around Seattle and reported to the U.S. Weather Bureau. For more statistics on the effects of the Depression, see Piers Brendon, *The Dark Valley: A Panorama of the 1930s* (New York: Vintage, 2002), p. 86, and Joyce Bryant's "The Great Depression and New Deal" in *American Political Thought*, vol. 4 (New Haven: Yale–New Haven Teachers' Institute, 1998). Interestingly, according to Erik Larson, in his excellent book *In the Garden of Beasts* (New York: Crown, 2012), 375, *King Kong* was also a particular favorite of Adolf Hitler. More on the performance of the stock market through this period can be found in the *Wall Street Journal*'s table of "Dow Jones Industrial Average All-Time Largest One-Day Gains and Losses," which is available at http://online.wsj.com/mdc/public/page/2_3024-djia_alltime.html. The Dow next passed 381 on November 23, 1954. At its low in 1932, the Dow had lost 89.19 percent of its value. See Harold Bierman, *The Causes of the 1929 Stock Market Crash* (Portsmouth, NH: Greenwood Publishing, 1998). Hoover's full remarks are available in *U.S. Presidential Inaugural Addresses* (Whitefish, MT: Kessinger Publishing Company, 2004), 211.

Descriptions of the students' appearance and mode of dress are derived from photographs taken on the Washington campus that fall. My account of Joe's and Roger's first day at the shell house is based in part on my interview with Roger Morris on October 2, 2008. For more about Royal Brougham, see Dan Raley, "The Life and Times of Royal Brougham," *PI*, October 29, 2003. The description of the shell house is based partly on my own observations and partly on Al Ulbrickson's description in "Row, Damit, Row,"

Esquire, April 1934. Facts and figures on the boys assembled on the dock that day are from *WD*, "New Crew Men Board Old Nero," October 12, 1933. Years later, Ulbrickson would turn out to be one of three men on the shell house dock that afternoon—along with Royal Brougham and Johnny White—to be inducted into Franklin High's Hall of Fame.

An enormous amount of information about the construction of the Olympic facilities in Berlin can be found in Organisationskomitee für die XI Olympiade Berlin 1936, *The XIth Olympic Games Berlin, 1936: Official Report*, vol. 1 (Berlin: Wilhelm Limpert, 1937). For more about Hitler's initial attitude regarding the Olympics, see Paul Taylor, *Jews and the Olympic Games: The Clash Between Sport and Politics* (Portland, OR: Sussex Academic Press, 2004), 51. The Dodd family's impressions of Goebbels are documented in Larson's *In the Garden of Beasts*. See "Foreign News: Consecrated Press," in *Time*, October 16, 1933, for a telling story about Goebbels and the press.

Astronomical data—references to sunrise, sunset, moonrise, etc.—throughout are drawn from the U.S. Naval Observatory's website. The best single source of information about the history of the Washington crew program is Eric Cohen's marvelous online compendium, "Washington Rowing: 100+ Year History," available at http://www.huskycrew.com. Among the eight Yale oarsmen who crewed the gold-medal-winning shell in 1924 was the future Dr. Benjamin Spock.

CHAPTER TWO

The epigraph is from Pocock, quoted in Newell (94–95). The facts regarding the Wright brothers' flight are derived from "A Century of Flight," *Atlantic Monthly*, December 17, 2003. For more about George Wyman's motorcycle odyssey, see the entry on him at the AMA Motorcycle Hall of Fame website: http://motorcyclemuseum.org/halloffame. More interesting facts and figures about the rather remarkable year of 1903 can be found in Kevin Maney's article "1903 Exploded with Tech Innovation, Social Change," *USA Today*, May 1, 2003. Confusingly, the first Model A was an entirely different automobile from the well-known Model A of 1927–31, which followed the wildly successful Model T.

Some of the details of this phase of Joe's life are derived from an unpublished typescript, "Autobiography of Fred Rantz." The names and dates of Thula LaFollette's parents are from monument inscriptions at the LaFollette Cemetery in Lincoln County, Washington. I gleaned many facts about Thula's life from my interview with Harry Rantz Jr. on July 11, 2009. For an overview of the history of the Gold and Ruby mine, I consulted "It's No Longer Riches That Draw Folks to Boulder City," in the *Spokane Spokesman-Review*, September 28, 1990, and "John M. Schnatterly" in N. N. Durham, *Spokane and the Inland Empire*, vol. 3 (Spokane, WA: S. J. Clarke, 1912), 566. The anecdote regarding Thula's "second sight" is drawn from an unpublished monograph, "Remembrance," authored by one of Thula's daughters, Rose Kennebeck.

CHAPTER THREE

The Pocock epigraph is quoted in Newell (144). Royal Brougham's colorful description of the rigors of rowing is from "The Morning After: Toughest Grind of Them All?" *PI*, May 32, 1934. My discussion of the physiology of rowing and rowing injuries is drawn in part from the following sources: "Rowing Quick Facts" at the U.S. Rowing website: http://www.usrowing.org/About/Rowing101; Alison McConnell, *Breathe Strong, Perform Better* (Champaign, IL: Human Kinetics, 2011), 10; and J. S. Rumball, C. M. Lebrun, S. R. Di Ciacca, and K. Orlando, "Rowing Injuries," *Sports Medicine* 35, no. 6 (2005): 537–55.

Pocock studied and emulated the rowing style of one of the greatest of the Thames watermen, Ernest Barry, who won the Doggett's Coat and Badge in 1903 and was the world's sculling champion in 1912, 1913, 1914, and 1920. For much more on the history of the Pocock family, see Newell, on whom I have relied heavily here, though many details also come from my two interviews with Stan Pocock and some from Clarence Dirks, "One-Man Navy Yard," *Saturday Evening Post*, June 25, 1938, 16, as well as an unpublished typescript, "Memories," written by Pocock himself in 1972. Many years later Rusty Callow, who coached at Washington before Ulbrickson, would say of Pocock, "Honesty of effort and pride in his work are a religion with him."

Much of the information regarding Hiram Conibear is derived from an unpublished 1923 typescript by Broussais C. Beck, "Rowing at Washington," available in the Beck Papers in the University of Washington Archives, accession number 0155-003. Additional information is from "Compton Cup and Conibear," *Time*, May 3, 1937; David Eskenazi, "Wayback Machine: Hiram Conibear's Rowing Legacy," *Sports Press Northwest*, May 6, 2011, available at http://sportspressnw.com/2011/05/wayback-machine-hiram-conibears-rowing-legacy/; and Eric Cohen's website cited above. Bob Moch's remark about the reverence with which oarsmen regarded Pocock can be found in Christopher Dodd, *The Story of World Rowing* (London: Stanley Paul, 1992).

Apparently there was an earlier version of *Old Nero*, with seats for only ten oarsmen, as described by Beck. Al Ulbrickson refers to sixteen seats in "Row, Damit, Row." Some details of Roger Morris's early life are drawn from my interview with him. My description of the basic stroke taught by Ulbrickson in the 1930s is based on his own description of it in "Row, Damit, Row." Over time the stroke used at the University of Washington has continued to evolve in various ways. The golf ball analogy is from Pocock himself, in his "Memories" (110).

CHAPTER FOUR

The epigraph is from the already cited letter Pocock wrote to C. Leverich Brett, printed in the *Rowing News Bulletin*. Many of the details of life in Sequim are from Joe Rantz's memory, some from Harry Rantz Jr.'s recollection, and some from Doug McInnes, *Sequim Yesterday: Local History Through the Eyes of Sequim Old-Timers*, self-published in May 2005. A few additional facts are from Michael Dashiell, "An Olympic Hero," *Sequim Gazette*, January 18, 2006. A discussion of the role farm prices played in the Depression can be found in Piers Brendon's *The Dark Valley* (87) and also in Timothy Egan's *The Worst Hard Time* (Boston: Mariner, 2006), 79. Joe recounted his abandonment in Sequim and his subsequent efforts to survive in great detail many times over his lifetime, and my account is based on his own telling to me as well as on details gleaned from my interviews with Judy Willman and with Harry Rantz Junior. Some of the facts concerning Charlie McDonald and his horses, as well as other details about the McDonald household, were outlined in an e-mail from Pearlie McDonald to Judy Willman, June 1, 2009.

The biographical material on Joyce Simdars, here and throughout, is drawn from my interviews with Judy Willman, Joyce's daughter, as well as from photos and documents that Judy shared with me. Ulbrickson's discovery of Joe in the gym at Roosevelt High School was one of the first things that Joe talked about when I began to interview him.

CHAPTER FIVE

The epigraph is Pocock, quoted in Newell (144). The biographical information about Roger Morris is largely from my interview with him on October 2, 2008. For more on home foreclosures early in the Depression, see David C. Wheelock, "The Federal Response to Home Mortgage Distress: Lessons from the Great Depression," *Federal Reserve Bank of Saint Louis Review*, available online at http://research.stlouisfed.org/. See also Brian Albrecht, "Cleveland Eviction Riot of 1933 Bears Similarities to Current Woes," *Cleveland Plain Dealer*, March 8, 2009.

A scrapbook that Joe kept for much of his rowing career is the source of many of the small details of his life at the shell house, his job, his living conditions, and the things he and Joyce did together throughout their college years. The sketch of life on the UW campus in the fall of 1933 is drawn from various issues of *WD* from that fall.

My account of the dust storms of 1933 is derived largely from "Dust Storm at Albany," *NYT*, November 14, 1933. Facts pertaining to the state of affairs in Germany that fall are from Edwin L. James, "Germany Quits League; Hitler Asks 'Plebiscite,'" *NYT*, October 15, 1933; "Peace Periled When Germany Quits League," *ST*, October 14, 1933; Larson, *Garden of Beasts* (152); Samuel W. Mitcham Jr., *The Panzer Legions: A Guide to the German Army Tank Divisions of World War II and Their Commanders* (Mechanicsburg, PA: Stackpole, 2006), 8; and "U.S. Warns Germany," *ST*, October 12, 1933. The reference to nitrates passing through the Panama Canal is from "Munitions Men," *Time*, March 5, 1934. The Will Rogers quote is from "Mr. Rogers Takes a Stand on New European Dispute," in *Will Rogers' Daily Telegrams*, vol. 4, *The Roosevelt Years*, edited by James M. Smallwood and Steven K. Gragert (Stillwater: Oklahoma State University Press), 1997.

Some meteorologists argue that November 2006 eclipsed the December 1933 record, but the official rainfall measurements in 2006 were taken at Sea-Tac Airport, eight miles south of Seattle, where rainfall tends to be higher. See Sandi Doughton, "Weather Watchdogs Track Every Drop," *ST*, December 3, 2006. Also Melanie Connor, "City That Takes Rain in Stride Puts on Hip Boots," *NYT*, November 27, 2006.

CHAPTER SIX

The epigraph appears in Newell (88). The freshmen can be seen rowing under the bowsprits of an old schooner in a photograph from the *ST*, February 18, 1934. "Tolo" refers, in western Washington and British Columbia, to what most of the country knows as a Sadie Hawkins dance—one in which the girl asks the boy to the event. The term apparently derives from *tulu* (to win) in Chinook, the jargon spoken in the nineteenth century by many Northwest Indians.

Ulbrickson's running commentary on the performance of different boys and different crews, here and throughout, is taken from his "Daily Turnout Log of University of Washington Crew," vol. 4 (1926; 1931–43), housed in the Alvin Edmund Ulbrickson Papers in the University of Washington's Special Collections, accession number 2941-001. Hereafter referred to as "Ulbrickson's logbook."

One of Ebright's later oarsmen and devoted disciples was Gregory Peck. The Buzz Schulte quote is from Gary Fishgall, *Gregory Peck: A Biography* (New York: Scribner, 2001), 41. The Don Blessing quote is from a newspaper clipping, "Ebright: Friend, Tough Coach," *Daily Californian*, November 3, 1999. Much of the information on Ebright's early years at Cal and the rivalry with Washington—including the "vicious and bloody" quote—comes from an interview with Ebright conducted by Arthur M. Arlett in 1968, housed in the Regional Oral History office of the Bancroft Library at the University of California, Berkeley. The testy exchange of letters between Ebright and Pocock took place between October 1931 and February 1933. The letters are also housed in the Bancroft Library. Pocock states in "Memories" (63) that it was he who first suggested Ebright for the job at Cal.

The principal sources of my account of the lead-up to the 1934 Cal-Washington race are "Freshmen Win, Bear Navy Here," *ST*, April 1934; "Bear Oarsmen Set for Test with Huskies," *San Francisco Chronicle*, April 5, 1934; "Bear Oarsmen to Invade North," *San Francisco Chronicle*, April 6, 1934; "Huskies Have Won Four Out of Six Races," *San Francisco Chronicle*, April 6, 1934; and "California Oarsmen in Washington Race Today," Associated Press, April 13, 1934.

Joyce's experience watching from the ferry as Joe raced for the first time was something she remembered well, and my account of her feelings and thoughts comes from her many conversations with her daughter Judy. The reference to John Dillinger is from "John Dillinger Sends U.S. Agents to San Jose Area," *San Francisco Chronicle*, April 13, 1936. The estimate of 300-plus strokes in two miles is based on Susan Saint Sing's figure of 200 strokes in 2,000 meters, or one stroke every 10 meters, in her *The Wonder Crew* (New York: St Martin's, 2008), 88. Two miles is 3,218 meters, which would yield a result of 321 strokes; however, the stroke rate is inevitably lower in a two-mile race than in a 2,000-meter sprint. My account of the 1934 Cal-Washington freshman races is based primarily on Frank G. Gorrie, "Husky Shell Triumphs by ¼ Length," Associated Press, April 13, 1934; and Royal Brougham, "U.W. Varsity and Freshmen Defeat California Crews," *PI*, April 14, 1934.

For much more on Joseph Goebbels's family life, see Anja Klabunde, *Magda Goebbels* (London: Time Warner, 2003). The additional facts presented here about the Reichssportfeld are drawn from *The XIth Olympic Games: Official Report*; Duff Hart-Davis, *Hitler's Games* (New York: Harper & Row, 1986), 49; and Christopher Hilton, *Hitler's Olympics* (Gloucestershire: Sutton Publishing, 2006), 17. The torch-relay idea is often credited to Dr. Carl Diem, chief organizer of the 1936 Olympics, but according to *The XIth Olympic Games: Official Report* (58), the proposal originally came from within the Ministry of Propaganda.

For an up-to-date assessment of Leni Riefenstahl's relationship with Nazi Party leaders, I highly recommend Steven Bach, *Leni: The Life and Work of Leni Riefenstahl* (New York: Abacus, 2007). See also Ralf Georg Reuth, *Goebbels* (New York: Harvest, 1994), 194; and Jurgen Trimborn, *Leni Riefenstahl: A Life* (New York: Faber and Faber, 2002). After the war, Riefenstahl would deny that she had been on social terms with the Goebbels family and other top Nazis, but Goebbels's diary from 1933 and other documents that have come to light since make clear that she was, in fact, very much a part of their social circle.

CHAPTER SEVEN

The Pocock quote that opens this chapter is, interestingly, from a note he sent wrapped around an oar to a Washington crew rowing at Henley in 1958; see Newell (81). My account of the 1934 varsity race here is, like the freshman race, based largely on Gorrie, "Husky Shell Triumphs by ¼ Length," and Brougham, "U.W. Varsity and Freshmen Defeat California Crews," cited above, as well as Ulbrickson's logbook.

Joe's unease mixed with excitement as he boarded the train to Poughkeepsie for the first time was one of the things he often brought up with Judy, as were other details of the trip east, particularly his moment of humiliation when he began to sing.

For much more about the history of the Poughkeepsie Regatta, see the many resources available at the Intercollegiate Rowing Association's Poughkeepsie Regatta website, at http://library.marist.edu/archives/regatta/index.html. The account of Washington's first win at Poughkeepsie is based on my interviews with Stan Pocock; George Pocock, quoted in "One-Man Navy Yard" (49); "From Puget Sound," *Time*, July 9, 1923; Saint Sing, *Wonder Crew* (228); and Newell (73). The mention of Ulbrickson's injury in the 1926 regatta is from "Unstarred Rowing Crew Champions: They Require Weak But Intelligent Minds, Plus

Strong Backs," *Literary Digest* 122:33–34. For more on the East versus West theme, see Saint Sing (232–34).

Many elements of my description of Poughkeepsie on the day of the 1934 regatta are drawn from a wonderful piece by Robert F. Kelley, "75,000 See California Win Classic on Hudson," *NYT*, June 17, 1934. The reference to Jim Ten Eyck having rowed in 1863 comes from Brougham, "The Morning After," *PI*, May 27, 1937. In that piece Ten Eyck also proclaimed the 1936–37 University of Washington varsity crew the greatest he ever saw.

My description of the 1934 Poughkeepsie races is based on the Robert F. Kelley piece cited above, as well as "Washington Crew Beats California," *NYT*, April 13, 1934; "Ebright Praises Washington Eight," *NYT*, June 17, 1934; George Varnell, "Bolles' Boys Happy," *ST* (a clipping in Joe Rantz's scrapbook with no date); "U.W. Frosh Win" (no date, Joe Rantz's scrapbook); and "Syracuse Jayvees Win Exciting Race," *NYT*, June 17, 1934.

Weather data for the spring and summer of 1934 is, in part, from Joe Sheehan, "May 1934: The Hottest May on Record," available at the National Weather Service Weather Forecast Office website, http://www.crh.noaa.gov/fsd/?n=joe_may1934; W. R. Gregg and Henry A. Wallace, *Report of the Chief of the Weather Bureau, 1934* (Washington, D.C.: United States Department of Agriculture, 1935); "Summer 1934: Statewide Heat Wave," available at http://www.ohiohistory.org; and "Grass from Gobi," *Time*, August 20, 1934. For more on the dust storms that year, see Egan, *Worst Hard Time* (particularly 5 and 152).

A great deal more information about the 1934 West Coast labor disputes is available on Rod Palmquist's Waterfront Workers' History Project website: http://depts.washington .edu/dock. A small sampling of the rhetorical assaults on Roosevelt can be found in "New Deal Declared 3-Ring Circus by Chairman of Republican Party," *PI*, July 3, 1934; and "American Liberty Threatened by New Deal, Borah Warns," *PI*, July 5, 1934. The full text of Roosevelt's remarks at Ephrata are recorded in "Remarks at the Site of the Grand Coulee Dam, Washington," August 4, 1934, on the American Presidency Project website: http:// www.presidency.ucsb.edu.

CHAPTER EIGHT

The Pocock quote is from Newell (156). My description of working with a mallet and froe to split cedar is based in part on lessons given to me by Joe's daughter Judy, to whom he taught the skills. Ulbrickson's speech to the boys on the shell house ramp is derived from assorted press accounts of it as well as his own description of such speeches as told to Clarence Dirks in *Esquire* a few months earlier. The boat assignments in this section are taken from Al Ulbrickson's logbook for the spring of 1935 and from articles in the *WD*.

Details of the Rantz family's years in Seattle are drawn primarily from my interview with Harry Rantz Jr. and from his unpublished typescript, "Memories of My Mother." For more on the commissaries and the socialist movement in Seattle, see "Communism in Washington State," at http://depts.washington.edu/labhist/cpproject. For more about the Golden Rule labor dispute, see The Great Depression in Washington State website, "Labor Events Yearbook: 1936," at http://depts.washington.edu/depress/yearbook1936.shtml. Joe's encounter with Thula at her house on Bagley was seared in his memory, as it was in Joyce's, and both of them recalled it and their conversation in the car afterward in considerable detail. The respect that was paid to Pocock, especially when he was at work in his shop, was made emphatically clear to me in a discussion I had with Jim Ojala, February 22, 2011. I am indebted to Jim—author, publisher, oarsman, and friend of the Pococks—for a number of other insights into what Pocock's shop was like, as well as for his help in obtaining some of the photographs in this book. The correspondence between Pocock and Ebright quoted here took place between September 1 and October 30, 1934.

I learned much about how Pocock crafted his shells from the following: Stan Pocock's *Way Enough!* (Seattle: Blabla, 2000); my own interviews with Stan; Newell (95–97, 149); "George Pocock: A Washington Tradition," *WD*, May 6, 1937; and George Pocock's "Memories."

My account of the great windstorm of 1934 is based largely on "15 Killed, 3 Ships Wrecked As 70-Mile Hurricane Hits Seattle," *PI*, October 22, 1934. Some figures from this source, such as the ultimate death toll, were later updated. Some facts are from Wolf Read, "The Major Windstorm of October 21, 1934," available at http://www.climate.washington .edu/stormking/October1934.html, and from the *WD* for October 23, 1934. I am indebted to Bob Ernst, director of rowing at the University of Washington, for his colorful description of the rowing tanks used by eastern schools.

My discussion of Leni Riefenstahl's *Triumph of the Will* is based on Trimborn, Bach, and Brendon, cited above, but also in part on Riefenstahl's own autobiography, *Leni Riefenstahl: A Memoir* (New York: St. Martins Press, 1993). One has to be very cautious in relying on Riefenstahl's own account of many of these events. I have tried to point out areas where she may be unreliable.

Joe kept the "Senior Men Face Life with Debts" clipping in his scrapbook and still recalled near the end of his life the feelings that reading it had provoked in him.

CHAPTER NINE

The epigraph is from a letter Pocock wrote to the National Association of Amateur Oarsmen, reprinted in the *Rowing News Bulletin* for 1944. I have reassembled Ulbrickson's remarks based on the press coverage in Clarence Dirks, "Husky Mentor Sees New Era for Oarsmen: Crews Adopt 'On to Olympics' Program as They Launch 1935 Campaign," *PI*, January 15, 1935, and "Husky Crew Can Be Best Husky Oarsmen," *WD*, January 15, 1935. For more on Broussais Beck Sr., see the "Broussais C. Beck labor spy reports and ephemera" in the Beck Papers at the University of Washington Library's Special Collections, accession number 0155-001. The unusually cold weather that January is documented in a series of articles in the Seattle press. See my online notes for full citations. The anecdote about the interaction between Moch and Green is based in part on my interview with Marilynn Moch and in part on Moch himself in his interview with Michael J. Socolow, November 2004, as recorded in a transcript from the Moch family collection. The attendees at Ulbrickson's "chat" with the sophomore boys are listed in his logbook entry for February 13, 1935.

Some of the details of my sketch of Shorty Hunt are based on my interview with his daughters, Kristin Cheney and Kathy Grogan. The character sketch of Don Hume is drawn in part from Royal Brougham, "Varsity Crew to Poughkeepsie," *ST*, June 1936. The brief characterization of Chuck Day is based in part on my interview with Kris Day.

Ulbrickson's experimentations with different boatings are chronicled in his logbook as well as in coverage by the *ST* and *PI*. Their canoe ride on the first warm day that spring was something that stuck in the minds of both Joe and Joyce and they often shared details of it fondly with Judy. Joe's conversation with his father in the car at the Golden Rule bakery was another of those key moments that he shared in detail with me as he had with Judy over a lifetime. My description of "the swing" is based on conversations with a number of oarsmen; however, Eric Cohen's input on this question was particularly valuable. Ulbrickson's equivocations over who should row as varsity against California are documented in a series of articles in the *ST*, *PI*, and *NYT* throughout April 1935, all cited in my online notes. Some facts are from Ulbrickson's logbook for that month. Bob Moch, as quoted in Michael Socolow's 2004 interview with him, is the source of Ulbrickson's "I'm sorry" comment on April 12, 1935. My account of the races on the Oakland Estuary is based on Bill Leiser, "Who Won?" *San Francisco Chronicle*, April 14, 1935; "Husky Crews Make Clean Sweep," *ST*, April 14, 1935; Bruce Helberg, "Second Guesses," *WD* (no date, clipping from Bob Moch's scrapbook); "Husky Crews Win Three Races," *ST*, April 14, 1935; and "Washington Sweeps Regatta with Bears: Husky Varsity Crew Spurts to Turn Back U.C. Shell by 6 Feet," *San Francisco Chronicle*, April 14, 1935.

The homecoming parade in Seattle is documented in George Varnell, "Crew, Swim Team Welcomed Home," *ST*, April 19, 1935, and "City Greets Champions," *PI*, April 19, 1935. Jack Medica was himself destined for the 1936 Olympics, where he would earn a gold medal in the four-hundred-meter freestyle, as well as two silver medals. Joe's moment of surprise and pride as he basked in applause still brought tears to his eyes as he talked about it with me years later.

CHAPTER TEN

The Pocock quote is from Newell (85). The iron shoulder pads incident is mentioned in Pocock, *Way Enough* (51). My brief overview of early sports in Seattle is based on the following: Dan Raley, "From Reds to Ruth to Rainiers: City's History Has Its Hits, Misses," *PI*, June 13, 2011; C. J. Bowles, "Baseball Has a Long History in Seattle," available on MLB.com at http://seattle.mariners.mlb.com; "A Short History of Seattle Baseball," available at http://seattlepilots.com/history1.html; Dan Raley, "Edo Vanni, 1918–2007: As player, manager, promoter, he was '100 percent baseball,'" *PI*, April 30, 2007; "Seattle Indians: A Forgotten Chapter in Seattle Baseball," available at Historylink.org; and Jeff Obermeyer, "Seattle Metropolitans," at http://www.seattlehockey.net/Seattle_Hockey_Homepage/Metropolitans.html. It wasn't until 1969—with the arrival of the Seattle Pilots—that Seattle finally got a major-league baseball team. And they went bankrupt within a year.

My discussion of Black Sunday is based on Egan, *Worst Hard Time* (8); "Black Sunday Remembered," April 13, 2010, on the Oklahoma Climatological Survey website: http://climate.ok.gov; and Sean Potter, "Retrospect: April 14, 1935: Black Sunday," available at http://www.weatherwise.org. The effect on Seattle of the subsequent exodus from the Plains states is based, in part, on "Great Migration Westward About to Begin," *PI*, May 4, 1935. The anonymous "Rowing is like a beautiful duck . . ." has been floating around for years, though no one seems to know its source. Al Ulbrickson discussed the complexities caused by oarsmen with different physical abilities rowing together in the International Olympic Committee's *Olympische Rundschau (Olympic Review)* 7 (October 1939). I am indebted to Bob Ernst for the essential idea that great crews require a blend of both physical abilities and personality types.

The continuing struggle between Joe's all-sophomore boat and the JV boat ultimately chosen as varsity for the Poughkeepsie Regatta is chronicled in a series of articles in the *PI*, *ST*, *NYT*, and *New York American* between early May and early June 1935. See full notes online for specific references. I found Bobby Moch's table of codes in his scrapbook, kindly made available by Marilynn Moch.

Descriptive details in my account of the 1935 Poughkeepsie Regatta are drawn largely from the following: "Huge Throng Will See Regatta," *ST*, June 17, 1935; "California Varsity Wins, U.W. Gets Third," *PI*, June 19, 1935; "Western Crews Supreme Today," *ST*, June 19, 1935; Robert F. Kelley, "California Varsity Crew Victor on Hudson for 3rd Successive Time," *NYT*, June 19, 1935; "Sport: Crews," *Time*, July 1, 1935; Hugh Bradley, "Bradley Says: 'Keepsie's

Regatta Society Fete, With Dash of Coney, Too,'" *New York Post*, June 25, 1935; and Brougham, "The Morning After," *PI*, June 20, 1935.

CHAPTER ELEVEN

The Pocock quote is from Newell (85–87). Joe's trip out to Grand Coulee and his subsequent experiences there were favorite topics of conversation for him, and he shared countless details with Judy, Joyce, and later me. In places here I have supplemented his description of the physical environment with my own observations, drawn while driving his route and exploring the site myself; however, the specifics of his experiences and his feelings during that summer are all his as conveyed directly to me or conveyed to me through Judy. For more about Lake Missoula and the epic prehistoric floods, see "Ice Age Floods: Study of Alternatives," section D: "Background," available at http://www.nps.gov/iceagefloods/d.htm; William Dietrich, "Trailing an Apocalypse," *ST*, September 30, 2007; and "Description: Glacial Lake Missoula and the Missoula Floods," available on the USGS website at http://vulcan.wr.usgs.gov/Glossary/Glaciers/IceSheets/description_lake_missoula.html.

Facts pertaining to the two-thousand-meter race at Long Beach are from "Crew Goes West," *ST*, June 20, 1935, and Theon Wright, "Four Boats Beat Olympic Record," United Press, June 30, 1935.

The statistics regarding food consumption at Mason City are from "Here's Where Some Surplus Food Goes," *Washington Farm News*, November 29, 1935. For much more about Grand Coulee and B Street, see Roy Bottenberg, *Grand Coulee Dam* (Charleston: Arcadia Press, 2008), and Lawney L. Reyes, *B Street: The Notorious Playground of Coulee Dam* (Seattle: University of Washington Press, 2008).

Many details of the biographical sketch of Johnny White are from my interview with his sister, Mary Helen Tarbox. Others are from her unpublished typescript, "Mary Helen Tarbox, Born November 11, 1918 in Seattle, Washington." Aspects of my characterization of Chuck Day are based on my conversation with his daughter, Kris Day.

CHAPTER TWELVE

The epigraph is from Newell (78). Some of the details about construction of the Olympic Stadium are from Berlin Olympic Stadium website: http://www.olympiastadion-berlin.de. Others are from Dana Rice, "Germany's Olympic Plans," *NYT*, November 24, 1935, and from *The XIth Olympic Games: Official Report*. The reference to Nazi officers executing German boys is from David Large, *Nazi Games: The Olympics of 1936* (New York: W. W. Norton, 2007), 324. My discussion of the history of rowing at Grünau is drawn in part from a translation, helpfully provided by Isabell Schober, of "Geschichte des Wassersports" on the website of the Wassersportmuseum at Grünau, available at http://www.wassersportmuseum-gruenau.de. Other facts about the facility are from my interview with Werner Phillip at the museum.

Much of the information about Harry and Thula Rantz's excursions to eastern Washington comes from my interviews with Harry Rantz Jr. The anecdote regarding Ulbrickson's determination to win gold at Berlin is based in large part on a video interview with Hazel Ulbrickson, "U of W Crew—The Early Years," produced by American Motion Pictures Video Laboratory, Seattle, 1987. Joe only learned about the conversation between Ulbrickson and Pocock, and Pocock's mission to "fix" him, years later. Pocock's several subsequent talks with him left an enormous impression on Joe, and he recounted them in vivid detail to me as he had earlier to Judy. Pocock took "only God can make a tree" from

Joyce Kilmer's "Trees," in *Trees and Other Poems* (New York: George H. Doran, 1914). An English translation of the Nuremberg Laws is available on the U.S. Holocaust Museum's website: http://www.ushmm.org. I also consulted Tom Kuntz, "Word for Word/The Nuremberg Laws: On Display in Los Angeles: Legal Foreshadowing of Nazi Horror," *NYT*, July 4, 1999. For more on their immediate effect in Germany, see William Shirer's classic *The Rise and Fall of the Third Reich* (New York: Simon and Schuster, 1960), 233–34. The banning of the Jewish Helvetia Rowing Club in 1933 is mentioned in "Geschichte des Wassersports."

My sketch of McMillin working in the shell house is drawn primarily from Joe's memory, along with details provided by McMillin himself in transcripts of his interview with Michael Socolow on November 2004, from the Moch family collection as well as an obituary, "Legendary U.W. Rower Jim McMillin Dies at Age 91," August 31, 2005, available at http://www.gohuskies.com. The details of Thula's death are from my interview with Harry Rantz Jr.; Charlie McDonald's, from Pearlie McDonald's e-mail, cited above. Joe's first conversation with his father following Thula's passing was another of these moments that stuck with Joe throughout his lifetime.

The pro-boycott demonstration in New York is described in "10,000 in Parade Against Hitlerism," *NYT*, November 22, 1935. The final demise of the boycott is documented in "A.A.U. Backs Team in Berlin Olympic; Rejects Boycott," *NYT*, December 9, 1935. For my discussion of the boycott movement, and particularly the forces arrayed around Avery Brundage to oppose it, I have relied on Susan D. Bachrach, *The Nazi Olympics: Berlin 1936* (Boston: Little, Brown, 2000), 47–48; Guy Walters, *Berlin Games: How the Nazis Stole the Olympic Dream* (New York: Harper Perennial, 2007), 24; "U.S. Olympic Chief Brands Boycotters as Communists," *PI*, October 25, 1935; Stephen R. Wenn, "A Tale of Two Diplomats: George S. Messersmith and Charles H. Sherrill on Proposed American Participation in the 1936 Olympics," *Journal of Sport History* 16, no. 1 (Spring 1989); "Sport: Olympic Wrath," *Time*, November 4, 1935; and "Brundage Demands U.S. Entry," *ST*, October 24, 1935.

CHAPTER THIRTEEN

The epigraph is again taken from Newell (85). Ulbrickson's frustration is evident in his logbook, from mid-January into February. Emmett Watson quotes Ulbrickson—"George, tell them what I'm trying to teach them . . ."—in his *Once Upon a Time in Seattle* (Seattle: Lesser Seattle, 1992), 109. The "typical coxswain abuse" remark is from Eric Cohen, as are a number of details related to coxes in this section of the book. The Don Blessing quote is reprinted in Benjamin Ivry, *Regatta: A Celebration of Oarsmanship* (New York: Simon and Schuster, 1988), 75. My biographical sketch of Bobby Moch is based on interviews with Marilynn and Michael Moch, with some additional details from Amy Jennings, "Bob Moch: Monte's Olympian," *Vidette*, January 1, 1998. Joe's second shell house encounter with Pocock is again based on Joe's own recollection of it.

Joe's moment of reflection and insight as he stood on the dock in front of his father's house was a key memory for him—a momet things began to turn around in his personal life. The details of that moment are drawn from his own telling to me and from Judy's recollection of earlier accounts.

Some biographical facts about Gordy Adam and Don Hume are from Wayne Cody's KIRO Radio interview with Adam, Hume, Hunt, and White, August 1, 1986. More about Gordy is from George A. Hodak's interview with Gordon B. Adam, May 1988, published by the Amateur Athletic Foundation of Los Angeles and available at http://www.la84foundation.org/6oic/OralHistory/OHAdam.pdf. More about Hume is from Wallie Funk, "Hume Rowed from Guemes to Berlin in '36," *Anacortes American*, August 7, 1996, and "The Laurel Wreath to Don Hume," *WD*, April 21, 1936.

Ulbrickson noted Joe's addition to the boat and its immediate effect in his logbook on March 21, 1936. Entries over the following days confirm his growing confidence in the new arrangement. The various greetings that Joe's new crewmates gave him meant a great deal to Joe and he delighted in recalling them after some prompting from Judy. The sauerkraut christening of the *Husky Clipper* is described in Newell (137). Ebright's pulling names out of a hat is revealed in Sam Jackson, "Ky Ebright Pulls Crew Champions Out of His Hat," *Niagara Falls Gazette*, February 22, 1936. Jim Lemmon discusses Ebright's use of a training table in his *Log of Rowing at the University of California Berkeley, 1870–1987* (Berkeley: Western Heritage Press, 1989), 97–98. Paul Simdars, who later rowed for Ulbrickson, described Ulbrickson's alternative—a calcium solution and liquid gelatin. Laura Hillenbrand mentions Tom Smith's search for high-calcium hay, and his awareness of the Washington crew's supplements, in *Seabiscuit: An American Legend* (New York: Ballantine, 2001).

Royal Brougham asserts that the 1936 regatta drew the largest crowd ever to see a crew race in "U.W. Crews Win All Three Races: California Crushed," *PI* (an undated clipping in John White's collection of materials). Joyce recalled, in a conversation she had with Judy late in life, how nervous both she and Joe were that day as they awaited the race. My descriptions of the races that day are drawn both from that article and from the following: "75,000 Will See Crews Battle," *WD*, April 17, 1936; Clarence Dirks, "U.W. Varsity Boat Wins by 3 Lengths," *PI*, April 19, 1936; George Varnell, "U.W. Crews in Clean Sweep," *ST*, April 19, 1936; "Coaches Happy, Proud, Says Al, Grand, Says Tom," *ST*, April 19, 1936; and Ulbrickson's logbook entry for April 18, 1936.

CHAPTER FOURTEEN

The Pocock quote is from Newell (106). An interesting and chilling contemporaneous overview of Berlin in this time frame can be found in "Changing Berlin," *National Geographic*, February 1937. More about the state of affairs in Germany at this time can be found in "Hitler's Commemorative Timepiece," *Daily Mail Reporter*, March 7, 2011; Claudia Koonz, *The Nazi Conscience* (Cambridge: Harvard University Press, 2003), 102; and Walters, *Berlin Games* (90–92). The precise mechanism by which Riefenstahl, Goebbels, and the Nazi government concealed the source of Riefenstahl's funding for *Olympia* is documented at length in Bach, *Leni* (174–76).

The crisis over some of the boys' eligibility is recounted in George Varnell, "Varsity Quartet to Make Up Work Before Leaving," *ST* (a clipping without date in Roger Morris's scrapbook), and mentioned in Ulbrickson's logbook on May 18, 1936. Their increasingly impressive times are also noted in the logbook throughout this period.

Beginning with their departure for Poughkeepsie, we begin to get firsthand accounts of events in the journals of three of the boys: Johnny White, Chuck Day, and, later, Roger Morris. The race strategy for Poughkeepsie, hatched on the train trip east and reported by George Varnell in "Varnell Says: New Tactics for U.W. Plan," *ST*, June 13, 1936, is important partly for how little regard Bobby Moch paid to it in the actual event. Details of the atmosphere in the shell house at Poughkeepsie and other events leading up to the regatta are drawn from a wide variety of news reports, cited individually in the online version of the notes. Bob Moch describes the almost mystical night row on the Hudson in "Washington Rowing: 100+ Year History," on Eric Cohen's website: http://huskycrew.com/1930 .htm.

Facts pertaining to the Louis-Schmeling fight are drawn from James P. Dawson, "Schmeling Stops Louis in Twelfth as 45,000 Look On," *NYT*, June 20, 1936, and "Germany Acclaims Schmeling as National Hero for Victory Over Louis," *NYT*, June 21, 1936. The trouble in Harlem that night is reported in "Harlem Disorders Mark Louis Defeat," *NYT*,

June 20, 1936, as is the celebrating in German American neighborhoods. Goebbels's "the white man prevailed" is quoted from his diary entry for June 20, 1936.

The account of the visit to Hyde Park is derived mostly from a letter from Shorty Hunt to his family, published in the *Puyallup Press*, June 25, 1936, under the title "Local Youth Meets Son of President on Visit to Hyde Park."

Washington's 1936 varsity win at Poughkeepsie was one of the great crew races of all time. My account of it is drawn from a large number of sources, of which these are the most important: Robert F. Kelley's "Rowing Fans Pour into Poughkeepsie for Today's Regatta," *NYT*, June 22, 1936, and "Washington Gains Sweep in Regatta at Poughkeepsie," *NYT*, June 23, 1936; Ed Alley, "Ulbrickson's Mighty Western Crew Defeats Defending Golden Bears," *Poughkeepsie Star-Enterprise*, June 23, 1936; Hugh Bradley, "Bradley Says: 'Keepsie Regatta Society Fete with Dash of Coney Too," *NYP*, June 23, 1936; Harry Cross, "Washington Sweeps Poughkeepsie Regatta as Varsity Beats California by One Length," *HT*, June 23, 1936; "Husky Crews Take Three Races at Poughkeepsie," *PI*, June 23, 1936; James A. Burchard, "Varsity Coxswain Hero of Huskies' Sweep of Hudson," *New York World-Telegram*, June 23, 1936; "Huskies Sweep All Three Races on Hudson," *PI*, June 23, 1936; Malcolm Roy, "Washington Sweeps Hudson," *New York Sun*, June 23, 1936; Herbert Allan, "Moch Brains Enable Husky Brawn to Score First 'Keepsie Sweep," *NYP*, June 23, 1936; and Royal Brougham, "U.W. Varsity Boat Faces Games Test," *PI*, June 23, 1936. Jim McMillin is the source of his comment about breathing through his nose, as recorded in his November 2004 interview with Michael Socolow; Hazel Ulbrickson's account is from the video "U of W Crew—The Early Years," cited above, as is Bob Moch's "Go to hell, Syracuse" remark. A few additional details are from Johnny White's journal.

CHAPTER FIFTEEN

The Pocock quote can be found in Newell (156). The first mention of Don Hume fighting some kind of "nasty cold" appears in George Varnell, "Shells Late in Arriving; Drill Due Tomorrow," *ST*, July 1, 1936, six full weeks before the gold medal race in Berlin. The boys' mounting anxiety and difficulty sleeping are chronicled in White's and Day's journals beginning on July 4. Their victory in the final race at Princeton is chronicled in "Washington's Huskies Berlin Bound After Crew Win at Princeton," *Trenton Evening Times*, July 6, 1936; Harry Cross, "Washington Crew Beats Penn by Sixty Feet and Wins Olympic Final on Lake Carnegie," *New York Herald Tribune*, July 6, 1936; Robert F. Kelley, "Splendid Race Establishes Washington Crew as U.S. Olympic Standard Bearer," *NYT*, July 6, 1936; George Varnell, "Huskies Win with Ease Over Penn, Bears, and N.Y.A.C.," *ST*, July 6, 1936; and Royal Brougham, "Huskies Win Olympic Tryouts in Record Time," *PI*, July 6, 1936. Additional details are from Johnny White's journal, George A. Hodak's 1988 interview with Gordon Adam cited above, and one of several letters Shorty Hunt began to write home at this time, reprinted in the *Puyallup Valley Tribune*, July 10, 1936. Joyce took great delight in reliving for Judy her memories of listening to the Princeton race that day and her pride at the moment when she realized that Joe would be going to the Olympics. Bob Moch is the source of the mention of a tug-of-war over the silver cup in his November 2004 interview with Michael Socolow. George Pocock's "Coming from Al" comment can be found in Newell (101).

The crisis over the shortage of funds for Berlin and the subsequent drive to raise money in Seattle are documented in a series of articles in the Seattle press over the next few days; see the online notes. Statistics regarding the terrible heat wave of 1936 are primarily from "Mercury Hits 120, No Rain in Sight as Crops Burn in the Drought Area," *NYT*, July 8, 1936, and "130 Dead in Canada as Heat Continues," *NYT*, July 12, 1936. The boys' stay at Travers

Island and their excursions are chronicled in the journals of Johnny White and Chuck Day, as well as in the continuing series of letters that Shorty Hunt wrote home. Joe's trip to the top of the Empire State Building made a large impression on him, and the feelings he had there about the upcoming trip were something he shared often with Judy, who in turn shared them with me. Marilynn Moch explained the contents of the letter Bob Moch received from his father, and his reaction to it, in my interviews with her. Much of the description of loading the *Husky Clipper* onto the *Manhattan* is from George Pocock's "Memories." Other details of those final hours in New York are from Day's and White's journals.

The 1936 U.S. Olympic team consisted of 382 individuals, but not all were aboard the *Manhattan*. Some of the details concerning the history and construction of the *Manhattan* are from "S.S. *Manhattan* & S.S. *Washington*," *Shipping Wonders of the World*, no. 22 (1936). My account of the departure is based in part on "United States Olympic Team Sails for Games Amid Rousing Send-Off," *NYT*, July 16, 1936.

CHAPTER SIXTEEN

The epigraph is from Newell (79). For more on the Olympic preparations in Berlin, see Walters, *Berlin Games* (164–65); Brendon, *Dark Valley* (522); Bach, *Leni* (177); and Richard D. Mandell, *The Nazi Olympics* (New York: Macmillan, 1971), 143–44. Additional details are from *The XIth Olympic Games: Official Report*. For Riefenstahl's preparations, I have relied primarily on her own account in her memoir, cited above.

For my description of life on the *Manhattan*, I have drawn from Joe's recollections and a letter Shorty Hunt wrote home, published in the *Puyallup Press*, July 31, 1936. Day's and White's journals also offered many interesting tidbits. Other facts are from George Pocock's "Memories"; Arthur J. Daley, "Athletes Give Pledge to Keep Fit," *NYT*, July 16, 1936; and M. W. Torbet, "United States Lines Liner S.S. *Manhattan*: Description and Trials," *Journal of the American Society for Naval Engineers* 44, no. 4 (November 1932): 480–519. Al Ulbrickson tells the anecdote about Jim McMillin and the pancakes in "Now! Now! Now!" *Collier's*, June 26, 1937.

My sources for the Eleanor Holm incident include *The Report of the American Olympic Committee: Games of the XIth Olympiad* (New York: American Olympic Committee, 1937), 33; Day's and White's journals; "Mrs. Jarrett Back, Does Not Plan Any Legal Action Against A.A.U.," *NYT*, August 21, 1936; Richard Goldstein, "Eleanor Holm Whalen, 30's Swimming Champion, Dies," *NYT*, February 2, 2004; and Walters, *Berlin Games* (157).

I have drawn mostly from Day's and White's journals to recount the boys' arrival in Europe, with additional information from Shorty Hunt's letter home, cited above. Their reception in Hamburg and Berlin is chronicled in Arthur J. Daley, "Tens of Thousands Line Streets to Welcome U.S. Team to Berlin," *NYT*, July 25, 1936, and "Olympic Squad Receives Warm Nazi Welcome," Associated Press, July 24, 1936. Richard Wingate's response to Brundage's triumphant arrival in Berlin appears in "Olympic Games Comment," *NYT*, July 24, 1936.

The crew's impressions of Köpenick, Grünau, and the German crew are derived from Roger Morris's journal; George Pocock's impressions recorded in Newell (104) and "Memories"; and Lewis Burton, "Husky Crew Gets Lengthy Workout," Associated Press, July 27, 1936. The boys' ramblings in Berlin and Köpenick are chronicled in all three journals—Day, White, and Morris—and Gordon Adam's interview with Hodak, cited above. Peter Mallory discusses the Italian crew in his *Sport of Rowing* (Henley on Thames: River Rowing Museum, 2011), 735–38. Pocock's tale of the outraged Australians at Henley is recounted in Newell (104).

My account of the opening ceremonies draws from Albion Ross, "Nazis Start Olympics as Gigantic Spectacle," *NYT*, July 26, 1936; Shorty Hunt's letter home published in the *Puyallup Press*, August 21, 1936; Riefenstahl in her memoir (191–92); Goebbels's diary quoted in Trimborn, *Leni Riefenstahl* (141); Christopher Hudson, "Nazi Demons Laid to Rest in World Cup Stadium," *Daily Mail*, July 6, 2006; the Day, White, and Morris journals; my 2011 interview with Mike and Marilynn Moch; Bob Moch's account as given in Michael Socolow's November 2004 interview with him; Frederick T. Birchall, "100,000 Hail Hitler; U. S. Athletes Avoid Nazi Salute to Him," *NYT*, August 2, 1936; Royal Brougham, "120,000 Witness Olympic Opening," *PI*, August 2, 1936; John Kiernan, "Sports of the Times," *NYT*, August 2, 1936; "Olympic Games," *Time*, August 10, 1936; Bethlehem Steel, "John White Rowed for the Gold . . . and Won It," *Bottom Line* 6, no. 2 (1984); and Pocock's "Memories."

CHAPTER SEVENTEEN

The Pocock quote is from Newell (79). The boys' adventures in Berlin, Köpenick, and Grünau are drawn, again, primarily from the journals of the three who kept them. Throughout this time, press reports surfaced concerning the ongoing worries about Don Hume's health. For more on Noel Duckworth, see Julia Smyth's brief biographical sketch on the Churchill College Boat Club website, available at http://www.chu.cam.ac.uk/societies/boatclub/history.html#duckworth. Also of interest is the transcript of a radio broadcast from Singapore to London, September 12, 1945, available at http://www.history infilm.com/kwai/padre.htm. An article about the 1936 Boat Race, featuring Ran Laurie and Duckworth, "Beer Scores Over Milk," *NYT*, April 5, 1936, is the source of some of my information about Laurie. Laurie was so modest, it is said, that his son Hugh did not know that his father had won an Olympic gold medal (in 1948) until he happened across it in his father's sock drawer many years later. The drenching of the police cadets and the near brawl with the Yugoslavians are documented in the journals and mentioned in Newell (105).

The British assessment that the American eight was "perfect" appears in "Chances of British Oarsmen," *Manchester Guardian*, August 11, 1936. Hume's weight and condition are discussed again in "Hume Big Worry," Associated Press, August 12, 1936. My account of the qualifying race is based on the boys' journals, as well as Royal Brougham, "U.S. Crew Wins Olympic Trial," *PI*, August 13, 1936; Arthur J. Daley, "Grünau Rowing Course Mark Smashed by Washington in Beating British Crew," *NYT*, August 1936 (no specific date on clipping); and "Leander's Great Effort," *Manchester Guardian*, August 13, 1936.

For more on the Nazi atrocities in Köpenick, see "Nazi Tortures Told in 'Blood Week' Trial," *Stars and Stripes*, June 14, 1950, and Richard J. Evans, *The Coming of the Third Reich* (New York: Penguin, 2005), 360. For more on the Sachsenhausen camp, see the entry in the Holocaust Encyclopedia at the U.S. Holocaust Memorial Museum website: http://www .ushmm.org, and the Brandenburg Memorials Foundation website: http://www.stiftung-bg .de/gums/en/index.htm. For a listing of firms complicit with the Nazis, see "German Firms That Used Slave or Forced Labor During the Nazi Era," on the Jewish Virtual Library website, available at http://www.jewishvirtuallibrary.org/jsource/Holocaust/germancos .html. For a chilling firsthand account of what the forced labor camps were like, see "Record of Witness Testimony number 357," Voices from Ravensbrück, Lund University Library website, available at http://www3.ub.lu.se/ravensbruck/interview357-1.html. My account of the ordeal of the Hirschhahn family is based primarily on a transcript of Eva Lauffer Deutschkron's oral history in "Wisconsin Survivors of the Holocaust," at the Wisconsin Historical Society's website: http://www.wisconsinhistory.org.

The new rules for lane selection are mentioned in *The XIth Olympic Games: Official Report* (1000). For a bit more on Germany's lane assignments, see Albion Ross, "Germany Leads in Olympic Rowing as U.S. Fares Poorly in Consolation Round," *NYT*, August 14, 1936. For the rest of their lives the boys and their coaches believed that Germany and Italy had been assigned the best lanes and they the worst—deliberately.

George Pocock describes his feelings upon hearing "God Save the King" in his "Memories." Photographs taken before and after the gold medal race, as well as footage of the race itself, seem to confirm that the American boys were wearing mismatched outfits, not their official uniforms, during the race.

The psychological importance of having Don Hume in the boat can't be overstated. All the boys brought it up when they talked about the race in later years. Al Ulbrickson is quoted as saying after the race, "When Don came back they simply decided nothing could stop them," in Alan Gould's "Huskies, It's Revealed, All But Ready for Sick Beds Before Winning Race," Associated Press, August 14, 1936.

CHAPTER EIGHTEEN

The Pocock epigraph is again from Newell (81). My account of what was happening inside the *Husky Clipper* during the gold medal race is based to a large extent on the journals, along with Joe's own recollections. Other sources include Hodak's 1988 interview with Gordon Adam; my interviews with Marilynn and Michael Moch; a voice recording of Moch's account, available at http://huskycrew.com/bobmoch.mp3; Wayne Cody's KIRO Radio interview with Adam, Hume, Hunt, and White, August 1, 1986; the video "U of W Crew—The Early Years," cited above; and Pocock's "Memories." Bob Moch mentions counting down the remaining strokes in his November 2004 interview with Michael Socolow; Jim McMillin, in his November 2004 interview with Socolow, mentions shouting the F word.

Major sources for that day also include "Beresford's Third Gold Medal," *Manchester Guardian*, August 15, 1936; Arthur J. Daley, "Fifth Successive Eight-Oared Rowing Title Is Captured by U.S.," *NYT*, August 15, 1936; Grantland Rice, "In the Sportlight," *Reading Eagle*, January 21, 1937; J. F. Abramson, "Washington 8 Wins Title of World's Greatest Crew," *HT*, August 15, 1936; Tommy Lovett, "Went to Town as Bob Knocked" (an undated clipping in the John White materials, no source); Alan Gould, "U.W. Crew Noses Out Italians," Associated Press, August 14, 1936; Al Ulbrickson's already-cited "Now! Now! Now!" in *Collier's*; and *The XIth Olympic Games: Official Report*. My descriptions of Hitler and his entourage are based on photographs and several contemporaneous newsreels shot that day.

CHAPTER NINETEEN

The Pocock quote is from his previously cited letter to the National Association of Amateur Oarsmen, reprinted in *Rowing News Bulletin*. Royal Brougham's firsthand account of the race was never published because of the news writers' strike in Seattle; however, he hearkened back to it in "That Day Recalled," *PI*, July 24, 1976. The comment about Moch's shortness is from my interview with Marilynn Moch. The boys' tears on the podium are documented in Gail Wood, "Olympians to Be Honored," an undated clipping from the *Olympian* in Joe Rantz's scrapbook. The all-night escapade in Berlin is documented in some detail in the three journals. Among other things, it involved many bottles of champagne, a visit to Berlin's notorious Femina nightclub, and winding up on the wrong train and arriving far out in Potsdam as the sun rose the next morning.

EPILOGUE

The epigraph is once again Pocock, this time from a speech he gave to the University of Washington Varsity Boat Club in 1965. Audio is available on the Husky Crew website at http://www.huskycrew.org/audio-video/Pocock65mp3.mp3. McMillin mentions stopping to visit relatives in New York in his 2004 interview with Socolow. Johnny White's journey home was explained to me in my interview with Mary Helen Tarbox. Shorty Hunt's arrival home is celebrated in "When Olympic Athletes Were Honored by Valley," *Puyallup Valley Tribune*, September 29, 1936. Pocock's side trip to England is discussed in "One-Man Navy Yard" (49) and Newell (111). Bobby Moch's post-Olympics experiences were explained to me in my interviews with Marilynn Moch, with some details also from the Montesano *Vidette*, November 11, 1999.

The boys' extraordinary accomplishment in the 1937 Poughkeepsie Regatta is best chronicled in "Washington Crews Again Sweep Hudson Regatta," *NYT*, June 23, 1937. Royal Brougham describes the evening the boys parted ways in "Ulbrickson Plans Arrival on July 5," *PI*, June 23, 1937.

Göring's "All that is lacking" proclamation can be found in Shirer, *Rise and Fall* (300). The unidentified American's comment is from a chilling piece of prewar propaganda, Stanley McClatchie, *Look to Germany: The Heart of Europe* (Berlin: Heinrich Hoffmann, 1936). For much more on the reception Riefenstahl's *Olympia* received, see Bach, *Leni* (196–213).

Many details of the boys' subsequent lives are drawn from a series of obituaries. See the online notes for individual citations. Ulbrickson's clear recollection of the day he first put Joe in the 1936 varsity boat is recounted in George Varnell, "Memories of Crew: Al Recalls the Highlights of a Long, Honored Career," *ST* (no date, a clipping in Joe Rantz's scrapbook). Some details of Ebright's later career are from Arthur M. Arlett's 1968 interview with him. The ten-year anniversary rows are chronicled in a series of news articles and local television broadcasts through these years.

It is a small but noteworthy irony that among the first Allied troops who crossed the Elbe River and met up with Russian troops in April of 1945—encircling Berlin and sealing Hitler's fate—was a small band of resourceful American boys, rowing a captured German racing shell.

INDEX

Page numbers in *italics* refer to illustrations.

Read on for a selection from
Daniel James Brown's
newest book . . .

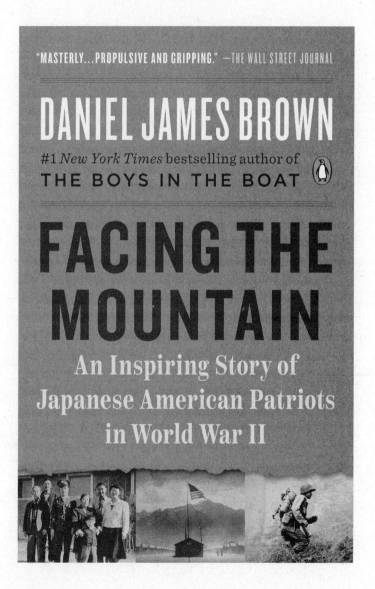

"MASTERLY...PROPULSIVE AND GRIPPING." —THE WALL STREET JOURNAL

DANIEL JAMES BROWN

#1 *New York Times* bestselling author of
THE BOYS IN THE BOAT

FACING THE
MOUNTAIN

An Inspiring Story of
Japanese American Patriots
in World War II

CHAPTER THREE

The news had gotten around that my father was going to be taken soon after. And so my father was all prepared and he was dressed in his coat and tie. They had these gun bayonets. They said, "Hey! You are arrested! Come with us!" And they just grabbed him. Oh, we were all so scared, and we didn't know what to do.

Laura Iida Miho

In 1941, there were forty-five million radios in the United States, and on any given Sunday most of them were likely to be turned on. Radio programming was enormously popular throughout the country, particularly on Sunday afternoons, after church, when life offered working Americans an opportunity to finally sit down, pick up some knitting needles or a newspaper or a panful of peas in need of shelling, and enjoy a broadcast. But when the first bulletins about Pearl Harbor came crackling across the airwaves that day, whatever they had been doing, whatever they had been listening to, faded instantly into insignificance for millions of Americans and their allies around the world. In Los Angeles and in Omaha, in London and in Toronto, people leaned closer to their radios, beckoned others to gather around, and listened intently. In those first few minutes, most of them understood that whatever else the news signified, it meant that a generation, their generation, was about to be defined forever.

One of the radios turned on that day was in a small apartment over a commercial laundry in a beaten-down neighborhood called Hillyard, on the shabby side of Spokane, Washington.

Hillyard was a rough-hewn place, a mile or so of old brick storefronts and small, wood-frame houses squatting on weedy lots alongside the sprawling, five-hundred-acre rail yard of James J. Hill's Great Northern Railway. With a roundhouse capable of holding twenty locomotives at a time, massive sheds for the manufacture and repair of more locomotives, enormous tanks for storing oil, a lumber mill for making railroad ties, gravel pits, machine shops, and rows of boxcars with their wheels removed and converted into cheap housing for workers, the Great Northern yard was a bedlam of clanging steel, shrieking whistles, and engines belching steam, day and night. It was a world of grime and grease and grit, of soot and sweat, of perpetually soiled overalls and grubby work shirts—the kind of place that needed a laundry nearby.

Just half a block from the yard, the Hillyard Laundry occupied the downstairs portion of a narrow two-story building on East Olympic Avenue. The laundry's busy proprietors, Kisaburo and Tori Shiosaki, were at their ease that morning after another long week of work. Six days a week, the Shiosakis arose well before dawn to begin their sixteen-hour workdays, firing up the laundry's huge boilers, operating the whirring extractor that spun most of the water out of hundreds of pounds of wet clothes and bedsheets, wrestling the still wet laundry into two large electric dryers, pulling it all out, and then ironing, shaking, and folding it, until it was finally time to open the shop at 7:00 a.m. and greet the day's first customers.

Most of the Shiosakis' customers, indeed most of Hillyard's residents, were recent immigrants—mainly German, Irish, Scandinavian, or Italian laborers, the majority of whom worked for the Great Northern in one capacity or an-

Tori and Kisaburo Shiosaki at work in the Hillyard Laundry

other. A few were Japanese, from a colony of railroad workers who lived in the boxcars on the other side of the tracks in a place called Dogtown, the only place in the Spokane area that could be called a step down from Hillyard. Whichever side of the tracks they came from, their customers were almost universally fond of the Shiosakis, whom they called Kay and Mrs. Kay, monikers that the pair liked and happily embraced for themselves. Pretty much everyone in town enjoyed stopping in for a few minutes to exchange pleasantries and a bit of morning gossip with Kay and Mrs. Kay before they dropped off their laundry and got on with their day's work.

But that December Sunday was a day for resting up, for Kisaburo to sit back, read the *Spokane Spokesman-Review*, and enjoy a few of the big White Owl cigars that he favored. It was a cold, mostly clear day in Hillyard, not quite freezing, but just on the edge of it. The snow from a storm the week before had mostly melted, but the streets were still icy, the ground rock hard, the vegetation in James J. Hill Park over on Nebraska Avenue brown and withered. Driven by a chilling north wind, a few high clouds scudded rapidly across a nearly white sky. Small as it was—just two bedrooms, a sitting room, and a kitchen—the apartment over the laundry was pleasant, cozy, and warm, the wet heat rising from the big boilers downstairs steaming up the windows. And it was full of the usual comfortable Sunday morning smells— eggs frying, toast browning, tea brewing on the stove. If she had time, Tori Shiosaki thought she might go downtown to the Methodist Mission Church in Spokane to visit with some of the Japanese ladies there. After a week of struggling to communicate with her customers in English, she always enjoyed being able to speak Japanese.

The Shiosakis' seventeen-year-old son, Fred, had turned the radio on. He wasn't really looking forward to the next morning. The school week usually dragged for Fred. He was a competent but not particularly enthusiastic student at John R. Rogers High. He was vice president of the school's photography club and popular on the track team, but he really lived for his weekends, particularly his Saturdays. His Saturday mornings, like his weekday mornings, began at dawn with chores, mostly cutting and splitting the seemingly endless supply of firewood required for the boilers, but by afternoon he was free to play baseball with his friends in one of the town's many vacant lots, take photographs around town, ride his bike down to the

Rialto Theater on Diamond Avenue to catch a matinee western, or wander among the sagebrush and ponderosa pines up in Spokane's dry, dusty hills, plinking at tin cans with his .22 rifle.

At five feet six, Fred was a slight, bespectacled young man, light-skinned with a tendency to pink up in the cheeks when the weather turned cold or he got excited. He had a twinkle in his eye, a ready smile, a surprisingly hearty laugh, and a ready willingness to poke fun at himself. He was polite and courteous as a first instinct. In a tough town like Hillyard—and it was a very tough town, particularly if you were a kid trying to hold your own out on its potholed streets—he looked at first glance like someone you could steamroll, pick a fight with, and walk away a winner. More than a few Hillyard boys had made that calculation over the years, and nearly all of them had quickly come to regret it.

For all his genuine good nature, Fred had a core of steel. If someone tried to take advantage of him, the politeness melted away in an instant. He wound up in so many scuffles that his father threatened to stop buying him new eyeglasses if he kept coming home with smashed pairs. At fifteen dollars a pair, it was straining the family budget. More often than not, the fights arose because in the ethnic stew of Hillyard race and ethnicity were often a bully's first and most potent line of attack. Fred would not abide being bullied, and above all he would not abide being called a Jap. It didn't matter a whit how big the boy hurling the epithet at him was. Defiance would rise in Fred like a cobra. With narrowed eyes and a clenched jaw, he would hiss out the first cussword he could think of, tighten his fists, and go at the offender in a flash. He didn't always win, but he never backed down.

At 11:30 a.m., Fred was listening to the opening of *The World Today*, a regular CBS news show, when an agitated voice abruptly broke into the broadcast: "Go ahead, New York!" Then a different voice, the show's anchor, John Charles Daly, was suddenly on the air. This voice was urgent, crackling through the speaker: "The Japanese have attacked Pearl Harbor, Hawaii, by air, President Roosevelt has just announced." Fred looked up, startled, trying to comprehend it. Daly went on, "The attack also was made on all naval and military activities on the principal island of Oʻahu."* Fred called to his father in the next

*Though Daly actually mispronounced the island's name as "Ohau."

room, "Hey, Pop. The Japanese have attacked Hawaii." Fred's parents, his brother Floyd, and his sister, Blanche, all gathered around Fred and the radio. His parents suddenly looked drawn, pale, tense. After listening for a while, Kisaburo murmured, "It's not going to last long." But he didn't look convinced, and Fred couldn't decipher what exactly his father meant. Why wouldn't it last long? Troubling thoughts began to worm their way through his mind: What would happen to the laundry? What would his friends and neighbors do? What would happen at school the next day?

As the noon hour passed, Fred put his homework aside unfinished and sat in front of the radio stunned as the word began to pour out, over and over again, sounding more and more venomous each time. "The Japs." "The dirty Japs." "The dirty yellow Japs." This time, though, the word wasn't coming from adolescent bullies on the streets of Hillyard; it was coming from adults, from stern-voiced news announcers, from military officials issuing emergency proclamations, from figures of respect and authority. It was serious, sober, cold, official, and it seemed to be coming from the heart of America itself.

For Fred's parents the word, and the tone, came as no surprise. They had traveled a long, hard road from their previous lives in Japan. Since arriving in America they had been mistreated often enough, heard the word hurled at them often enough to know that as friendly as their customers in Hillyard might be, much of the country had long since hardened its heart against people who looked like them. Now, instinctively, Tori Shiosaki pulled down the blinds on the apartment's two little upstairs windows looking out onto the mean streets of Hillyard.

In Japan, it was already December 8 when word of the attack reached civilians going about their morning business. Kats Miho's sister Fumiye was in suburban Tokyo, standing in the classroom where she taught English at a women's college when another teacher, a young Russian named Miss Zabriaski, rushed into her classroom.

"Miss Miho, Miss Miho! War between Japan, America!"

Fumiye smiled and laughed her off. "No, no, that's just propaganda," she said, and went on teaching. Miss Zabriaski, with little English, looked exasperated, stuttered something in Russian, and ran from the room.

Fumiye—fed up with the racial discrimination she had faced growing up on Maui—had come to Japan in the spring of 1940, shortly after graduating from the University of Hawai'i. The impetus for the move had come when a famous Oxford-educated Buddhist scholar, Dr. Junjiro Takakusu, visited the university, saw Fumiye's extraordinary academic potential, and suggested that she enroll for graduate studies at Japan's most prestigious university, Tokyo Imperial. Fumiye had enthusiastically embraced the chance and set sail for Japan almost without a second thought. Only when she arrived in Yokohama did she discover that her new mentor had overlooked one crucial detail: women were not allowed to enroll at Tokyo Imperial. Nevertheless, she moved in with her older sister Tsukie and her husband, a dentist.

Fumiye threw herself into her new life. She found jobs teaching English part-time. She took advanced lessons in ikebana and dutifully wore kimonos for tea ceremony every Friday. She developed a deep interest in Kabuki. She stopped speaking English at home with Tsukie.* And she thrilled to the rhythms and opportunities of her new life. For the first time, she felt a fully fledged part of the society in which she lived, as if she truly belonged and would not be judged by her appearance or held back by her race.

She knew that tensions between the country where she had been born and the country where she chose to live were on the rise, but she paid little attention to the saber rattling that seemed to emanate every day from the Japanese press. It seemed like the hyperbolic rhetoric of old men, political men, and it seemed incomprehensible that her two worlds would collide in any real way. She knew too many good, kind people on both sides in both countries. So when Miss Zabriaski rushed into her classroom shouting about war that morning, Fumiye had immediately put it out of her mind and turned her attention to her students.

But walking home that afternoon, she began to realize that something unusual was, in fact, going on. People were gathered in small knots on the streets, agitated, their conversations animated. As she passed open windows, she heard martial music blaring from radios. Lines had formed in front of shops selling more radios. People were smiling for a change. There was something electric in the air. Then she passed a radio airing an official bulletin

*Tsukie had been born in Japan but had grown up on Maui and attended Maui High, where she went by Rosaline. But because Japanese-born immigrants could not become American citizens, she had returned to Japan in 1934.

from NHK, Japan's national broadcaster. Japan had "entered into a situation of war with the United States and Britain in the western Pacific before dawn." On a street corner she saw a shocking headline; apparently the entire U.S. Navy had been destroyed in Hawai'i.

Fumiye ran the rest of the way home, burst into the house, and fell into her sister's arms, the two young women sobbing, trying to comfort each other, quaking, wondering aloud and fearing silently what was happening to their parents and siblings back in Hawai'i.

Despite the flashes on the radio, the news reached many people in the United States that day more slowly than one might have expected. Because it was a Sunday, many Americans were still at church or in movie theaters for early afternoon matinees. A few theaters flashed cards on the screen or made announcements over the PA systems, but many didn't. Thousands of moviegoers walked out into the light of day later that afternoon and were stunned to find newsboys shouting and holding up extra editions of the papers with banner headlines like the *Oakland Tribune*'s—JAPS DECLARE WAR; HAWAII BOMBED, HEAVY LIFE LOSS—or the *San Francisco Chronicle*'s simpler, four-inch-tall proclamation: WAR. For others, the news arrived by telephone as family members reached out to one another. Young women in telephone exchanges around the country worked frantically to make connections, but there were not nearly enough operators working on a Sunday afternoon to keep up with the load. In quiet neighborhoods, on farms and in towns, word traveled by mouth, directly from one neighbor to another, a doorbell ringing after Sunday afternoon dinner or a quick, startling conversation over a hedge or a picket fence.

In the first few hours, Americans' reactions ran the gamut from rage to fear to relief. The last of those, relief, sometimes came as a surprise even to those who felt it most acutely. The country had spent the years since World War I assiduously trying to ignore what was happening in the rest of the world, convincing itself that the growing global mayhem was someone else's problem even as it became more and more obvious that it wasn't. Now that line of reasoning was suddenly extinct. The endless uncertainty was over. Benjamin Fox, a young police officer standing on Market Street in San Francisco that day, said the feeling was like a rubber band that had been stretched too far for too long and had finally been allowed to snap. "Now it's come and it's a good thing and I think everyone thinks so." A waitress in Boston proclaimed to her customers,

"There's been too much talk and not enough action. Let's get going." Many young men, particularly those already in uniform, suddenly saw their futures as more interesting, vibrant with the possibility of glory awaiting them just over the western horizon. A soldier on leave at the Rialto Theater in Atlanta crowed, "Oh boy. This is it!" A sailor added, "That's what we've been waiting for." Another soldier, in Portland, Oregon, turned to a friend, smiled, and said, "We'd better polish up our shootin' irons."

But most people were, unsurprisingly, just plain angry—deeply angry and raring to do something about it. At Pilgrim Congregational Church in St. Louis, Sunday worshippers agreed that "they ought to blow the Japanese navy out of the water." In Kansas City, a newsboy hawking an extra edition yelled, "Gotta whip those Japs," as his customers nodded, handed him coins, and took their papers. In Buffalo, ninety-five-year-old John Caudell—a man old enough to have fought in the Civil War—growled at a reporter, "I hope we knock hell out of them, but don't say hell. It won't look good."

And right from those first moments of realization, anti-Asian racial animus that had long festered—particularly in the American West—bubbled to the surface and fueled the fury of millions. A motorist in San Francisco pulled in to a filling station and exclaimed, "Down the street I almost ran over a Jap on a motorcycle. Maybe I should have hit him. That would be my contribution." In Topeka a man at a field trial for hunting dogs snarled, "I guess our hunting will be confined to those God-damned slant-eyed bastards from now on."

At the epicenter of it all, in Honolulu, Kats Miho found himself in a city gripped by terror that night. The widespread—and not unreasonable—assumption was that the air raids had merely been preparation for a full-scale invasion of Hawai'i. At 4:25 p.m., the territorial governor, Joseph Poindexter, had imposed martial law, and now a total blackout plunged the city into utter darkness. Virtually the only light illuminating the Pearl Harbor area was from the fires still burning on shattered battleships and in the ruins of aircraft hangars. Sirens wailed in the darkness. From time to time, thundering volleys of antiaircraft fire lit up the sky as anxious gunners at Pearl shot at imagined aircraft. Drivers desperate to get home or to find loved ones drove, without aid of headlights or traffic lights, through blackened streets, despite a military curfew. Except for occasional bulletins, commercial radio stations went off the air to prevent any additional Japanese aircraft from following their signals toward O'ahu.

In the official silence, wild rumors raced unchecked through the darkened city. Word was that Japanese nationals living in Hawai'i had poisoned the water supply; that SS *Lurline*—a Matson Company luxury liner that carried thousands between Honolulu and California each year—had been sunk en route to Los Angeles with 840 passengers aboard;* that Japanese plantation workers had cut large arrows in the cane fields to direct enemy planes toward Pearl; that Japanese troops had come ashore on certain beaches on the north shore of O'ahu; that Kaua'i was already occupied; that San Francisco was being bombed; that Japanese Americans armed with machine guns had opened fire on Hickam Field from milk trucks.

Kats stood in the dark on a street corner down in Iwilei—a raw industrial landscape of fuel-storage tanks, railroad tracks, cranes, and rusting machinery near Honolulu Harbor—carrying an old rifle he still didn't really know how to use, peering into the night. The waterfront was black all the way down through Waikīkī to Diamond Head, the lights of the grand hotels along the beach extinguished. Even the red and green navigation lights in the harbor had been turned off, so it was hard to make out anything but shadows and silhouettes in the moonlight. From time to time, an unexpected sound startled Kats—the sudden bark of a dog, someone dropping something into a trash can, a door slamming—and he flinched, crouched, and put his finger back on the trigger.

Earlier in the day he and his fellow ROTC cadets from the University of Hawai'i—virtually all Americans of Japanese ancestry—had been transferred into an entirely new entity, the Hawai'i Territorial Guard. Their mission was to guard O'ahu's critical infrastructure—power plants, pumping stations, fuel depots, and the like—against the expected Japanese invasion. The earlier reports of paratroopers landing on St. Louis Heights had turned out to be false, just some hikers apparently trying to get a better view of what was happening at Pearl Harbor. But now in the dark, everything that moved, every ambiguous shape, every unexpected sound, seemed a potentially lethal threat. More young men like Kats were stationed at other spots along the waterfront, every fifty yards or so. Everyone was jittery, trigger-happy. Occasionally someone

---

*In fact, the *Lurline* arrived safely at Pier 32 in San Francisco a little after 2:00 a.m. on December 10, but only after its crew had daubed black paint on all its portals and ordered passengers not even to strike a match after twilight, its skipper put it on a zigzag course and brought it up to its maximum speed, and terrorized passengers had tried vainly to fall asleep fully dressed and wearing life jackets.

actually pulled the trigger, and the crack of a shot split the night, boys unwittingly shooting at dogs and cats and rats, at anything that walked, crept, or crawled through shadows in the moonlight.

Still, Kats was proud. After a long day of feeling angry and helpless, he was in uniform, armed, and finally doing something—serving his country, protecting it from those who would do it harm. But what Kats didn't know was that while he stood guard with his gun in Honolulu, other men with guns were leading his father away into the Kahului night at the point of a bayonet as Ayano Miho stood in the doorway of their hotel, weeping. As he was taken out the door, Katsuichi, believing he was about to be executed, turned to his wife and hastily offered his final advice: "Don't do anything that will bring shame to the family and the Japanese race. Do your best no matter what. Keep your self-dignity."

Katsuichi Miho was just one of hundreds of mostly older men taken from their homes that evening and one of thousands taken over the next several weeks as federal agents arrested and jailed Japanese nationals both in Hawai'i and on the U.S. mainland. Almost all were Issei men—first-generation immigrants, the heads of households. Most of them had lived lawfully in the United States for decades, though by law they were not allowed to naturalize as citizens. Their second-generation, American-born children—the Nisei—were American citizens and theoretically protected by the Constitution from unwarranted arrest, though that protection would soon turn out to be illusory.

Well before the attack on Pearl Harbor, the U.S. government had laid detailed plans for what it might do about alien residents from hostile nations in the event of war. Relying on the authority of the Alien Enemies Act of 1798, the Office of Naval Intelligence, the War Department's Military Intelligence Division, and the FBI had begun during the 1930s to compile lists of Japanese, Italian, and German nationals living in the United States. By 1936, as tensions with Japan heightened, Japanese immigrants in Hawai'i came under particular scrutiny as authorities examined with whom they associated. One major point of focus was Japanese commercial ships stopping in Honolulu. Often, they carried Japanese naval personnel who mingled with local Issei and Nisei, carrying news and letters from family in Japan. On August 10 of that year, President Roosevelt proposed to the chief of naval operations that "every Japanese citizen or non-citizen on the Island of Oahu who meets these Japanese ships [arriving in Hawai'i] or has any connection with their officers or men should be secretly but definitely identified and his or her name placed on a special list of those who would be the first to be placed in a concentration camp in the event of trouble." By 1941, the military intelligence services and the FBI, at the direction of J. Edgar Hoover, had developed an extensive, hierarchical system for identifying and categorizing those whom they suspected might pose a danger. Termed the Custodial Detention List, the list was organized with the names of suspect individuals divided into three categories—A, B, and C. In the A category were the people considered most dangerous: members of ultranationalistic German, Italian, or Japanese organizations, as well as international fascist or communist organizations. One step down, in the B category, were members of cultural or religious organizations that might promote "foreign" values, such as Japanese community associations, Buddhist temples, and Shinto shrines. The C category included a much wider variety of people, such as those doing business in Japan or simply individuals whom someone had identified as "suspicious."

Now, in the wake of Pearl Harbor—both in Hawai'i and on the mainland—the FBI cast a wide net, working through the lists as quickly as they could, sweeping up everyone in all three categories, whether of Japanese, German, or Italian ancestry.* In Hawai'i and on the West Coast, most of the names on the list were far and away Japanese. FBI agents fanned out, seizing Buddhist and Shinto priests, Japanese-language schoolteachers, business leaders, anyone who had corresponded with the Japanese consulate, the owners of fishing boats, Japanese-language newspaper editors, members of Japanese literary societies, Japanese flower arranging clubs, and many others. Most of the people taken were men, and most were taken from their homes or businesses with only the clothes on their backs, without charges, and without a word to them or to their families about where they were being taken. The suddenness and seeming randomness of the arrests sent a shock wave of dread and uncertainty through Japanese families both on the mainland and in Hawai'i. Nobody could be sure who would be taken and who wouldn't.

---

*More than 1.2 million people in the United States had been born in Germany, and 5 million had two German-born parents. The nation's ethnic Italian community was even larger. During the war, the Department of Justice incarcerated roughly 11,500 individuals of German ancestry and 3,000 of Italian ancestry. However, neither Italian Americans nor German Americans were ever subject to the sweeping, all-inclusive incarcerations that would follow for Japanese Americans and their parents.

Agents arresting Issei men

At Sumi Okamoto's wedding in Spokane, agents raided the reception and led several Issei guests away. In San Pedro, California, as they climbed off their boats, unaware of what had happened in Hawai'i, several hundred fishermen were herded into chicken-wire enclosures on the waterfront. In San Diego, Margaret Ishino, a student at San Diego High, watched as federal agents searched her family home. Her mother lay in bed, having just delivered her little brother, Thomas. Suspecting the bed held contraband, one of the agents ripped away the blankets and sheets, exposing her mother. Then they took away her father. In Hood River, Oregon, agents pounded on doors at 3:30 on Monday morning, ransacking houses and taking away a dozen community leaders. Among them was Tomeshichi Akiyama, whose son George was then serving in the U.S. Army.* In Stockton, California, as Yasaburo Saiki was being led away from the boardinghouse he ran, he said, "Wait, wait, you might need these," reached into his pocket, and handed his son Barry—a student at the University of California at Berkeley—a bundle of U.S. defense bonds he had purchased before the attack. In Honolulu's Wai'alae neighborhood, Matsujiro Otani was sick in bed, dressed only in pajamas, when the FBI arrived. They stuck a pistol in his ribs, ordered him out of bed, and marched him out-

---

*George Akiyama would subsequently earn a Silver Star for his extraordinary courage in battle.

side barefoot. His wife pleaded with them, "If you are going to take him, take me along too!" The agents snapped, "You keep out of this," and shoved Otani toward their waiting car. Mrs. Otani dashed back into the house, grabbed a raincoat and a pair of shoes, and threw them into the car just before the doors closed and the car pulled away. In downtown Honolulu, the Yokohama Specie Bank on Merchant Street had been seized and turned into a station for booking the Issei men as they were brought in. One of them, a temple priest so bent and stooped by age that he could hardly walk, was escorted by a young Japanese American soldier. Mortified by what he was being required to do, the soldier stared glumly at the ground and refused to talk to anyone about it. Some of the older men being questioned spoke little English and simply did not understand what was happening to them. One asked his son and daughter-in-law, "What means Jap?"

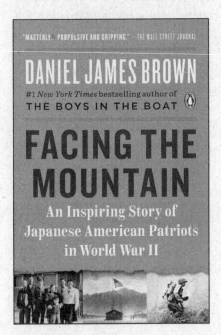